尾田栄一郎

There's a jump rope song that kids have been singing for ages.
I heard it recently and it really brought me back.
It goes, "The postal worker dropped some things ♪
Let's help him pick them up
One letter ♪ Two letters ♪ Three letters ♪ ... Ten letters ♪
Thank you sooo much ♪"
It's very cute. But is that one letter the only thing a postal
worker loses?
Honesty ♪ Youth ♪ Friendship ♪ Freedom ♪
The gleam in his eyes ♪ His spirit of adventure ♪
*Thank you sooo much (bawling)* ♪
Let's get volume 80 started!!

–Eiichiro Oda, 2015

iichiro Oda began his manga career at the age of
17, when his one-shot cowboy manga **Wanted!**
won second place in the coveted Tezuka manga
awards. Oda went on to work as an assistant to
some of the biggest manga artists in the industry,
including Nobuhiro Watsuki, before winning the
Hop Step Award for new artists. His pirate
adventure **One Piece**, which debuted in
**Weekly Shonen Jump** in 1997, quickly became
one of the most popular manga in Japan.

ONE PIECE VOL. 80
NEW WORLD PART 20

SHONEN JUMP Manga Edition

STORY AND ART BY EIICHIRO ODA

Translation/Stephen Paul
Touch-up Art & Lettering/Vanessa Satone
Design/Fawn Lau
Editor/Alexis Kirsch

ONE PIECE © 1997 by Eiichiro Oda. All rights reserved.
First published in Japan in 1997 by SHUEISHA Inc., Tokyo.
English translation rights arranged by SHUEISHA Inc.

The stories, characters and incidents mentioned
in this publication are entirely fictional.

No portion of this book may be reproduced or
transmitted in any form or by any means without
written permission from the copyright holders.

Printed in the U.S.A.

Published by VIZ Media, LLC
P.O. Box 77010
San Francisco, CA 94107

10 9 8 7 6 5 4
First printing, November 2016
Fourth printing, July 2022

viz.com

PARENTAL ADVISORY
ONE PIECE is rated T for Teen and is recommended
for ages 13 and up. This volume contains fantasy
violence and tobacco usage.

SHONEN JUMP MANGA

# ONE PIECE

**Vol. 80**
**OPENING SPEECH**

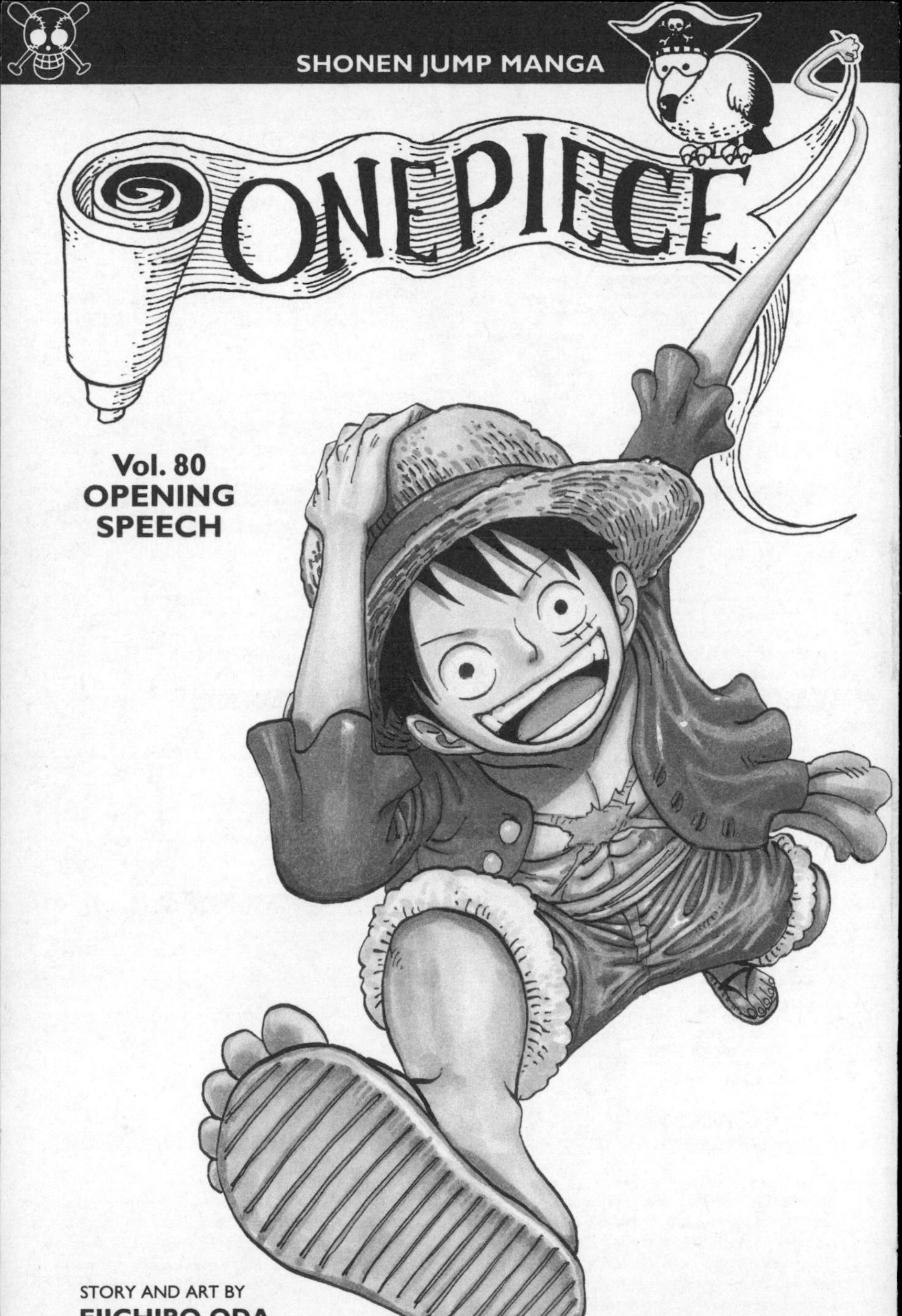

STORY AND ART BY
**EIICHIRO ODA**

# The Straw Hat Crew

## Tony Tony Chopper

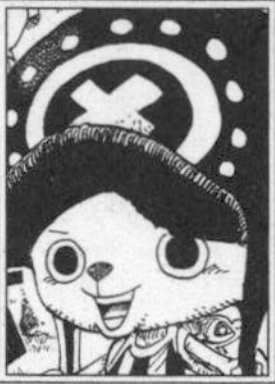

After researching powerful medicine in Birdie Kingdom, he reunited with the rest of the crew.

Ship's Doctor, Bounty: 50 berries

## Monkey D. Luffy

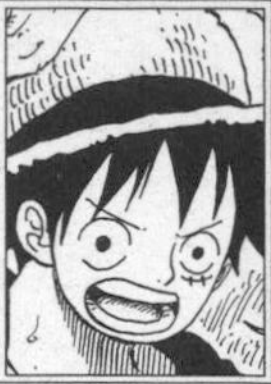

A young man who dreams of becoming the Pirate King. After training with Rayleigh, he and his crew head for the New World!

Captain, Bounty: 400 million berries

## Nico Robin

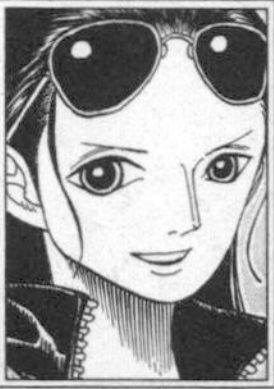

She spent her time in Baltigo with the leader of the Revolutionary Army: Luffy's father, Dragon.

Archeologist, Bounty: 80 million berries

## Roronoa Zolo

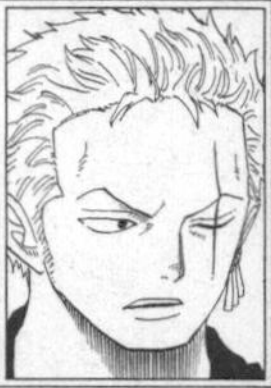

He swallowed his pride and asked to be trained by Mihawk on Gloom Island before reuniting with the rest of the crew.

Fighter, Bounty: 120 million berries

## Franky

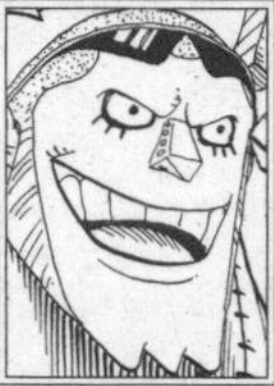

He modified himself in Future Land Baldimore and turned himself into Armored Franky before reuniting with the rest of the crew.

Shipwright, Bounty: 44 million berries

## Nami

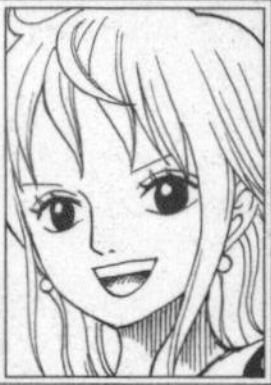

She studied the weather of the New World on the small Sky Island Weatheria, a place where weather is studied as a science.

Navigator, Bounty: 16 million berries

## Brook

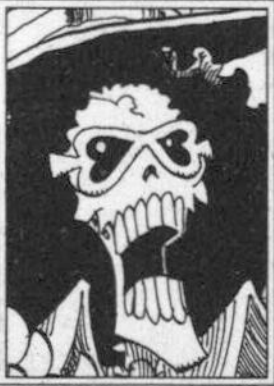

After being captured and used as a freak show by the Longarm Tribe, he became a famous rock star called "Soul King" Brook.

Musician, Bounty: 33 million berries

## Usopp

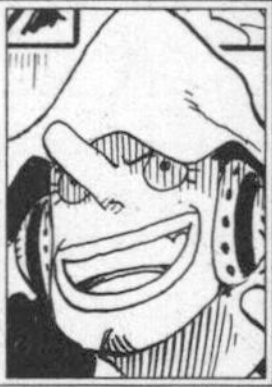

He trained under Heracles at the Bowin Islands to become the King of Snipers.

Sniper, Bounty: 30 million berries

## Shanks

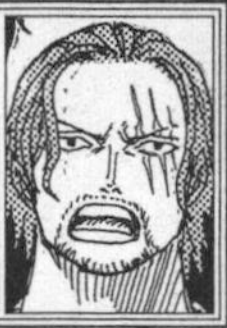

One of the Four Emperors. Waits for Luffy in the "New World," the second half of the Grand Line.

Captain of the Red-Haired Pirates

## Sanji

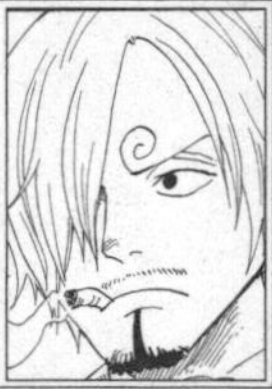

After fighting the New Kama Karate masters in the Kamabakka Kingdom, he returned to the crew.

Cook, Bounty: 77 million berries

one-legged toy soldier who informs them of the nation's hidden darkness, and they decide to help the little Tontattas in their fight for freedom. Their companions defeat the DQ Family officers, leaving only the wicked Doflamingo. Luffy then unleashes the tremendous Gear Four to ultimately topple the mighty foe, liberating Dressrosa from his rule. While they all celebrate their victory, Nami's group is under attack by mysterious enemies on a mysterious island. Meanwhile, Kaido, King of the Beasts, shows himself at last, sending foreboding waves throughout the world...

# The story of ONE PIECE 1»80

**Revolutionaries**

**Monkey D. Dragon**
Rev. Army Commander

**Sabo**
Rev. Army Chief of Staff

**Koala**
Rev. Army Fish-man Karate Master

**Hack**
Rev. Army Warrior

**Navy**

**Fujitora (Issho)**
Naval HQ Admiral

**"Great Advisor" Tsuru**
Naval HQ Vice Admiral

**Sengoku the Buddha**
Naval HQ Inspector General

**Trafalgar Law**
Captain of the Heart Pirates

**Corazon**
Ex-Heart Leader of DQ Family

**Ideo**
Long-Arm XXX-Class Boxer

**Bartolomeo**
Barto Club Captain

**Orlumbus**
Commodore of Yonta Maria Fleet

**Cavendish**
Beautiful Pirates Captain

**Don Quixote Doflamingo**
Captain of the DQ Family

**Hajrudin**
Giant Mercenary

**Don Sai**
13th Chieftain of Happosui

**Leo**
Tonta Corps Commander

**Mansherry**
Tontatta Princess

**Bellamy the Hyena**
Ex-captain of the Bellamy Pirates

**Dressrosa**

**Riku Doldo III**
Former King of Dressrosa

**Kyros** (One-Legged Soldier)
Rebecca's Father

**Rebecca**
Gladiator
(Riku's G.Daughter)

**Violet**
Riku's Second Daughter

**Foxfire Kin'emon**
Samurai of Wano

**Evening Shower Kanjuro**
Samurai of Wano

## Story

After two years of hard training, the Straw Hat pirates are back together, first at the Sabaody Archipelago and then through Fish-Man Island to their next stage: the New World!!

The crew happens across Trafalgar Law on the island of Punk Hazard. At his suggestion, they form a new pirate alliance that seeks to take down one of the Four Emperors. The group infiltrates the kingdom of Dressrosa in an attempt to set up Doflamingo, but Law is abducted after falling into a trap. The rest of the crew meets a

# NEW WORLD

## ONE PIECE

### Vol. 80
## OPENING SPEECH

## CONTENTS

# ONE PIECE

Hereafter, the 80th volume will start.

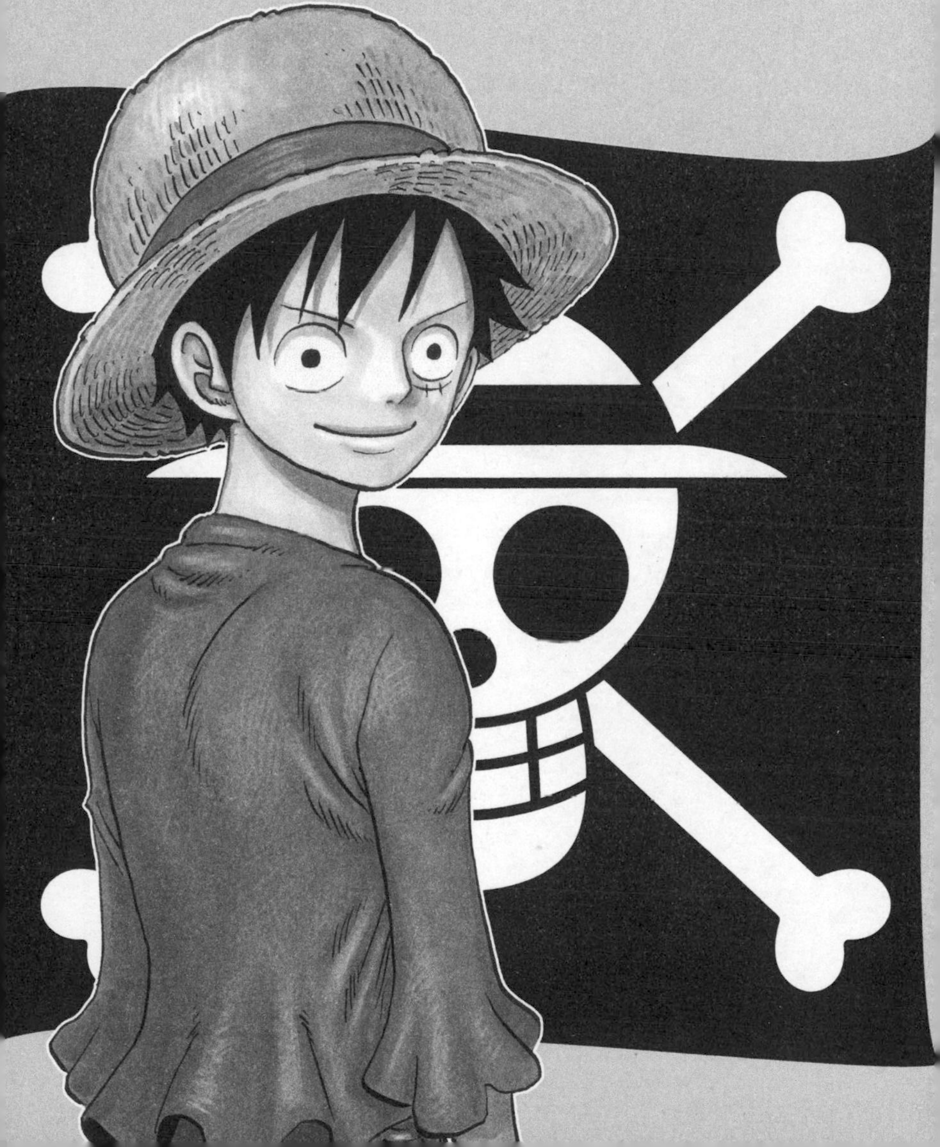

# SOLDIER'S CONVICTION

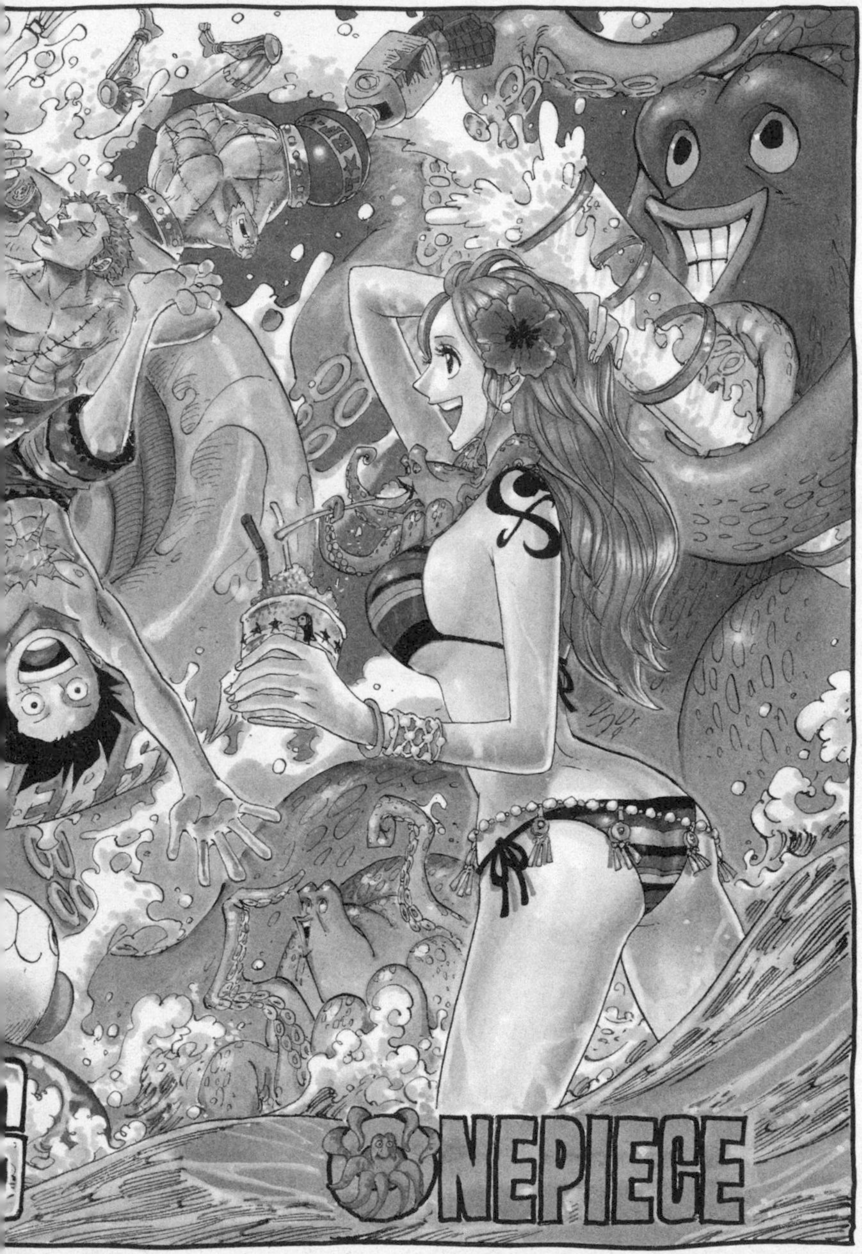

# Chapter 796:

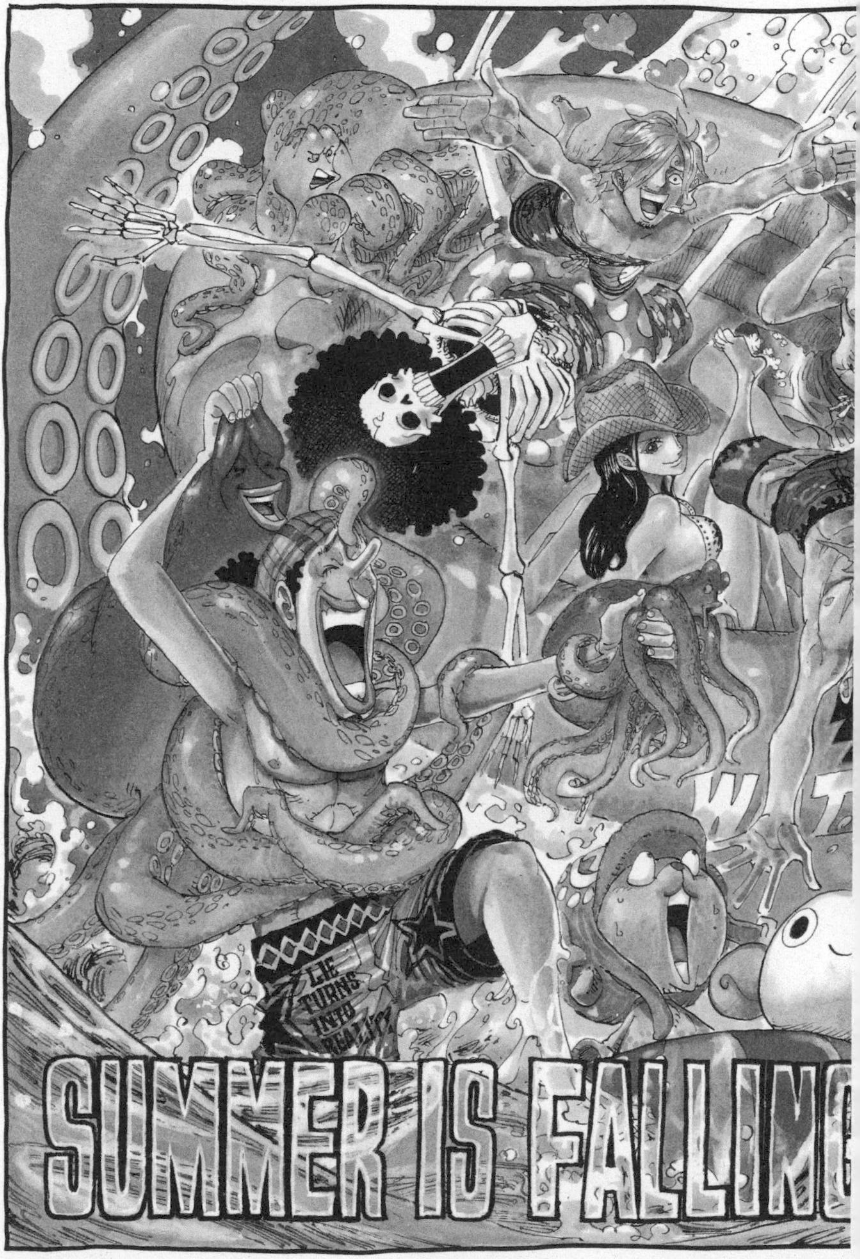
LIE TURNS INTO
SUMMER IS FALLIN

vol.80

ONE PIECE

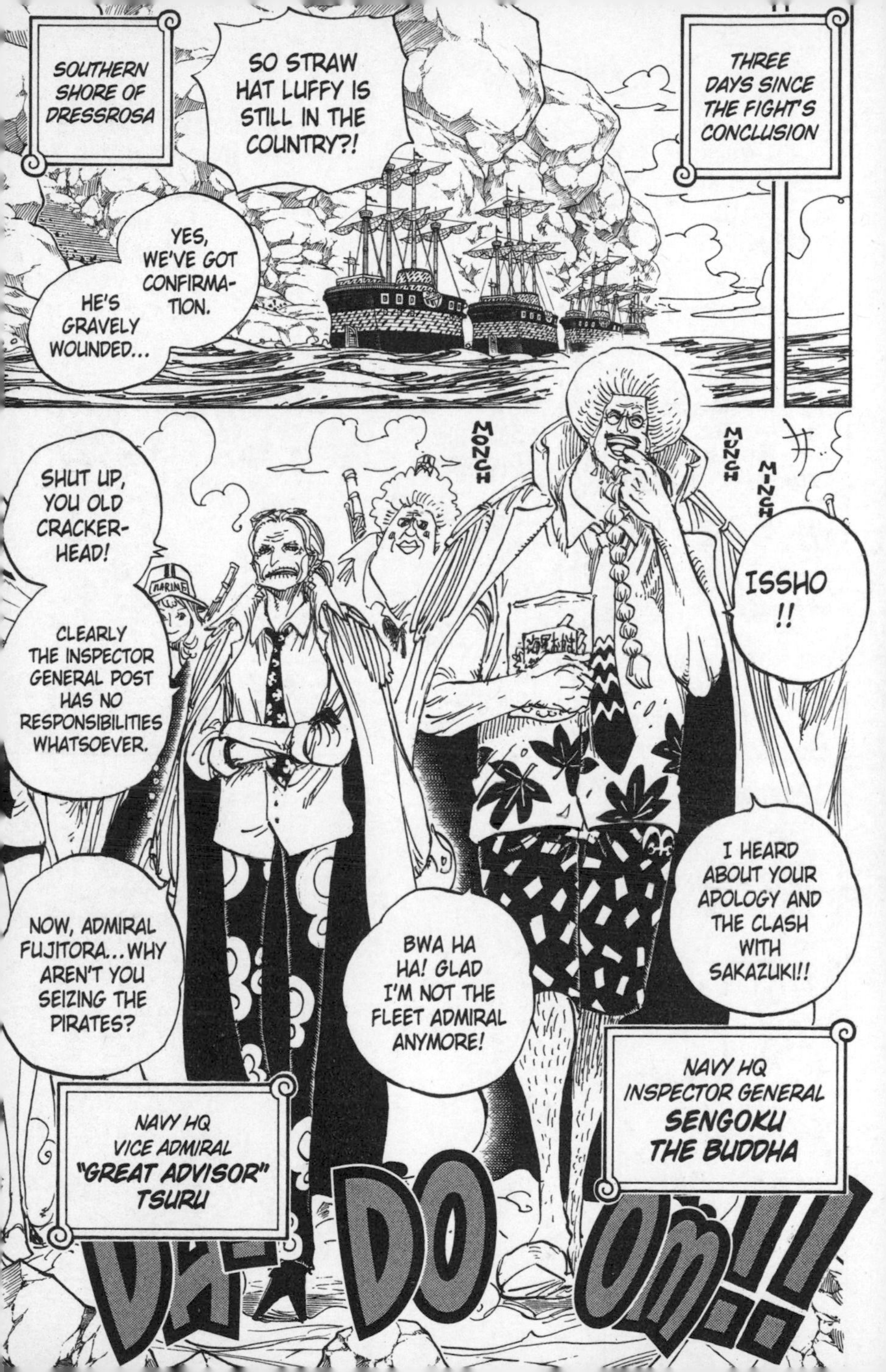
THREE DAYS SINCE THE FIGHT'S CONCLUSION
SO STRAW HAT LUFFY IS STILL IN THE COUNTRY?!
SOUTHERN SHORE OF DRESSROSA
YES, WE'VE GOT CONFIRMATION.
HE'S GRAVELY WOUNDED...
MUNCH
MINCH
MONCH
ISSHO!!
SHUT UP, YOU OLD CRACKER-HEAD!
CLEARLY THE INSPECTOR GENERAL POST HAS NO RESPONSIBILITIES WHATSOEVER.
I HEARD ABOUT YOUR APOLOGY AND THE CLASH WITH SAKAZUKI!!
BWA HA HA! GLAD I'M NOT THE FLEET ADMIRAL ANYMORE!
NOW, ADMIRAL FUJITORA...WHY AREN'T YOU SEIZING THE PIRATES?
NAVY HQ INSPECTOR GENERAL SENGOKU THE BUDDHA
NAVY HQ VICE ADMIRAL "GREAT ADVISOR" TSURU
DA-DO-OM!!

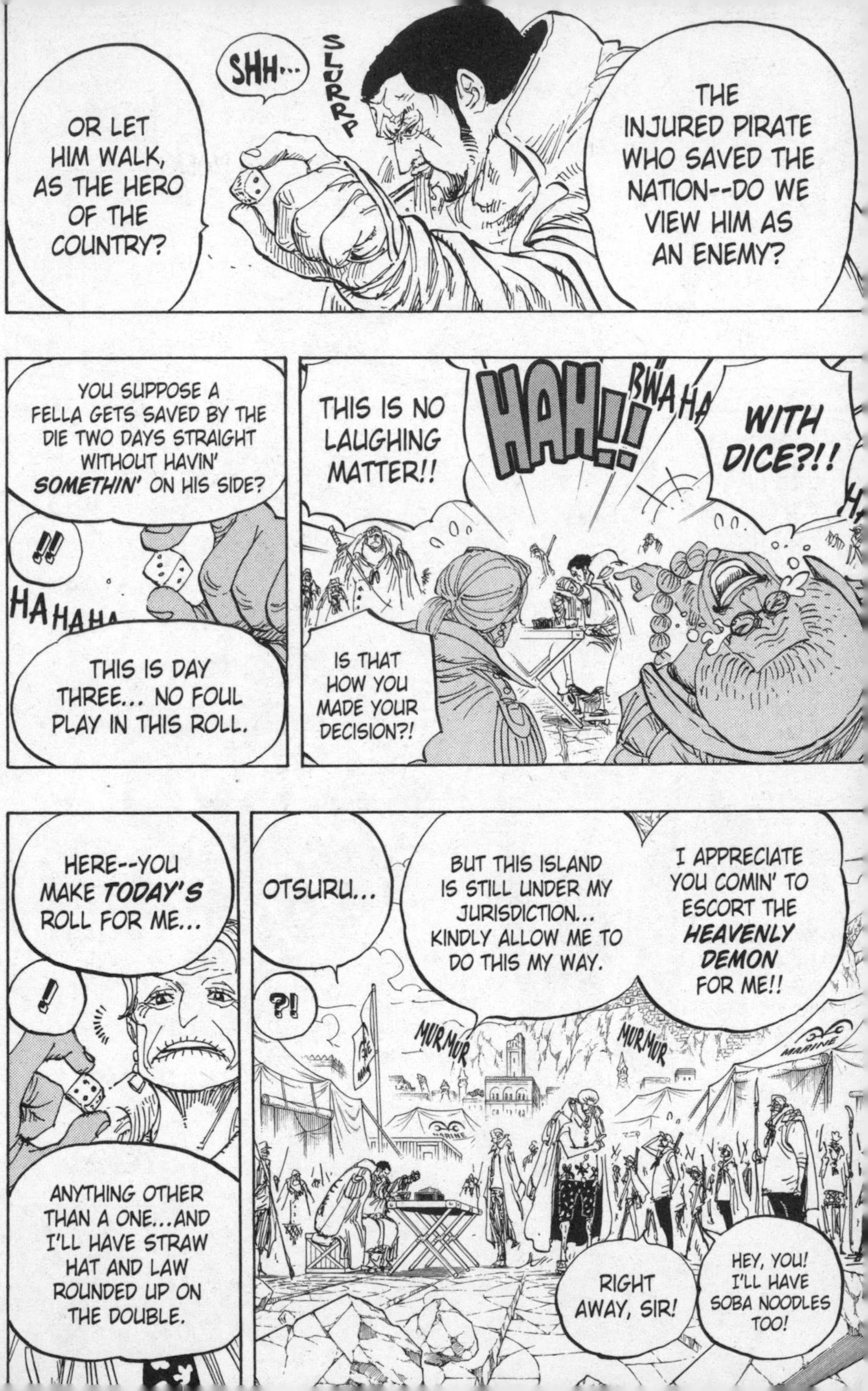
THE INJURED PIRATE WHO SAVED THE NATION--DO WE VIEW HIM AS AN ENEMY?
SLURRP
SHH...
OR LET HIM WALK, AS THE HERO OF THE COUNTRY?
WITH DICE?!!
BWAHAHA
HAH!!
THIS IS NO LAUGHING MATTER!!
IS THAT HOW YOU MADE YOUR DECISION?!
YOU SUPPOSE A FELLA GETS SAVED BY THE DIE TWO DAYS STRAIGHT WITHOUT HAVIN' *SOMETHIN'* ON HIS SIDE?
!!
HAHAHA
THIS IS DAY THREE... NO FOUL PLAY IN THIS ROLL.
I APPRECIATE YOU COMIN' TO ESCORT THE *HEAVENLY DEMON* FOR ME!!
BUT THIS ISLAND IS STILL UNDER MY JURISDICTION... KINDLY ALLOW ME TO DO THIS MY WAY.
OTSURU...
?!
MURMUR
MURMUR
MARINE
HEY, YOU! I'LL HAVE SOBA NOODLES TOO!
RIGHT AWAY, SIR!
HERE--YOU MAKE *TODAY'S* ROLL FOR ME...
!
ANYTHING OTHER THAN A ONE...AND I'LL HAVE STRAW HAT AND LAW ROUNDED UP ON THE DOUBLE.

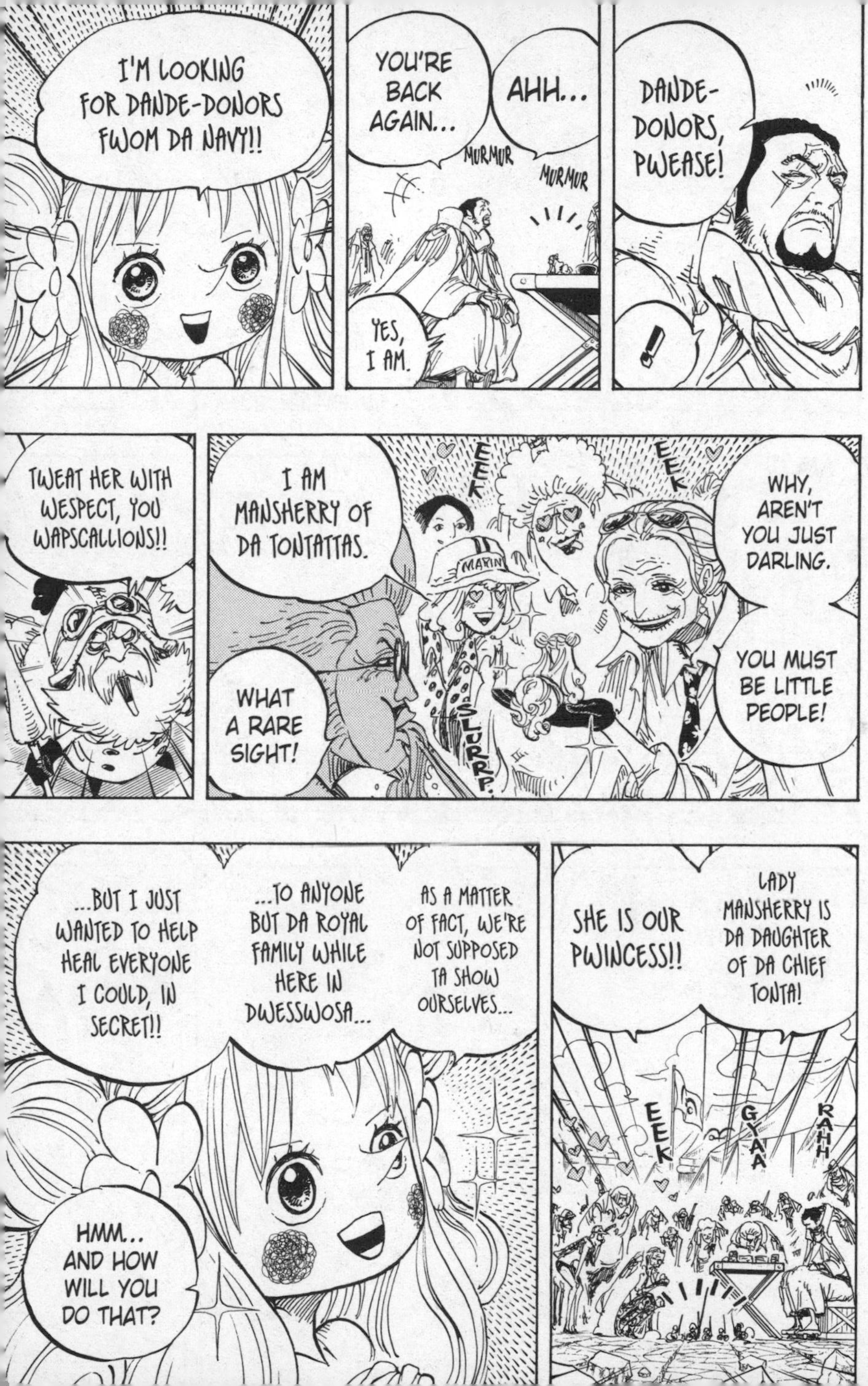
DANDE-DONORS, PWEASE!
!
AHH...
YOU'RE BACK AGAIN...
MURMUR
MURMUR
YES, I AM.
I'M LOOKING FOR DANDE-DONORS FWOM DA NAVY!!
WHY, AREN'T YOU JUST DARLING.
YOU MUST BE LITTLE PEOPLE!
EEK
EEK
I AM MANSHERRY OF DA TONTATTAS.
SLURRP
WHAT A RARE SIGHT!
TWEAT HER WITH WESPECT, YOU WAPSCALLIONS!!
LADY MANSHERRY IS DA DAUGHTER OF DA CHIEF TONTA!
SHE IS OUR PWINCESS!!
RAHH
GYAA
EEK
AS A MATTER OF FACT, WE'RE NOT SUPPOSED TA SHOW OURSELVES...
...TO ANYONE BUT DA ROYAL FAMILY WHILE HERE IN DWESSWOSA...
...BUT I JUST WANTED TO HELP HEAL EVERYONE I COULD, IN SECRET!!
HMM... AND HOW WILL YOU DO THAT?

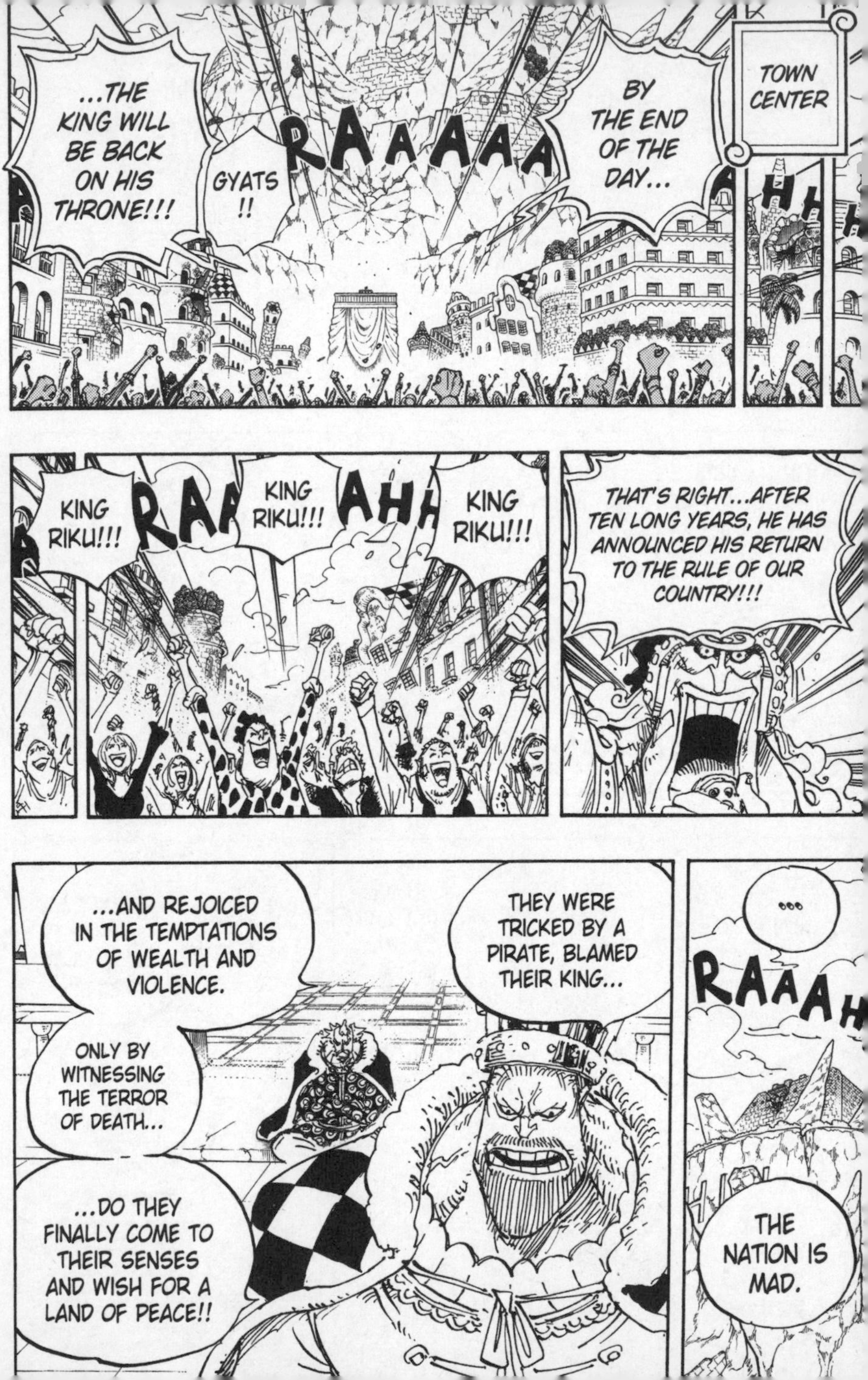
TOWN CENTER
AHHH
BY THE END OF THE DAY...
RAAAAA
GYATS !!
...THE KING WILL BE BACK ON HIS THRONE!!!
THAT'S RIGHT...AFTER TEN LONG YEARS, HE HAS ANNOUNCED HIS RETURN TO THE RULE OF OUR COUNTRY!!!
KING RIKU!!!
AHH
KING RIKU!!!
RAA
KING RIKU!!!
...
RAAAH
THE NATION IS MAD.
THEY WERE TRICKED BY A PIRATE, BLAMED THEIR KING...
...AND REJOICED IN THE TEMPTATIONS OF WEALTH AND VIOLENCE.
ONLY BY WITNESSING THE TERROR OF DEATH...
...DO THEY FINALLY COME TO THEIR SENSES AND WISH FOR A LAND OF PEACE!!

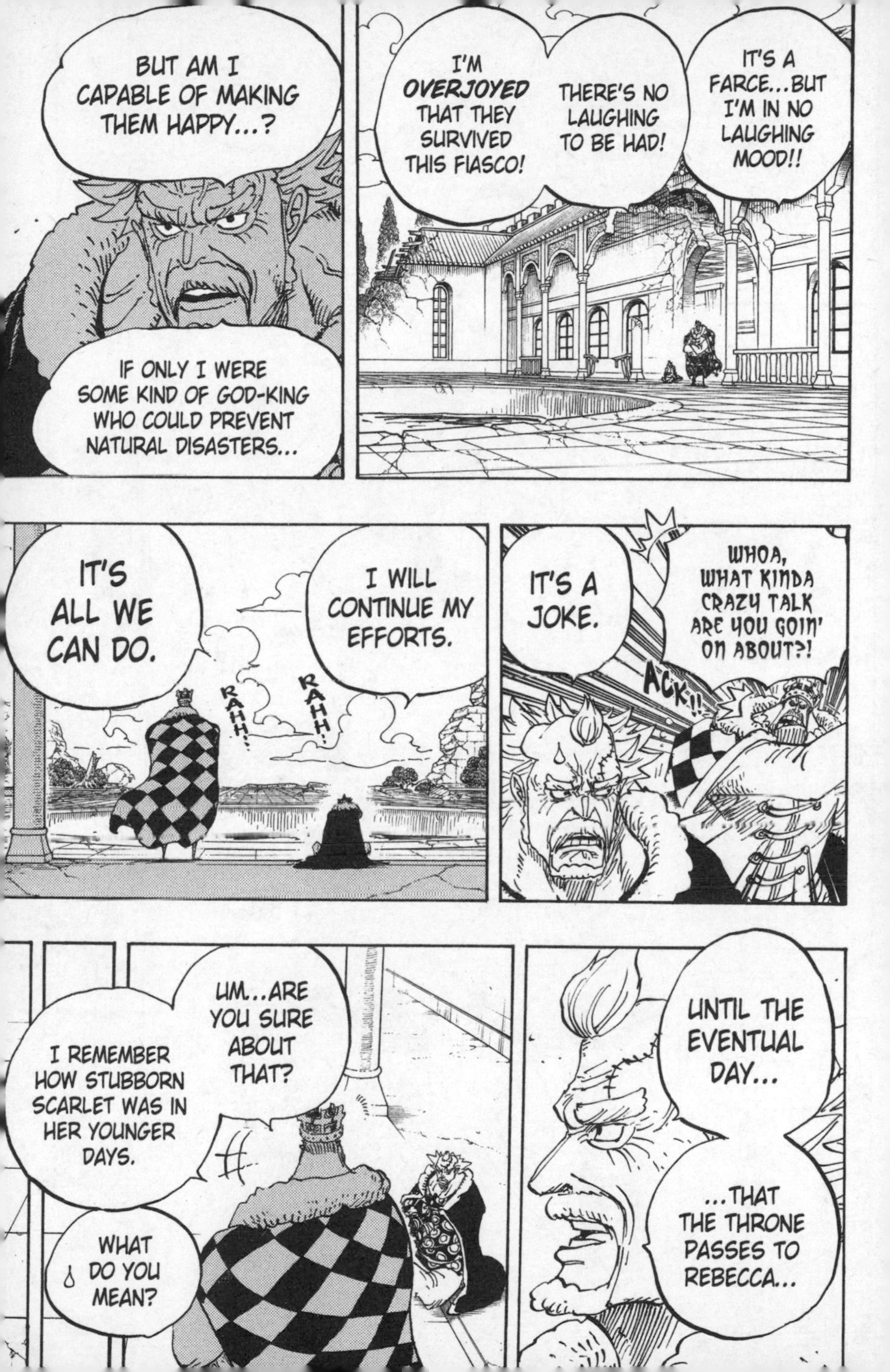
IT'S A FARCE...BUT I'M IN NO LAUGHING MOOD!!
THERE'S NO LAUGHING TO BE HAD!
I'M *OVERJOYED* THAT THEY SURVIVED THIS FIASCO!
BUT AM I CAPABLE OF MAKING THEM HAPPY...?
IF ONLY I WERE SOME KIND OF GOD-KING WHO COULD PREVENT NATURAL DISASTERS...
WHOA, WHAT KINDA CRAZY TALK ARE YOU GOIN' ON ABOUT?!
IT'S A JOKE.
ACK!!
I WILL CONTINUE MY EFFORTS.
RAHH!
RAHH!
IT'S ALL WE CAN DO.
UNTIL THE EVENTUAL DAY...
...THAT THE THRONE PASSES TO REBECCA...
UM...ARE YOU SURE ABOUT THAT?
I REMEMBER HOW STUBBORN SCARLET WAS IN HER YOUNGER DAYS.
WHAT DO YOU MEAN?

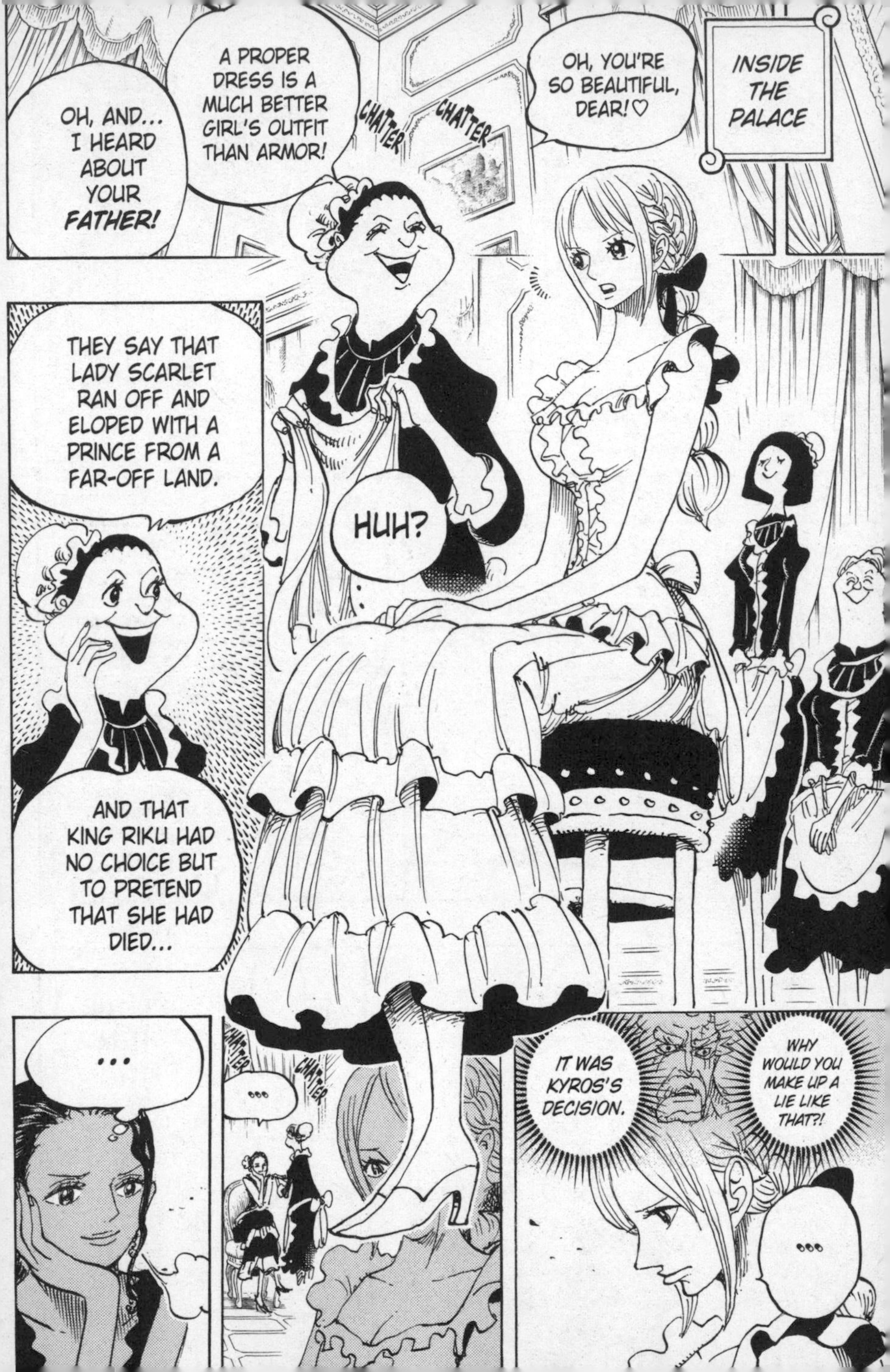
INSIDE THE PALACE
OH, YOU'RE SO BEAUTIFUL, DEAR!♡
CHATTER
CHATTER
A PROPER DRESS IS A MUCH BETTER GIRL'S OUTFIT THAN ARMOR!
OH, AND... I HEARD ABOUT YOUR FATHER!
HUH?
THEY SAY THAT LADY SCARLET RAN OFF AND ELOPED WITH A PRINCE FROM A FAR-OFF LAND.
AND THAT KING RIKU HAD NO CHOICE BUT TO PRETEND THAT SHE HAD DIED...
WHY WOULD YOU MAKE UP A LIE LIKE THAT?!
IT WAS KYROS'S DECISION.
...
CHATTER
...
...

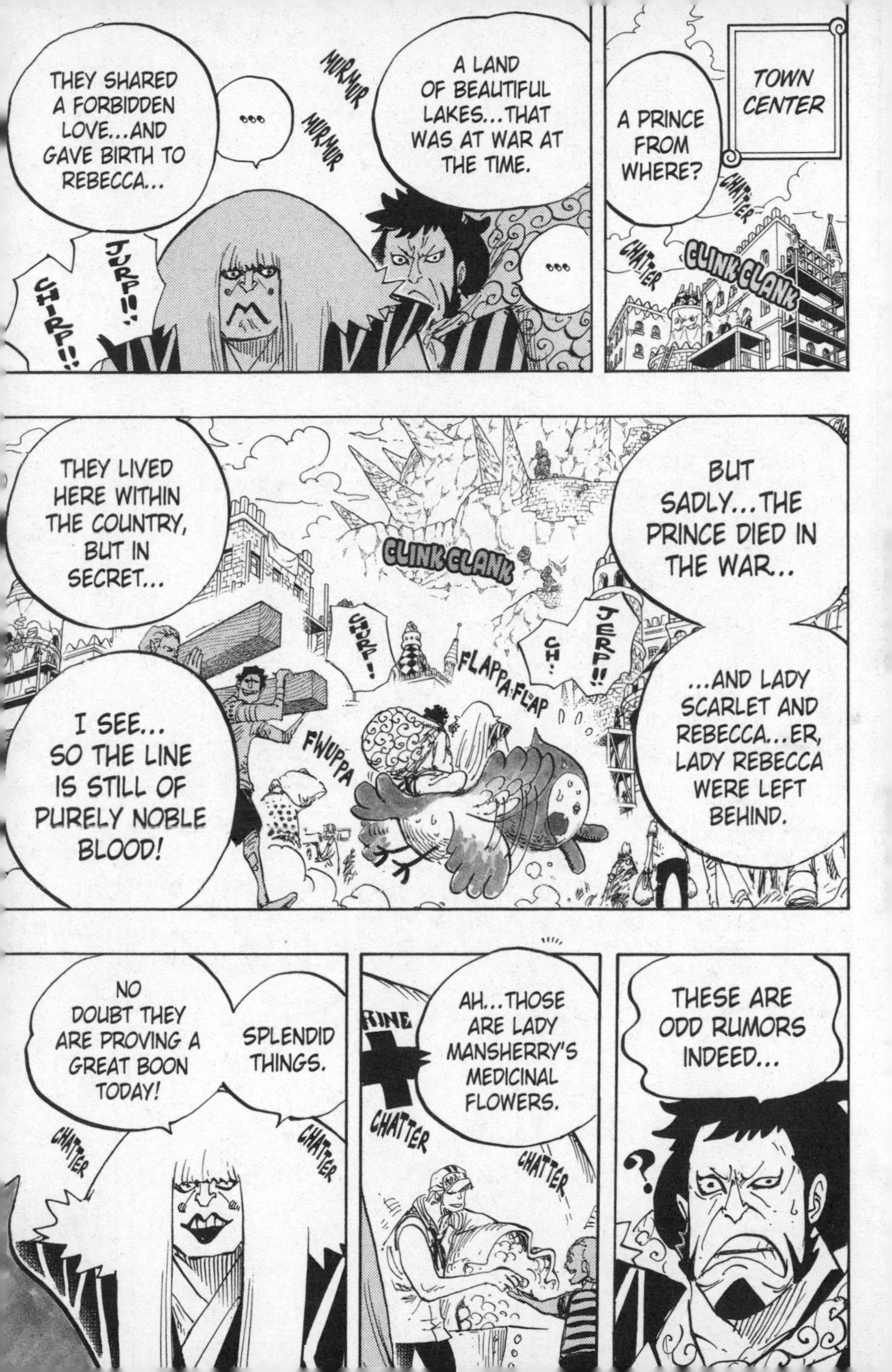
TOWN CENTER
A PRINCE FROM WHERE?
CHATTER
CHATTER
CLINK CLANK
A LAND OF BEAUTIFUL LAKES...THAT WAS AT WAR AT THE TIME.
...
MURMUR
MURMUR
...
THEY SHARED A FORBIDDEN LOVE...AND GAVE BIRTH TO REBECCA...
JURP!!
CHIRP!!
BUT SADLY...THE PRINCE DIED IN THE WAR...
THEY LIVED HERE WITHIN THE COUNTRY, BUT IN SECRET...
CLINK CLANK
JERP!!
CH!
CHURP!
FLAPPA FLAP
...AND LADY SCARLET AND REBECCA...ER, LADY REBECCA WERE LEFT BEHIND.
FWUPPA
I SEE... SO THE LINE IS STILL OF PURELY NOBLE BLOOD!
THESE ARE ODD RUMORS INDEED...
AH...THOSE ARE LADY MANSHERRY'S MEDICINAL FLOWERS.
RINE
CHATTER
CHATTER
SPLENDID THINGS.
NO DOUBT THEY ARE PROVING A GREAT BOON TODAY!
CHATTER
CHATTER

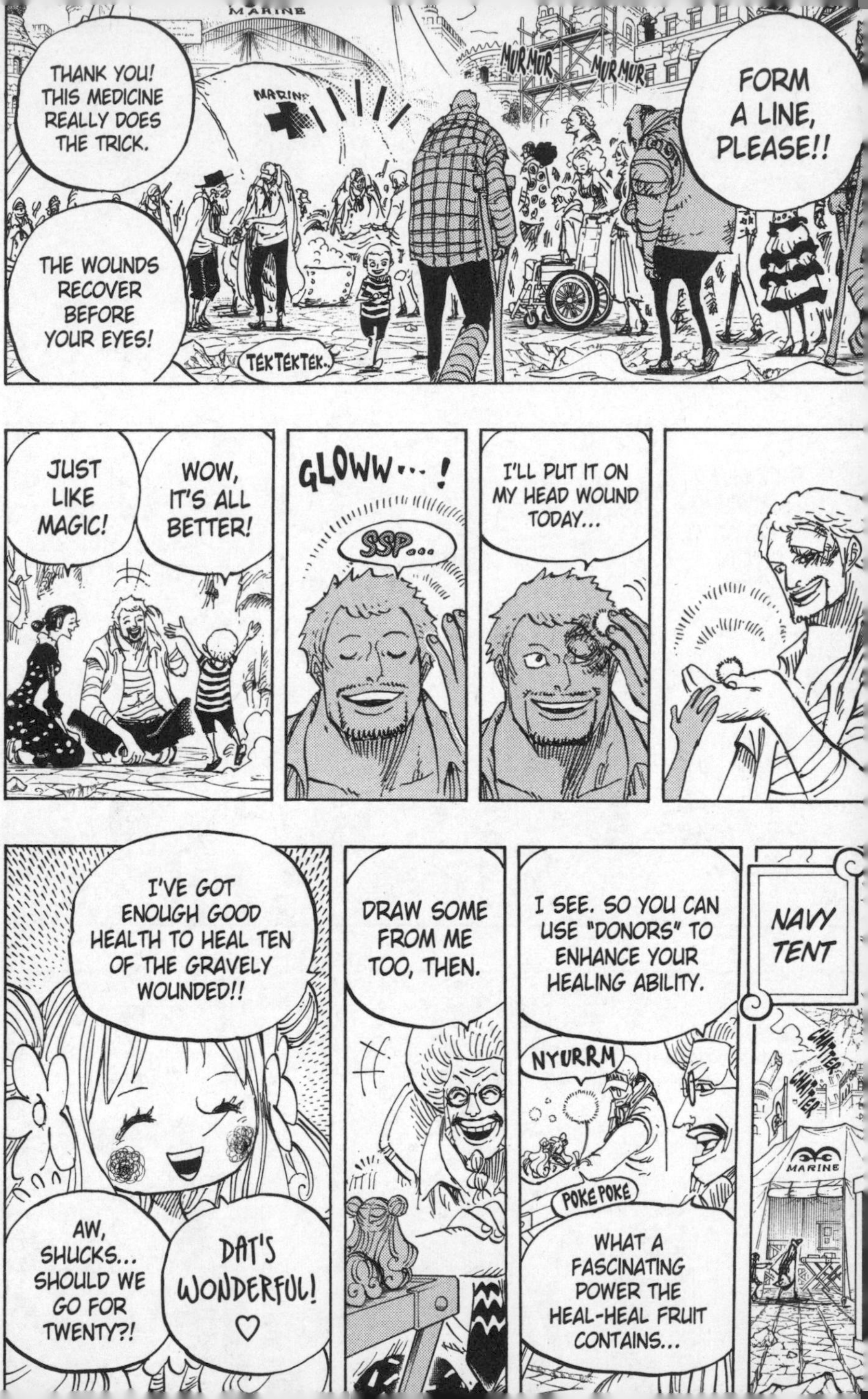

MARINE
FORM A LINE, PLEASE!!
MURMUR
MURMUR
THANK YOU! THIS MEDICINE REALLY DOES THE TRICK.
MARINE
THE WOUNDS RECOVER BEFORE YOUR EYES!
TEKTEKTEK..
I'LL PUT IT ON MY HEAD WOUND TODAY...
GLOWW...!
SSP...
WOW, IT'S ALL BETTER!
JUST LIKE MAGIC!
NAVY TENT
CHATTER
CHATTER
MARINE
I SEE. SO YOU CAN USE "DONORS" TO ENHANCE YOUR HEALING ABILITY.
NYURRM
POKE POKE
WHAT A FASCINATING POWER THE HEAL-HEAL FRUIT CONTAINS...
DRAW SOME FROM ME TOO, THEN.
I'VE GOT ENOUGH GOOD HEALTH TO HEAL TEN OF THE GRAVELY WOUNDED!!
DAT'S WONDERFUL! ♡
AW, SHUCKS... SHOULD WE GO FOR TWENTY?!

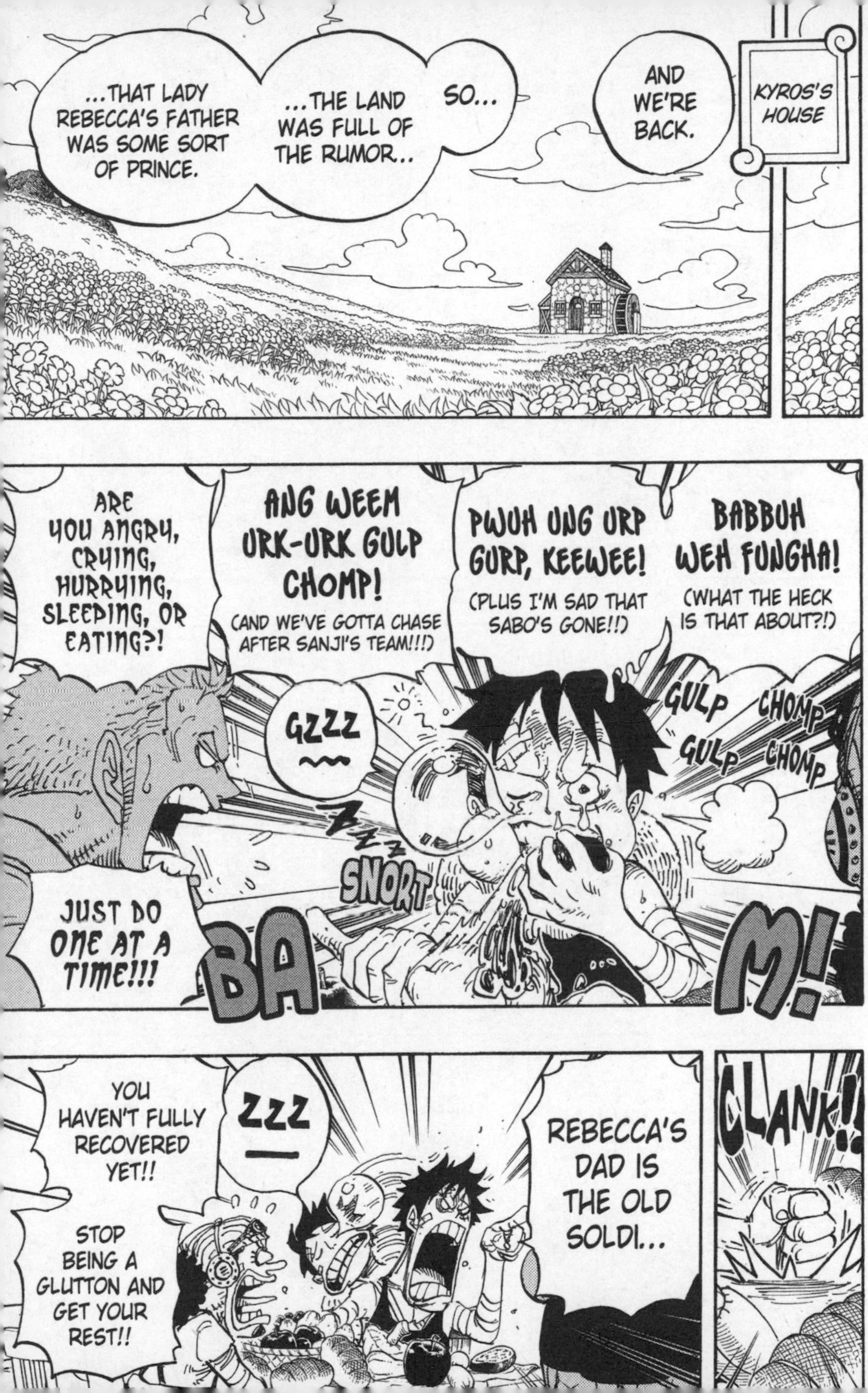
KYROS'S HOUSE
AND WE'RE BACK.
SO...
...THE LAND WAS FULL OF THE RUMOR...
...THAT LADY REBECCA'S FATHER WAS SOME SORT OF PRINCE.
BABBUH WEH FUNGHA!
(WHAT THE HECK IS THAT ABOUT?!)
PWUH UNG URP GURP, KEEWEE!
(PLUS I'M SAD THAT SABO'S GONE!!)
ANG WEEM URK-URK GULP CHOMP!
(AND WE'VE GOTTA CHASE AFTER SANJI'S TEAM!!!)
ARE YOU ANGRY, CRYING, HURRYING, SLEEPING, OR EATING?!
CHOMP CHOMP
GULP GULP
GZZZ ~~~
SNORT
JUST DO ONE AT A TIME!!!
BAM!
CLANK!!
REBECCA'S DAD IS THE OLD SOLDI...
ZZZ —
YOU HAVEN'T FULLY RECOVERED YET!!
STOP BEING A GLUTTON AND GET YOUR REST!!

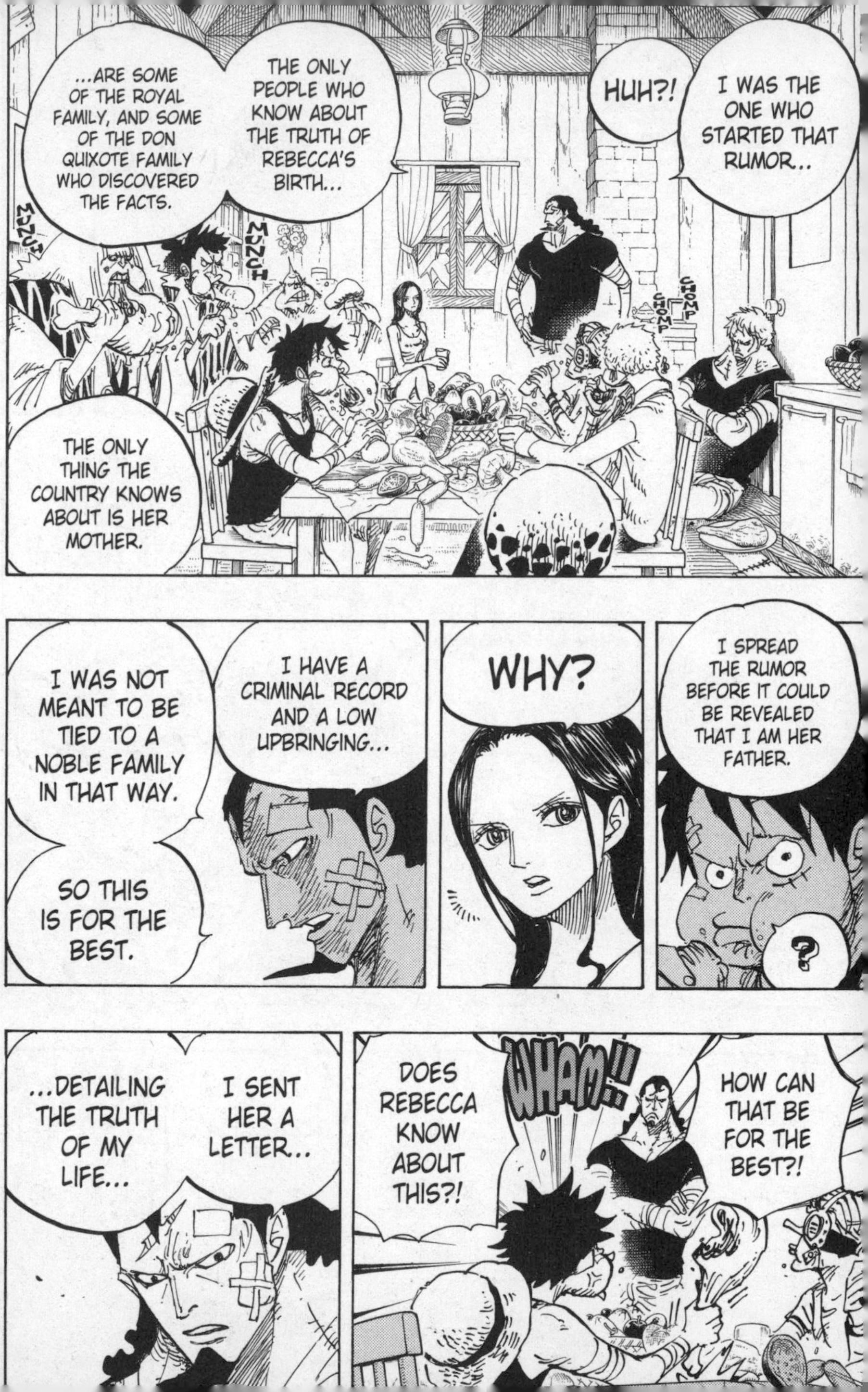
I WAS THE ONE WHO STARTED THAT RUMOR...
HUH?!
THE ONLY PEOPLE WHO KNOW ABOUT THE TRUTH OF REBECCA'S BIRTH...
...ARE SOME OF THE ROYAL FAMILY, AND SOME OF THE DON QUIXOTE FAMILY WHO DISCOVERED THE FACTS.
CHOMP
CHOMP
MUNCH
MUNCH
THE ONLY THING THE COUNTRY KNOWS ABOUT IS HER MOTHER.
I SPREAD THE RUMOR BEFORE IT COULD BE REVEALED THAT I AM HER FATHER.
?
WHY?
I HAVE A CRIMINAL RECORD AND A LOW UPBRINGING...
I WAS NOT MEANT TO BE TIED TO A NOBLE FAMILY IN THAT WAY.
SO THIS IS FOR THE BEST.
HOW CAN THAT BE FOR THE BEST?!
WHAM!!
DOES REBECCA KNOW ABOUT THIS?!
I SENT HER A LETTER...
...DETAILING THE TRUTH OF MY LIFE...

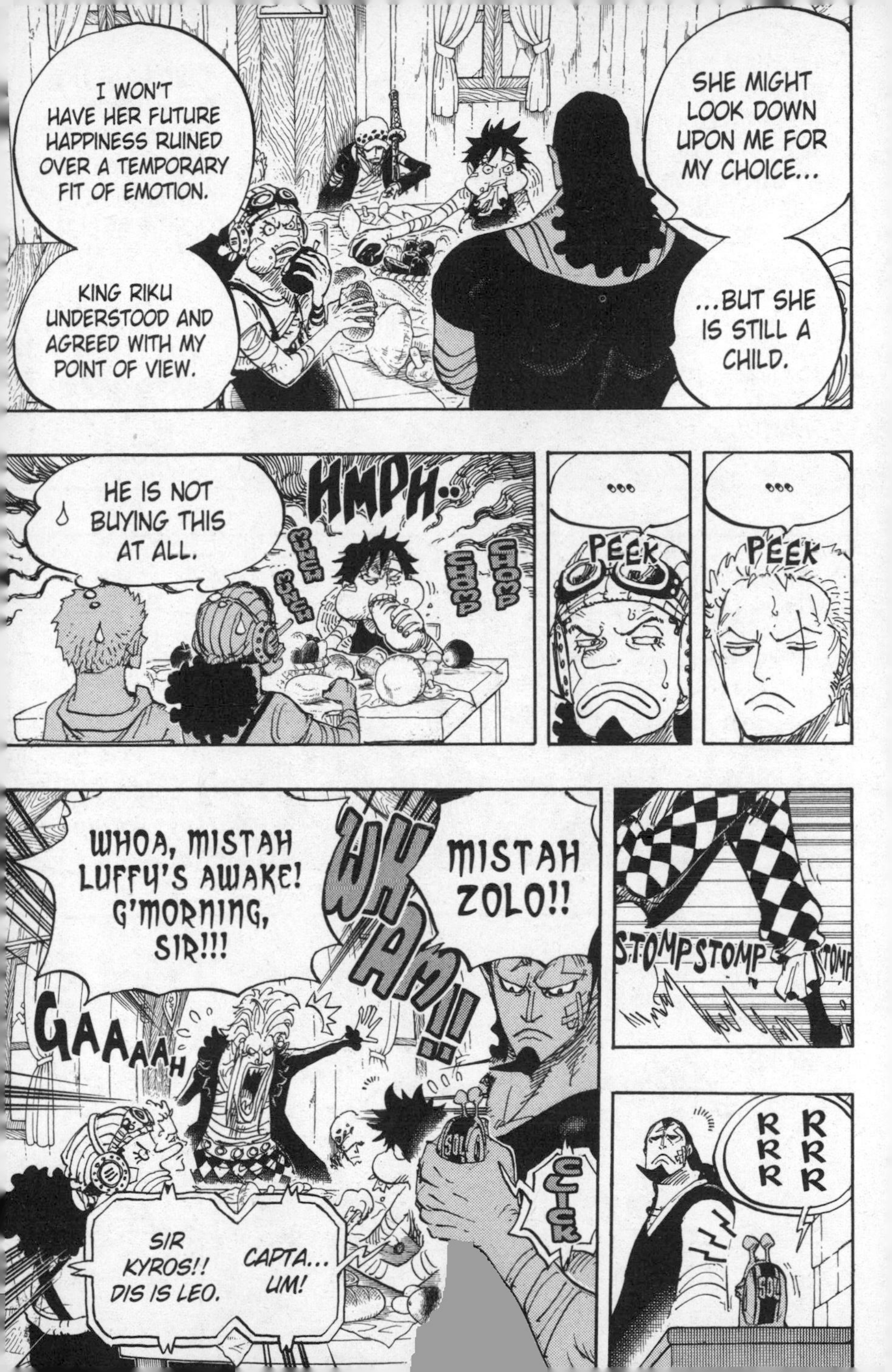
SHE MIGHT LOOK DOWN UPON ME FOR MY CHOICE...
...BUT SHE IS STILL A CHILD.
I WON'T HAVE HER FUTURE HAPPINESS RUINED OVER A TEMPORARY FIT OF EMOTION.
KING RIKU UNDERSTOOD AND AGREED WITH MY POINT OF VIEW.
...
PEEK
...
PEEK
HMPH..
CHOMP
CHOMP
MUNCH MUNCH
HE IS NOT BUYING THIS AT ALL.
STOMP STOMP STOMP
RRR RRR
MISTAH ZOLO!!
WHOA, MISTAH LUFFY'S AWAKE! G'MORNING, SIR!!!
WHAM!!
GAAAAH
CLICK
CAPTA... UM!
SIR KYROS!! DIS IS LEO.

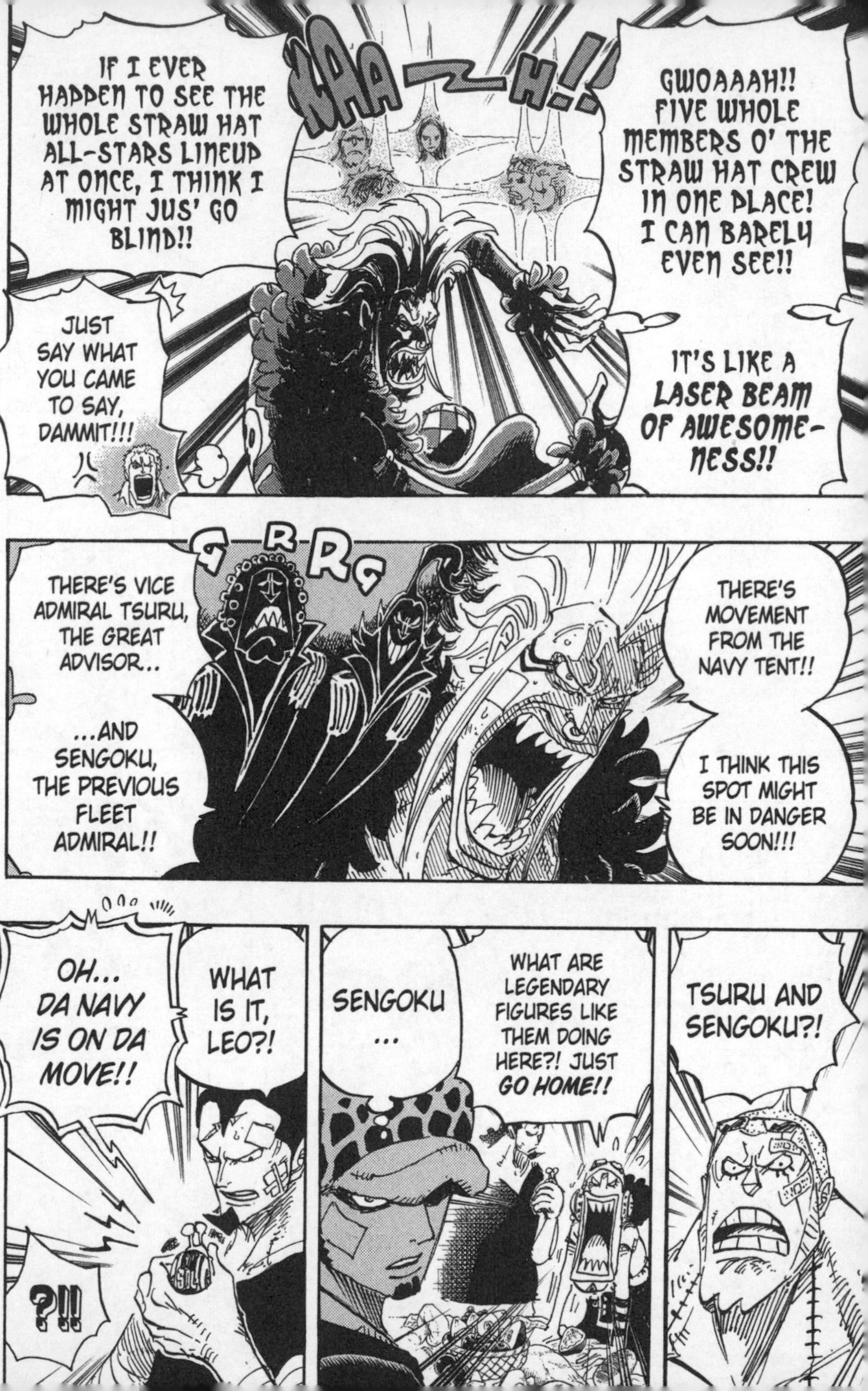
WAA—H!!
GWOAAAH!! FIVE WHOLE MEMBERS O' THE STRAW HAT CREW IN ONE PLACE! I CAN BARELY EVEN SEE!!
IF I EVER HAPPEN TO SEE THE WHOLE STRAW HAT ALL-STARS LINEUP AT ONCE, I THINK I MIGHT JUS' GO BLIND!!
IT'S LIKE A LASER BEAM OF AWESOME-NESS!!
JUST SAY WHAT YOU CAME TO SAY, DAMMIT!!!
THERE'S MOVEMENT FROM THE NAVY TENT!!
I THINK THIS SPOT MIGHT BE IN DANGER SOON!!!
GRRRG
THERE'S VICE ADMIRAL TSURU, THE GREAT ADVISOR...
...AND SENGOKU, THE PREVIOUS FLEET ADMIRAL!!
TSURU AND SENGOKU?!
WHAT ARE LEGENDARY FIGURES LIKE THEM DOING HERE?! JUST GO HOME!!
SENGOKU ...
WHAT IS IT, LEO?!
OH... DA NAVY IS ON DA MOVE!!
?!!

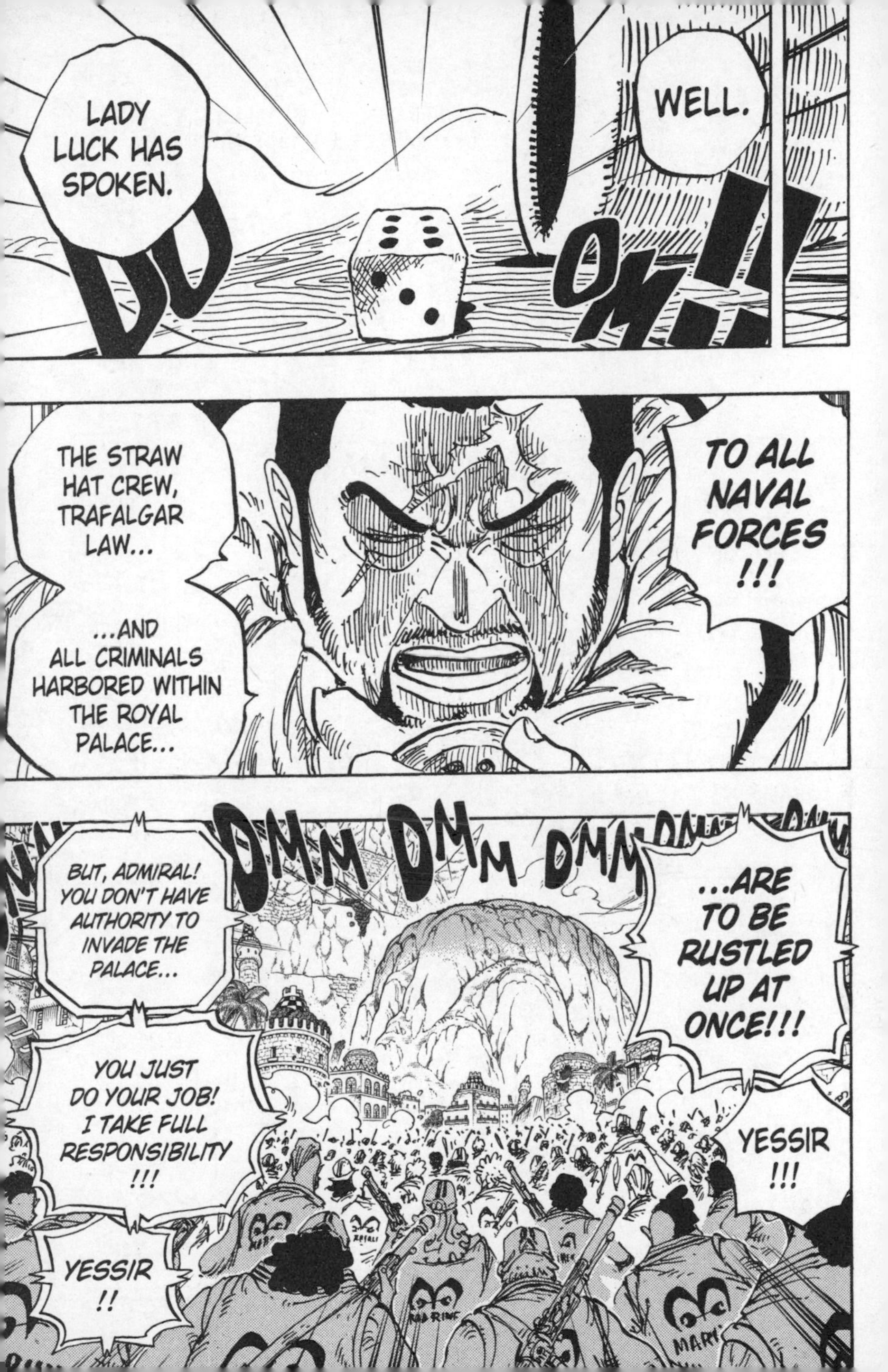
WELL.
OM!!
LADY LUCK HAS SPOKEN.
DO
TO ALL NAVAL FORCES!!!
THE STRAW HAT CREW, TRAFALGAR LAW...
...AND ALL CRIMINALS HARBORED WITHIN THE ROYAL PALACE...
DMM DMM DMM
...ARE TO BE RUSTLED UP AT ONCE!!!
YESSIR!!!
BUT, ADMIRAL! YOU DON'T HAVE AUTHORITY TO INVADE THE PALACE...
YOU JUST DO YOUR JOB! I TAKE FULL RESPONSIBILITY!!!
YESSIR!!

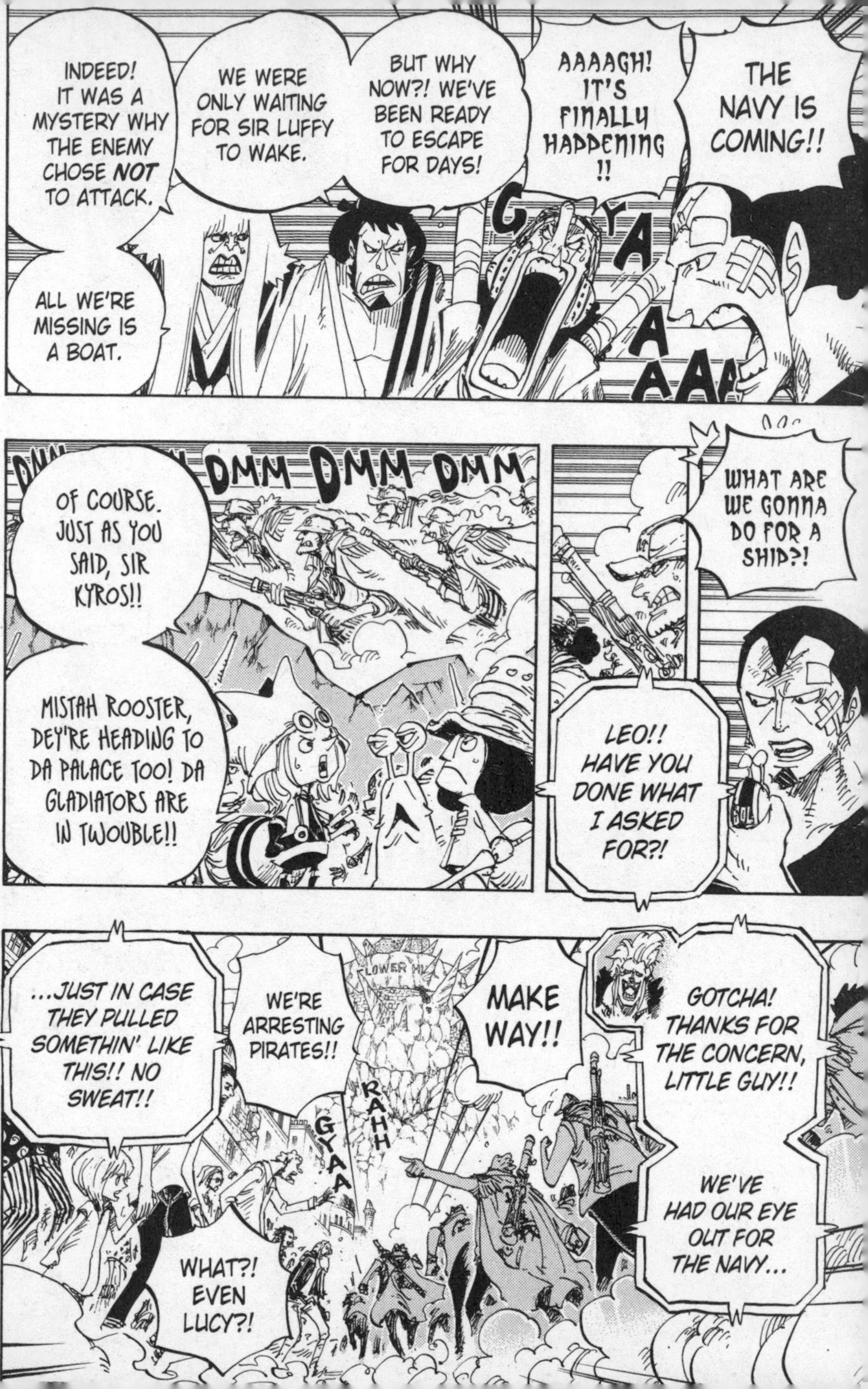
THE NAVY IS COMING!!
AAAAGH! IT'S FINALLY HAPPENING!!
GYAAAAA
BUT WHY NOW?! WE'VE BEEN READY TO ESCAPE FOR DAYS!
WE WERE ONLY WAITING FOR SIR LUFFY TO WAKE.
INDEED! IT WAS A MYSTERY WHY THE ENEMY CHOSE *NOT* TO ATTACK.
ALL WE'RE MISSING IS A BOAT.
WHAT ARE WE GONNA DO FOR A SHIP?!
LEO!! HAVE YOU DONE WHAT I ASKED FOR?!
DMM DMM DMM
OF COURSE. JUST AS YOU SAID, SIR KYROS!!
MISTAH ROOSTER, DEY'RE HEADING TO DA PALACE TOO! DA GLADIATORS ARE IN TWOUBLE!!
GOTCHA! THANKS FOR THE CONCERN, LITTLE GUY!!
WE'VE HAD OUR EYE OUT FOR THE NAVY...
MAKE WAY!!
WE'RE ARRESTING PIRATES!!
RAHH
GYAA
...JUST IN CASE THEY PULLED SOMETHIN' LIKE THIS!! NO SWEAT!!
WHAT?! EVEN LUCY?!

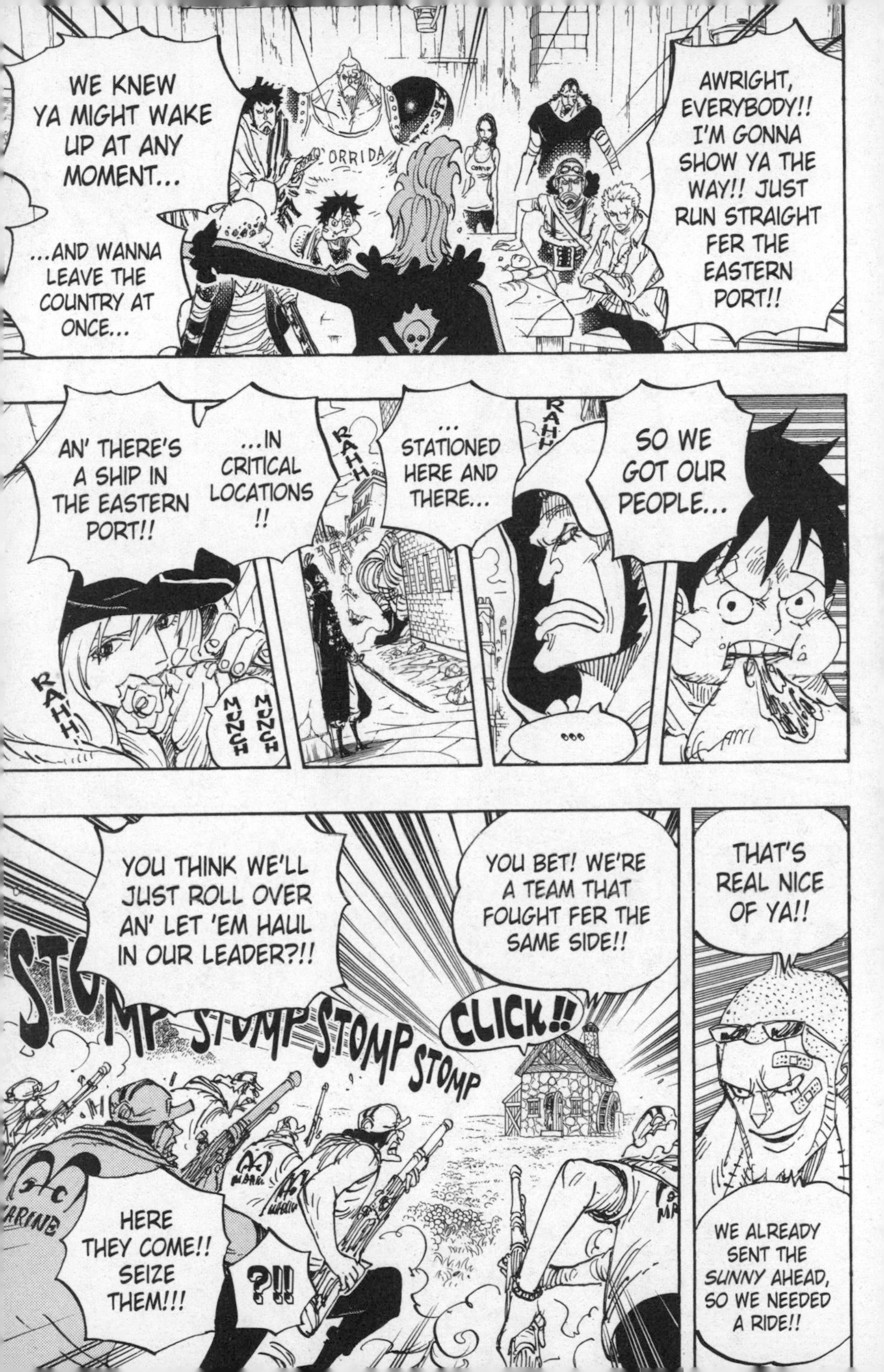
AWRIGHT, EVERYBODY!! I'M GONNA SHOW YA THE WAY!! JUST RUN STRAIGHT FER THE EASTERN PORT!!
WE KNEW YA MIGHT WAKE UP AT ANY MOMENT...
...AND WANNA LEAVE THE COUNTRY AT ONCE...
SO WE GOT OUR PEOPLE...
RAHH
...
... STATIONED HERE AND THERE...
RAHH
...IN CRITICAL LOCATIONS !!
RAHH
AN' THERE'S A SHIP IN THE EASTERN PORT!!
MUNCH MUNCH
RAHH
THAT'S REAL NICE OF YA!!
WE ALREADY SENT THE *SUNNY* AHEAD, SO WE NEEDED A RIDE!!
YOU BET! WE'RE A TEAM THAT FOUGHT FER THE SAME SIDE!!
CLICK!!
YOU THINK WE'LL JUST ROLL OVER AN' LET 'EM HAUL IN OUR LEADER?!!
STOMP STOMP STOMP STOMP
HERE THEY COME!! SEIZE THEM!!!
?!!

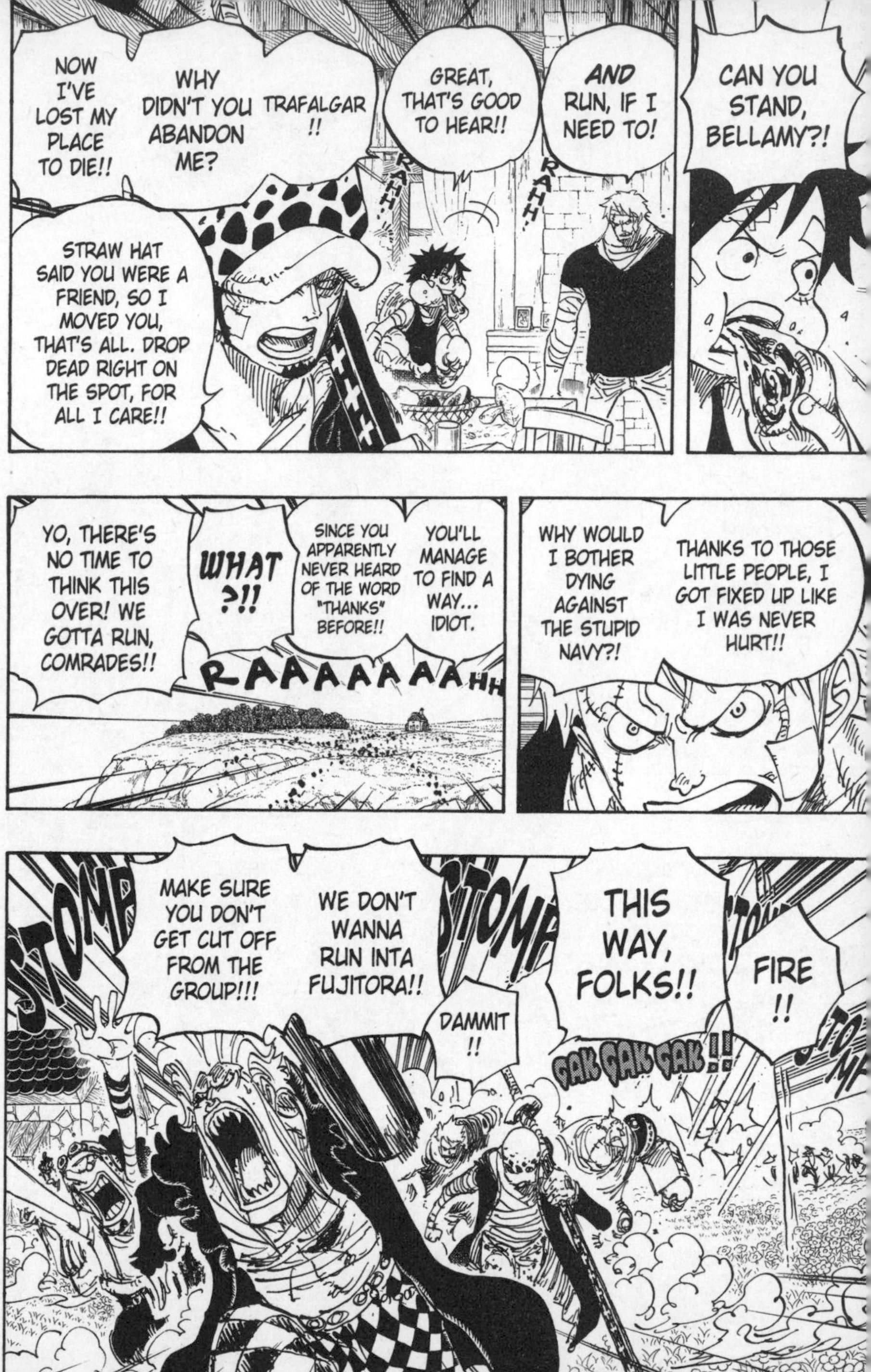
CAN YOU STAND, BELLAMY?!
AND RUN, IF I NEED TO!
RAHH!!
GREAT, THAT'S GOOD TO HEAR!!
RAHH!!
TRAFALGAR !!
WHY DIDN'T YOU ABANDON ME?
NOW I'VE LOST MY PLACE TO DIE!!
STRAW HAT SAID YOU WERE A FRIEND, SO I MOVED YOU, THAT'S ALL. DROP DEAD RIGHT ON THE SPOT, FOR ALL I CARE!!
THANKS TO THOSE LITTLE PEOPLE, I GOT FIXED UP LIKE I WAS NEVER HURT!!
WHY WOULD I BOTHER DYING AGAINST THE STUPID NAVY?!
YOU'LL MANAGE TO FIND A WAY... IDIOT.
SINCE YOU APPARENTLY NEVER HEARD OF THE WORD "THANKS" BEFORE!!
WHAT ?!!
YO, THERE'S NO TIME TO THINK THIS OVER! WE GOTTA RUN, COMRADES!!
RAAAAAAAAHH
STOMP
FIRE !!
STOMP
THIS WAY, FOLKS!!
GAK GAK GAK !!
DAMMIT !!
WE DON'T WANNA RUN INTA FUJITORA!!
MAKE SURE YOU DON'T GET CUT OFF FROM THE GROUP!!!
STOMP
STOMP

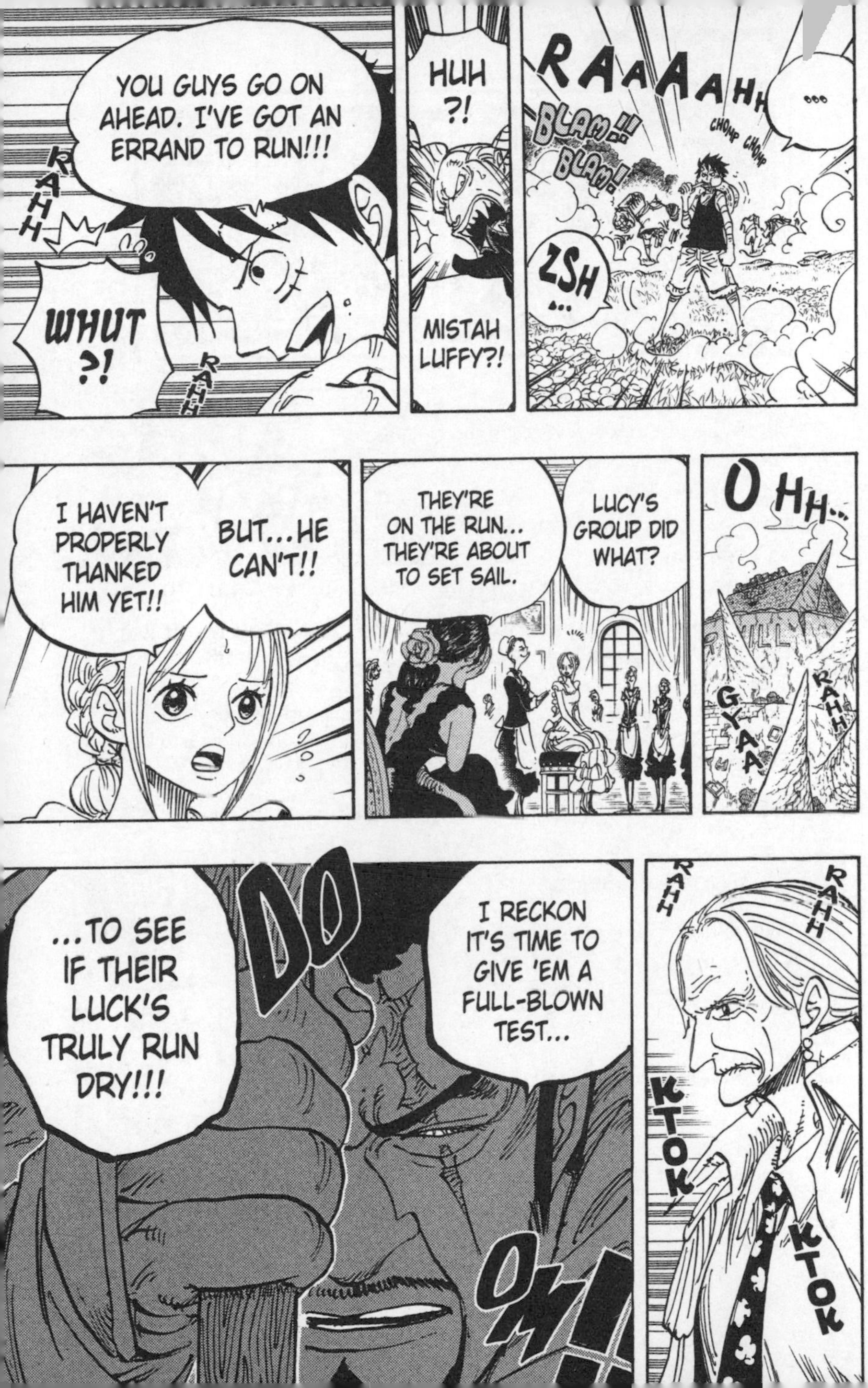
...
RAAAAAHH
CHOMP CHOMP
BLAM!! BLAM!
ZSH...
HUH ?!
MISTAH LUFFY?!
YOU GUYS GO ON AHEAD. I'VE GOT AN ERRAND TO RUN!!!
RAHH
RAHH
WHUT ?!
OHH...
RAHH
GYAA
LUCY'S GROUP DID WHAT?
THEY'RE ON THE RUN... THEY'RE ABOUT TO SET SAIL.
BUT...HE CAN'T!!
I HAVEN'T PROPERLY THANKED HIM YET!!
RAHH
RAHH
KTOK
KTOK
I RECKON IT'S TIME TO GIVE 'EM A FULL-BLOWN TEST...
...TO SEE IF THEIR LUCK'S TRULY RUN DRY!!!
DO
OM!!

## 質問コーナー SBS Question Corner

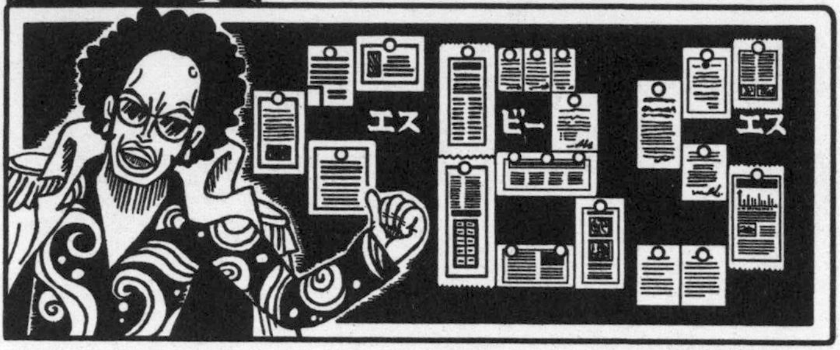
エス
ビー
エス

(Fujima, Fukuoka)

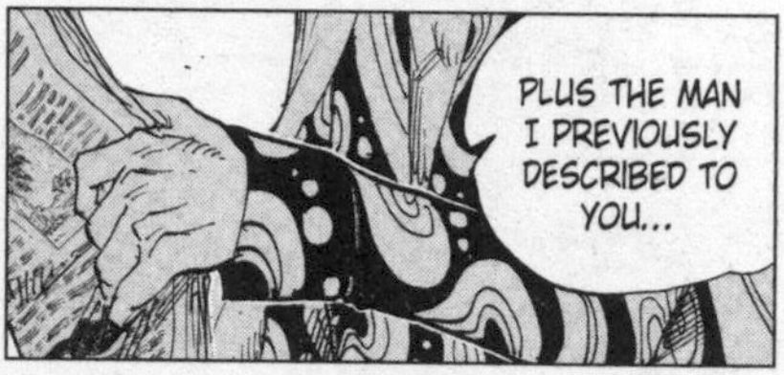
PLUS THE MAN I PREVIOUSLY DESCRIBED TO YOU...

**Q:** Hello, Odacchi. I'll be frank with you. When Brannew mentions the "man previously described" in Chapter 700, Volume 70, who is he talking about? Is it someone we've already seen?

--Someone who wants Odacchi to say "Start the SBS"

**A:** Aww, what a nice pen name. What's that? You want me? To start the...? Oh!! It already started!!!
Okay, let's go.
Yes, the final warlord shall be revealed in this very book. Check out Chapter 802, scream your lungs out, and look forward to what this character does in the future.

**Q:** What does the "SOL" on the one-legged soldier's hat mean?

--Takaaki T.

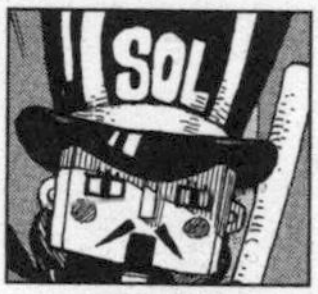
SOL

**A:** It's short for "Soldier."

**Q:** Can you turn into Hentai Kamen (Pervert Mask), Odacchi?

--Takaaki T.

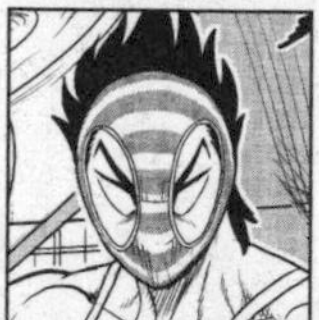

©Keishu Ando/Shueisha

**A:** I can.

**Q:** Why is Corazon's fruit called the Calm-Calm Fruit?

--Takaaki T.

**A:** Because that is the adjective that describes no wind and quiet waves on the sea.

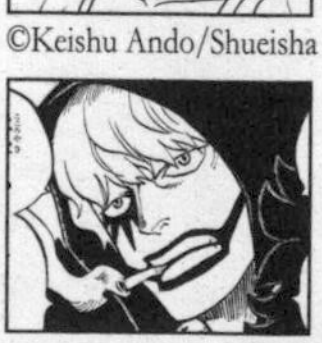

# Chapter 797:
# REBECCA

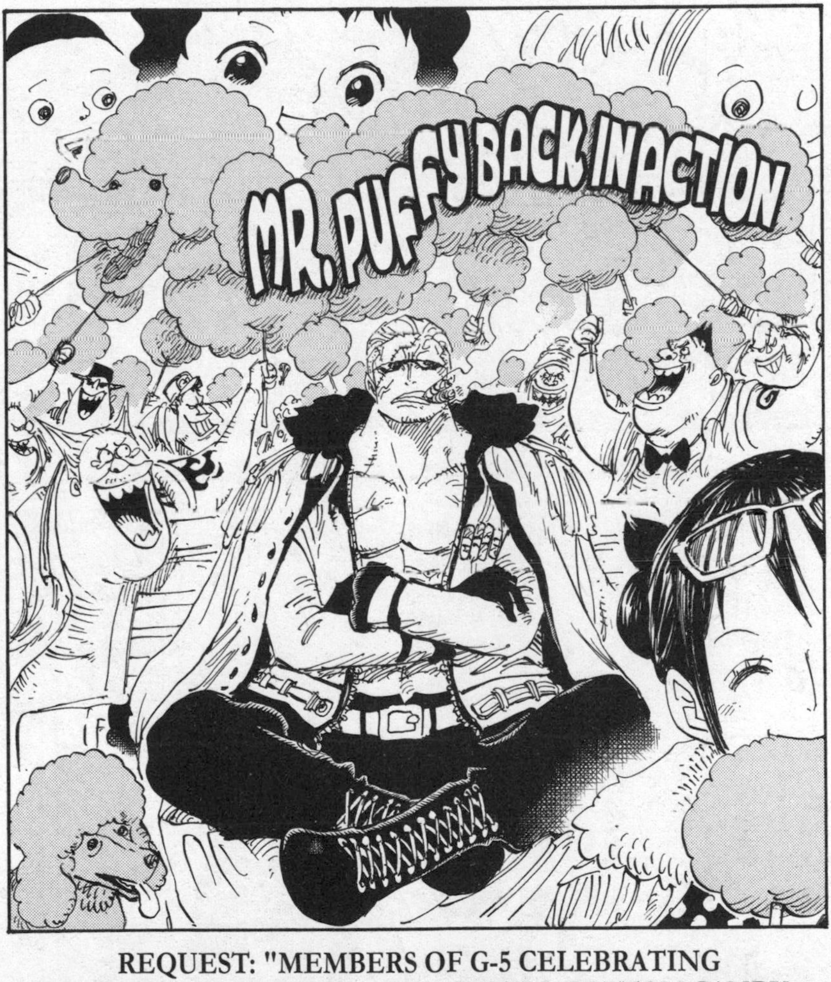
MR. PUFFY BACK IN ACTION

REQUEST: "MEMBERS OF G-5 CELEBRATING SMOKER'S RETURN TO DUTY WITH A COTTON CANDY PARTY" BY SHEENA FROM AICHI

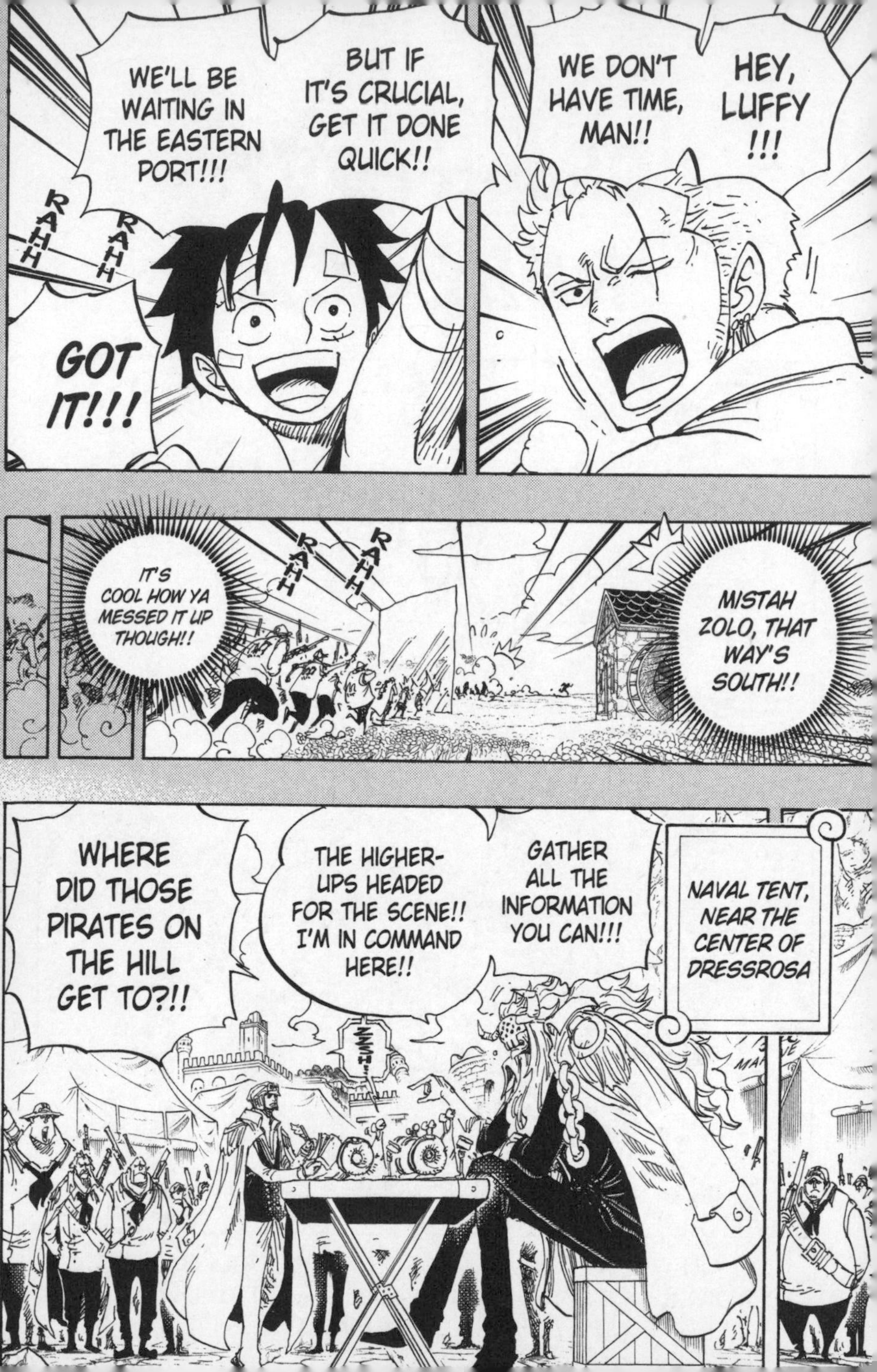
HEY, LUFFY!!!
WE DON'T HAVE TIME, MAN!!
BUT IF IT'S CRUCIAL, GET IT DONE QUICK!!
WE'LL BE WAITING IN THE EASTERN PORT!!!
RAHH
RAHH
GOT IT!!!
MISTAH ZOLO, THAT WAY'S SOUTH!!
RAHH
RAHH
IT'S COOL HOW YA MESSED IT UP THOUGH!!
NAVAL TENT, NEAR THE CENTER OF DRESSROSA
GATHER ALL THE INFORMATION YOU CAN!!!
THE HIGHER-UPS HEADED FOR THE SCENE!! I'M IN COMMAND HERE!!
WHERE DID THOSE PIRATES ON THE HILL GET TO?!!
ZSSH

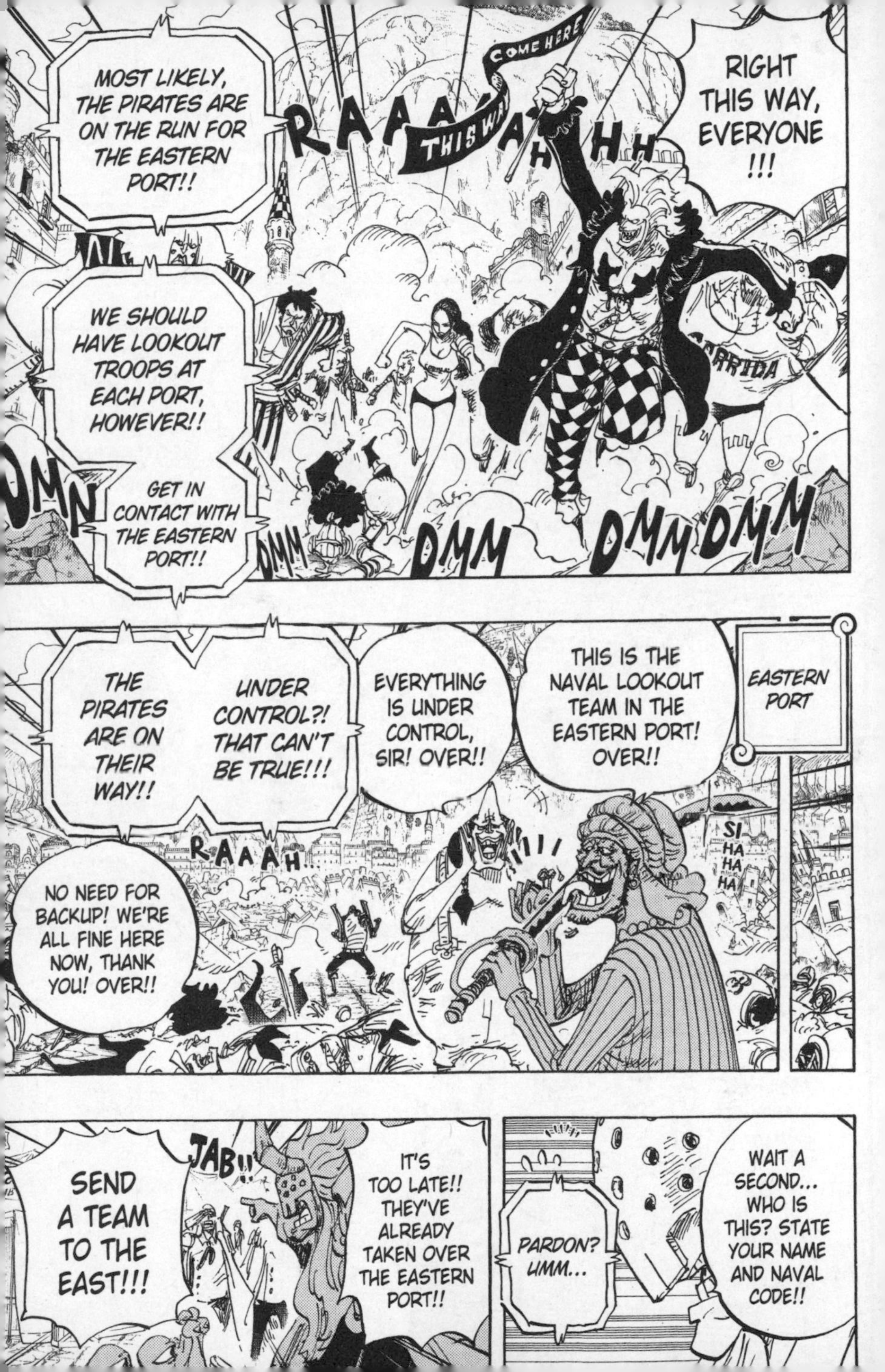

RIGHT THIS WAY, EVERYONE!!!
COME HERE
THIS WAY
RAAAAHHH
MOST LIKELY, THE PIRATES ARE ON THE RUN FOR THE EASTERN PORT!!
WE SHOULD HAVE LOOKOUT TROOPS AT EACH PORT, HOWEVER!!
DMM DMM
DMM
GET IN CONTACT WITH THE EASTERN PORT!!
DMM
DMM
EASTERN PORT
THIS IS THE NAVAL LOOKOUT TEAM IN THE EASTERN PORT! OVER!!
EVERYTHING IS UNDER CONTROL, SIR! OVER!!
UNDER CONTROL?! THAT CAN'T BE TRUE!!!
THE PIRATES ARE ON THEIR WAY!!
SI HA HA HA
RAAAH..
NO NEED FOR BACKUP! WE'RE ALL FINE HERE NOW, THANK YOU! OVER!!
WAIT A SECOND... WHO IS THIS? STATE YOUR NAME AND NAVAL CODE!!
PARDON? UMM...
IT'S TOO LATE!! THEY'VE ALREADY TAKEN OVER THE EASTERN PORT!!
JAB!!
SEND A TEAM TO THE EAST!!!

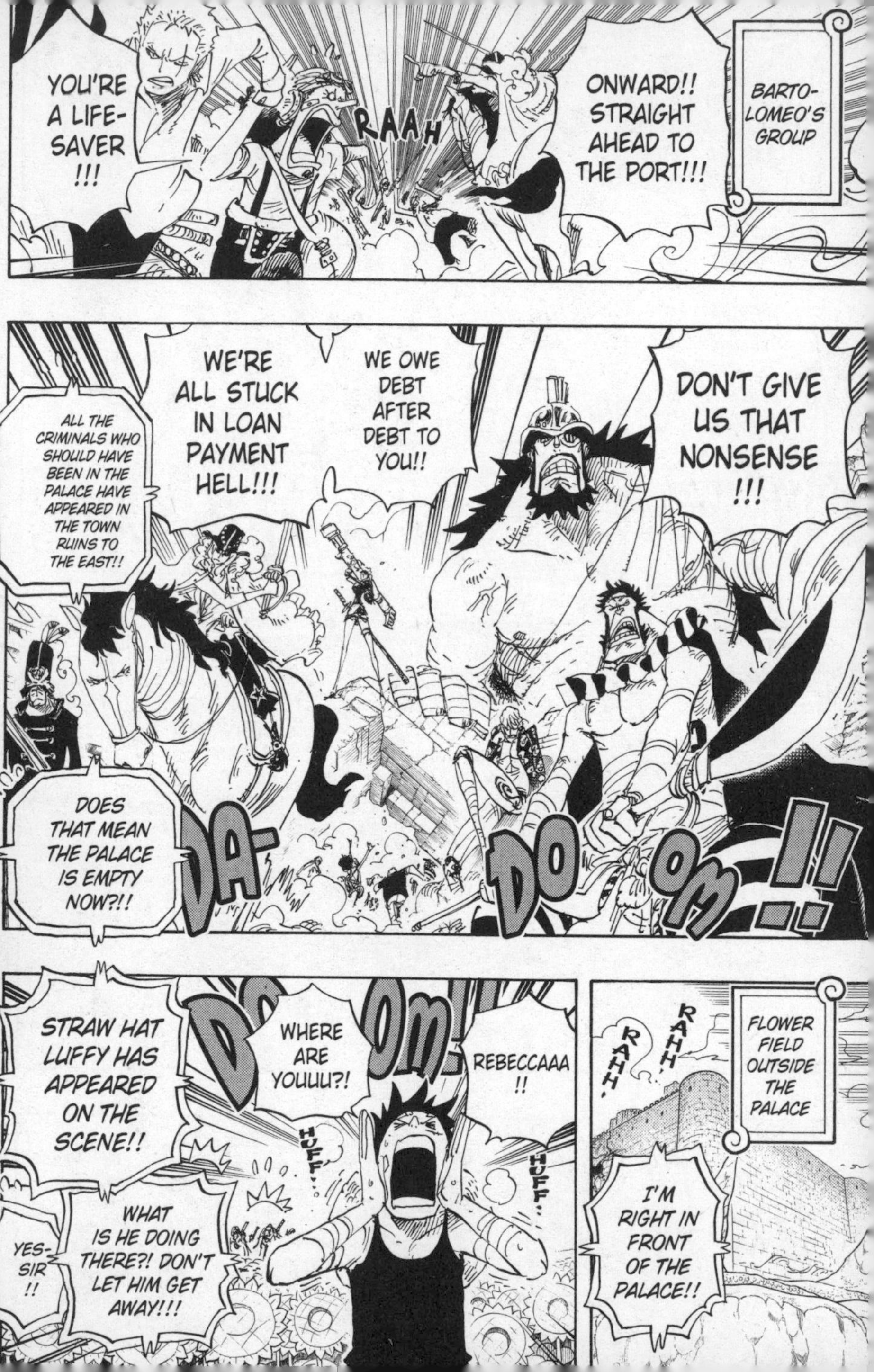
BARTO-LOMEO'S GROUP
ONWARD!! STRAIGHT AHEAD TO THE PORT!!!
RAAH
YOU'RE A LIFE-SAVER!!!
DON'T GIVE US THAT NONSENSE!!!
WE OWE DEBT AFTER DEBT TO YOU!!
WE'RE ALL STUCK IN LOAN PAYMENT HELL!!!
ALL THE CRIMINALS WHO SHOULD HAVE BEEN IN THE PALACE HAVE APPEARED IN THE TOWN RUINS TO THE EAST!!
DOES THAT MEAN THE PALACE IS EMPTY NOW?!!
DA-DOOM..!!
FLOWER FIELD OUTSIDE THE PALACE
RAHH
RAHH
I'M RIGHT IN FRONT OF THE PALACE!!
REBECCAAA!!
WHERE ARE YOUUU?!
STRAW HAT LUFFY HAS APPEARED ON THE SCENE!!
HUFF...
HUFF...
WHAT IS HE DOING THERE?! DON'T LET HIM GET AWAY!!!
YES-SIR!!

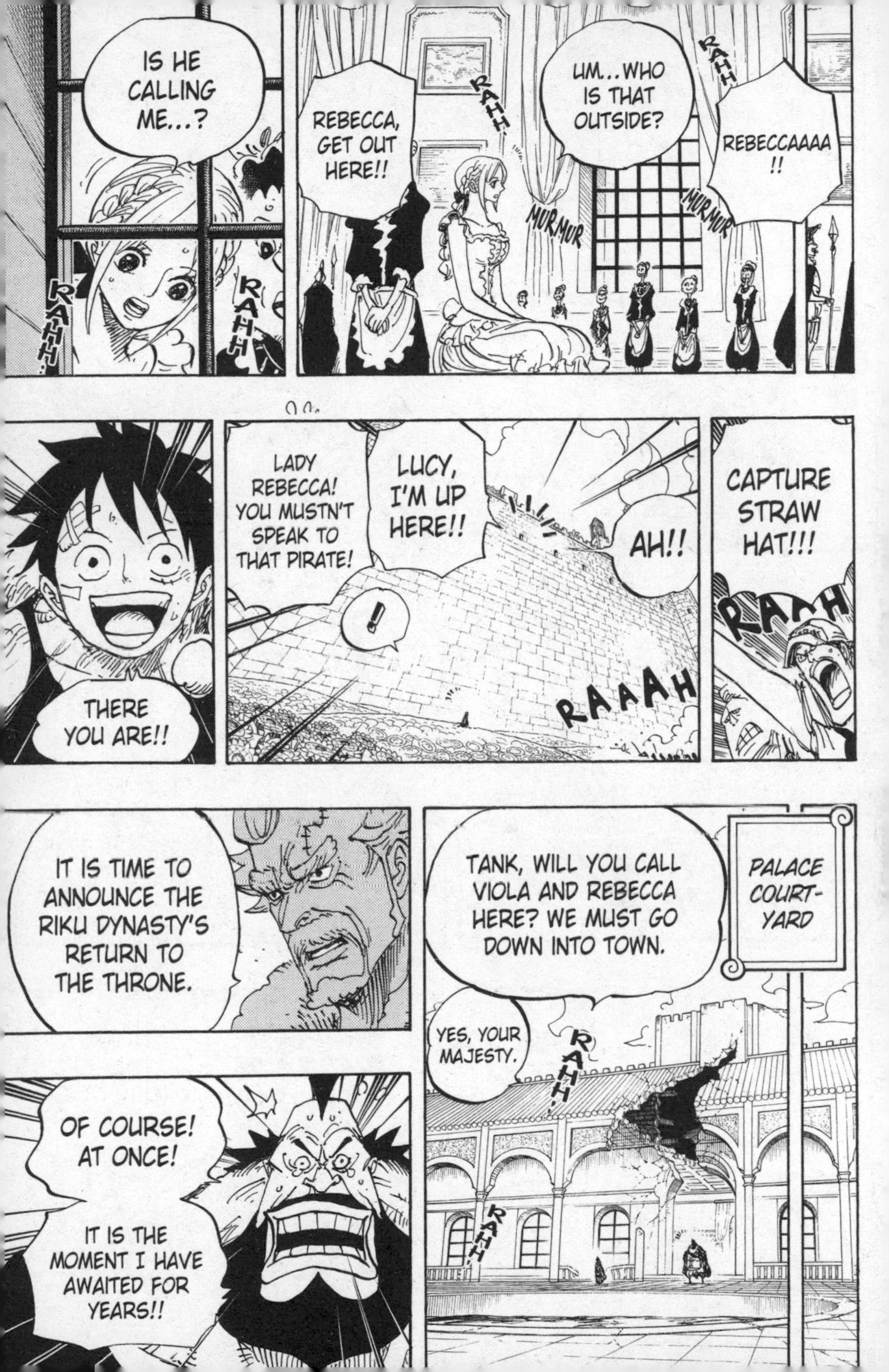
RAHH
UM...WHO IS THAT OUTSIDE?
REBECCAAAA !!
MURMUR
MURMUR
REBECCA, GET OUT HERE!!
RAHH
IS HE CALLING ME...?
RAHH
RAHH...
CAPTURE STRAW HAT!!!
RAAH
AH!!
LUCY, I'M UP HERE!!
LADY REBECCA! YOU MUSTN'T SPEAK TO THAT PIRATE!
!
RAAAH
THERE YOU ARE!!
PALACE COURT-YARD
TANK, WILL YOU CALL VIOLA AND REBECCA HERE? WE MUST GO DOWN INTO TOWN.
YES, YOUR MAJESTY.
RAHH!
RAHH
IT IS TIME TO ANNOUNCE THE RIKU DYNASTY'S RETURN TO THE THRONE.
OF COURSE! AT ONCE!
IT IS THE MOMENT I HAVE AWAITED FOR YEARS!!

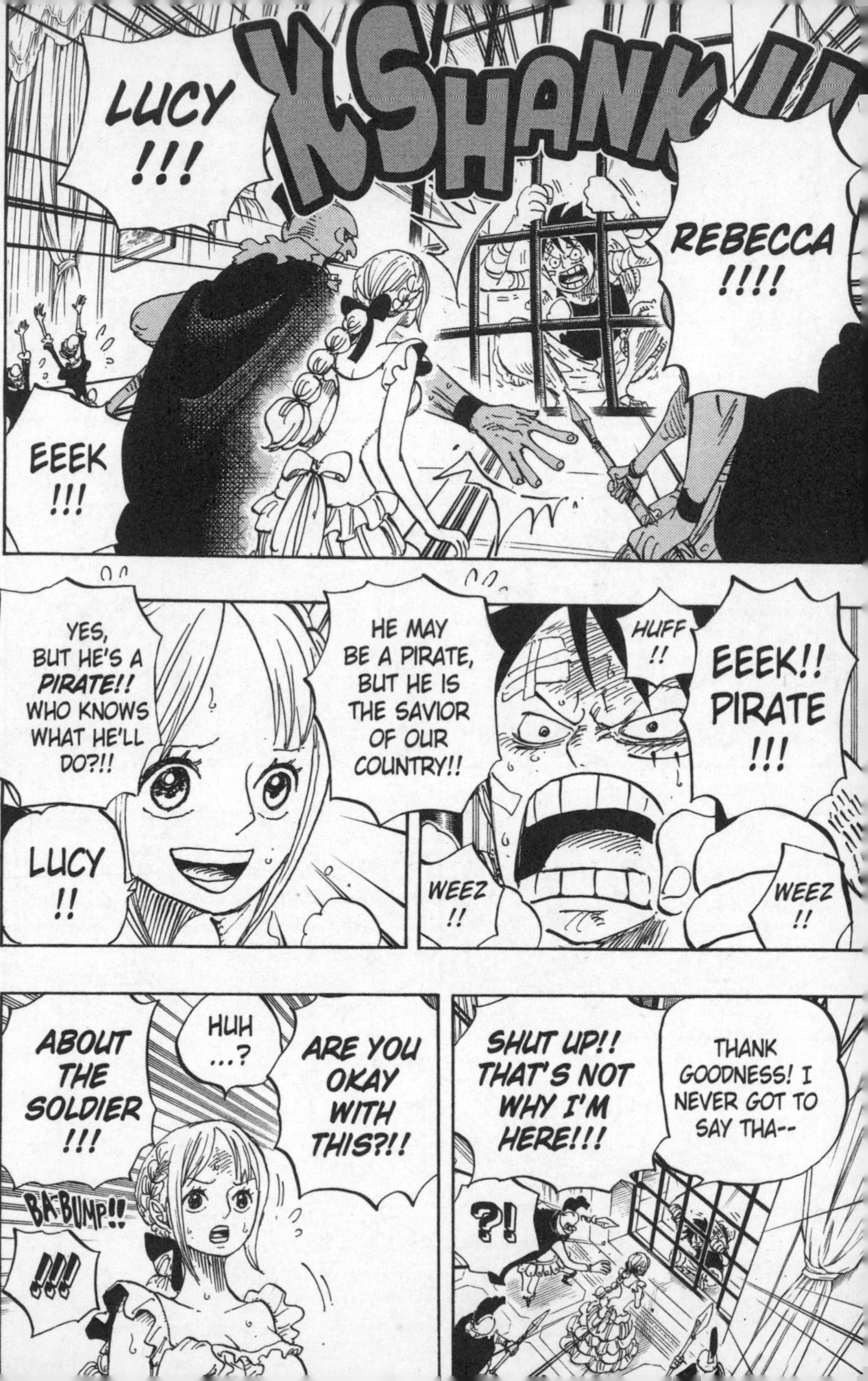
KSHANK!!
REBECCA !!!!
LUCY !!!
EEEK !!!
HUFF !!
EEEK!! PIRATE !!!
WEEZ !!
WEEZ !!
HE MAY BE A PIRATE, BUT HE IS THE SAVIOR OF OUR COUNTRY!!
YES, BUT HE'S A PIRATE!! WHO KNOWS WHAT HE'LL DO?!!
LUCY !!
THANK GOODNESS! I NEVER GOT TO SAY THA--
SHUT UP!! THAT'S NOT WHY I'M HERE!!!
?!
ARE YOU OKAY WITH THIS?!!
HUH ...?
ABOUT THE SOLDIER !!!
BA-BUMP!!
!!!

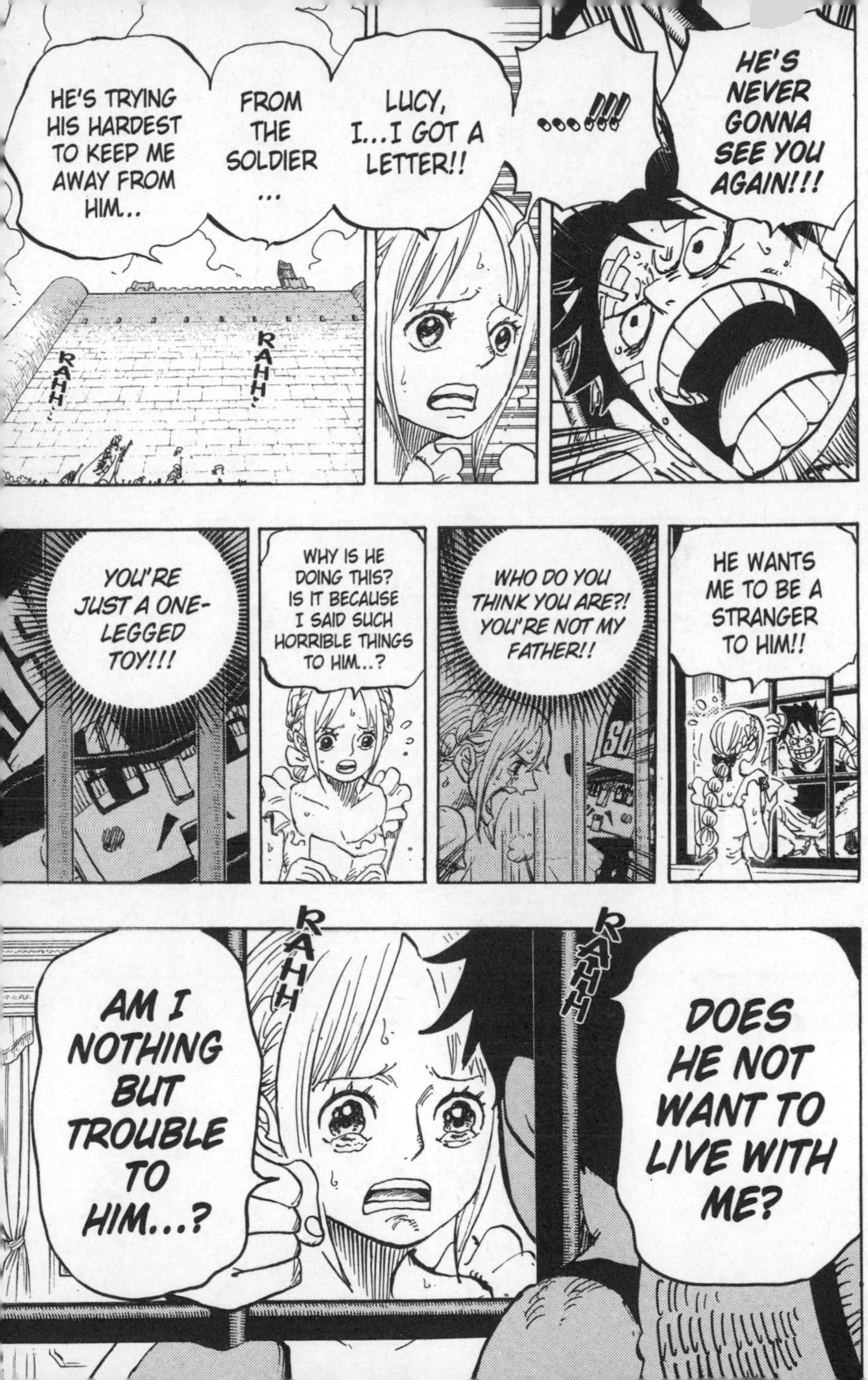
HE'S NEVER GONNA SEE YOU AGAIN!!!
...!!!
LUCY, I...I GOT A LETTER!!
FROM THE SOLDIER ...
HE'S TRYING HIS HARDEST TO KEEP ME AWAY FROM HIM...
RAHH
RAHH
HE WANTS ME TO BE A STRANGER TO HIM!!
WHO DO YOU THINK YOU ARE?! YOU'RE NOT MY FATHER!!
WHY IS HE DOING THIS? IS IT BECAUSE I SAID SUCH HORRIBLE THINGS TO HIM...?
YOU'RE JUST A ONE-LEGGED TOY!!!
DOES HE NOT WANT TO LIVE WITH ME?
RAHH
RAHH
AM I NOTHING BUT TROUBLE TO HIM...?

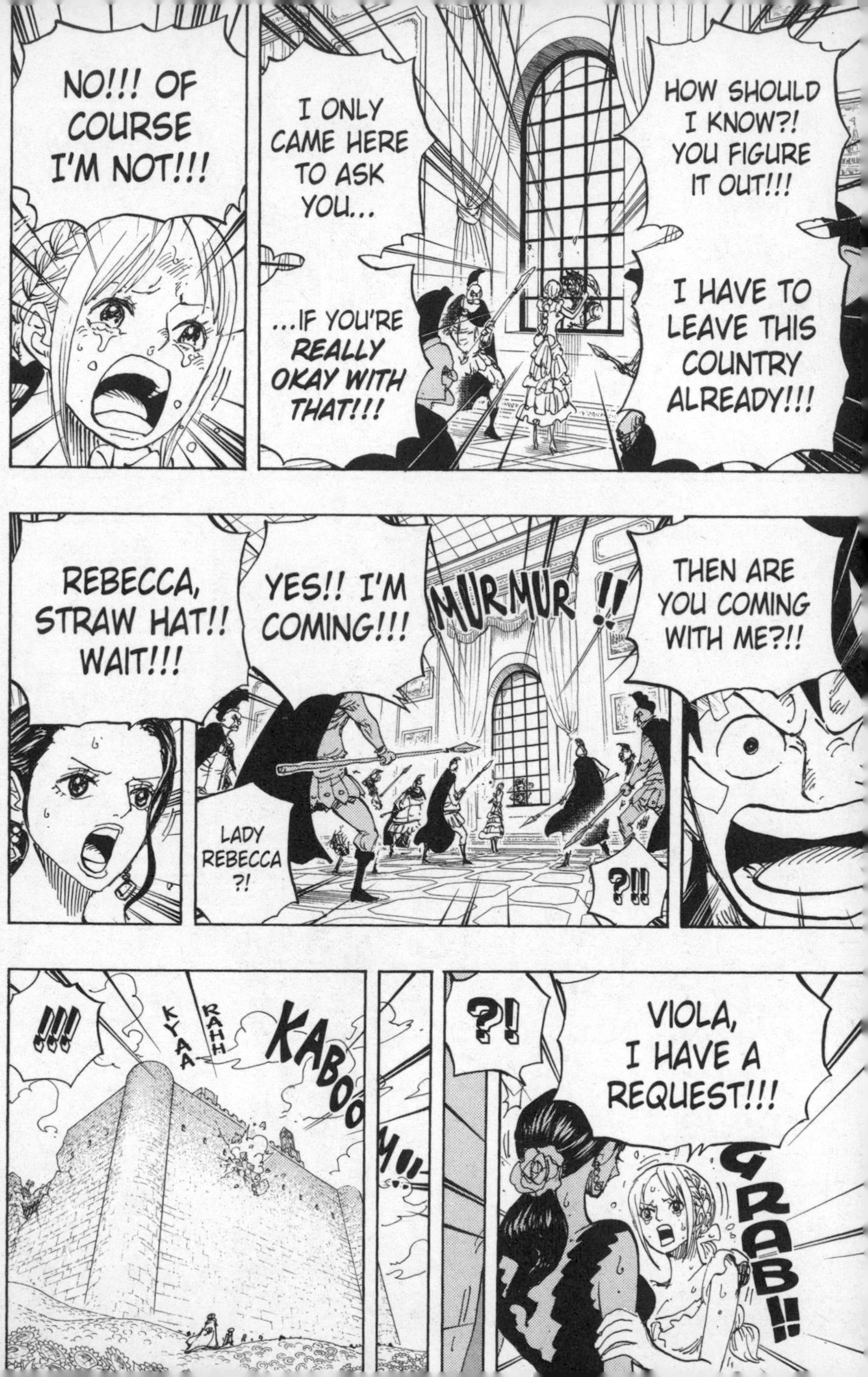
HOW SHOULD I KNOW?! YOU FIGURE IT OUT!!!
I HAVE TO LEAVE THIS COUNTRY ALREADY!!!
I ONLY CAME HERE TO ASK YOU...
...IF YOU'RE *REALLY OKAY WITH THAT!!!*
NO!!! OF COURSE I'M NOT!!!
THEN ARE YOU COMING WITH ME?!!
?!!
YES!! I'M COMING!!!
MURMUR !!
LADY REBECCA ?!
REBECCA, STRAW HAT!! WAIT!!!
?!
VIOLA, I HAVE A REQUEST!!!
GRAB!!
!!!
RAHH
KYAA
KABOOM!!

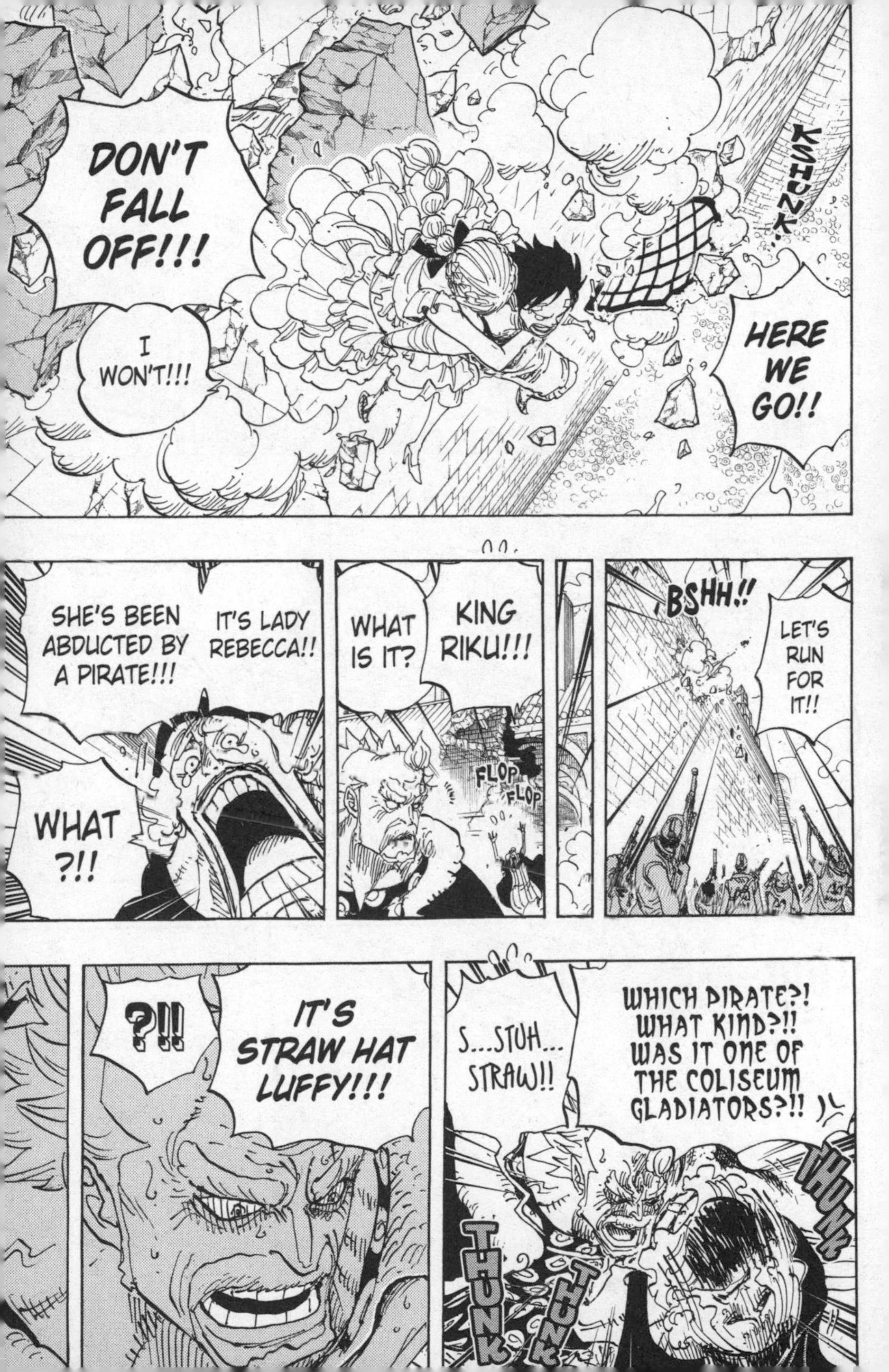
KSHUNK
HERE WE GO!!
DON'T FALL OFF!!!
I WON'T!!!
BSHH!!
LET'S RUN FOR IT!!
KING RIKU!!!
WHAT IS IT?
FLOP
FLOP
IT'S LADY REBECCA!!
SHE'S BEEN ABDUCTED BY A PIRATE!!!
WHAT ?!!
WHICH PIRATE?! WHAT KIND?!! WAS IT ONE OF THE COLISEUM GLADIATORS?!!
S...STUH... STRAW!!
THUNK
THUNK
THUNK
IT'S STRAW HAT LUFFY!!!
?!!

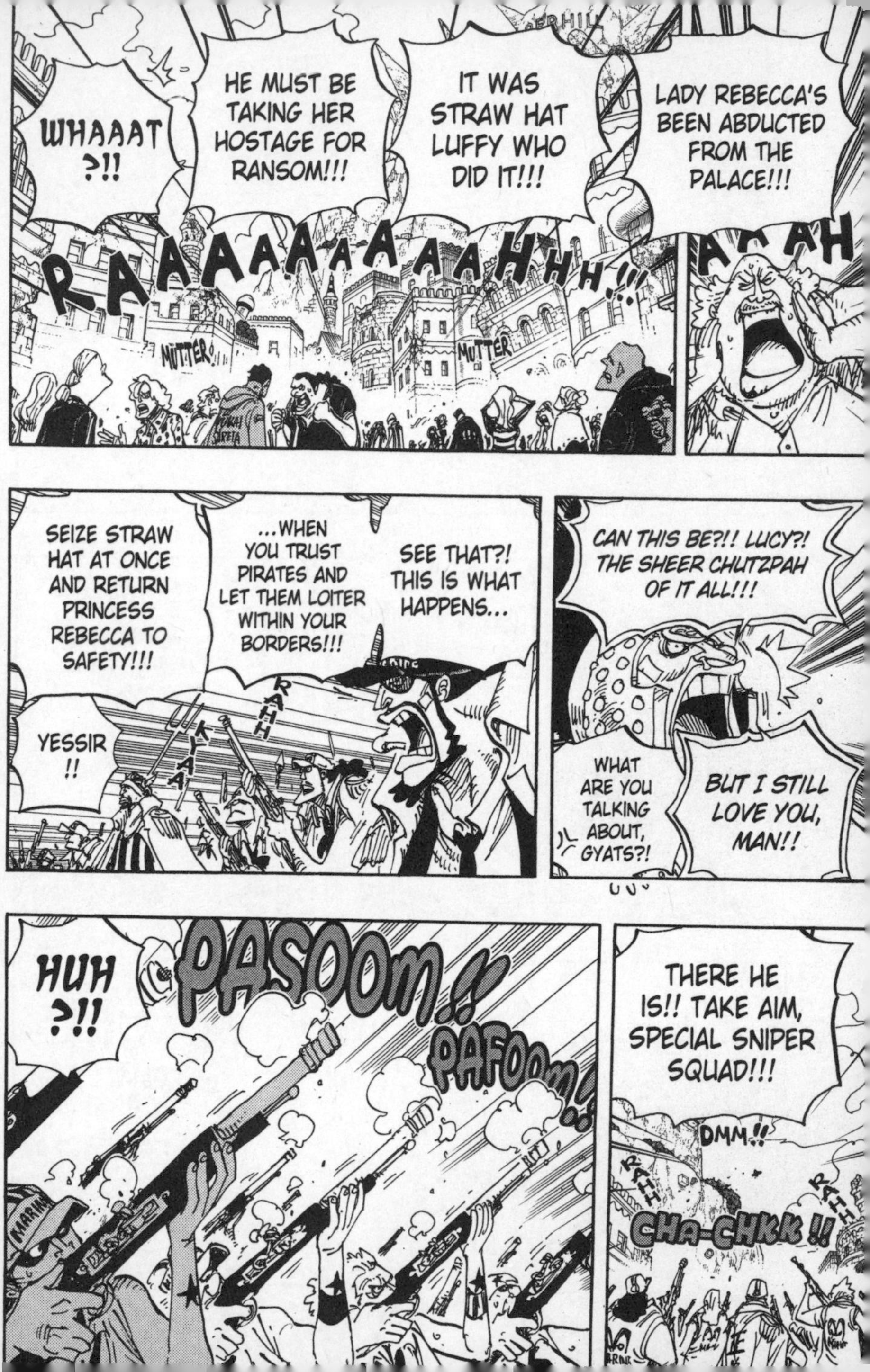

LADY REBECCA'S BEEN ABDUCTED FROM THE PALACE!!!
IT WAS STRAW HAT LUFFY WHO DID IT!!!
HE MUST BE TAKING HER HOSTAGE FOR RANSOM!!!
WHAAAT ?!!
AAAH
RAAAAAAAAAHHHH!!!
MUTTER
MUTTER
CAN THIS BE?!! LUCY?! THE SHEER CHUTZPAH OF IT ALL!!!
BUT I STILL LOVE YOU, MAN!!
WHAT ARE YOU TALKING ABOUT, GYATS?!
SEE THAT?! THIS IS WHAT HAPPENS...
...WHEN YOU TRUST PIRATES AND LET THEM LOITER WITHIN YOUR BORDERS!!!
SEIZE STRAW HAT AT ONCE AND RETURN PRINCESS REBECCA TO SAFETY!!!
RAHH
KYAA
YESSIR !!
THERE HE IS!! TAKE AIM, SPECIAL SNIPER SQUAD!!!
DMM!!
RAHH
CHA-CHKK!!
RAHH
PASOOM!!
PAFOOM!!
HUH ?!!

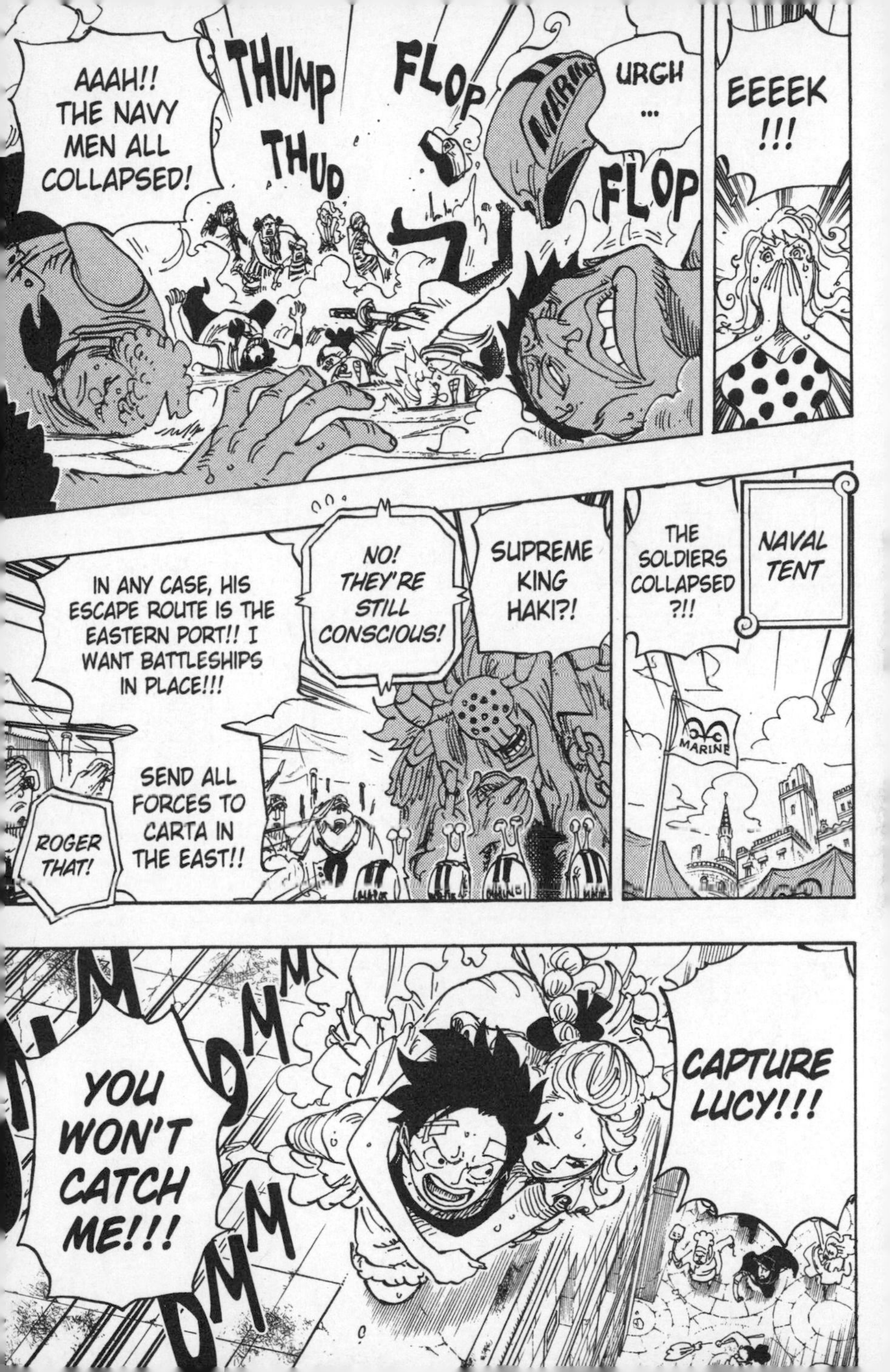
EEEEK!!!
URGH...
FLOP
FLOP
THUMP
THUD
AAAH!! THE NAVY MEN ALL COLLAPSED!
NAVAL TENT
THE SOLDIERS COLLAPSED?!!
SUPREME KING HAKI?!
NO! THEY'RE STILL CONSCIOUS!
IN ANY CASE, HIS ESCAPE ROUTE IS THE EASTERN PORT!! I WANT BATTLESHIPS IN PLACE!!!
SEND ALL FORCES TO CARTA IN THE EAST!!
ROGER THAT!
CAPTURE LUCY!!!
YOU WON'T CATCH ME!!!

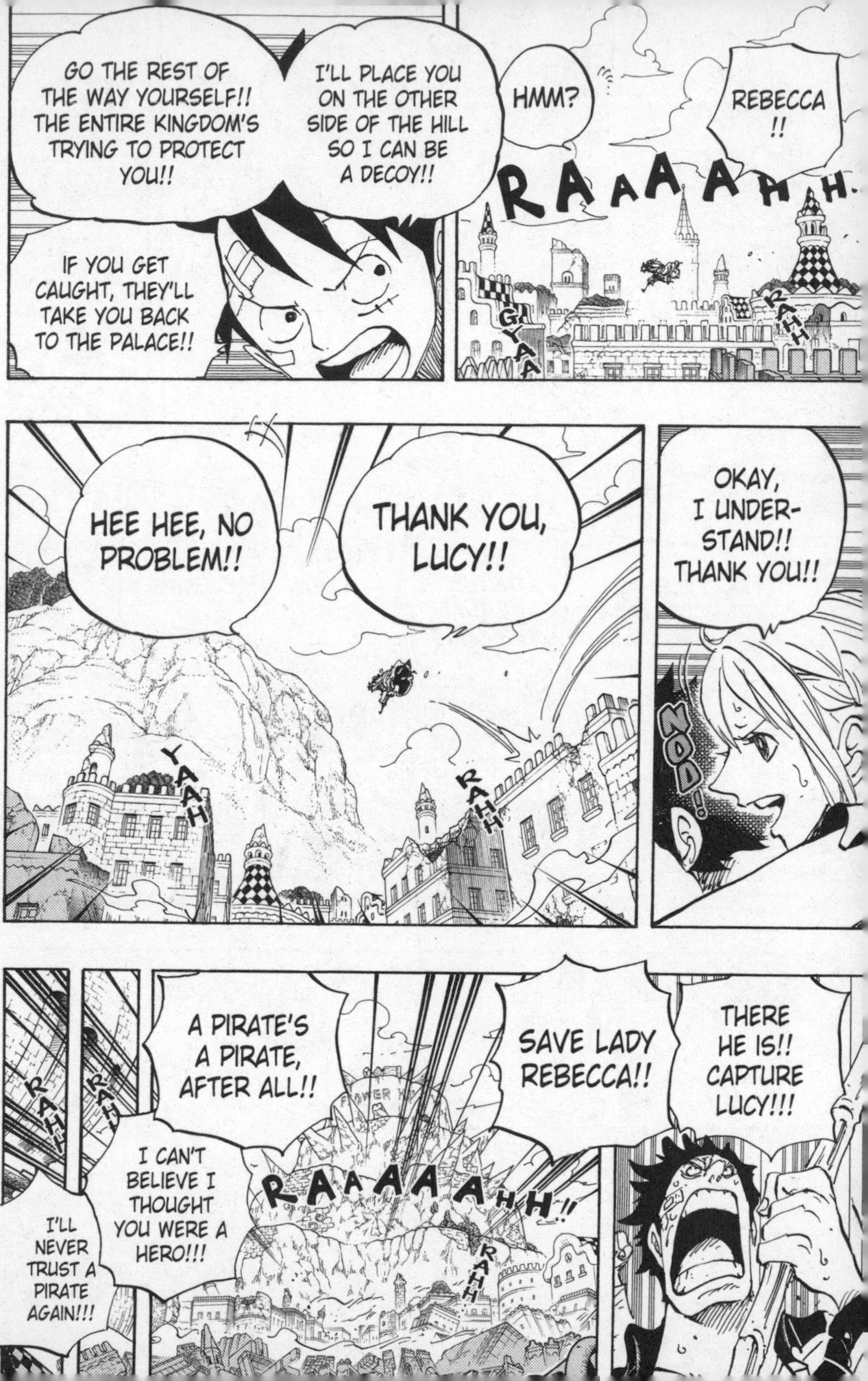
REBECCA!!
HMM?
RAAAAAHH
GYAA
RAHH
I'LL PLACE YOU ON THE OTHER SIDE OF THE HILL SO I CAN BE A DECOY!!
GO THE REST OF THE WAY YOURSELF!! THE ENTIRE KINGDOM'S TRYING TO PROTECT YOU!!
IF YOU GET CAUGHT, THEY'LL TAKE YOU BACK TO THE PALACE!!
OKAY, I UNDER-STAND!! THANK YOU!!
NOD!
THANK YOU, LUCY!!
HEE HEE, NO PROBLEM!!
RAHH
YAAH
THERE HE IS!! CAPTURE LUCY!!!
SAVE LADY REBECCA!!
A PIRATE'S A PIRATE, AFTER ALL!!
RAAAAAHH!!
RAHH
I CAN'T BELIEVE I THOUGHT YOU WERE A HERO!!!
RAHH
RAHH
I'LL NEVER TRUST A PIRATE AGAIN!!!

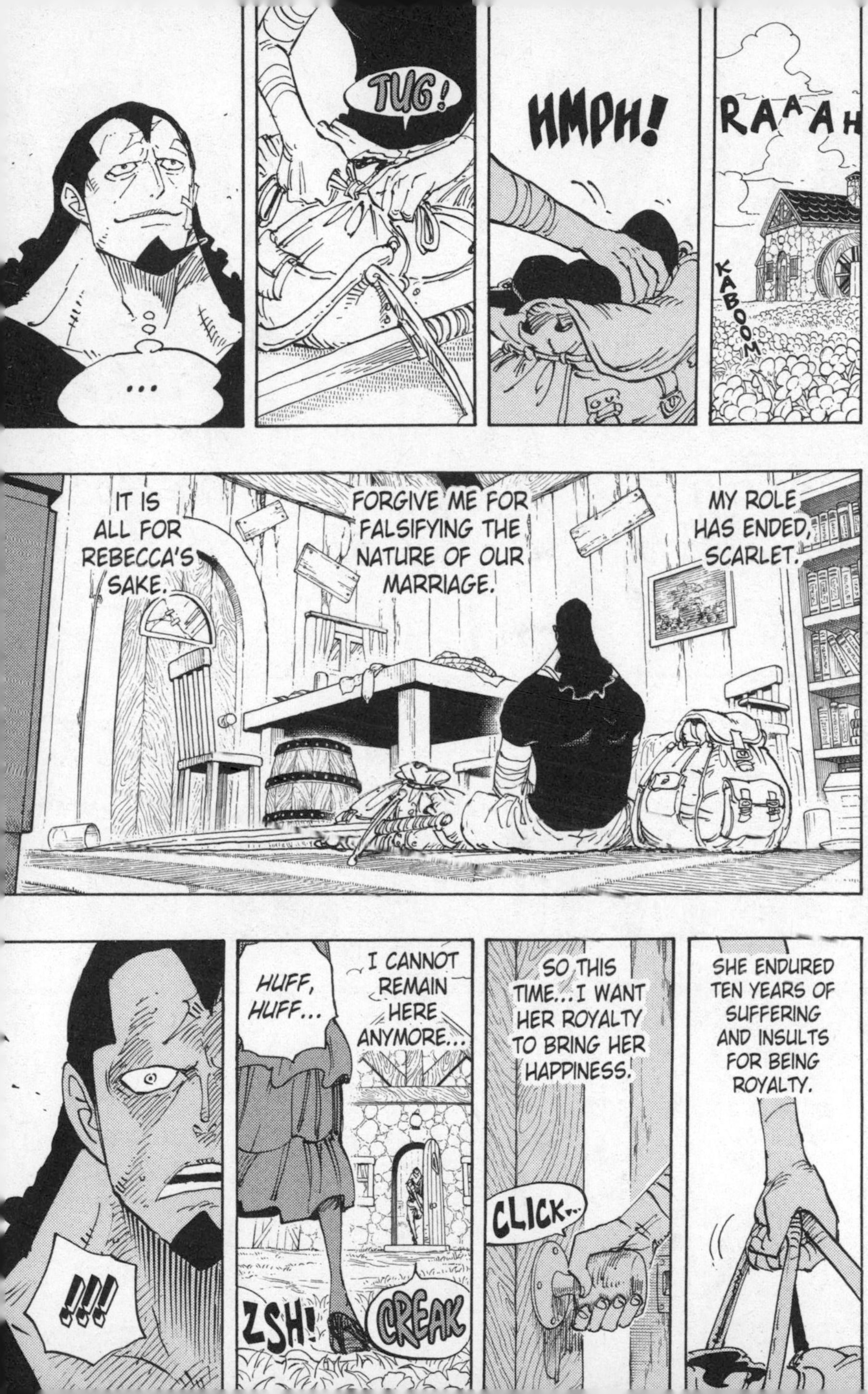
RAAAH
KABOOM
HMPH!
TUG!
...
MY ROLE HAS ENDED, SCARLET.
FORGIVE ME FOR FALSIFYING THE NATURE OF OUR MARRIAGE.
IT IS ALL FOR REBECCA'S SAKE.
SHE ENDURED TEN YEARS OF SUFFERING AND INSULTS FOR BEING ROYALTY.
SO THIS TIME...I WANT HER ROYALTY TO BRING HER HAPPINESS.
CLICK...
I CANNOT REMAIN HERE ANYMORE...
HUFF, HUFF...
CREAK
ZSH!
!!!

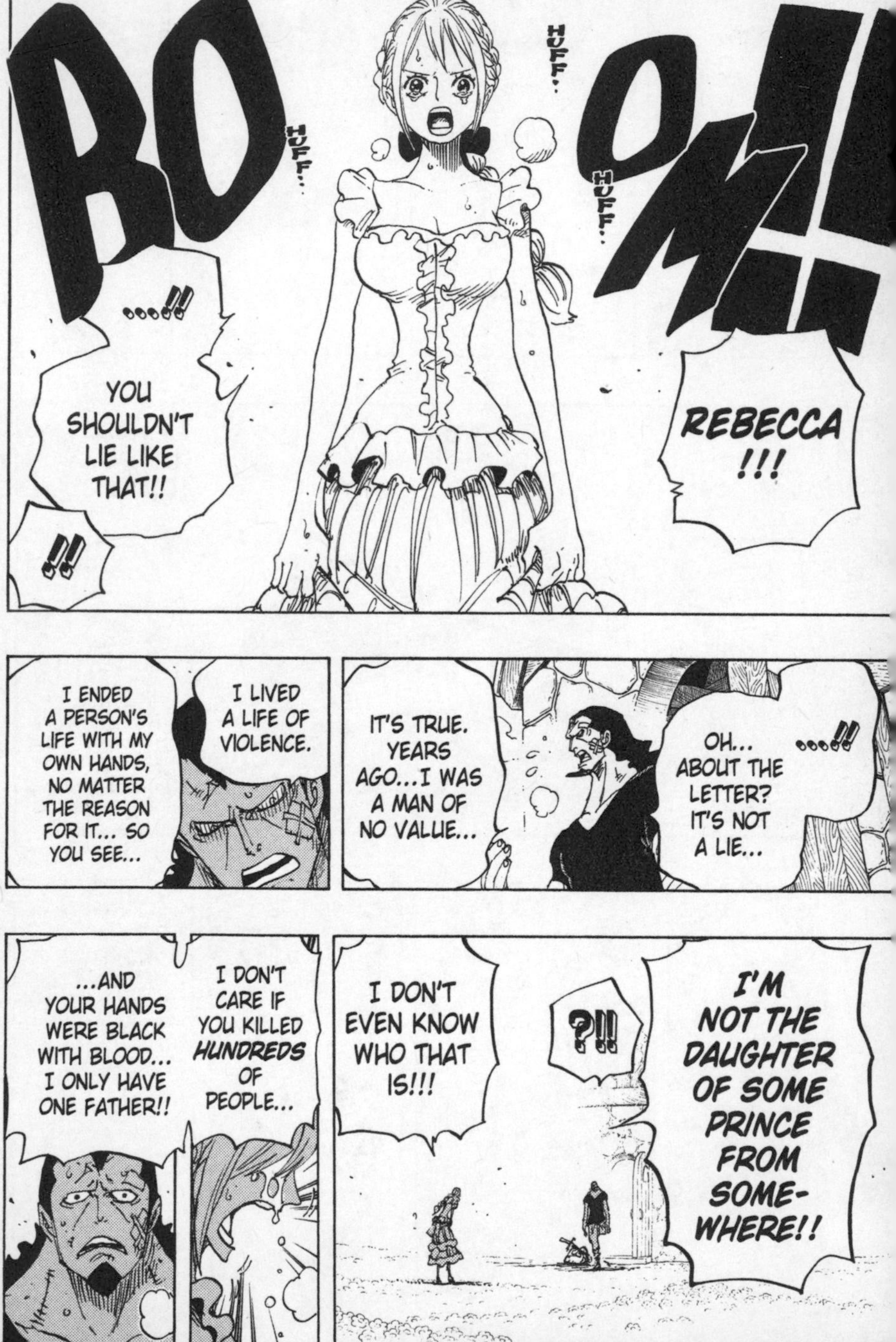
BOOM!!
HUFF HUFF HUFF
REBECCA!!!
...!!
YOU SHOULDN'T LIE LIKE THAT!!
!!
...!!
OH... ABOUT THE LETTER? IT'S NOT A LIE...
IT'S TRUE. YEARS AGO...I WAS A MAN OF NO VALUE...
I LIVED A LIFE OF VIOLENCE.
I ENDED A PERSON'S LIFE WITH MY OWN HANDS, NO MATTER THE REASON FOR IT... SO YOU SEE...
I'M NOT THE DAUGHTER OF SOME PRINCE FROM SOME-WHERE!!
?!!
I DON'T EVEN KNOW WHO THAT IS!!!
I DON'T CARE IF YOU KILLED HUNDREDS OF PEOPLE...
...AND YOUR HANDS WERE BLACK WITH BLOOD... I ONLY HAVE ONE FATHER!!

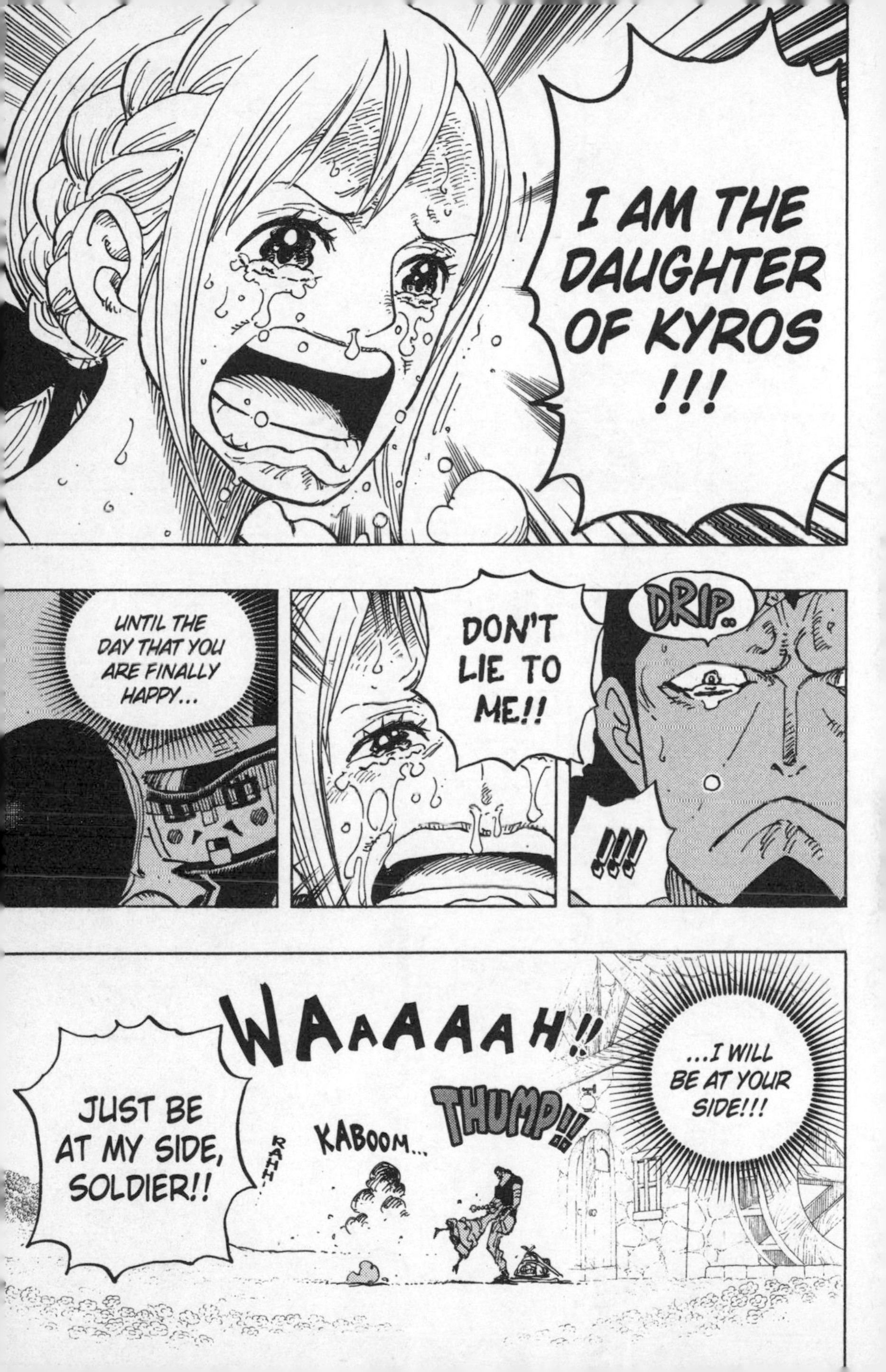
I AM THE DAUGHTER OF KYROS !!!
DRIP..
!!!
DON'T LIE TO ME!!
UNTIL THE DAY THAT YOU ARE FINALLY HAPPY...
...I WILL BE AT YOUR SIDE!!!
WAAAAAH!!
THUMP!!
KABOOM...
RAHH...
JUST BE AT MY SIDE, SOLDIER!!

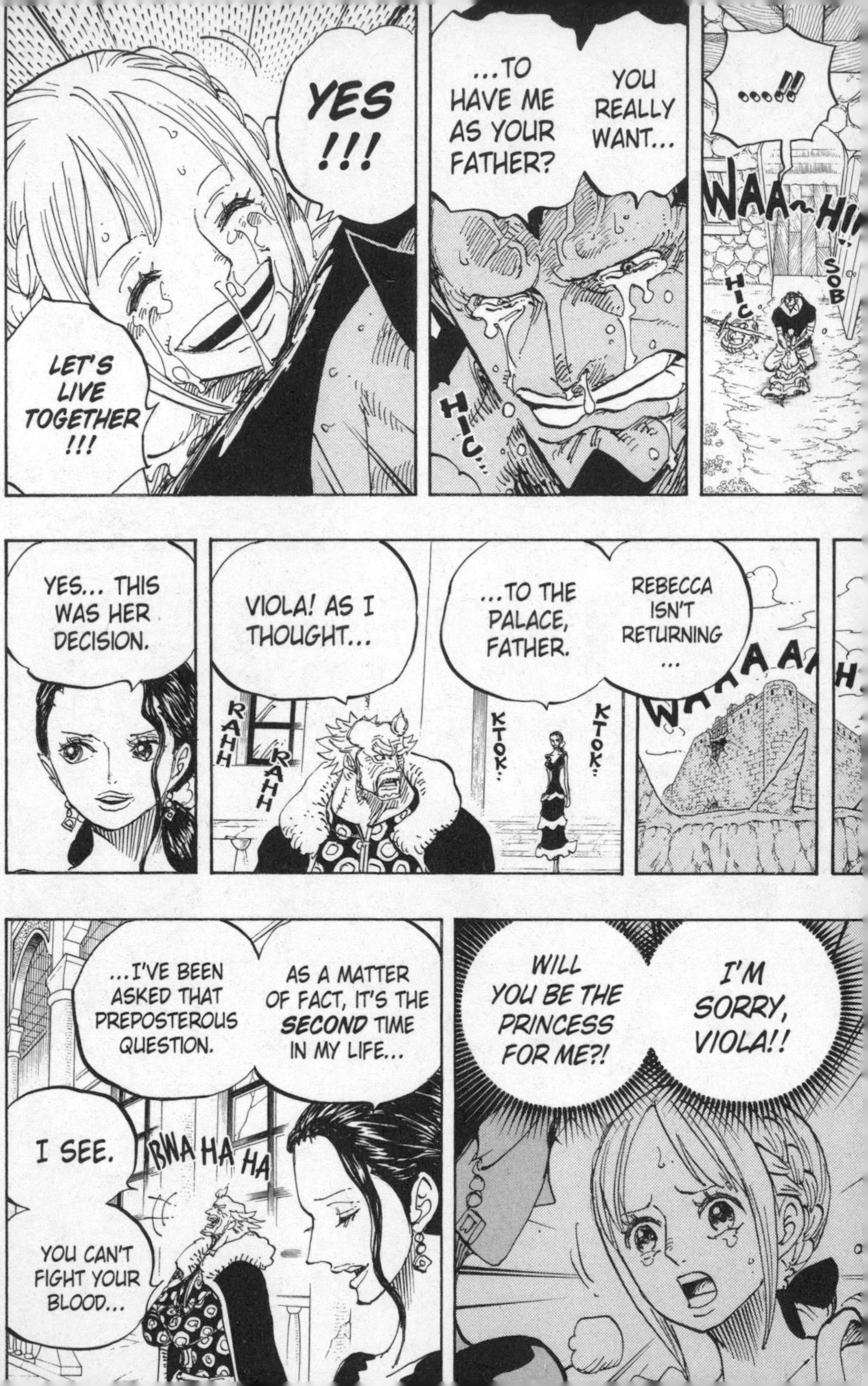
...!!
WAA~HI!!
HIC
SOB
YOU REALLY WANT...
...TO HAVE ME AS YOUR FATHER?
HIC...
YES!!!
LET'S LIVE TOGETHER!!!
WAAAAAH
REBECCA ISN'T RETURNING...
...TO THE PALACE, FATHER.
KTOK
KTOK
VIOLA! AS I THOUGHT...
RAHH
RAHH
YES... THIS WAS HER DECISION.
I'M SORRY, VIOLA!!
WILL YOU BE THE PRINCESS FOR ME?!
AS A MATTER OF FACT, IT'S THE SECOND TIME IN MY LIFE...
...I'VE BEEN ASKED THAT PREPOSTEROUS QUESTION.
I SEE.
BWA HA HA
YOU CAN'T FIGHT YOUR BLOOD...

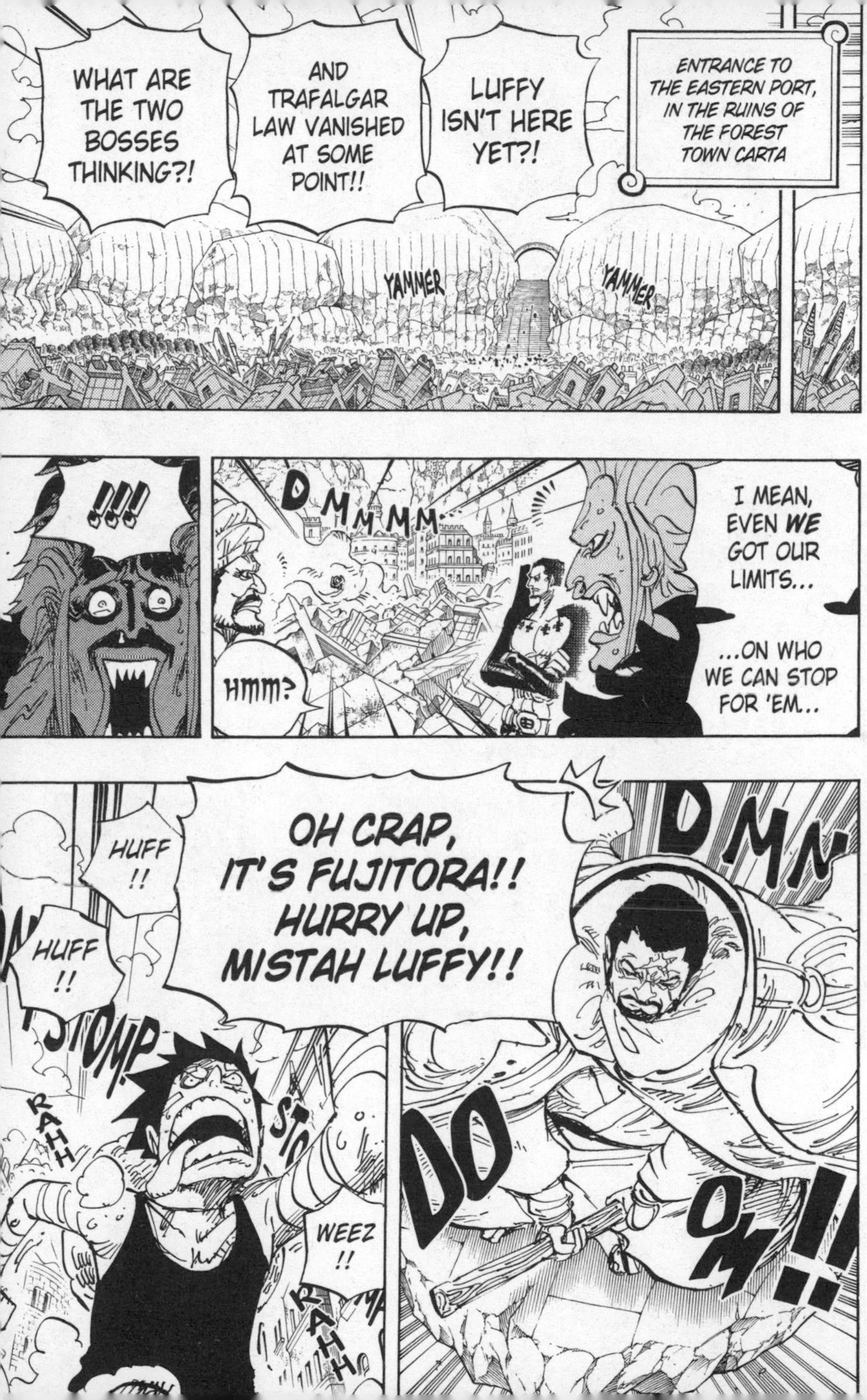
ENTRANCE TO THE EASTERN PORT, IN THE RUINS OF THE FOREST TOWN CARTA
LUFFY ISN'T HERE YET?!
AND TRAFALGAR LAW VANISHED AT SOME POINT!!
WHAT ARE THE TWO BOSSES THINKING?!
YAMMER
YAMMER
I MEAN, EVEN **WE** GOT OUR LIMITS...
...ON WHO WE CAN STOP FOR 'EM...
DMMMM
HMM?
!!!
DMN
DOOM!!
OH CRAP, IT'S FUJITORA!! HURRY UP, MISTAH LUFFY!!
HUFF !!
HUFF !!
STOMP
RAHH
STO
WEEZ !!
RAHH

## SBS Question Corner

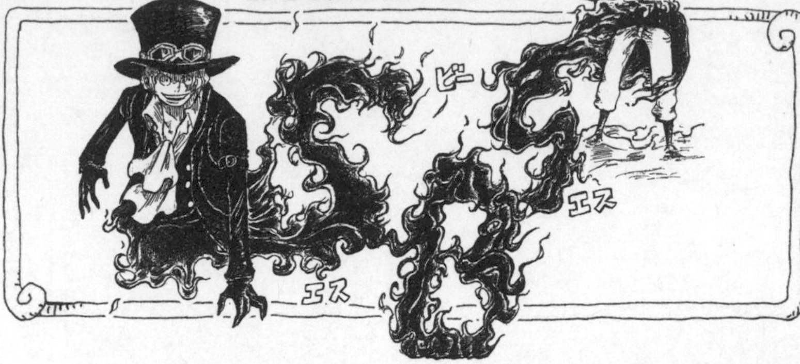
ビー
エス
エス

(Sasaaki, Okinawa)

**Q**: Ever since I started watching *One Piece,* I've been wondering why Sanji calls Nami "Nami-san," and Robin "Robin-chan" in Japanese? Robin's the older one, so she should get more respect!! Is there a deep meaning to this?!

--Miracle ♪

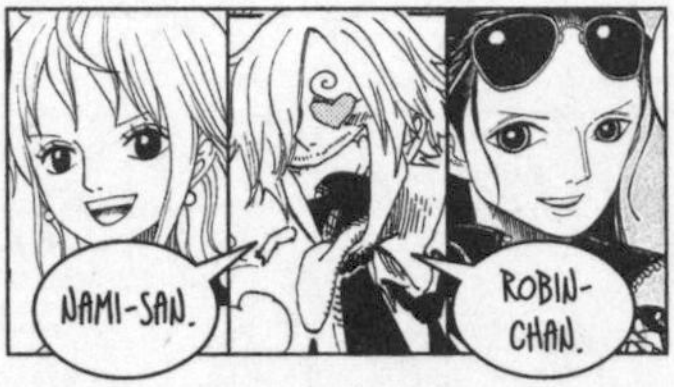
NAMI-SAN.
ROBIN-CHAN.

**A**: I've never really thought that deeply about it. Recently, one of my staff members asked an interesting question. He said that as women get older, they like to be treated as though they're younger, and they like to be treated older when they're young. He asked if Sanji realized that, and was acting accordingly. So I said, "Y-yes. Absolutely."

**Q**: I have a report to make! I was once printed in the fan art section of Volume 19 under the name "YapotPapi." Well, now I've made my debut as a manga artist, although my area is in educational manga, not entertainment.

--Takuma Takahashi

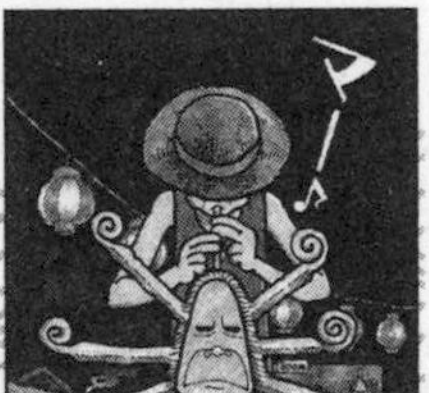

(YapotPapi, Miyagi)

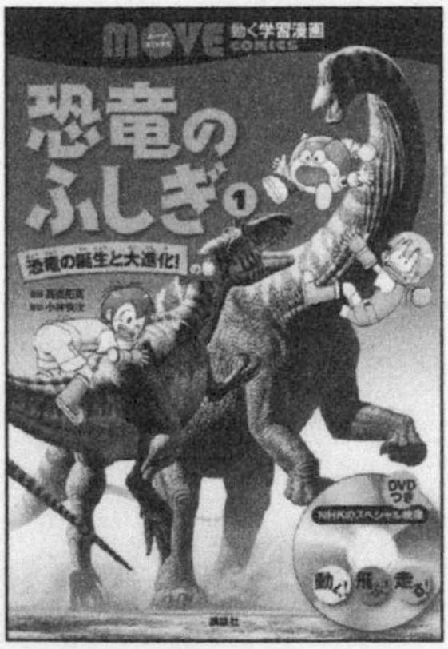
MOVE 動く学習漫画 COMICS
恐竜のふしぎ 1
恐竜の誕生と大進化!
DVDつき

**A**: Ooh, another one! It's wonderful to see your readers grow up like this after 18 years of being in this business! So if you happen to spot the book on the left (Mysteries of the Dinosaurs, Takuma Takahashi) in the store and you want to learn more about dinosaurs, check it out! Find our crewmate's book!

# Chapter 798:
# HEART

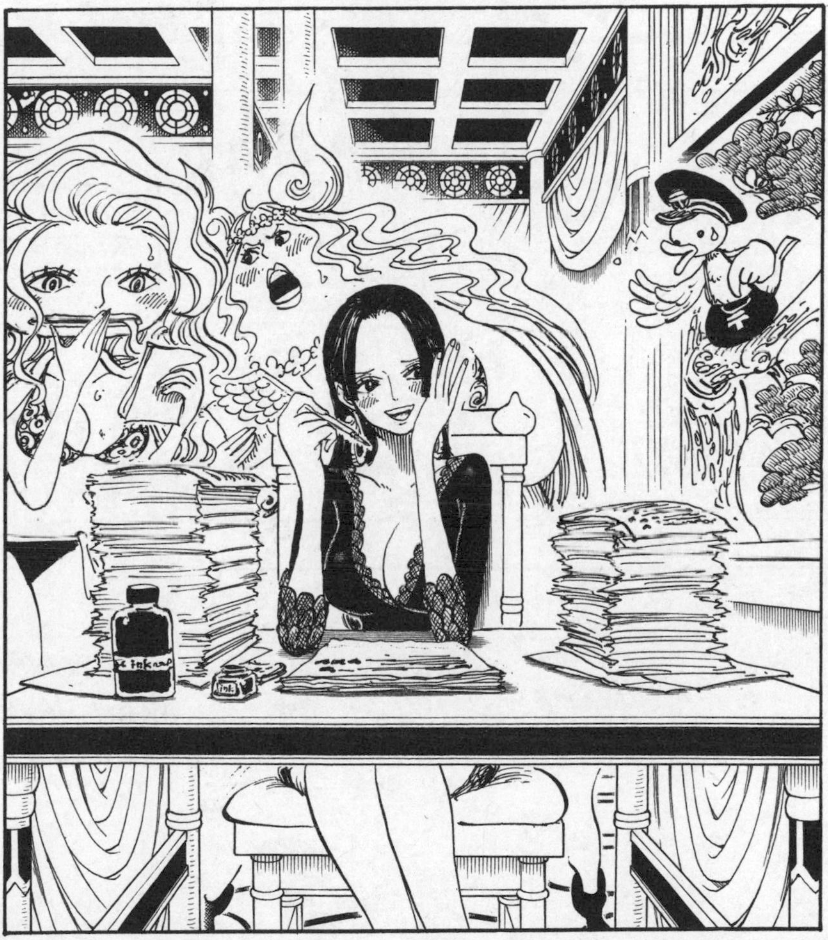

REQUEST: "HANCOCK WRITES A LETTER TO LUFFY"
BY LHAMS FROM SAITAMA

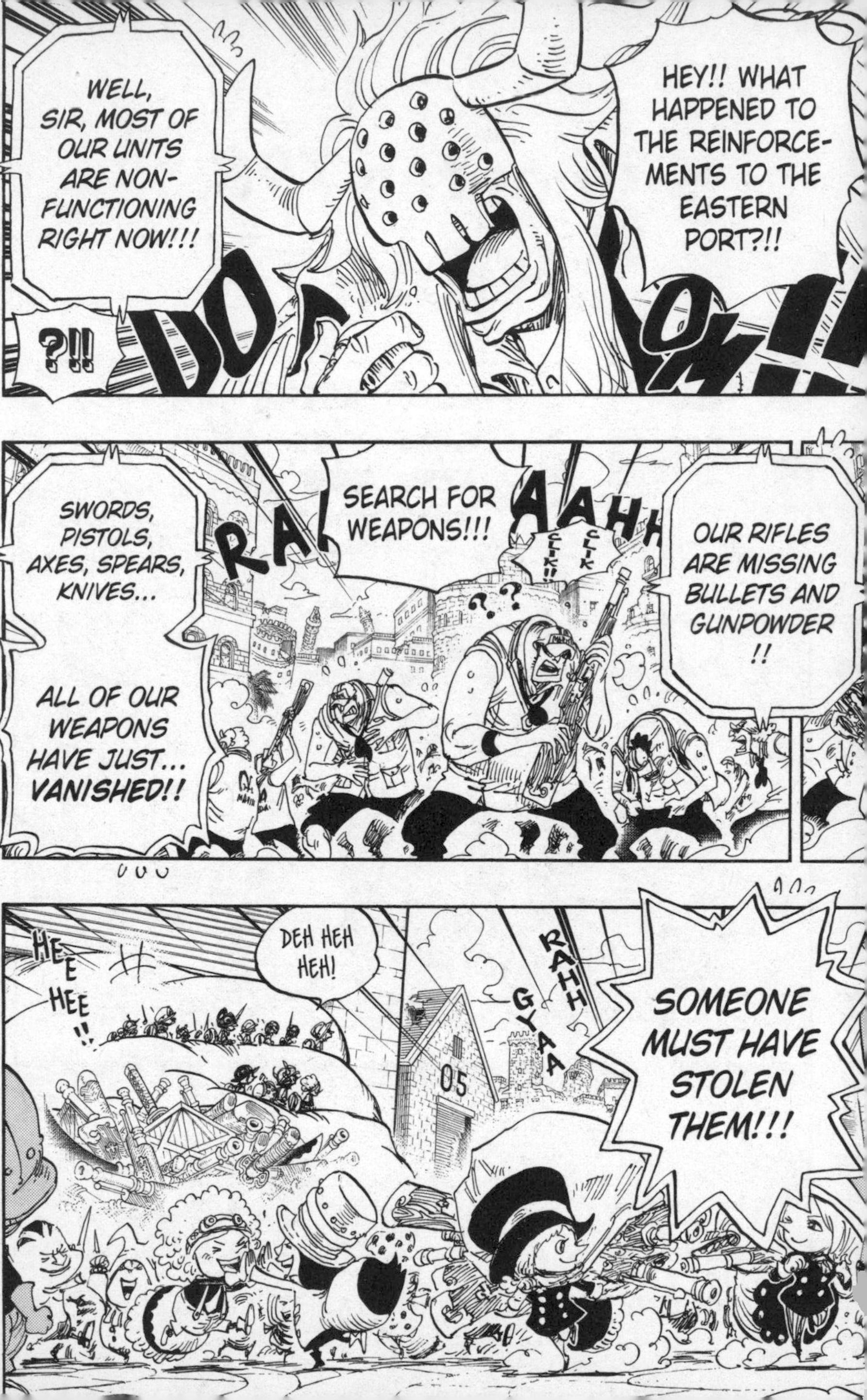
HEY!! WHAT HAPPENED TO THE REINFORCEMENTS TO THE EASTERN PORT?!!
WELL, SIR, MOST OF OUR UNITS ARE NON-FUNCTIONING RIGHT NOW!!!
?!!
OUR RIFLES ARE MISSING BULLETS AND GUNPOWDER !!
CLIK
CLIK!!
SEARCH FOR WEAPONS!!!
SWORDS, PISTOLS, AXES, SPEARS, KNIVES...
ALL OF OUR WEAPONS HAVE JUST... VANISHED!!
SOMEONE MUST HAVE STOLEN THEM!!!
RAHH
GYAA
05
DEH HEH HEH!
HEE HEE HEE!!

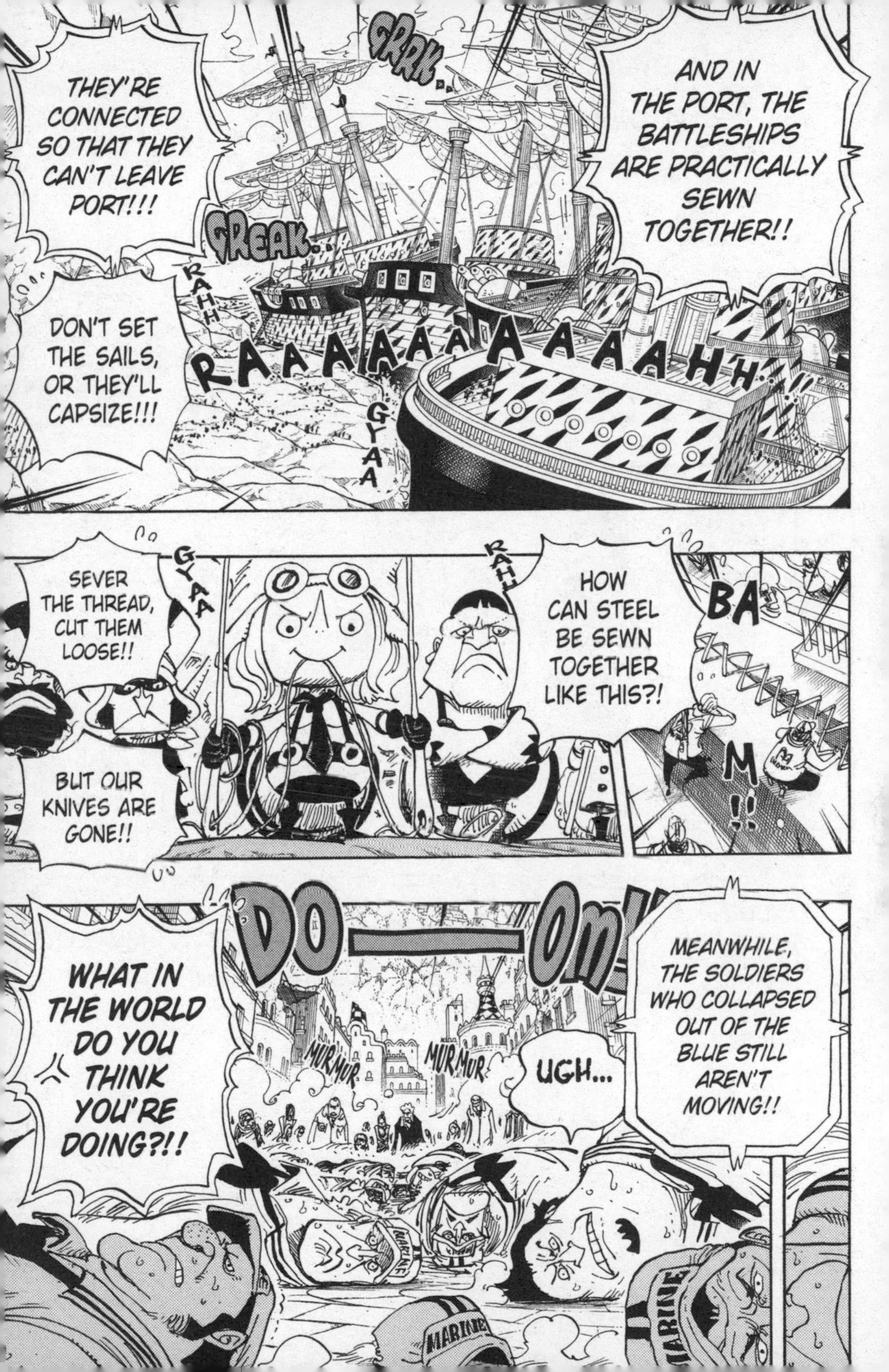
AND IN THE PORT, THE BATTLESHIPS ARE PRACTICALLY SEWN TOGETHER!!
GRRK
THEY'RE CONNECTED SO THAT THEY CAN'T LEAVE PORT!!!
GREAK
RAHH
DON'T SET THE SAILS, OR THEY'LL CAPSIZE!!!
RAAAAAAAAAHH
GYAA
BA
M!!
HOW CAN STEEL BE SEWN TOGETHER LIKE THIS?!
RAHH
SEVER THE THREAD, CUT THEM LOOSE!!
GYAA
BUT OUR KNIVES ARE GONE!!
MEANWHILE, THE SOLDIERS WHO COLLAPSED OUT OF THE BLUE STILL AREN'T MOVING!!
DO—OM!!
UGH...
MUR MUR
MUR MUR
WHAT IN THE WORLD DO YOU THINK YOU'RE DOING?!!
MARINE
MARINE
MARINE

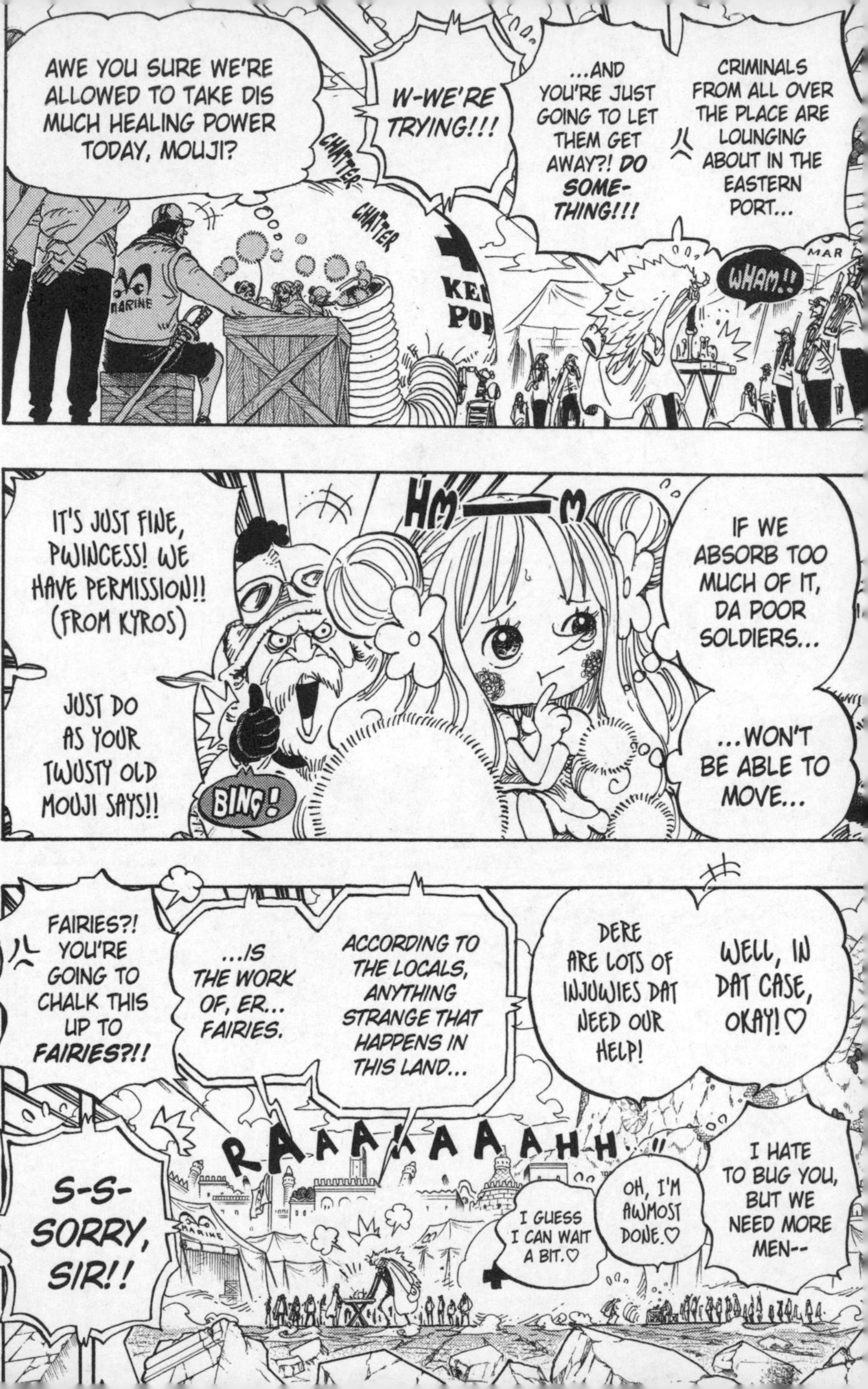
CRIMINALS FROM ALL OVER THE PLACE ARE LOUNGING ABOUT IN THE EASTERN PORT...
...AND YOU'RE JUST GOING TO LET THEM GET AWAY?! DO SOME-THING!!!
W-WE'RE TRYING!!!
CHATTER
CHATTER
WHAM!!
AWE YOU SURE WE'RE ALLOWED TO TAKE DIS MUCH HEALING POWER TODAY, MOUJI?
MARINE
IF WE ABSORB TOO MUCH OF IT, DA POOR SOLDIERS...
...WON'T BE ABLE TO MOVE...
HM—M
IT'S JUST FINE, PWINCESS! WE HAVE PERMISSION!! (FROM KYROS)
JUST DO AS YOUR TWUSTY OLD MOUJI SAYS!!
BING!
WELL, IN DAT CASE, OKAY!♡
DERE ARE LOTS OF INJUWIES DAT NEED OUR HELP!
ACCORDING TO THE LOCALS, ANYTHING STRANGE THAT HAPPENS IN THIS LAND...
...IS THE WORK OF, ER... FAIRIES.
FAIRIES?! YOU'RE GOING TO CHALK THIS UP TO FAIRIES?!!
I HATE TO BUG YOU, BUT WE NEED MORE MEN--
OH, I'M AWMOST DONE.♡
I GUESS I CAN WAIT A BIT.♡
RAAAAAAAAHH..!!
MARINE
S-S-SORRY, SIR!!

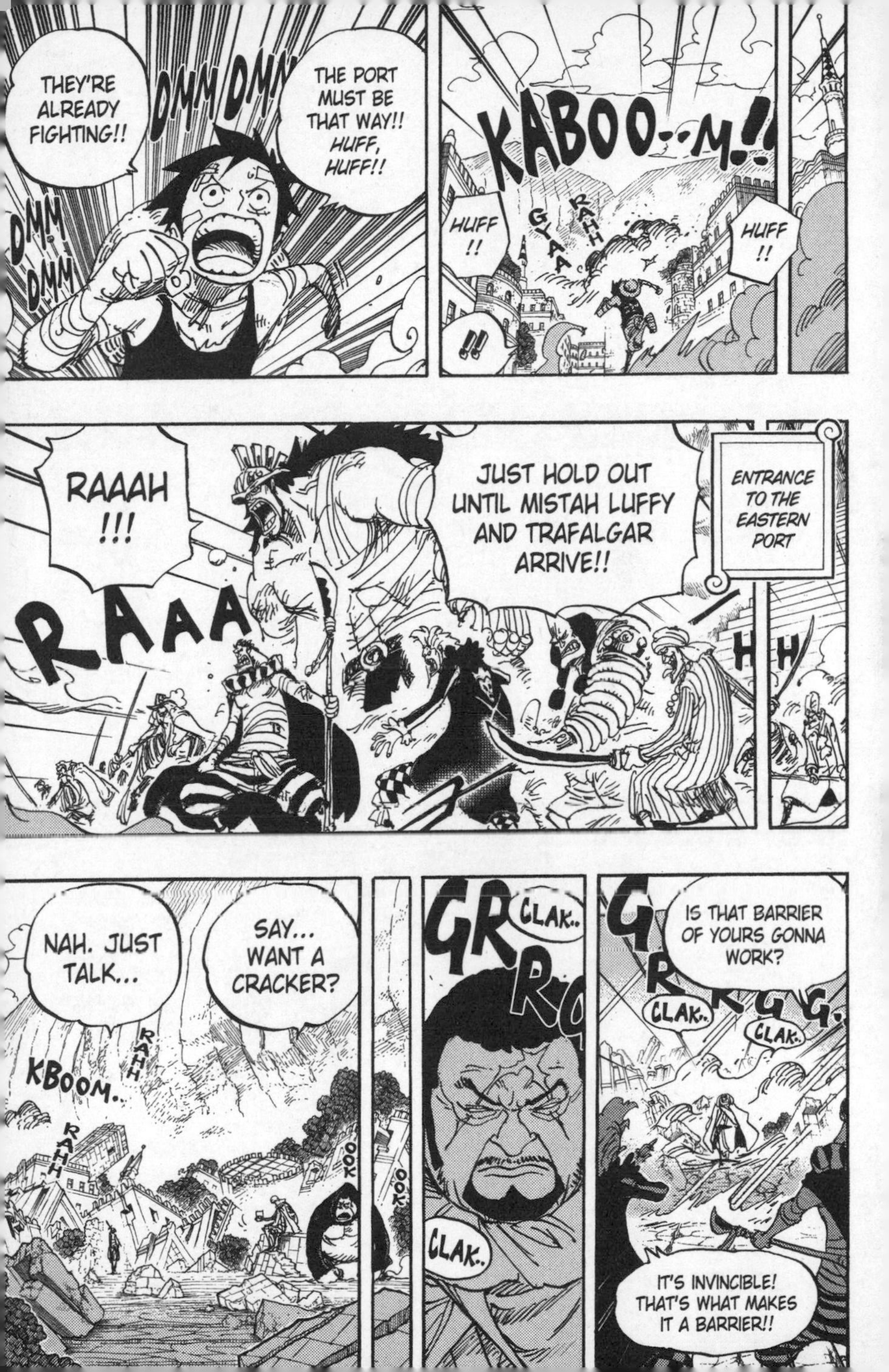
KABOO--M!!
HUFF !!
HUFF !!
RAHH
GYAA
!!
THE PORT MUST BE THAT WAY!! HUFF, HUFF!!
DMM DMM
THEY'RE ALREADY FIGHTING!!
DMM DMM
ENTRANCE TO THE EASTERN PORT
JUST HOLD OUT UNTIL MISTAH LUFFY AND TRAFALGAR ARRIVE!!
RAAAH !!!
RAAAHH
IS THAT BARRIER OF YOURS GONNA WORK?
GRRGG
CLAK..
CLAK..
IT'S INVINCIBLE! THAT'S WHAT MAKES IT A BARRIER!!
GRR
CLAK..
CLAK..
OOK
SAY... WANT A CRACKER?
NAH. JUST TALK...
RAHH
KBOOM..
RAHH
OOK

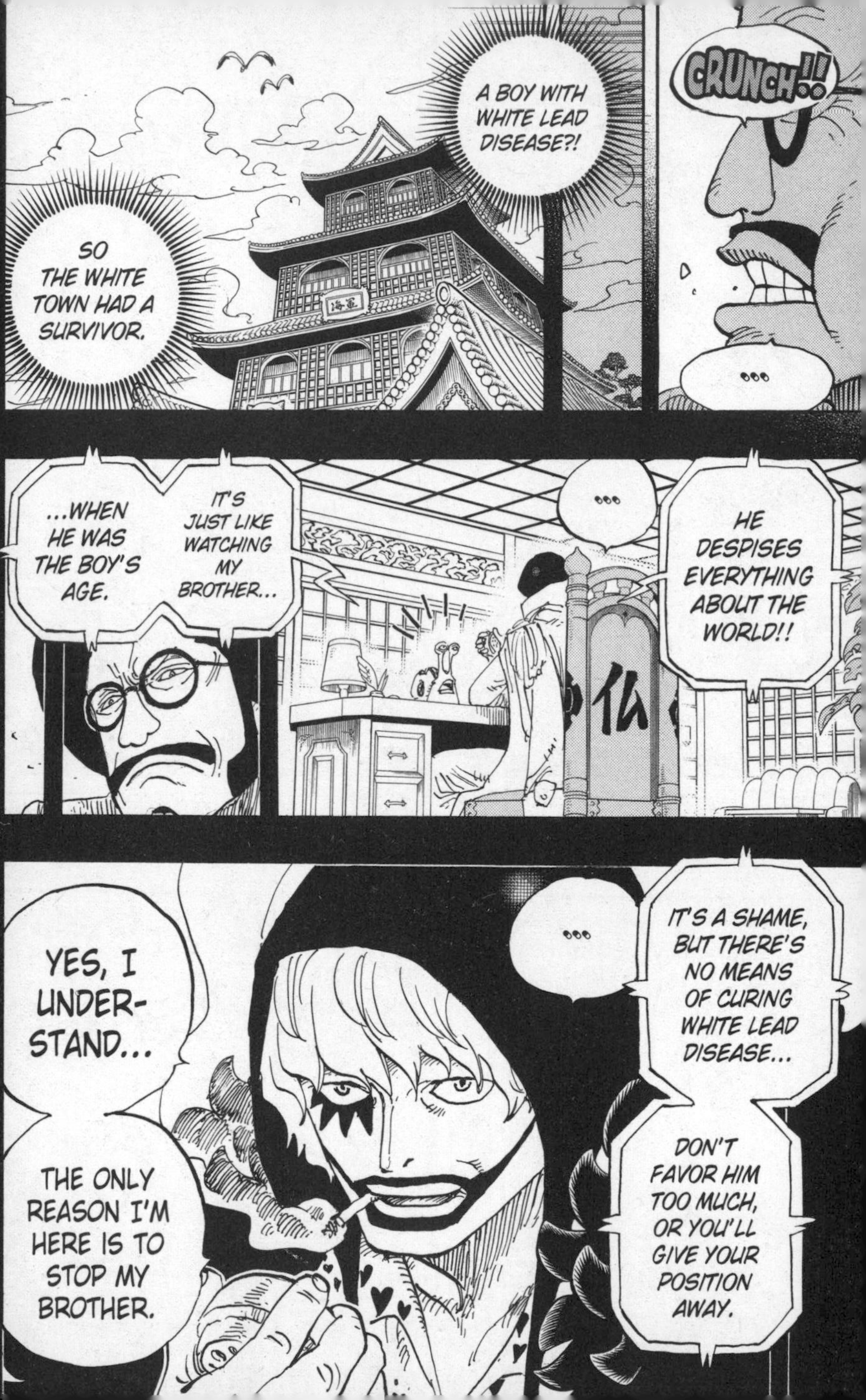
CRUNCH!!
...
A BOY WITH WHITE LEAD DISEASE?!
SO THE WHITE TOWN HAD A SURVIVOR.
...
HE DESPISES EVERYTHING ABOUT THE WORLD!!
IT'S JUST LIKE WATCHING MY BROTHER...
...WHEN HE WAS THE BOY'S AGE.
...
IT'S A SHAME, BUT THERE'S NO MEANS OF CURING WHITE LEAD DISEASE...
DON'T FAVOR HIM TOO MUCH, OR YOU'LL GIVE YOUR POSITION AWAY.
YES, I UNDER-STAND...
THE ONLY REASON I'M HERE IS TO STOP MY BROTHER.

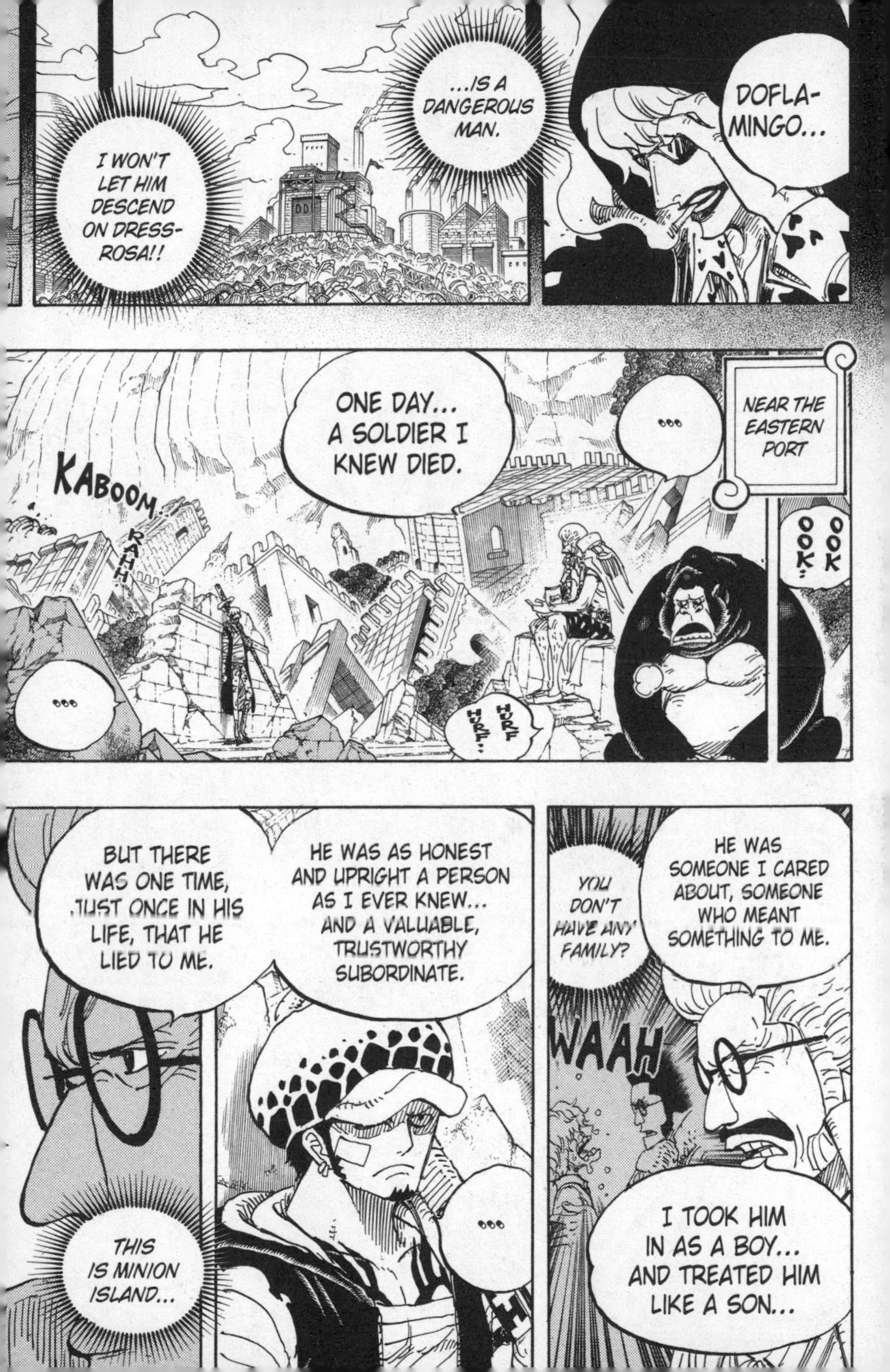
DOFLA-MINGO...
...IS A DANGEROUS MAN.
I WON'T LET HIM DESCEND ON DRESS-ROSA!!
NEAR THE EASTERN PORT
OOK OOK
...
ONE DAY... A SOLDIER I KNEW DIED.
KABOOM
RAHH
HURF HURF
...
HE WAS SOMEONE I CARED ABOUT, SOMEONE WHO MEANT SOMETHING TO ME.
YOU DON'T HAVE ANY FAMILY?
WAAH
I TOOK HIM IN AS A BOY... AND TREATED HIM LIKE A SON...
HE WAS AS HONEST AND UPRIGHT A PERSON AS I EVER KNEW... AND A VALUABLE, TRUSTWORTHY SUBORDINATE.
BUT THERE WAS ONE TIME, JUST ONCE IN HIS LIFE, THAT HE LIED TO ME.
...
THIS IS MINION ISLAND...

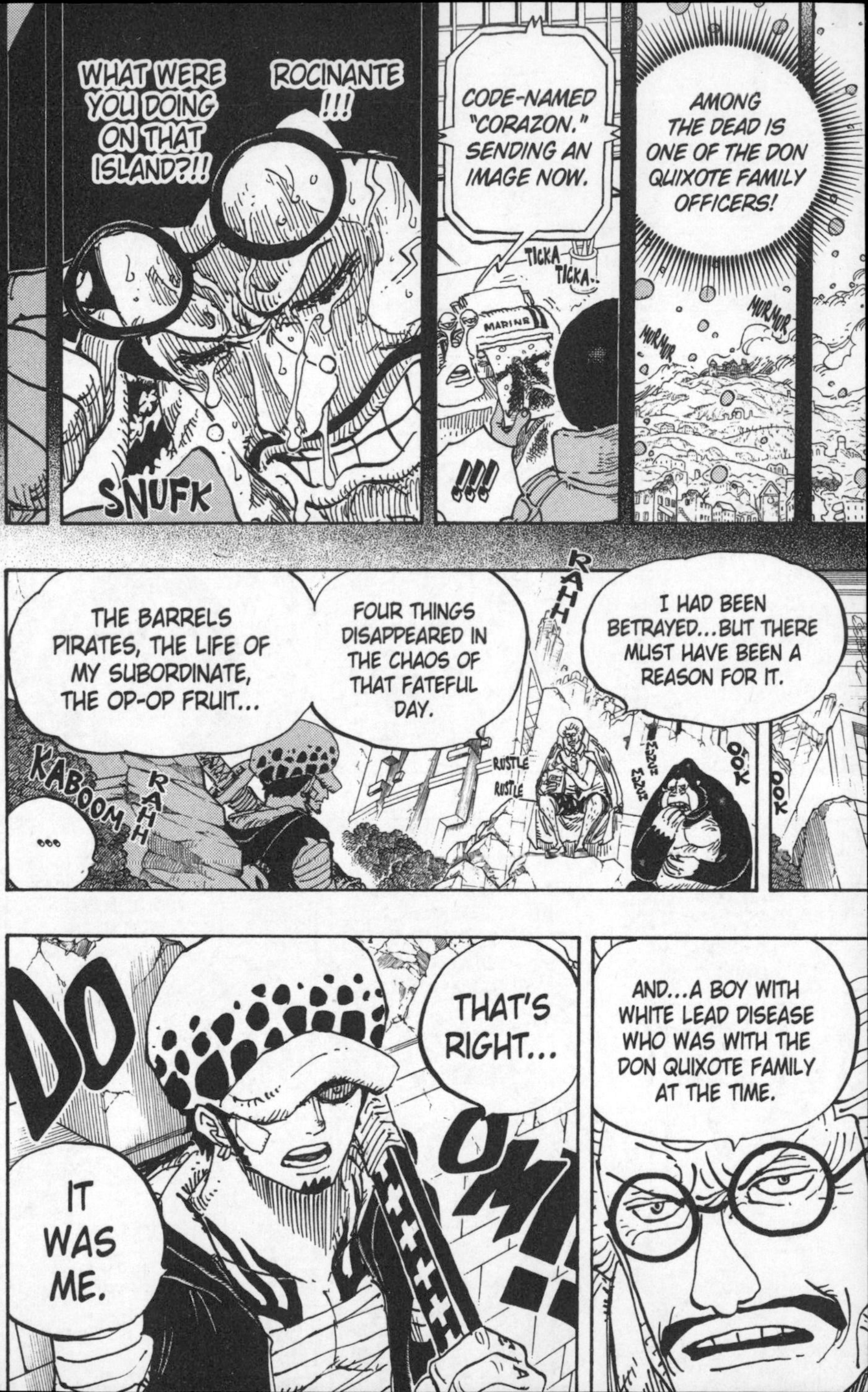
AMONG THE DEAD IS ONE OF THE DON QUIXOTE FAMILY OFFICERS!
MURMUR
MURMUR
CODE-NAMED "CORAZON." SENDING AN IMAGE NOW.
TICKA TICKA..
!!!
ROCINANTE!!!
WHAT WERE YOU DOING ON THAT ISLAND?!!
SNUFK
I HAD BEEN BETRAYED...BUT THERE MUST HAVE BEEN A REASON FOR IT.
OOK
OOK
MUNCH MUNCH
RUSTLE RUSTLE
RAHH
FOUR THINGS DISAPPEARED IN THE CHAOS OF THAT FATEFUL DAY.
THE BARRELS PIRATES, THE LIFE OF MY SUBORDINATE, THE OP-OP FRUIT...
RAHH
KABOOM
...
AND...A BOY WITH WHITE LEAD DISEASE WHO WAS WITH THE DON QUIXOTE FAMILY AT THE TIME.
THAT'S RIGHT...
DOOM
IT WAS ME.

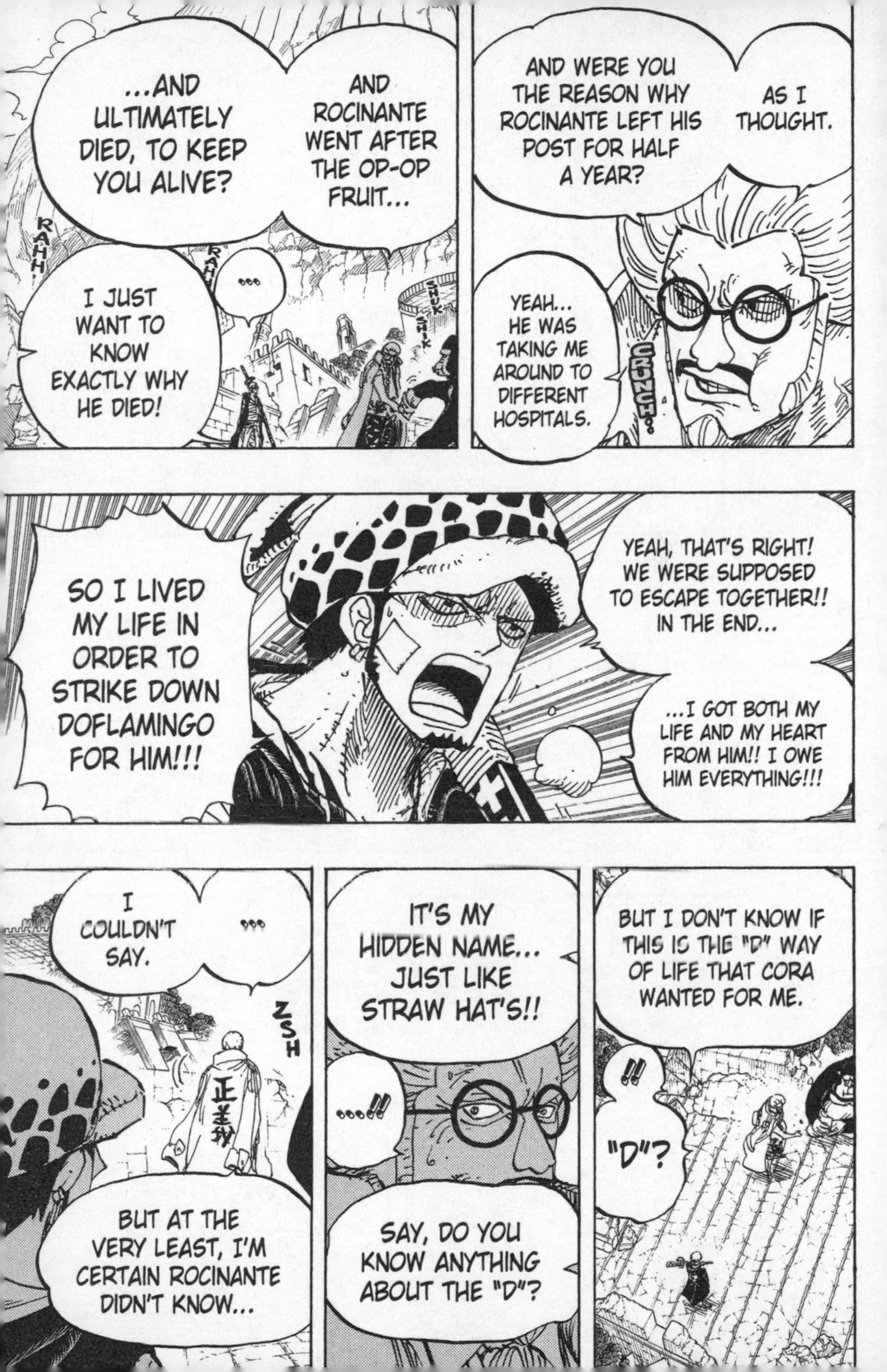

AS I THOUGHT.
AND WERE YOU THE REASON WHY ROCINANTE LEFT HIS POST FOR HALF A YEAR?
YEAH... HE WAS TAKING ME AROUND TO DIFFERENT HOSPITALS.
CRUNCH
AND ROCINANTE WENT AFTER THE OP-OP FRUIT...
...AND ULTIMATELY DIED, TO KEEP YOU ALIVE?
SHUK SHIK
...
RAHH
RAHH
I JUST WANT TO KNOW EXACTLY WHY HE DIED!
YEAH, THAT'S RIGHT! WE WERE SUPPOSED TO ESCAPE TOGETHER!! IN THE END...
...I GOT BOTH MY LIFE AND MY HEART FROM HIM!! I OWE HIM EVERYTHING!!!
SO I LIVED MY LIFE IN ORDER TO STRIKE DOWN DOFLAMINGO FOR HIM!!!
BUT I DON'T KNOW IF THIS IS THE "D" WAY OF LIFE THAT CORA WANTED FOR ME.
!!
"D"?
IT'S MY HIDDEN NAME... JUST LIKE STRAW HAT'S!!
...!!
SAY, DO YOU KNOW ANYTHING ABOUT THE "D"?
...
I COULDN'T SAY.
ZSH
BUT AT THE VERY LEAST, I'M CERTAIN ROCINANTE DIDN'T KNOW...

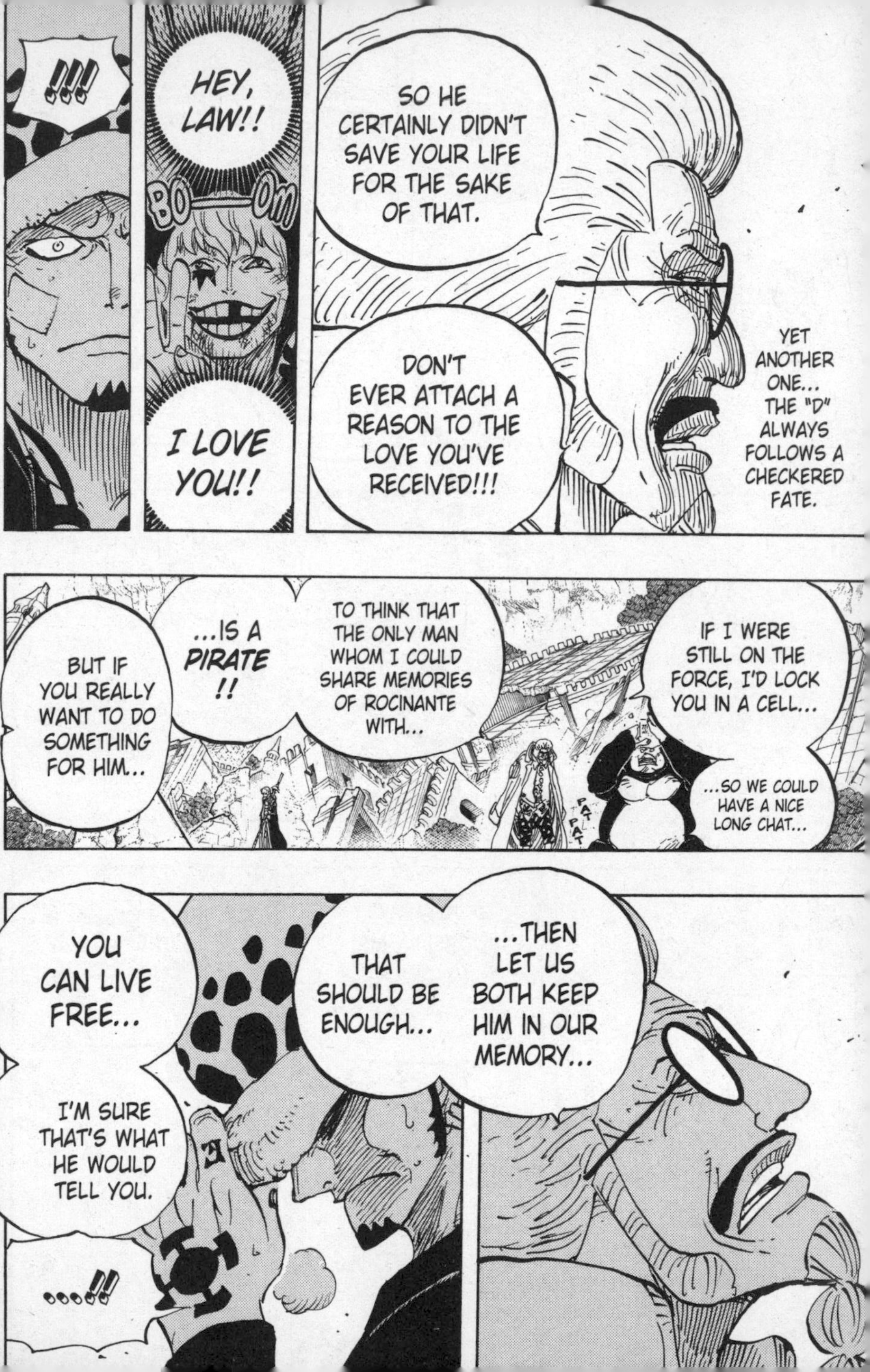
SO HE CERTAINLY DIDN'T SAVE YOUR LIFE FOR THE SAKE OF THAT.
YET ANOTHER ONE... THE "D" ALWAYS FOLLOWS A CHECKERED FATE.
DON'T EVER ATTACH A REASON TO THE LOVE YOU'VE RECEIVED!!!
HEY, LAW!!
BOOM
I LOVE YOU!!
!!!
IF I WERE STILL ON THE FORCE, I'D LOCK YOU IN A CELL...
...SO WE COULD HAVE A NICE LONG CHAT...
PAT PAT
TO THINK THAT THE ONLY MAN WHOM I COULD SHARE MEMORIES OF ROCINANTE WITH...
...IS A PIRATE!!
BUT IF YOU REALLY WANT TO DO SOMETHING FOR HIM...
...THEN LET US BOTH KEEP HIM IN OUR MEMORY...
THAT SHOULD BE ENOUGH...
YOU CAN LIVE FREE...
I'M SURE THAT'S WHAT HE WOULD TELL YOU.
....!!

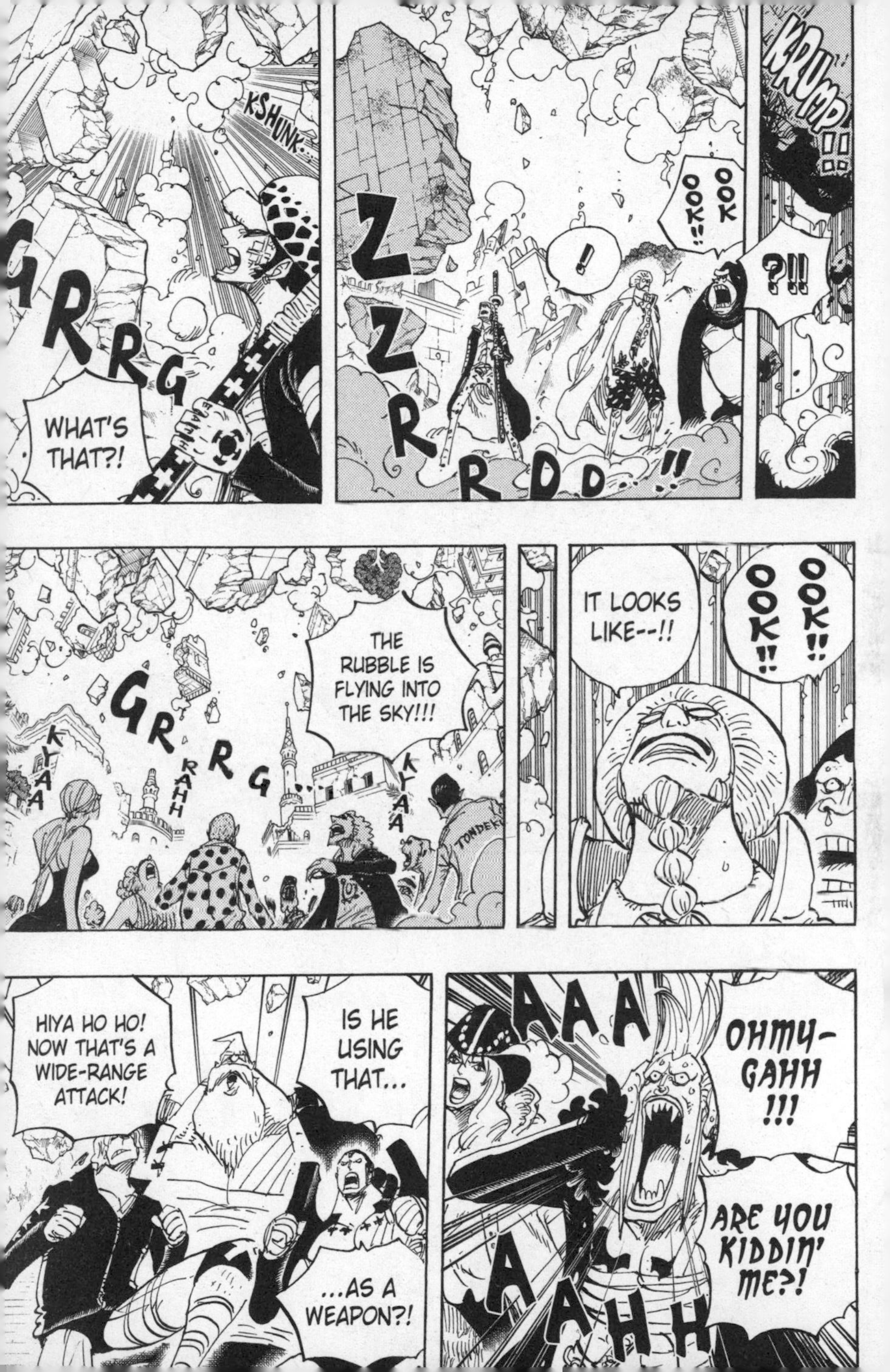
KRUMP!!
?!!
OOK OOK!!
!
ZZRRRDD..!!
KSHUNK...
GRRRG
WHAT'S THAT?!
OOK!! OOK!!
IT LOOKS LIKE--!!
THE RUBBLE IS FLYING INTO THE SKY!!!
GRRRG...
KYAA
RAHH
KYAA
AAAAHH
OHMY-GAHH!!!
ARE YOU KIDDIN' ME?!
IS HE USING THAT...
HIYA HO HO! NOW THAT'S A WIDE-RANGE ATTACK!
...AS A WEAPON?!

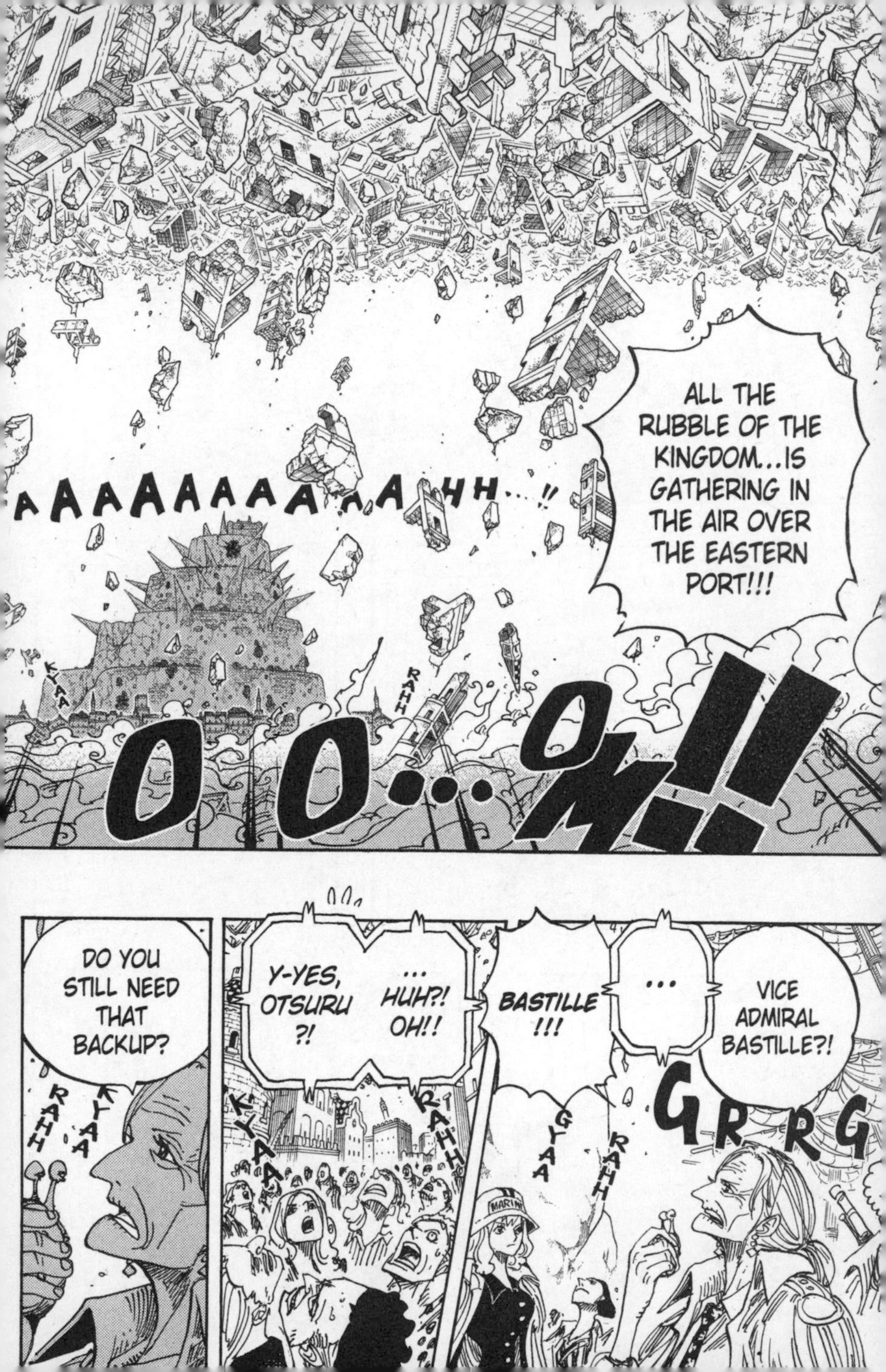
ALL THE RUBBLE OF THE KINGDOM...IS GATHERING IN THE AIR OVER THE EASTERN PORT!!!
AAAAAAAAAAHH...!!
RAHH
KYAA
O...O...OH!!
VICE ADMIRAL BASTILLE?!
GRRG
...
BASTILLE!!!
RAHH
GYAA
...HUH?! OH!!
Y-YES, OTSURU?!
RAHH
KYAA
DO YOU STILL NEED THAT BACKUP?
KYAA
RAHH

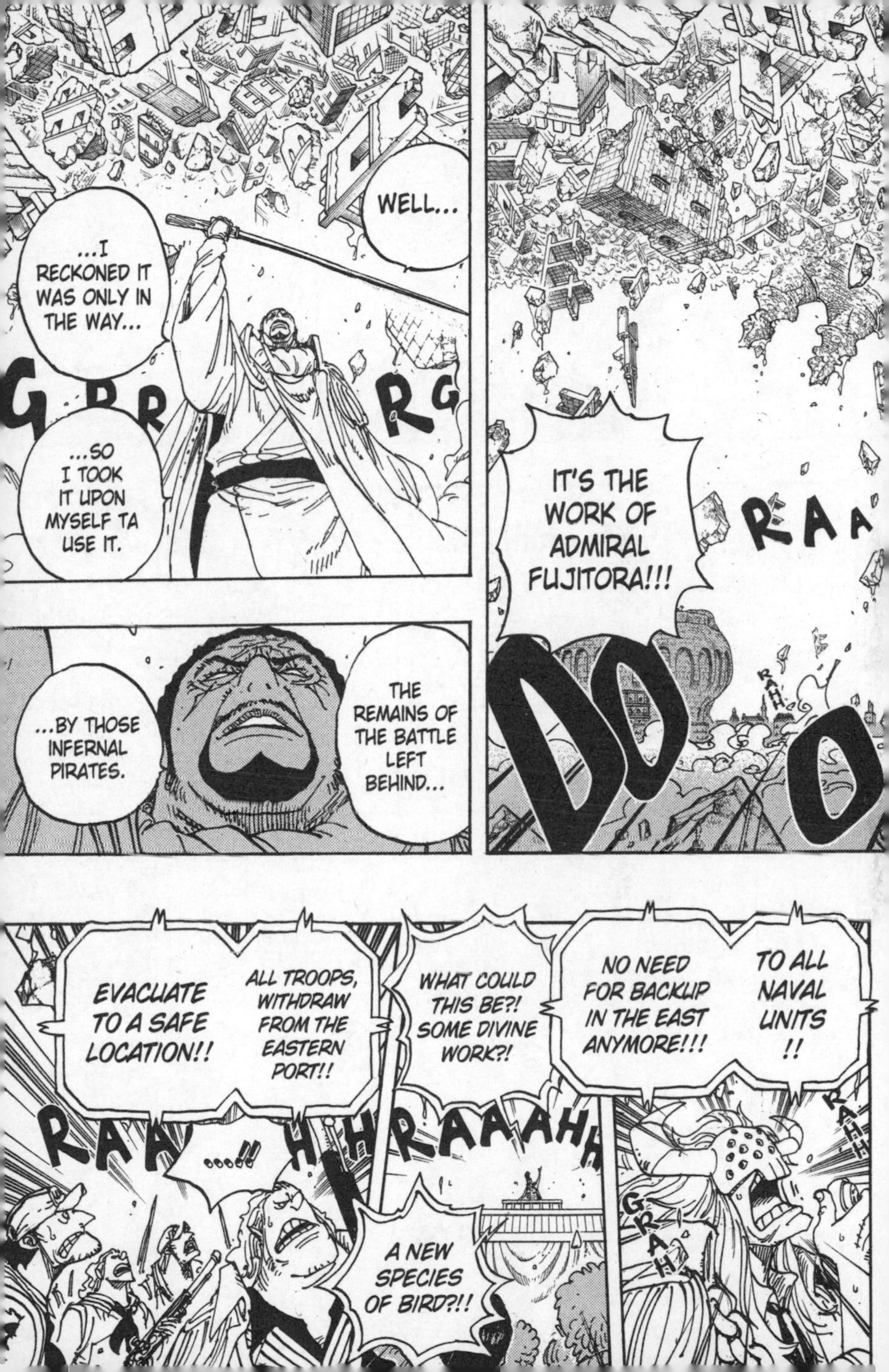
IT'S THE WORK OF ADMIRAL FUJITORA!!!
RAA
DOO
RAHH
WELL...
...I RECKONED IT WAS ONLY IN THE WAY...
GRRRG
...SO I TOOK IT UPON MYSELF TA USE IT.
THE REMAINS OF THE BATTLE LEFT BEHIND...
...BY THOSE INFERNAL PIRATES.
TO ALL NAVAL UNITS!!
NO NEED FOR BACKUP IN THE EAST ANYMORE!!!
WHAT COULD THIS BE?! SOME DIVINE WORK?!
ALL TROOPS, WITHDRAW FROM THE EASTERN PORT!!
EVACUATE TO A SAFE LOCATION!!
RAHH
GRAH
RAA.....!! HHRAAAAHH
A NEW SPECIES OF BIRD?!!

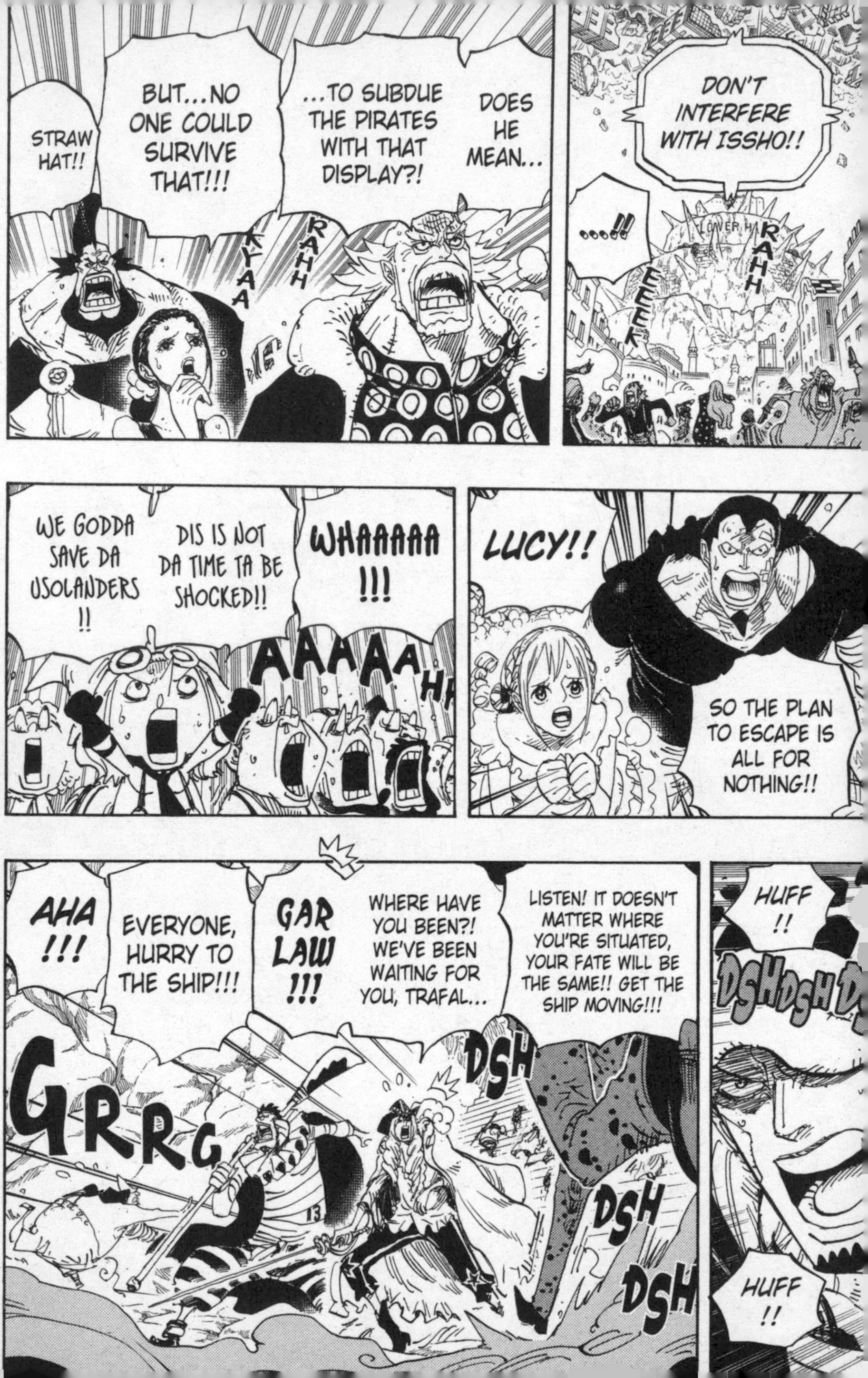
DON'T INTERFERE WITH ISSHO!!
...!!
RAHH
EEEEK
DOES HE MEAN...
...TO SUBDUE THE PIRATES WITH THAT DISPLAY?!
BUT...NO ONE COULD SURVIVE THAT!!!
STRAW HAT!!
RAHH
KYAA
LUCY!!
SO THE PLAN TO ESCAPE IS ALL FOR NOTHING!!
WHAAAAAA!!!
DIS IS NOT DA TIME TA BE SHOCKED!!
WE GODDA SAVE DA USOLANDERS!!
AAAAAHH
HUFF!!
DSHDSH
HUFF!!
LISTEN! IT DOESN'T MATTER WHERE YOU'RE SITUATED, YOUR FATE WILL BE THE SAME!! GET THE SHIP MOVING!!!
WHERE HAVE YOU BEEN?! WE'VE BEEN WAITING FOR YOU, TRAFAL...
GAR LAW!!!
EVERYONE, HURRY TO THE SHIP!!!
AHA!!!
DSH
DSH
DSH
GRRRG

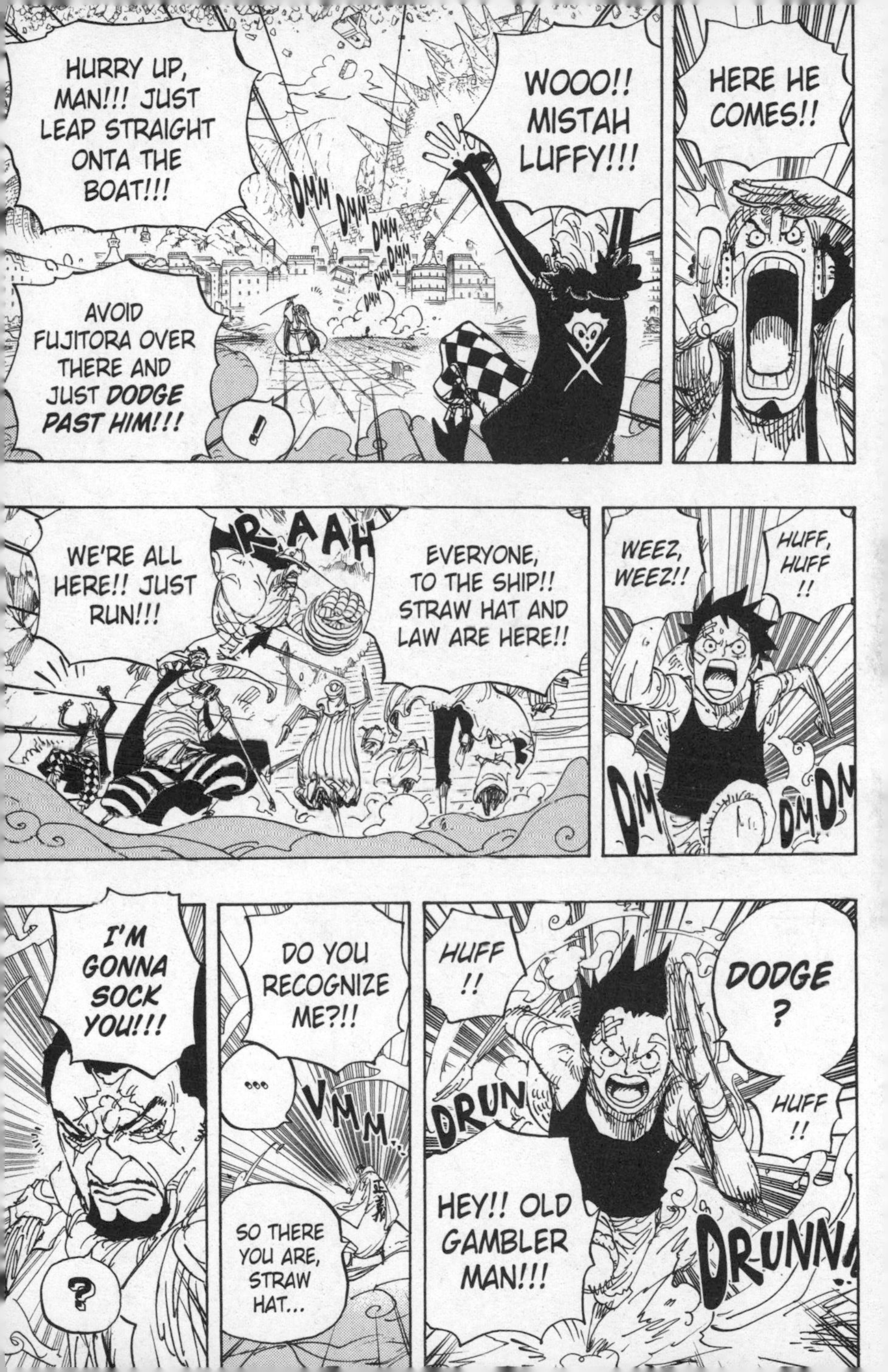
HERE HE COMES!!
WOOO!! MISTAH LUFFY!!!
HURRY UP, MAN!!! JUST LEAP STRAIGHT ONTA THE BOAT!!!
DMM DMM DMM DMM DMM DMM
AVOID FUJITORA OVER THERE AND JUST *DODGE PAST HIM!!!*
!
HUFF, HUFF !!
WEEZ, WEEZ!!
DM DM DM
EVERYONE, TO THE SHIP!! STRAW HAT AND LAW ARE HERE!!
RAAH
WE'RE ALL HERE!! JUST RUN!!!
DODGE ?
HUFF !!
HUFF !!
DRUN
HEY!! OLD GAMBLER MAN!!!
DRUNN
DO YOU RECOGNIZE ME?!!
...
VMM
SO THERE YOU ARE, STRAW HAT...
*I'M GONNA SOCK YOU!!!*
?

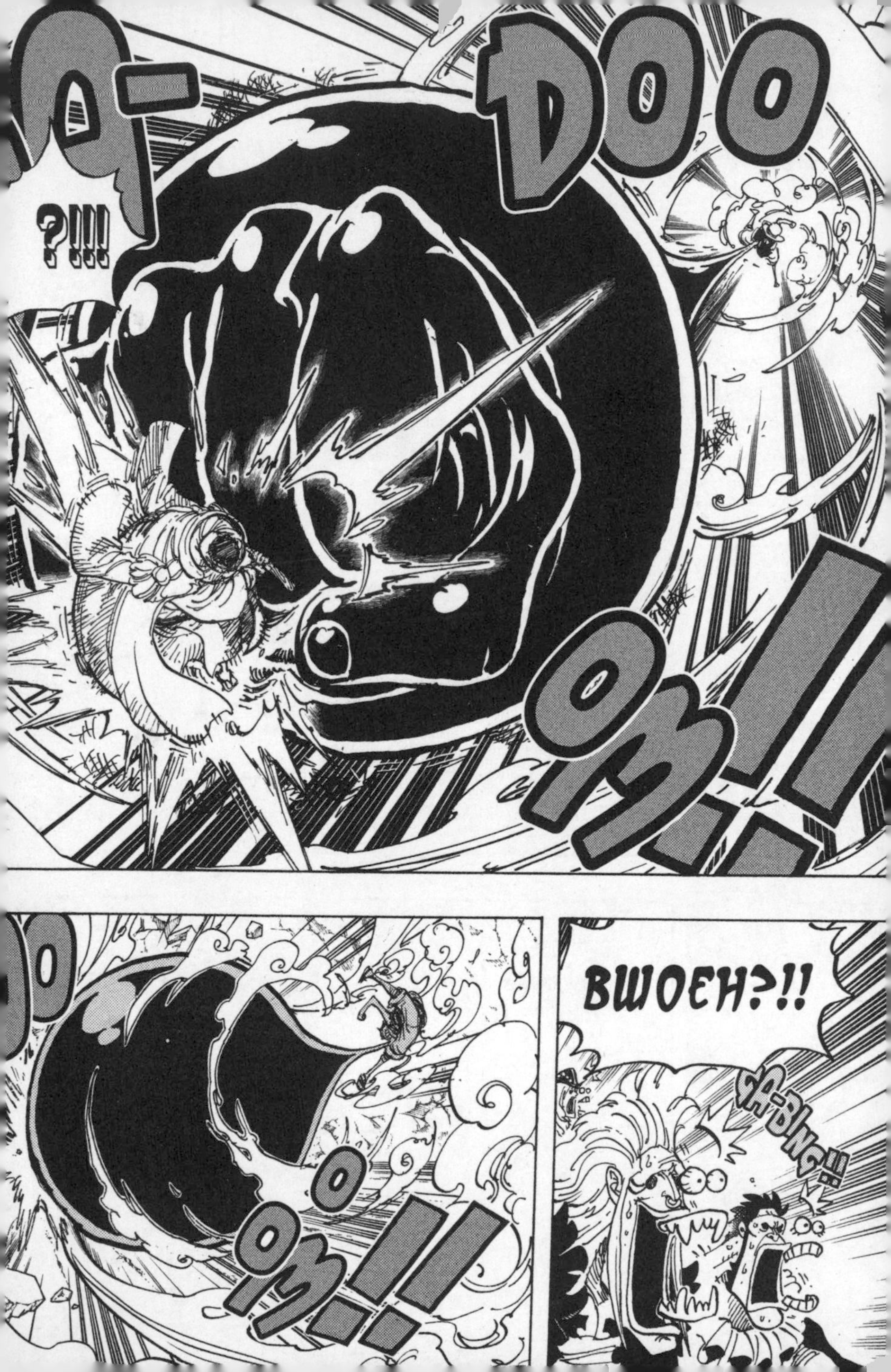
O-
DOO
OM!!
?!!!
BWOEH?!!
GA-BING!!
O
OOM!!

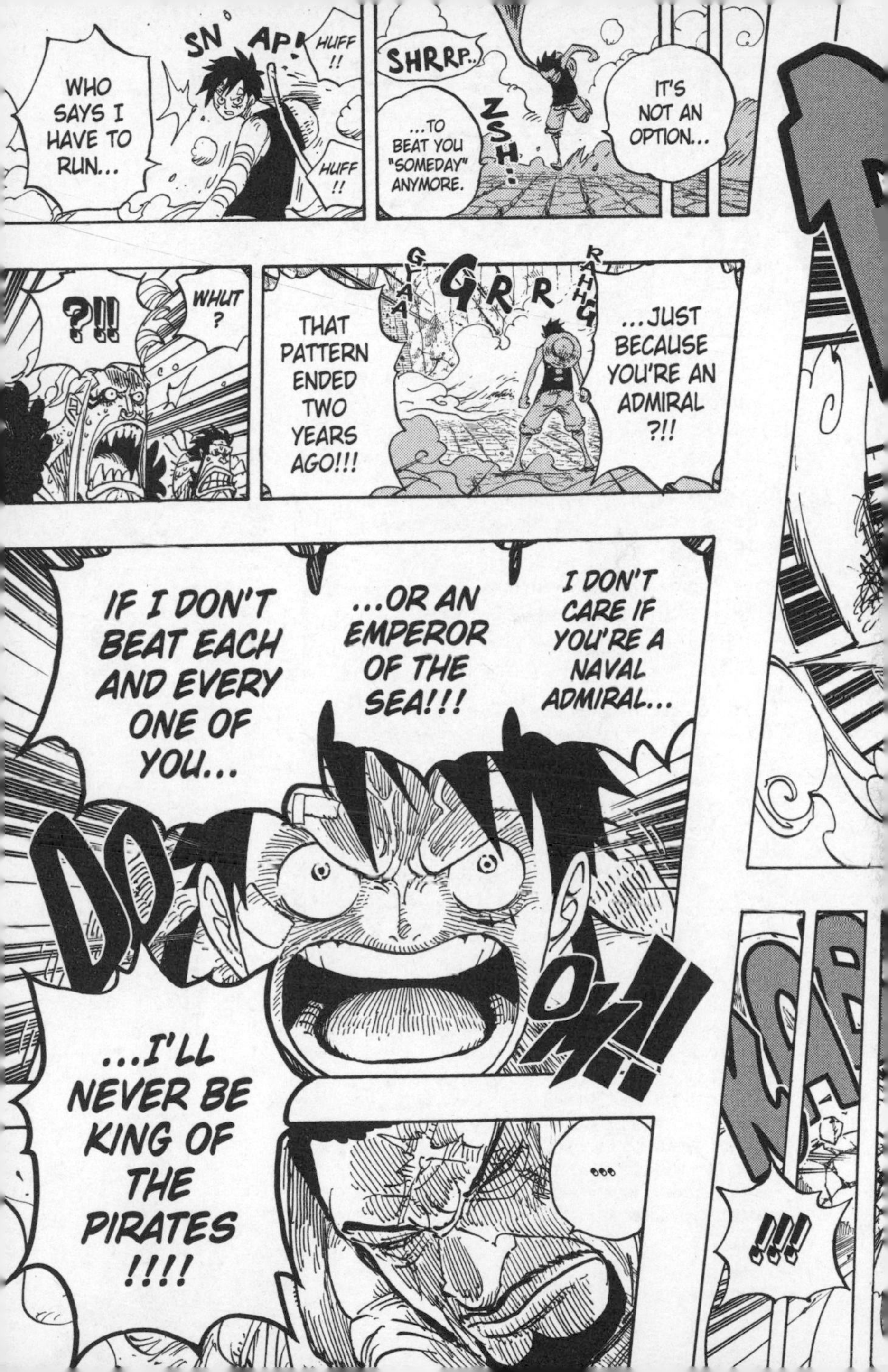
IT'S NOT AN OPTION...
...TO BEAT YOU "SOMEDAY" ANYMORE.
SHRRP..
ZSH!!
SNAP!
HUFF !!
WHO SAYS I HAVE TO RUN...
HUFF !!
...JUST BECAUSE YOU'RE AN ADMIRAL ?!!
THAT PATTERN ENDED TWO YEARS AGO!!!
GYAA
GRRR
RAHHG
WHUT ?
?!!
I DON'T CARE IF YOU'RE A NAVAL ADMIRAL...
...OR AN EMPEROR OF THE SEA!!!
IF I DON'T BEAT EACH AND EVERY ONE OF YOU...
...I'LL NEVER BE KING OF THE PIRATES !!!!
...
!!!

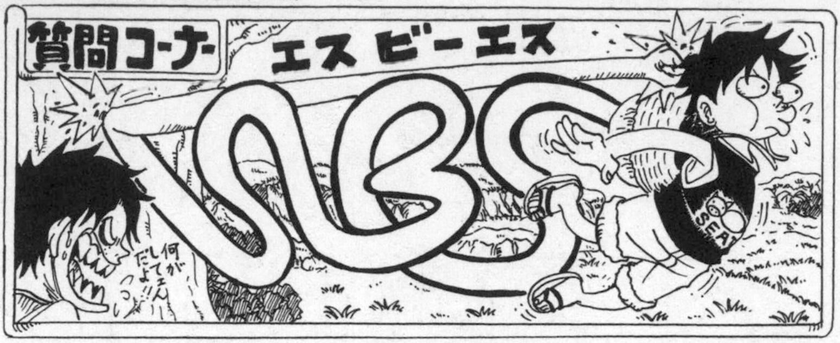
質問コーナー
エスビーエス
SBS
(Michi Nakahara, Tottori)

**Q:** Odacchi, I'll give you a nudie mag if you answer my question! Sanji will not allow people to leave food scraps behind, but what if a woman does it?

--Smoker's Cigar

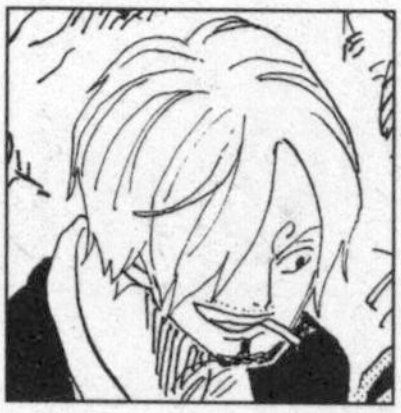

**A:** He'd probably eat the scraps off the dish once he took it away. Now where's my nudie mag?

**Q:** When Robin blooms more hands, there are petals in the air all around her. What type of flower are those petals from?

--One Piece Fanatic

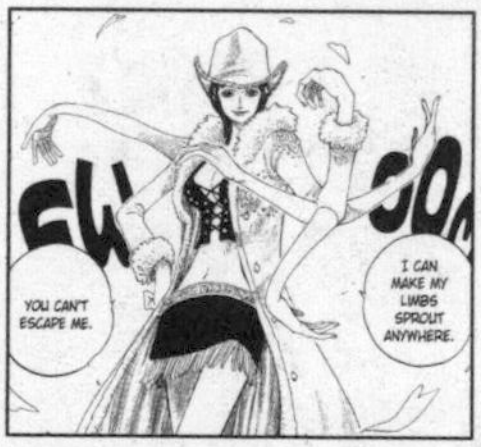
I CAN MAKE MY LIMBS SPROUT ANYWHERE.
YOU CAN'T ESCAPE ME.

**A:** That's quite a question. They just "fluff" out of nowhere and make her moves look graceful and elegant, so they're called Fluffflowers. They just fluff into being. Now where's my nudie mag?

**Q:** Hi, Mr. Oda. I wanted to ask you something. The cover of Chapter 518 is called the homeland of CP9, but it reminds me quite a bit of the eastern tower on Jiangxinyu Island in my hometown of Wenzhou, China. Did you model it on that?

--Haowii, Friend of Shrimp

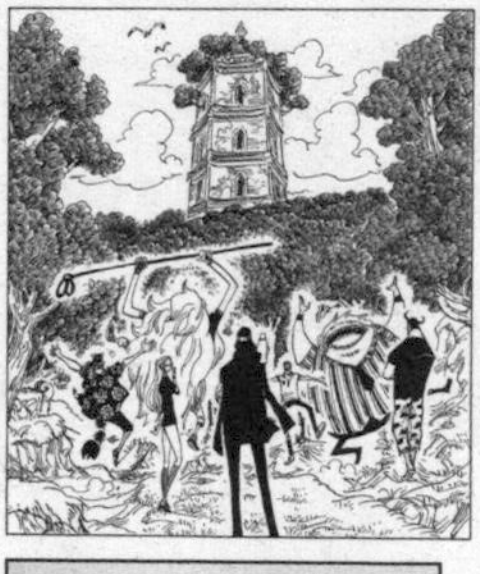

**A:** Oooh, that is the very tower. Having grown up in the kung-fu movie generation, I wanted CP9's training ground to be a Chinese-looking locale, and I think that's how I arrived at that image. I figured I was choosing a place in a far-off land, so the thought that a One Piece reader is there too brings me great joy. Thanks for the letter.

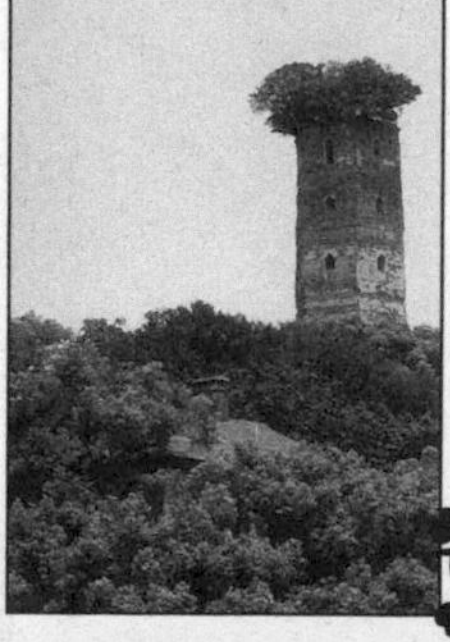

# Chapter 799:
# FATHER AND SONS

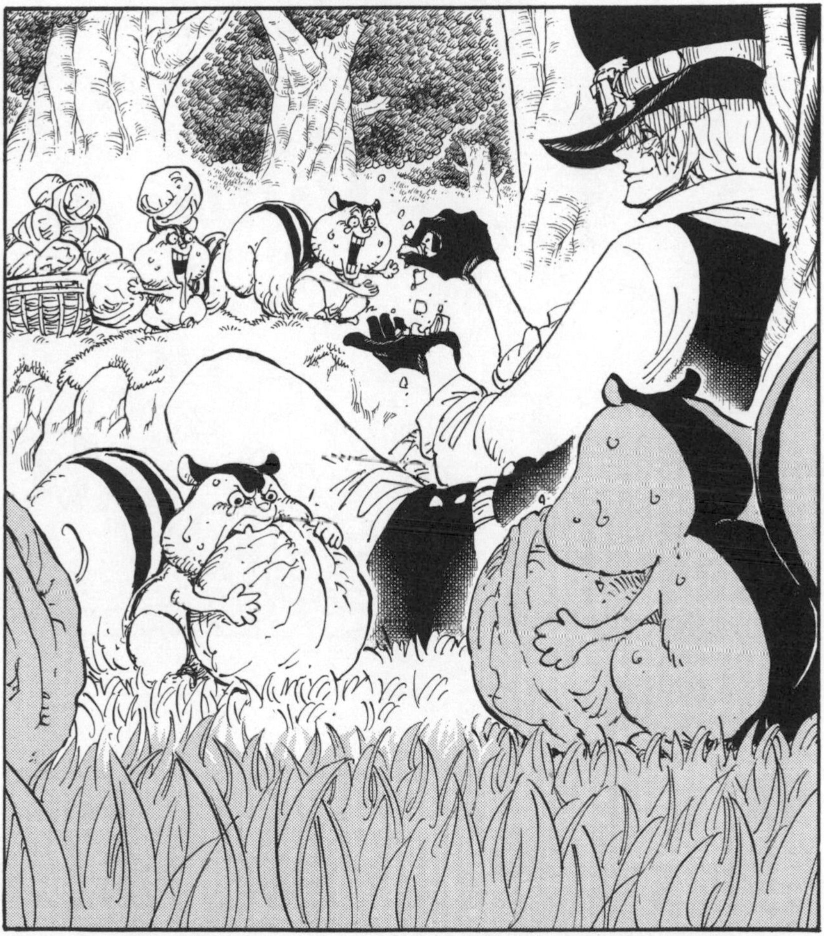

REQUEST: "SABO CRACKS WALNUTS FOR HUNGRY SQUIRRELS" BY NODA SKYWALKER FROM OSAKA

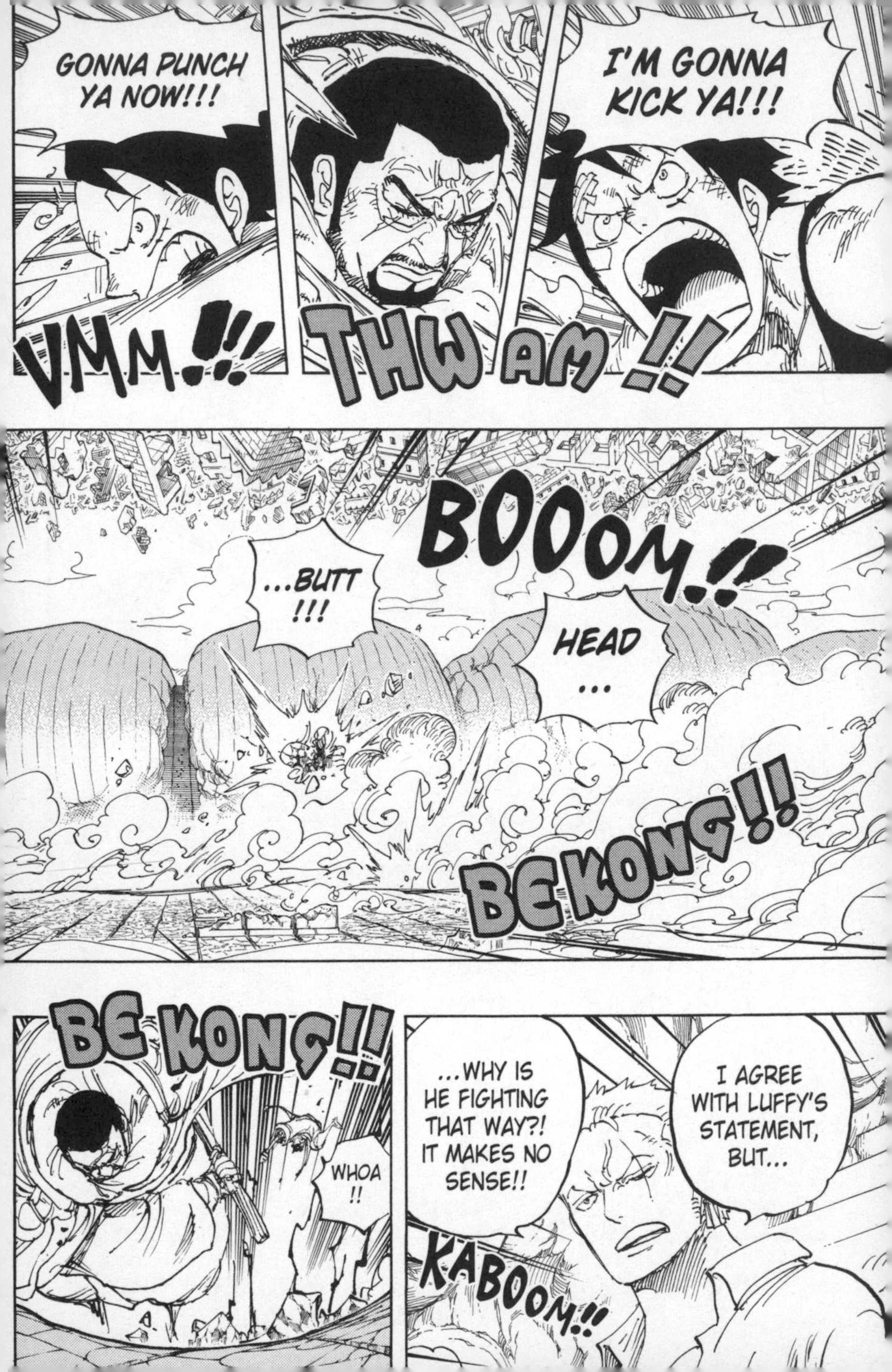
I'M GONNA KICK YA!!!
THWAM!!
GONNA PUNCH YA NOW!!!
VMM!!!
BOOOM!!
HEAD ...
...BUTT !!!
BEKONG!!
I AGREE WITH LUFFY'S STATEMENT, BUT...
...WHY IS HE FIGHTING THAT WAY?! IT MAKES NO SENSE!!
KABOOM!!
BEKONG!!!
WHOA !!

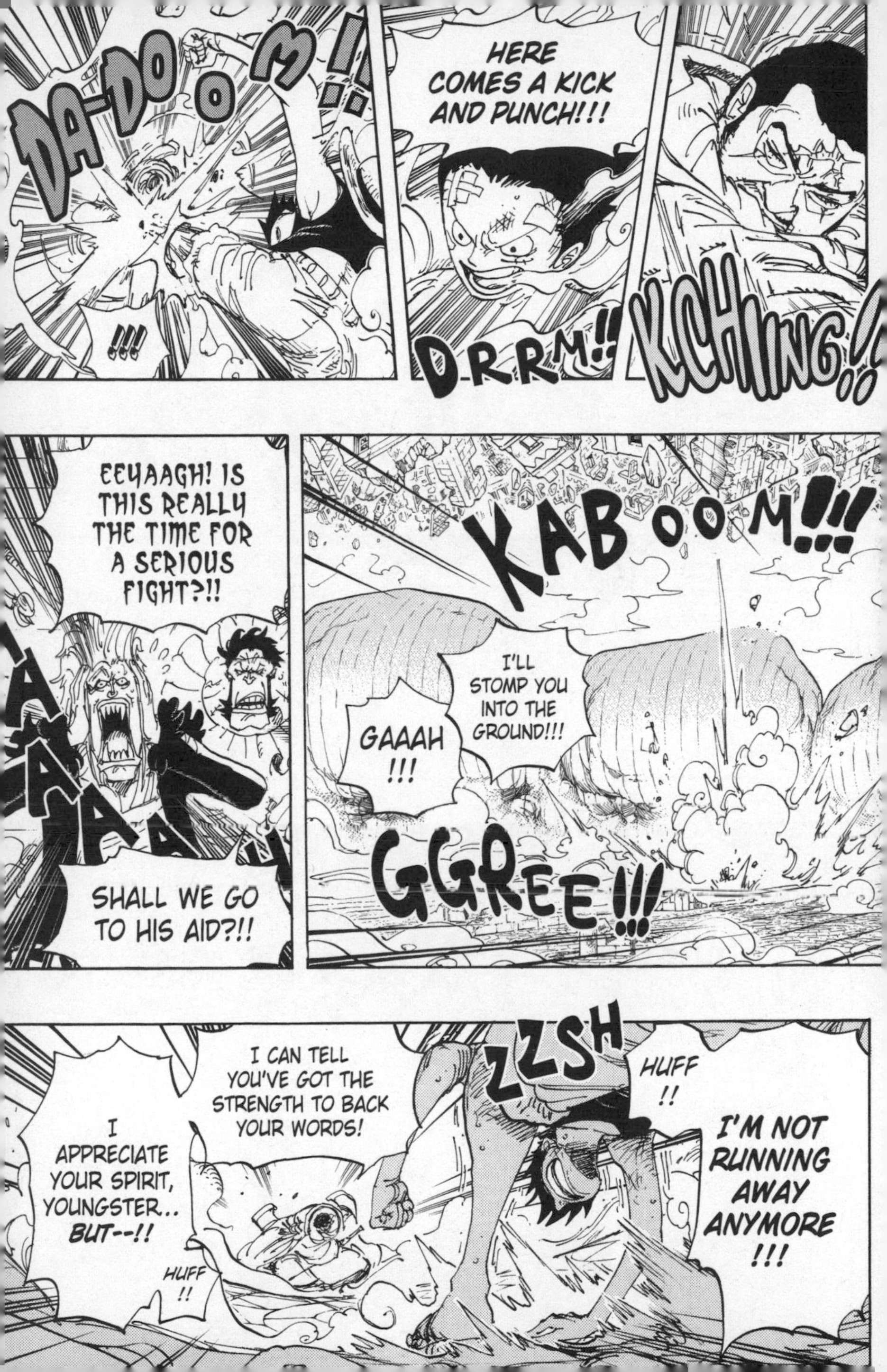
KCHING!!
HERE COMES A KICK AND PUNCH!!!
DRRM!!
DA-DOOOM!!
!!!
KABOOOM!!!
I'LL STOMP YOU INTO THE GROUND!!!
GAAAH!!!
GGREEE!!!
EEYAAGH! IS THIS REALLY THE TIME FOR A SERIOUS FIGHT?!!
SHALL WE GO TO HIS AID?!!
HUFF!!
I'M NOT RUNNING AWAY ANYMORE!!!
ZZSH
I CAN TELL YOU'VE GOT THE STRENGTH TO BACK YOUR WORDS!
I APPRECIATE YOUR SPIRIT, YOUNGSTER.. BUT--!!
HUFF!!

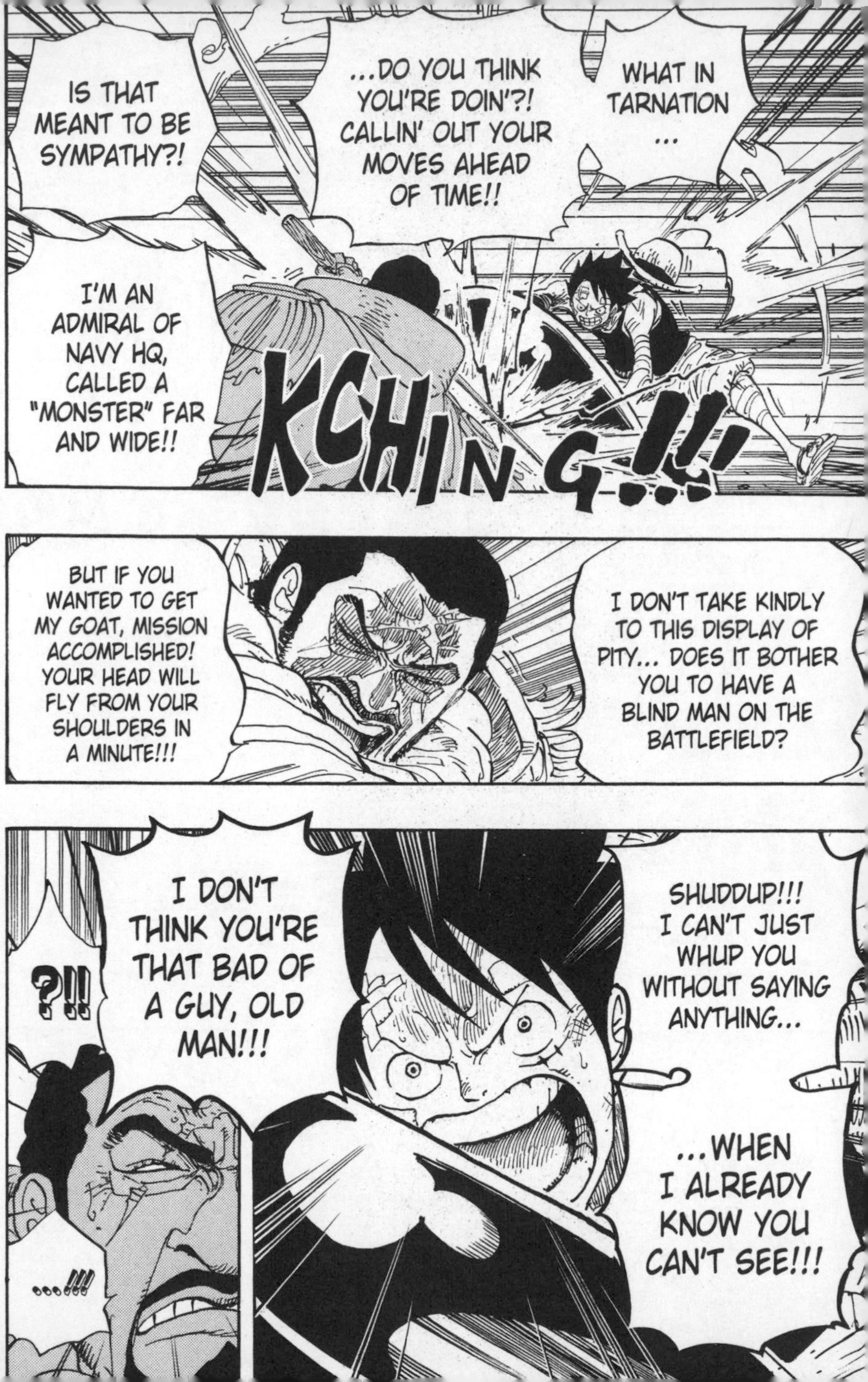
WHAT IN TARNATION ...
...DO YOU THINK YOU'RE DOIN'?! CALLIN' OUT YOUR MOVES AHEAD OF TIME!!
IS THAT MEANT TO BE SYMPATHY?!
KCHING...!!!
I'M AN ADMIRAL OF NAVY HQ, CALLED A "MONSTER" FAR AND WIDE!!
I DON'T TAKE KINDLY TO THIS DISPLAY OF PITY... DOES IT BOTHER YOU TO HAVE A BLIND MAN ON THE BATTLEFIELD?
BUT IF YOU WANTED TO GET MY GOAT, MISSION ACCOMPLISHED! YOUR HEAD WILL FLY FROM YOUR SHOULDERS IN A MINUTE!!!
SHUDDUP!!! I CAN'T JUST WHUP YOU WITHOUT SAYING ANYTHING...
...WHEN I ALREADY KNOW YOU CAN'T SEE!!!
I DON'T THINK YOU'RE THAT BAD OF A GUY, OLD MAN!!!
?!!
...!!!

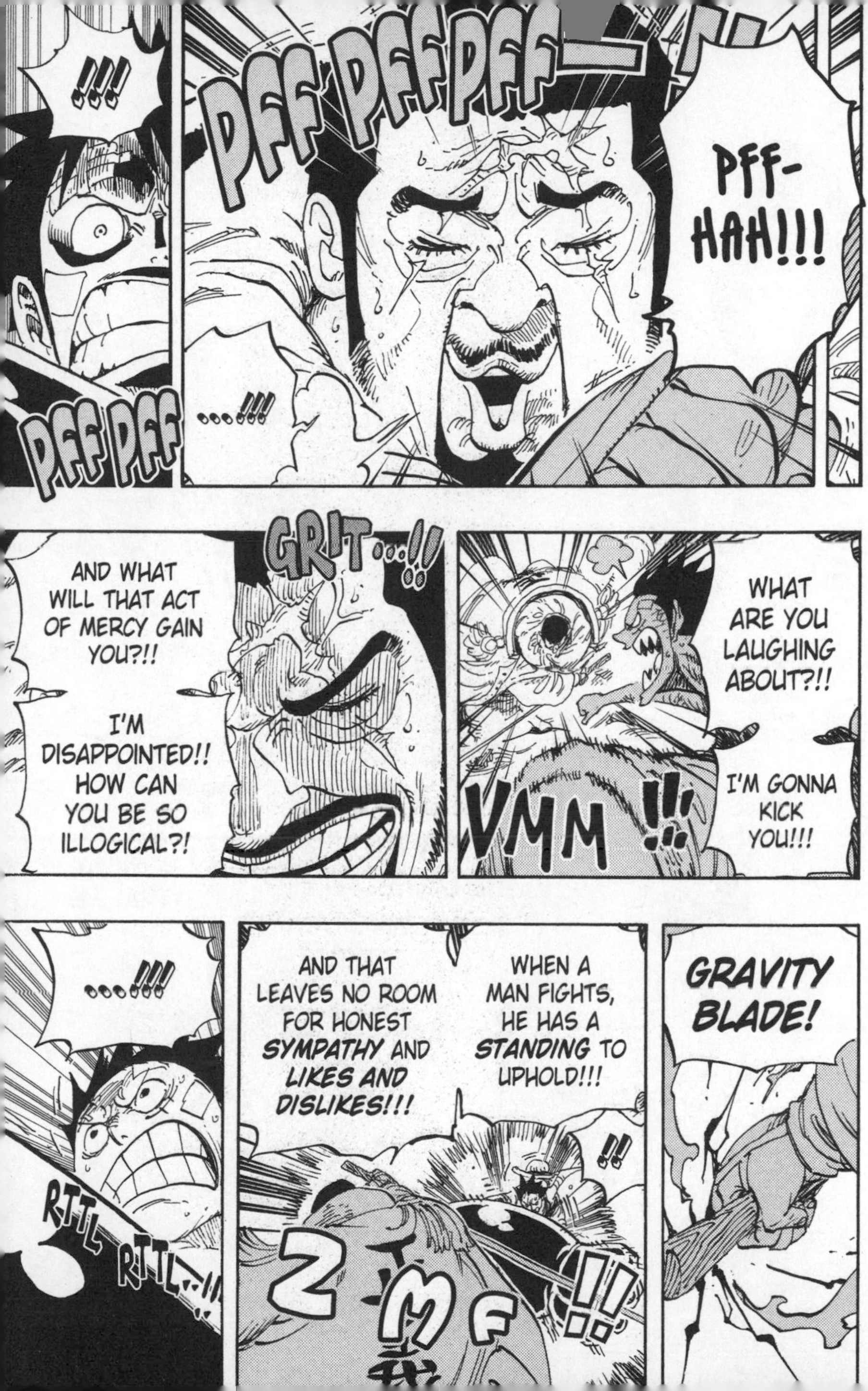
PFF-HAH!!!
PFF PFF PFF—
...!!!
!!!
PFF PFF
WHAT ARE YOU LAUGHING ABOUT?!!
I'M GONNA KICK YOU!!!
VMM !!
GRIT...!!
AND WHAT WILL THAT ACT OF MERCY GAIN YOU?!!
I'M DISAPPOINTED!! HOW CAN YOU BE SO ILLOGICAL?!
GRAVITY BLADE!
WHEN A MAN FIGHTS, HE HAS A *STANDING* TO UPHOLD!!!
AND THAT LEAVES NO ROOM FOR HONEST *SYMPATHY* AND *LIKES AND DISLIKES!!!*
!!
ZMF!!
...!!!
RTTL RTTL...!!

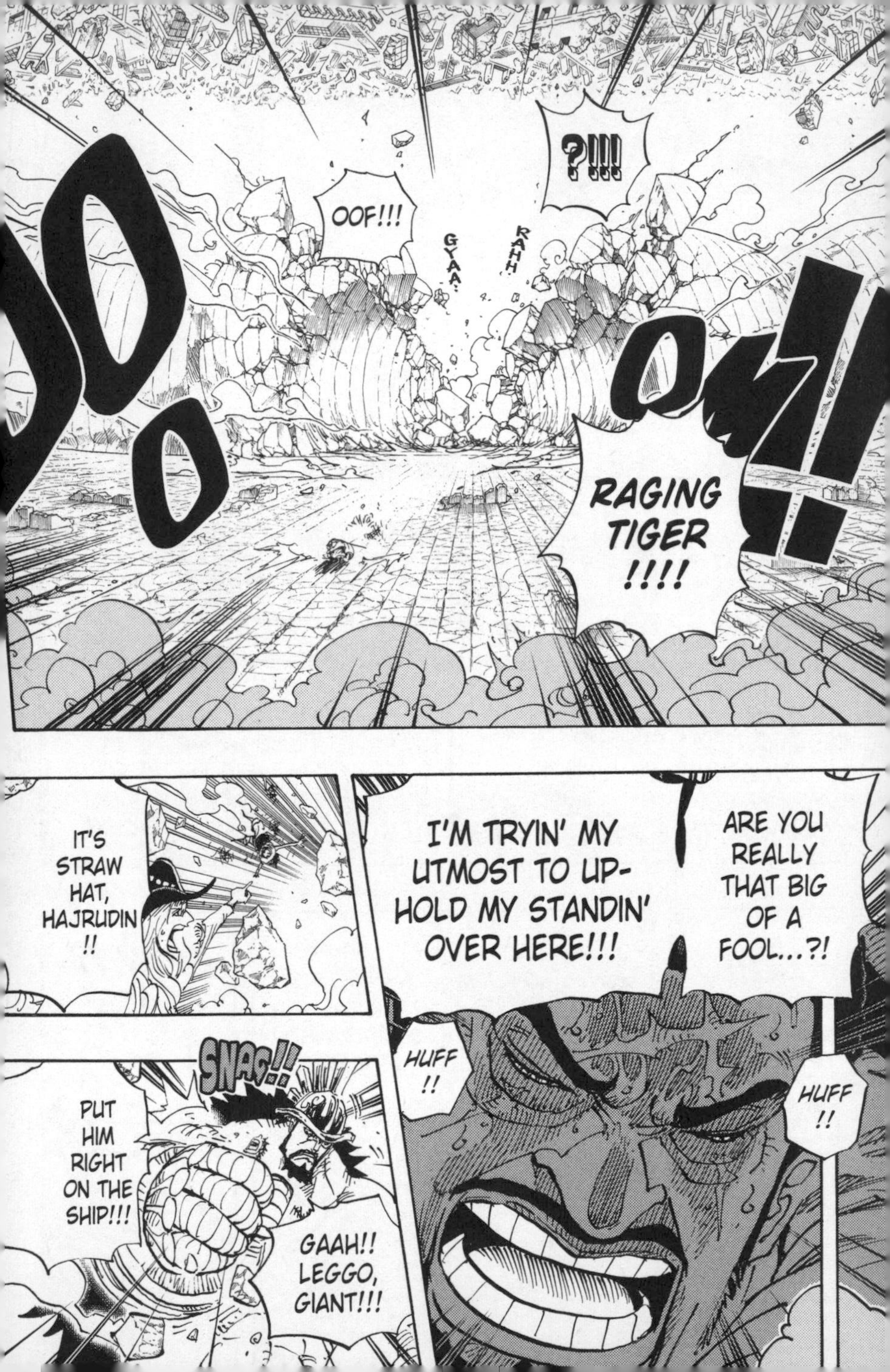
?!!!
OOF!!!
RAHH
GYAA
RAGING TIGER !!!!
ARE YOU REALLY THAT BIG OF A FOOL...?!
I'M TRYIN' MY UTMOST TO UP-HOLD MY STANDIN' OVER HERE!!!
HUFF !!
HUFF !!
IT'S STRAW HAT, HAJRUDIN !!
SNAG!!
PUT HIM RIGHT ON THE SHIP!!!
GAAH!! LEGGO, GIANT!!!

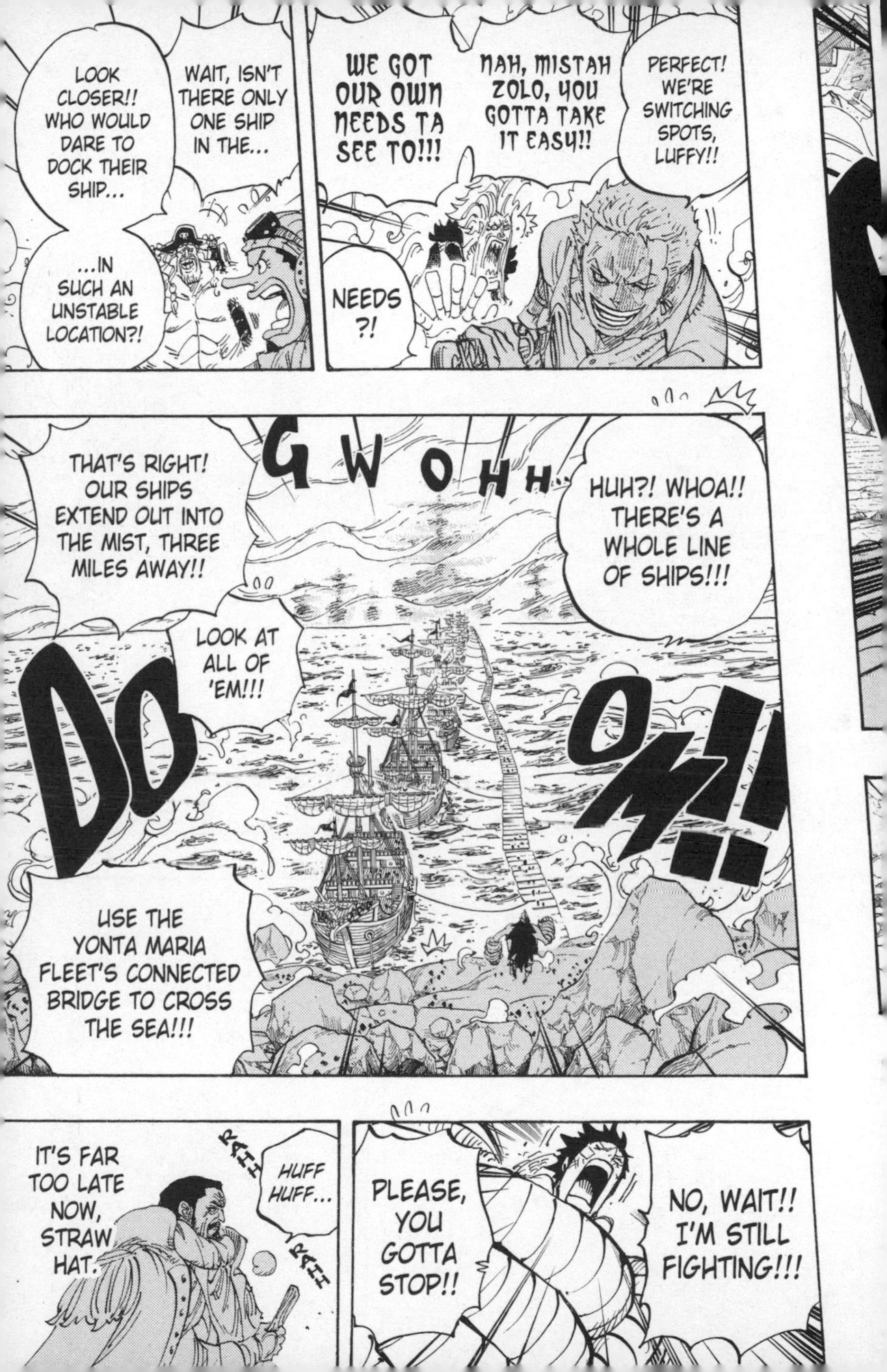
PERFECT! WE'RE SWITCHING SPOTS, LUFFY!!
NAH, MISTAH ZOLO, YOU GOTTA TAKE IT EASY!!
WE GOT OUR OWN NEEDS TA SEE TO!!!
NEEDS?!
WAIT, ISN'T THERE ONLY ONE SHIP IN THE...
LOOK CLOSER!! WHO WOULD DARE TO DOCK THEIR SHIP...
...IN SUCH AN UNSTABLE LOCATION?!
HUH?! WHOA!! THERE'S A WHOLE LINE OF SHIPS!!!
GWOHH...
THAT'S RIGHT! OUR SHIPS EXTEND OUT INTO THE MIST, THREE MILES AWAY!!
LOOK AT ALL OF 'EM!!!
DOOM!!
USE THE YONTA MARIA FLEET'S CONNECTED BRIDGE TO CROSS THE SEA!!!
NO, WAIT!! I'M STILL FIGHTING!!!
PLEASE, YOU GOTTA STOP!!
HUFF HUFF...
RAHH
RAHH
IT'S FAR TOO LATE NOW, STRAW HAT.

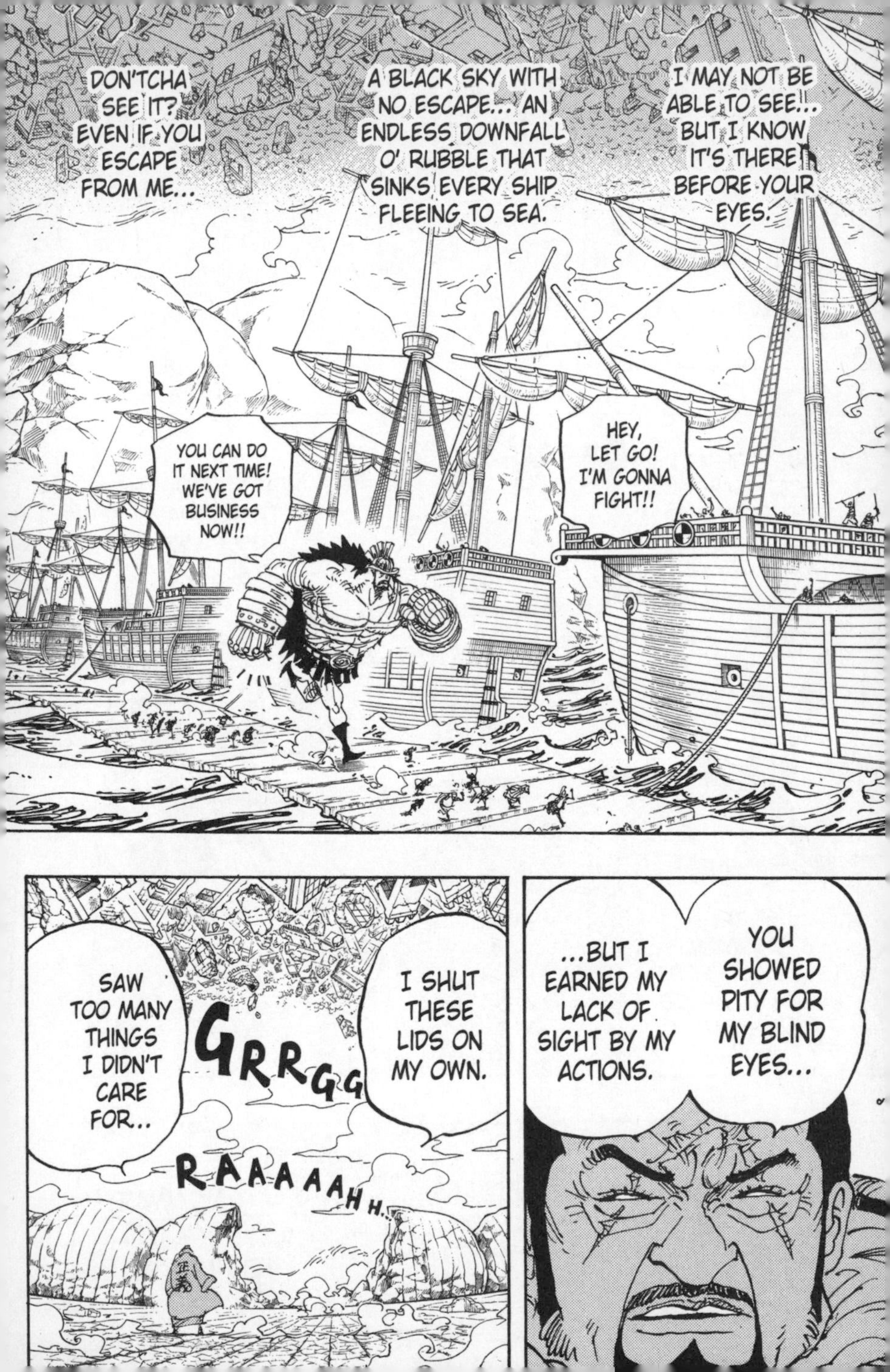
I MAY NOT BE ABLE TO SEE... BUT I KNOW IT'S THERE BEFORE YOUR EYES.
A BLACK SKY WITH NO ESCAPE... AN ENDLESS DOWNFALL O' RUBBLE THAT SINKS EVERY SHIP FLEEING TO SEA.
DON'TCHA SEE IT? EVEN IF YOU ESCAPE FROM ME...
HEY, LET GO! I'M GONNA FIGHT!!
YOU CAN DO IT NEXT TIME! WE'VE GOT BUSINESS NOW!!
YOU SHOWED PITY FOR MY BLIND EYES...
...BUT I EARNED MY LACK OF SIGHT BY MY ACTIONS.
I SHUT THESE LIDS ON MY OWN.
SAW TOO MANY THINGS I DIDN'T CARE FOR...
GRRRGG
RAAAAAHH...

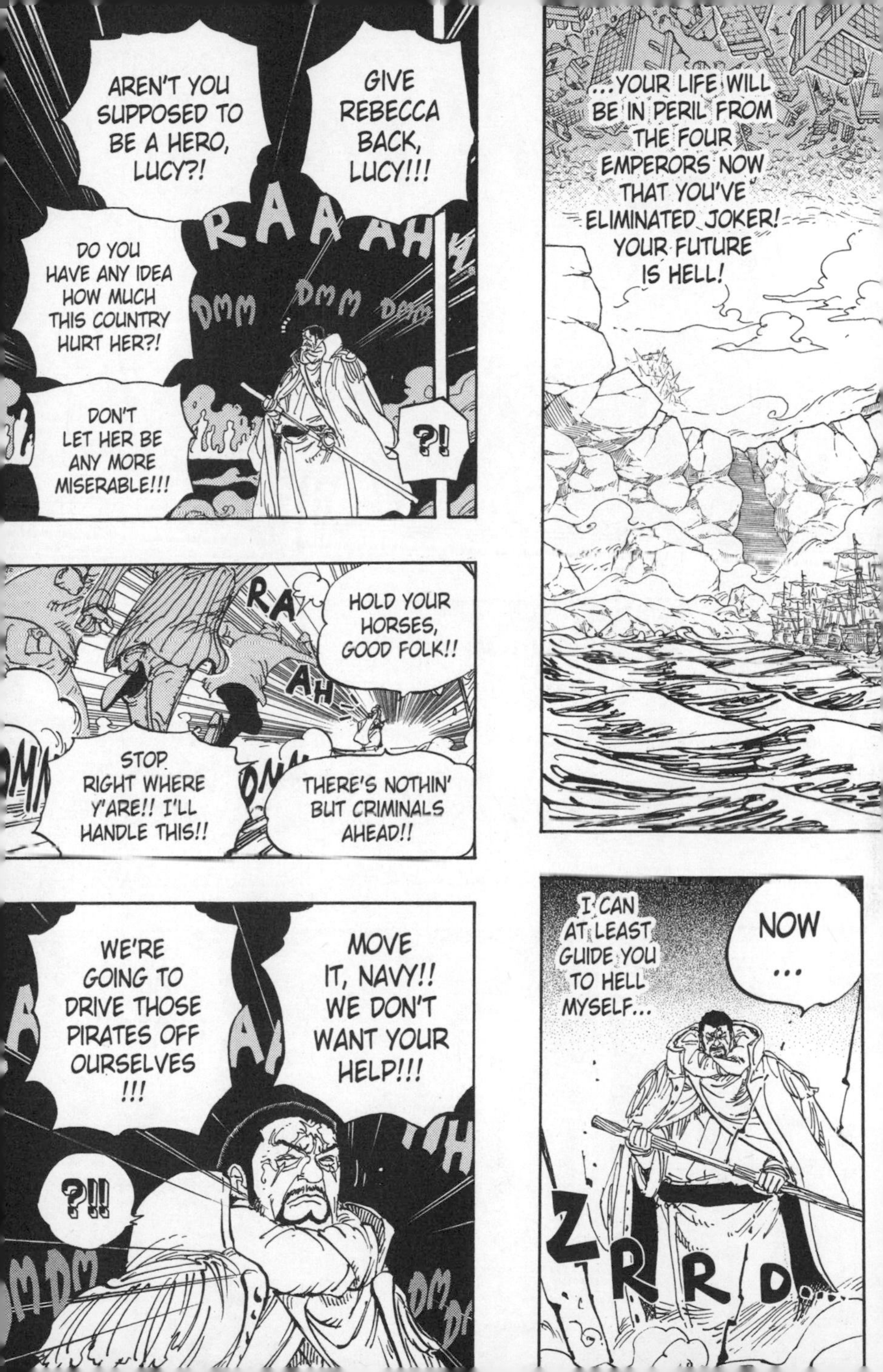
...YOUR LIFE WILL BE IN PERIL FROM THE FOUR EMPERORS NOW THAT YOU'VE ELIMINATED JOKER! YOUR FUTURE IS HELL!
GIVE REBECCA BACK, LUCY!!!
AREN'T YOU SUPPOSED TO BE A HERO, LUCY?!
RAAAAH
DO YOU HAVE ANY IDEA HOW MUCH THIS COUNTRY HURT HER?!
DMM DMM DMM
?!
DON'T LET HER BE ANY MORE MISERABLE!!!
HOLD YOUR HORSES, GOOD FOLK!!
RA
AH
THERE'S NOTHIN' BUT CRIMINALS AHEAD!!
STOP RIGHT WHERE Y'ARE!! I'LL HANDLE THIS!!
NOW ...
I CAN AT LEAST GUIDE YOU TO HELL MYSELF...
ZRRRD
MOVE IT, NAVY!! WE DON'T WANT YOUR HELP!!!
WE'RE GOING TO DRIVE THOSE PIRATES OFF OURSELVES!!!
?!!

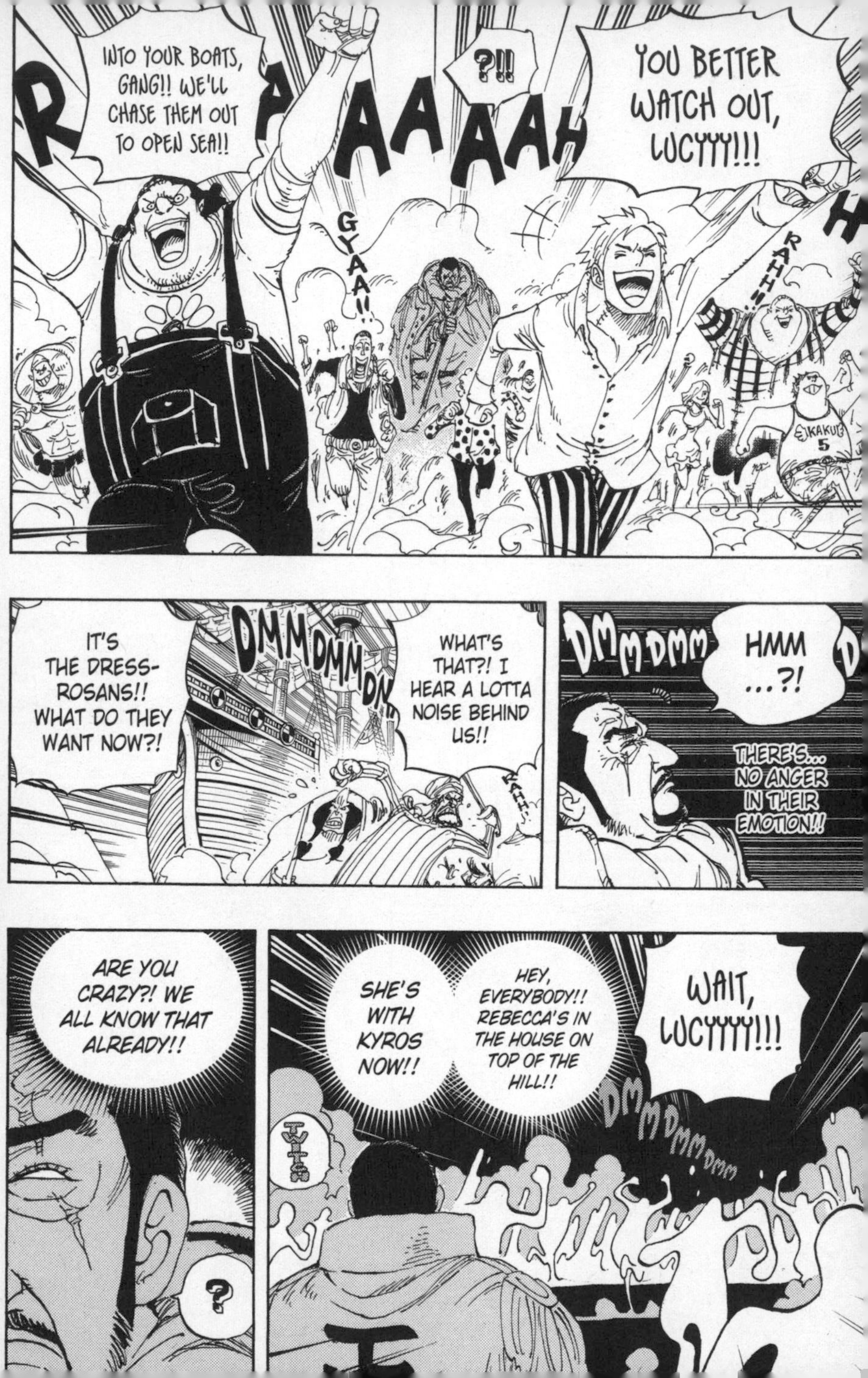
YOU BETTER WATCH OUT, LUCYYY!!!
?!!
AAAAAH
INTO YOUR BOATS, GANG!! WE'LL CHASE THEM OUT TO OPEN SEA!!
RAHH!!
GYAA!!
HMM ...?!
DMMDMM
THERE'S... NO ANGER IN THEIR EMOTION!!
WHAT'S THAT?! I HEAR A LOTTA NOISE BEHIND US!!
DMMDMMDM
IT'S THE DRESS-ROSANS!! WHAT DO THEY WANT NOW?!
RAHH!
WAIT, LUCYYYY!!!
HEY, EVERYBODY!! REBECCA'S IN THE HOUSE ON TOP OF THE HILL!!
SHE'S WITH KYROS NOW!!
DMMDMMDMM
ARE YOU CRAZY?! WE ALL KNOW THAT ALREADY!!
?

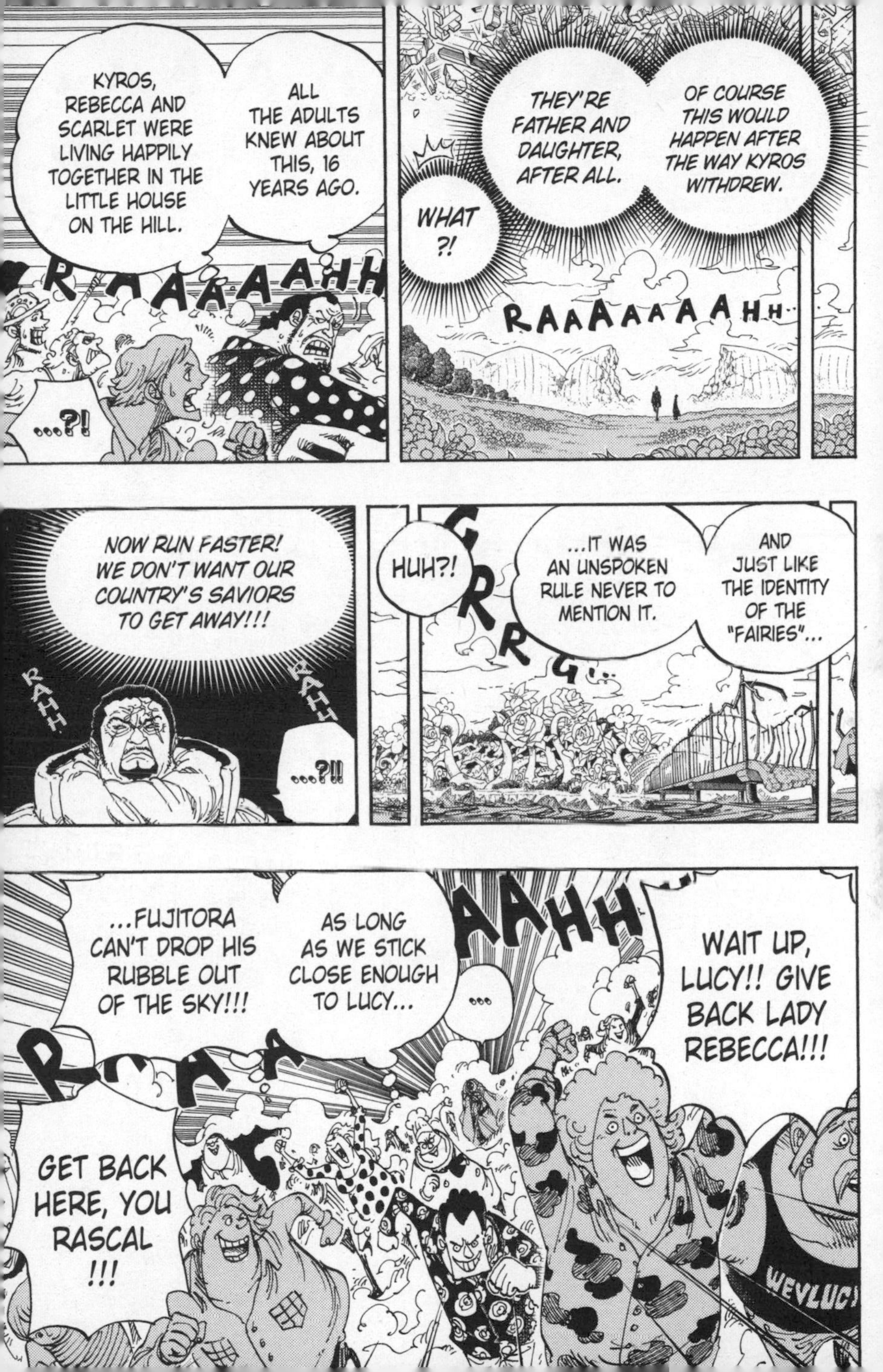
OF COURSE THIS WOULD HAPPEN AFTER THE WAY KYROS WITHDREW.
THEY'RE FATHER AND DAUGHTER, AFTER ALL.
WHAT ?!
RAAAAAAAAHH...
ALL THE ADULTS KNEW ABOUT THIS, 16 YEARS AGO.
KYROS, REBECCA AND SCARLET WERE LIVING HAPPILY TOGETHER IN THE LITTLE HOUSE ON THE HILL.
RAAAAAAAHH
...?!
AND JUST LIKE THE IDENTITY OF THE "FAIRIES"...
...IT WAS AN UNSPOKEN RULE NEVER TO MENTION IT.
HUH?!
GRRRG...
NOW RUN FASTER! WE DON'T WANT OUR COUNTRY'S SAVIORS TO GET AWAY!!!
RAHH
RAHH
...?!!
WAIT UP, LUCY!! GIVE BACK LADY REBECCA!!!
AAHH
...
AS LONG AS WE STICK CLOSE ENOUGH TO LUCY...
...FUJITORA CAN'T DROP HIS RUBBLE OUT OF THE SKY!!!
RAAA
GET BACK HERE, YOU RASCAL!!!

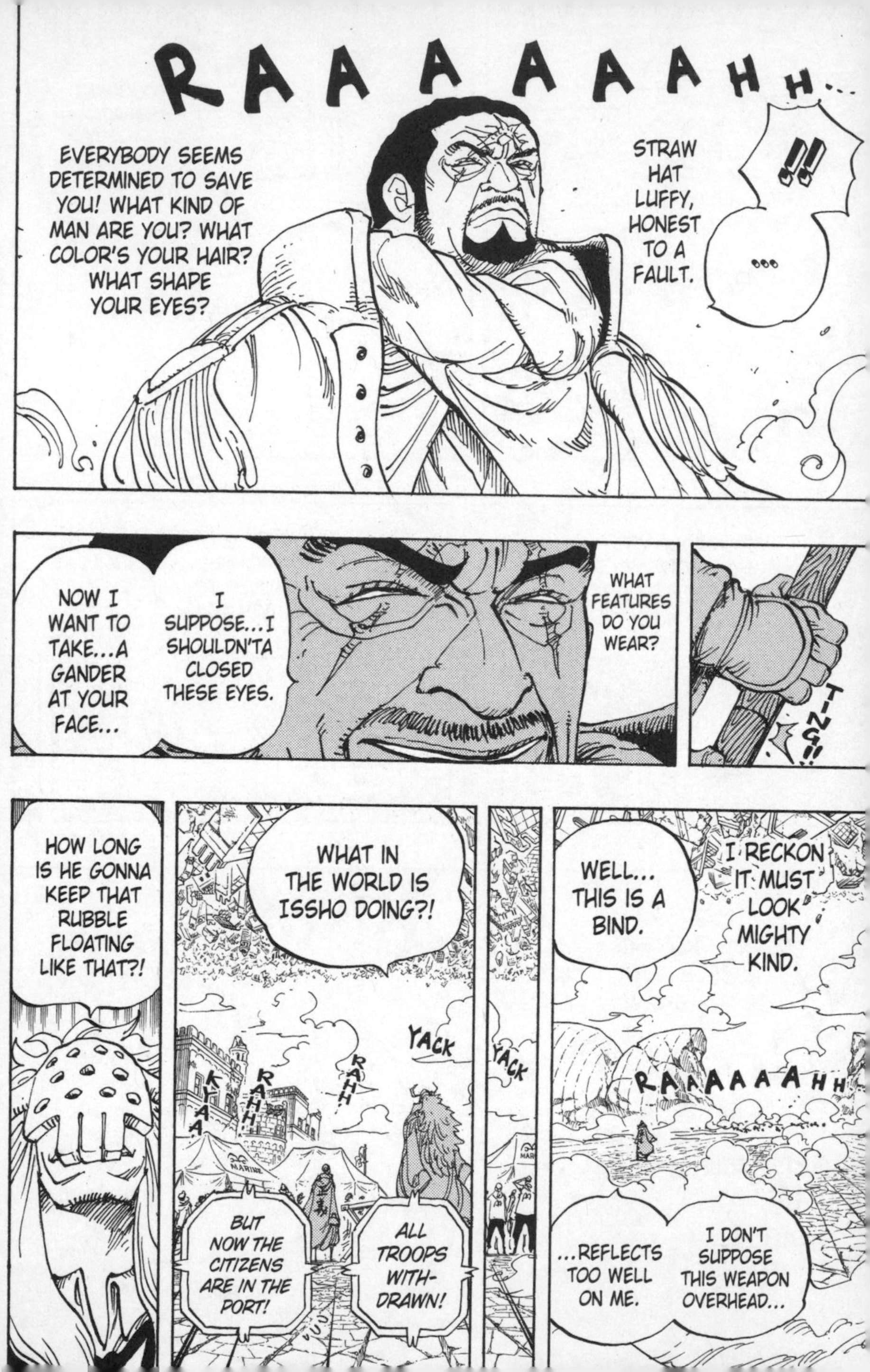
RAAAAAAHH...
!!
...
STRAW HAT LUFFY, HONEST TO A FAULT.
EVERYBODY SEEMS DETERMINED TO SAVE YOU! WHAT KIND OF MAN ARE YOU? WHAT COLOR'S YOUR HAIR? WHAT SHAPE YOUR EYES?
TING!!
WHAT FEATURES DO YOU WEAR?
I SUPPOSE...I SHOULDN'TA CLOSED THESE EYES.
NOW I WANT TO TAKE...A GANDER AT YOUR FACE...
I RECKON IT MUST LOOK MIGHTY KIND.
WELL... THIS IS A BIND.
RAAAAAAHH...
I DON'T SUPPOSE THIS WEAPON OVERHEAD...
...REFLECTS TOO WELL ON ME.
YACK
WHAT IN THE WORLD IS ISSHO DOING?!
YACK
RAHH
RAHH
KYAA
ALL TROOPS WITHDRAWN!
BUT NOW THE CITIZENS ARE IN THE PORT!
HOW LONG IS HE GONNA KEEP THAT RUBBLE FLOATING LIKE THAT?!

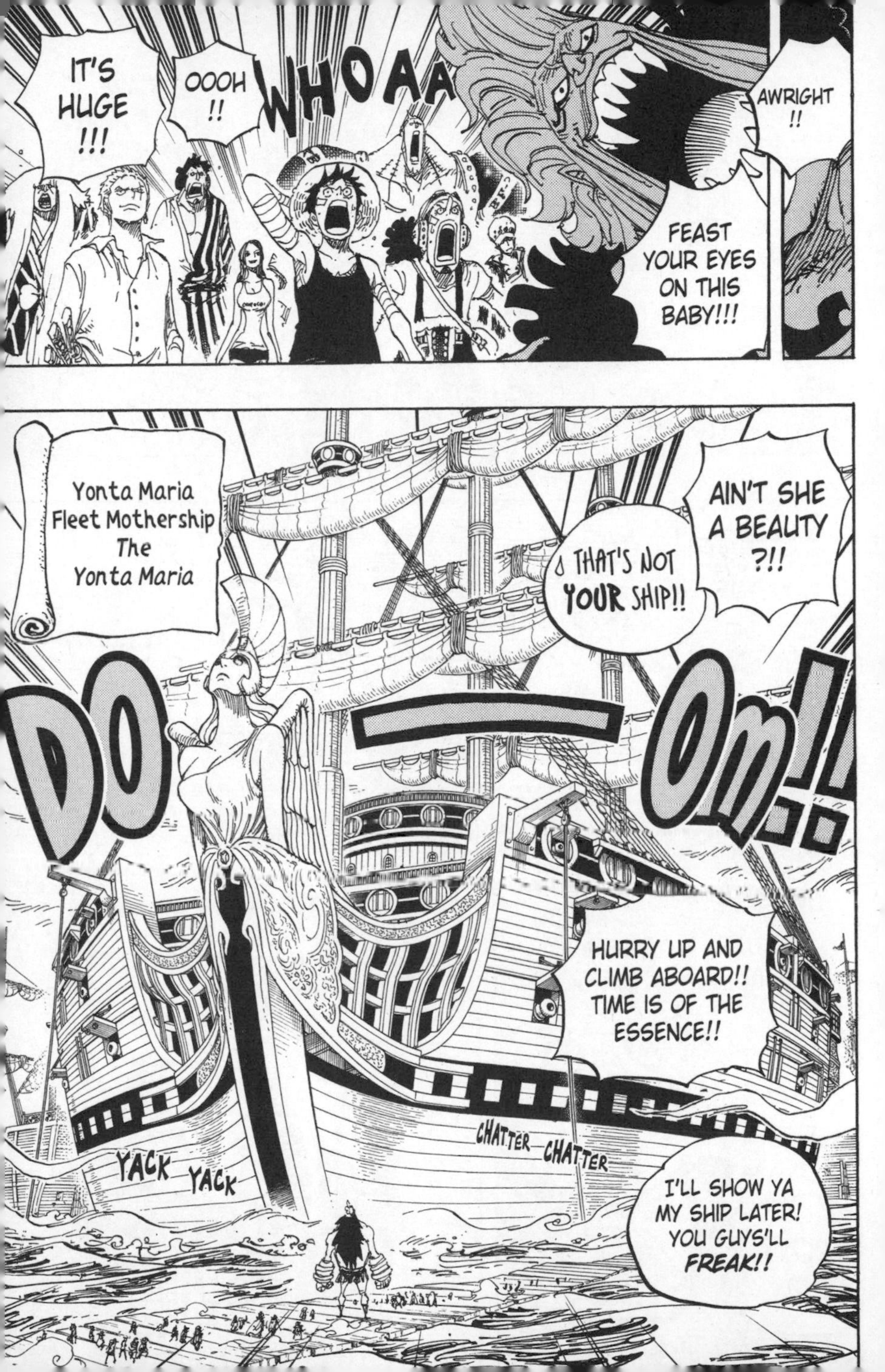
AWRIGHT!!
FEAST YOUR EYES ON THIS BABY!!!
WHOAA
OOOH!!
IT'S HUGE!!!
AIN'T SHE A BEAUTY?!!
THAT'S NOT YOUR SHIP!!
Yonta Maria Fleet Mothership The Yonta Maria
DO—OM!!
HURRY UP AND CLIMB ABOARD!! TIME IS OF THE ESSENCE!!
CHATTER CHATTER
YACK YACK
I'LL SHOW YA MY SHIP LATER! YOU GUYS'LL FREAK!!

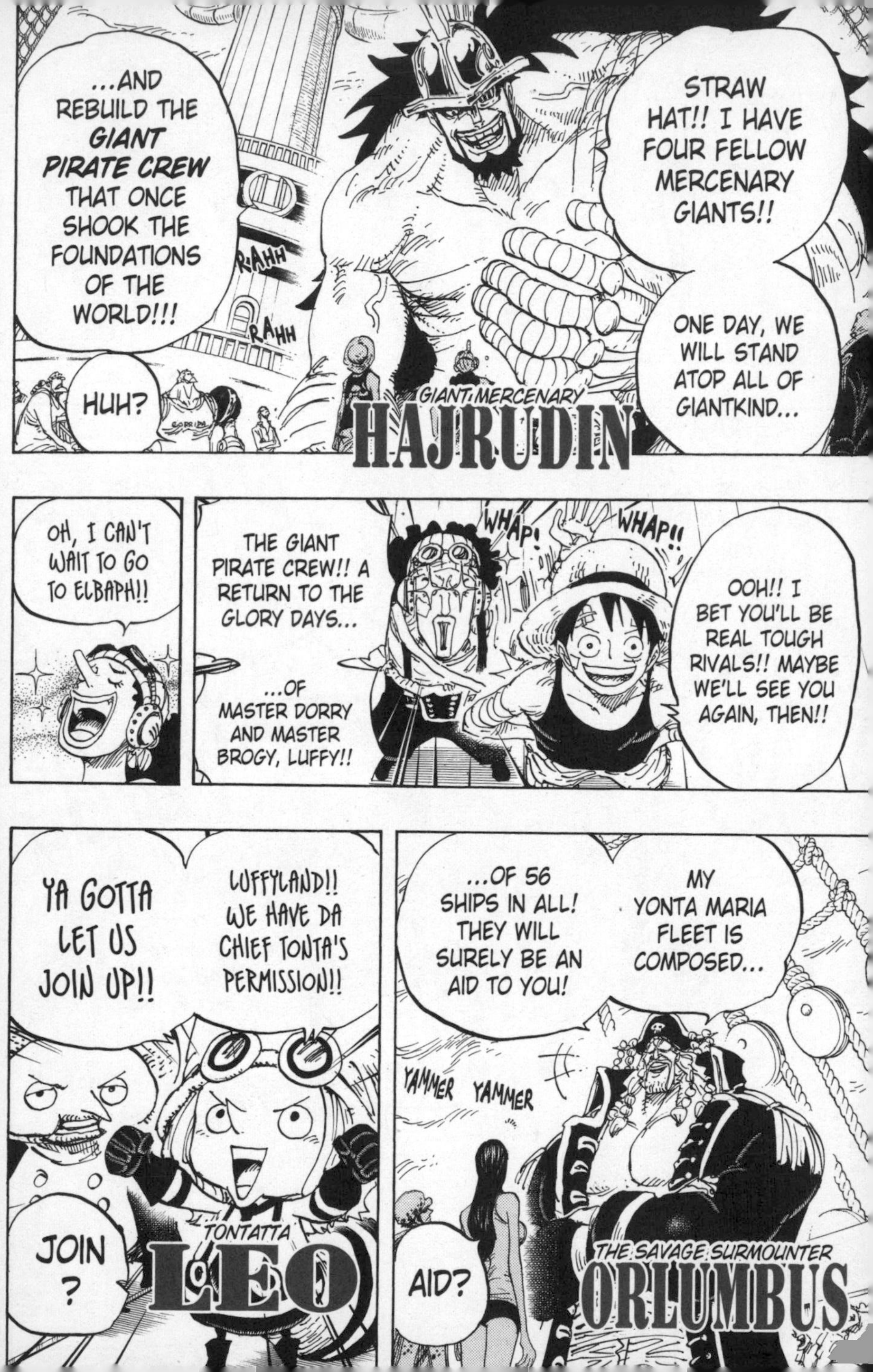
STRAW HAT!! I HAVE FOUR FELLOW MERCENARY GIANTS!!
ONE DAY, WE WILL STAND ATOP ALL OF GIANTKIND...
...AND REBUILD THE *GIANT PIRATE CREW* THAT ONCE SHOOK THE FOUNDATIONS OF THE WORLD!!!
RAHH
RAHH
HUH?
GIANT MERCENARY
HAJRUDIN
WHAP!!
WHAP!
OOH!! I BET YOU'LL BE REAL TOUGH RIVALS!! MAYBE WE'LL SEE YOU AGAIN, THEN!!
THE GIANT PIRATE CREW!! A RETURN TO THE GLORY DAYS...
...OF MASTER DORRY AND MASTER BROGY, LUFFY!!
OH, I CAN'T WAIT TO GO TO ELBAPH!!
MY YONTA MARIA FLEET IS COMPOSED...
...OF 56 SHIPS IN ALL! THEY WILL SURELY BE AN AID TO YOU!
YAMMER
YAMMER
AID?
THE SAVAGE SURMOUNTER
ORLUMBUS
LUFFYLAND!! WE HAVE DA CHIEF TONTA'S PERMISSION!!
YA GOTTA LET US JOIN UP!!
JOIN?
TONTATTA
LEO

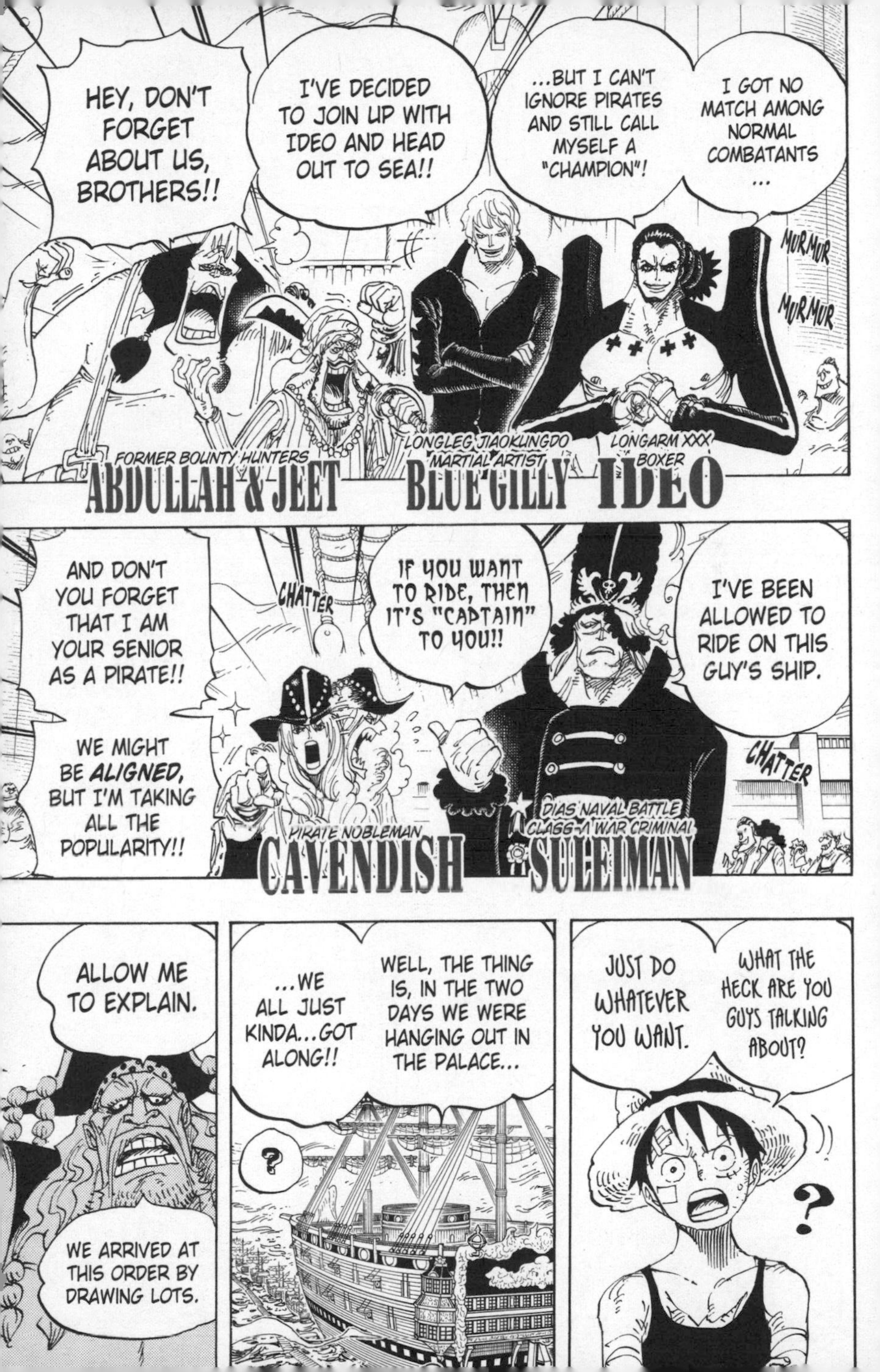
I GOT NO MATCH AMONG NORMAL COMBATANTS ...
...BUT I CAN'T IGNORE PIRATES AND STILL CALL MYSELF A "CHAMPION"!
I'VE DECIDED TO JOIN UP WITH IDEO AND HEAD OUT TO SEA!!
HEY, DON'T FORGET ABOUT US, BROTHERS!!
MURMUR
MURMUR
LONGARM XXX BOXER
IDEO
LONGLEG JIAOKUNGDO MARTIAL ARTIST
BLUE GILLY
FORMER BOUNTY HUNTERS
ABDULLAH & JEET
I'VE BEEN ALLOWED TO RIDE ON THIS GUY'S SHIP.
CHATTER
IF YOU WANT TO RIDE, THEN IT'S "CAPTAIN" TO YOU!!
CHATTER
AND DON'T YOU FORGET THAT I AM YOUR SENIOR AS A PIRATE!!
WE MIGHT BE ALIGNED, BUT I'M TAKING ALL THE POPULARITY!!
DIAS NAVAL BATTLE CLASS-A WAR CRIMINAL
SULEIMAN
PIRATE NOBLEMAN
CAVENDISH
WHAT THE HECK ARE YOU GUYS TALKING ABOUT?
JUST DO WHATEVER YOU WANT.
?
WELL, THE THING IS, IN THE TWO DAYS WE WERE HANGING OUT IN THE PALACE...
...WE ALL JUST KINDA...GOT ALONG!!
?
ALLOW ME TO EXPLAIN.
WE ARRIVED AT THIS ORDER BY DRAWING LOTS.

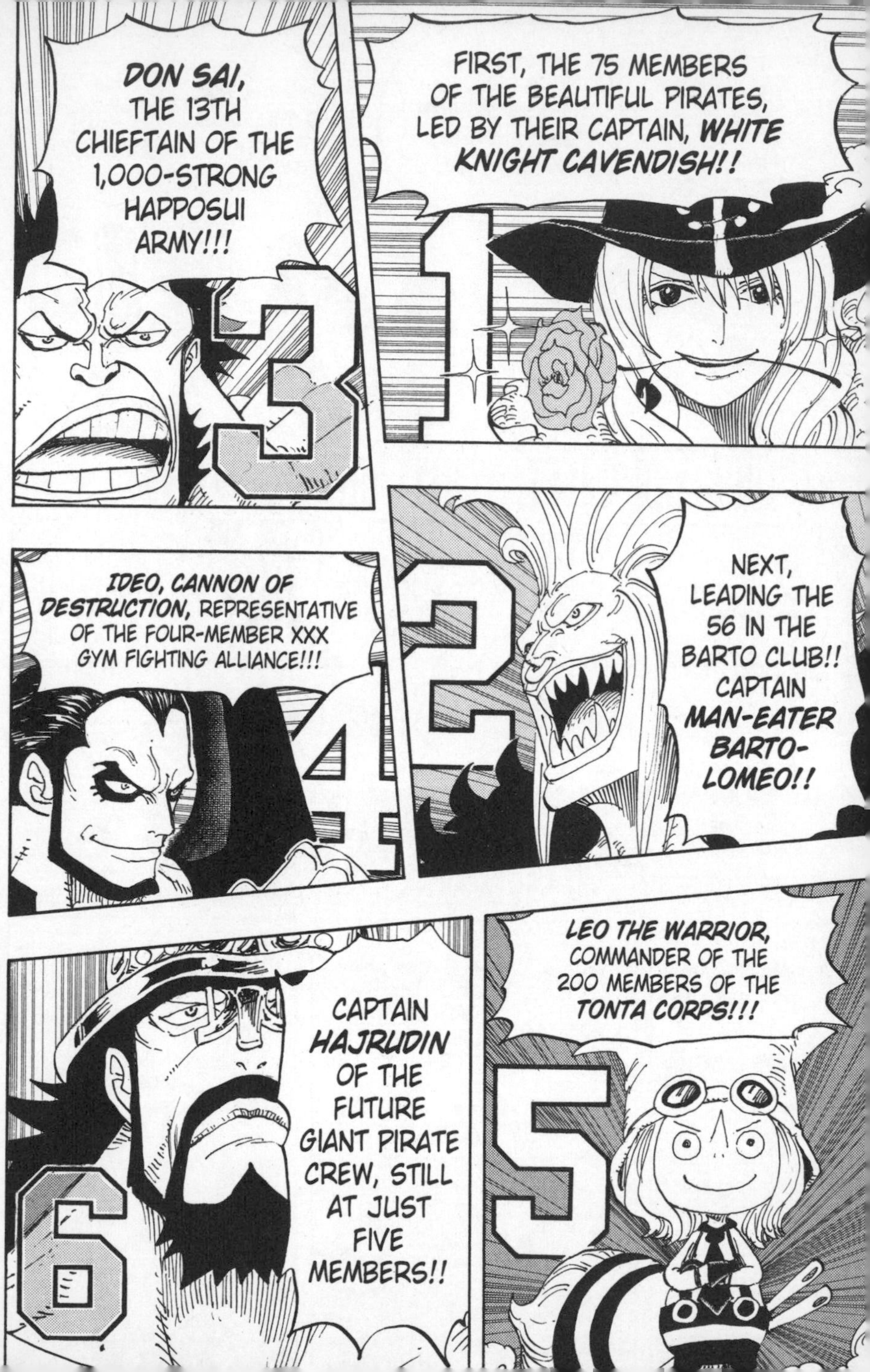
FIRST, THE 75 MEMBERS OF THE BEAUTIFUL PIRATES, LED BY THEIR CAPTAIN, ***WHITE KNIGHT CAVENDISH!!***
***DON SAI,*** THE 13TH CHIEFTAIN OF THE 1,000-STRONG HAPPOSUI ARMY!!!
NEXT, LEADING THE 56 IN THE BARTO CLUB!! CAPTAIN ***MAN-EATER BARTO-LOMEO!!***
***IDEO, CANNON OF DESTRUCTION,*** REPRESENTATIVE OF THE FOUR-MEMBER XXX GYM FIGHTING ALLIANCE!!!
***LEO THE WARRIOR,*** COMMANDER OF THE 200 MEMBERS OF THE ***TONTA CORPS!!!***
CAPTAIN ***HAJRUDIN*** OF THE FUTURE GIANT PIRATE CREW, STILL AT JUST FIVE MEMBERS!!

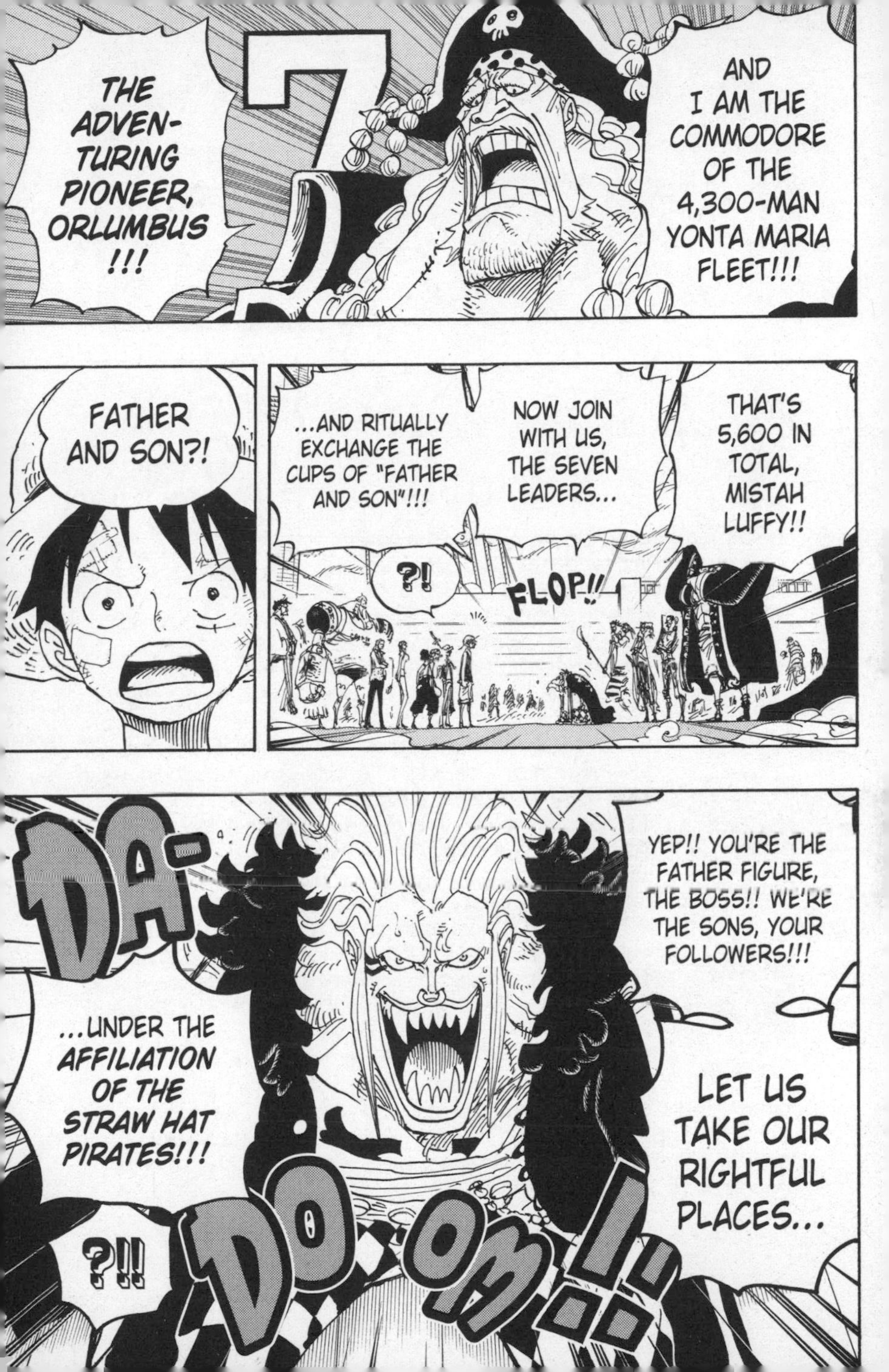
AND I AM THE COMMODORE OF THE 4,300-MAN YONTA MARIA FLEET!!!
THE ADVENTURING PIONEER, ORLUMBUS!!!
THAT'S 5,600 IN TOTAL, MISTAH LUFFY!!
NOW JOIN WITH US, THE SEVEN LEADERS...
...AND RITUALLY EXCHANGE THE CUPS OF "FATHER AND SON"!!!
FLOP!!
?!
FATHER AND SON?!
YEP!! YOU'RE THE FATHER FIGURE, THE BOSS!! WE'RE THE SONS, YOUR FOLLOWERS!!!
LET US TAKE OUR RIGHTFUL PLACES...
...UNDER THE AFFILIATION OF THE STRAW HAT PIRATES!!!
DA-
?!!
DOOM!!

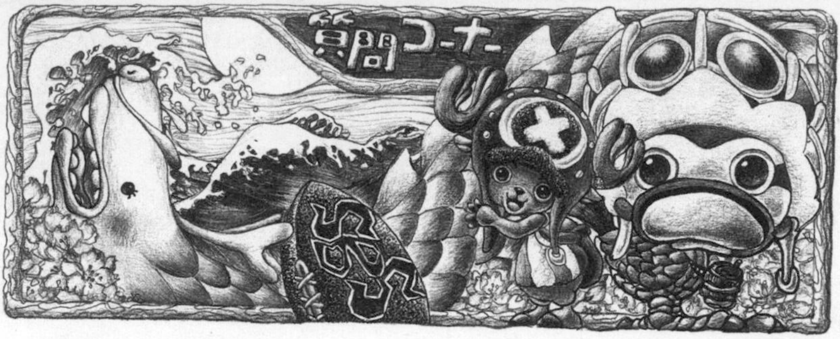
質問コーナー

(Takahisa Fujimoto, Nara)

**Q:** I fell in love with Koala the moment that she hugged Robin! \(^o^)/
How exactly did Koala, Sabo and Hack come together?

--One Piece Fanatic

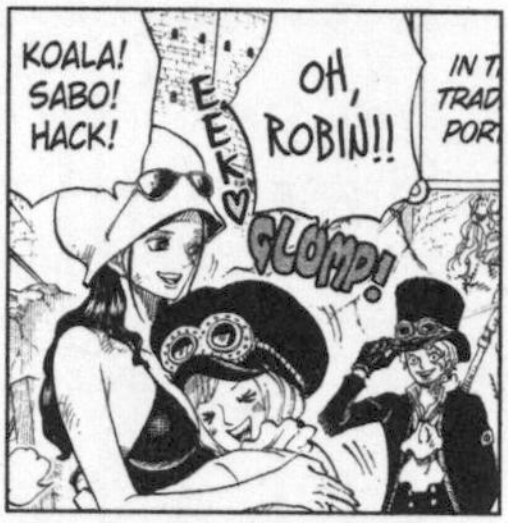
OH, ROBIN!!
KOALA! SABO! HACK!
EEK♥
GLOMP!

**A:** A lot of people seem curious about this, but that is three life stories to tell. It would never end if I got

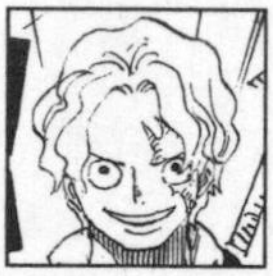

started on that. First, Sabo was ten years old when Dragon rescued him. As he met more revolutionaries and learned about what was happening in the world, their ideals resonated with his own. It was around that time that he met Hack, who was teaching fish-man karate to the orphans taken in by

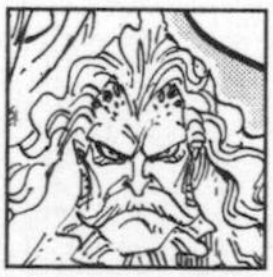

the Revolutionary Army. But while Sabo had no memory, he was already beyond the need for lessons in fighting. He took Dragon as his master, showed his skill in battle, and grew frightfully strong. When he was 13, a 14-year-old Koala joined the Revolutionaries through Hack's introduction. After some

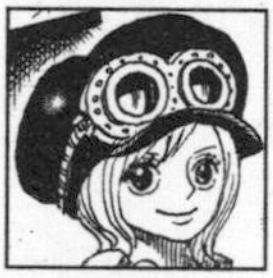

time, she learned fish-man karate from Hack and became an assistant instructor. Careful, watchful Hack and Koala were a good match for Sabo, and they were assigned various missions as a team. That's about the order of events that brought them together. There's a bit more elaboration in the anime, but there won't be time to tell the entire backstory, so go ahead and imagine it for yourself.

# Chapter 800:
# SONS' CUPS

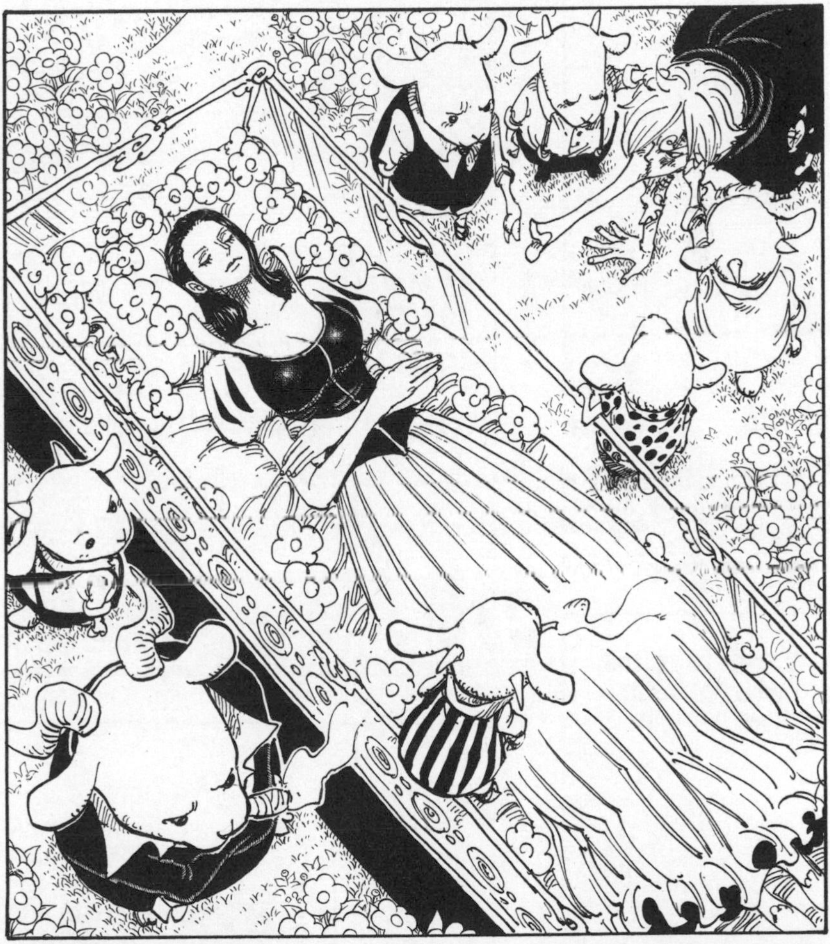

REQUEST: "THE SEVEN GOATS DESPERATELY TRYING TO KEEP PRINCE SANJI FROM KISSING SNOW ROBIN" BY I FEEL LIKE LAW'S REACTIONS ARE GETTING MORE EXAGGERATED FROM SAITAMA

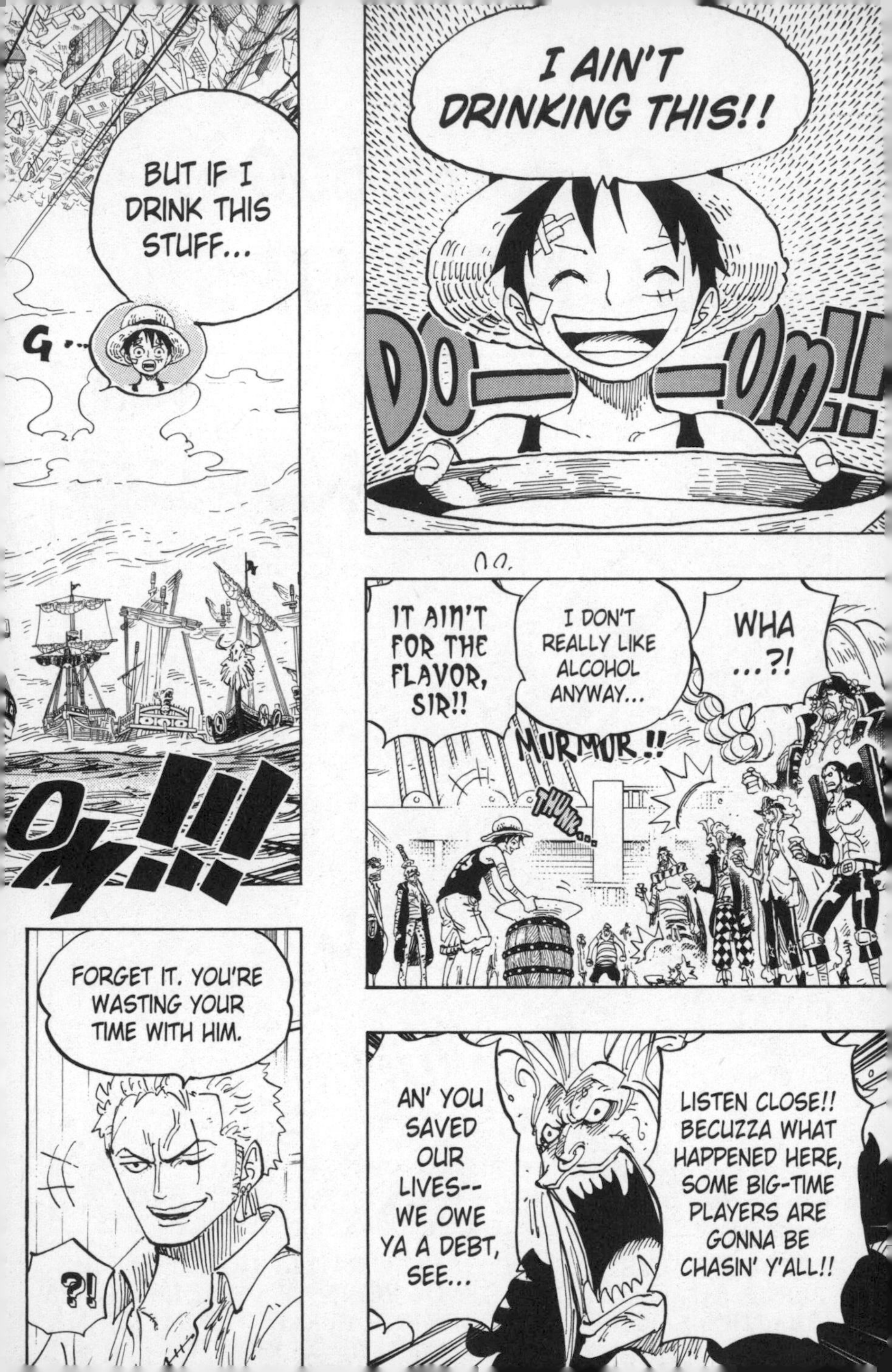

I AIN'T DRINKING THIS!!
DO——OM!!
WHA ...?!
I DON'T REALLY LIKE ALCOHOL ANYWAY...
IT AIN'T FOR THE FLAVOR, SIR!!
MURMUR!!
THUNK...
LISTEN CLOSE!! BECUZZA WHAT HAPPENED HERE, SOME BIG-TIME PLAYERS ARE GONNA BE CHASIN' Y'ALL!!
AN' YOU SAVED OUR LIVES-- WE OWE YA A DEBT, SEE...
BUT IF I DRINK THIS STUFF...
G...
OY...!!!
FORGET IT. YOU'RE WASTING YOUR TIME WITH HIM.
?!

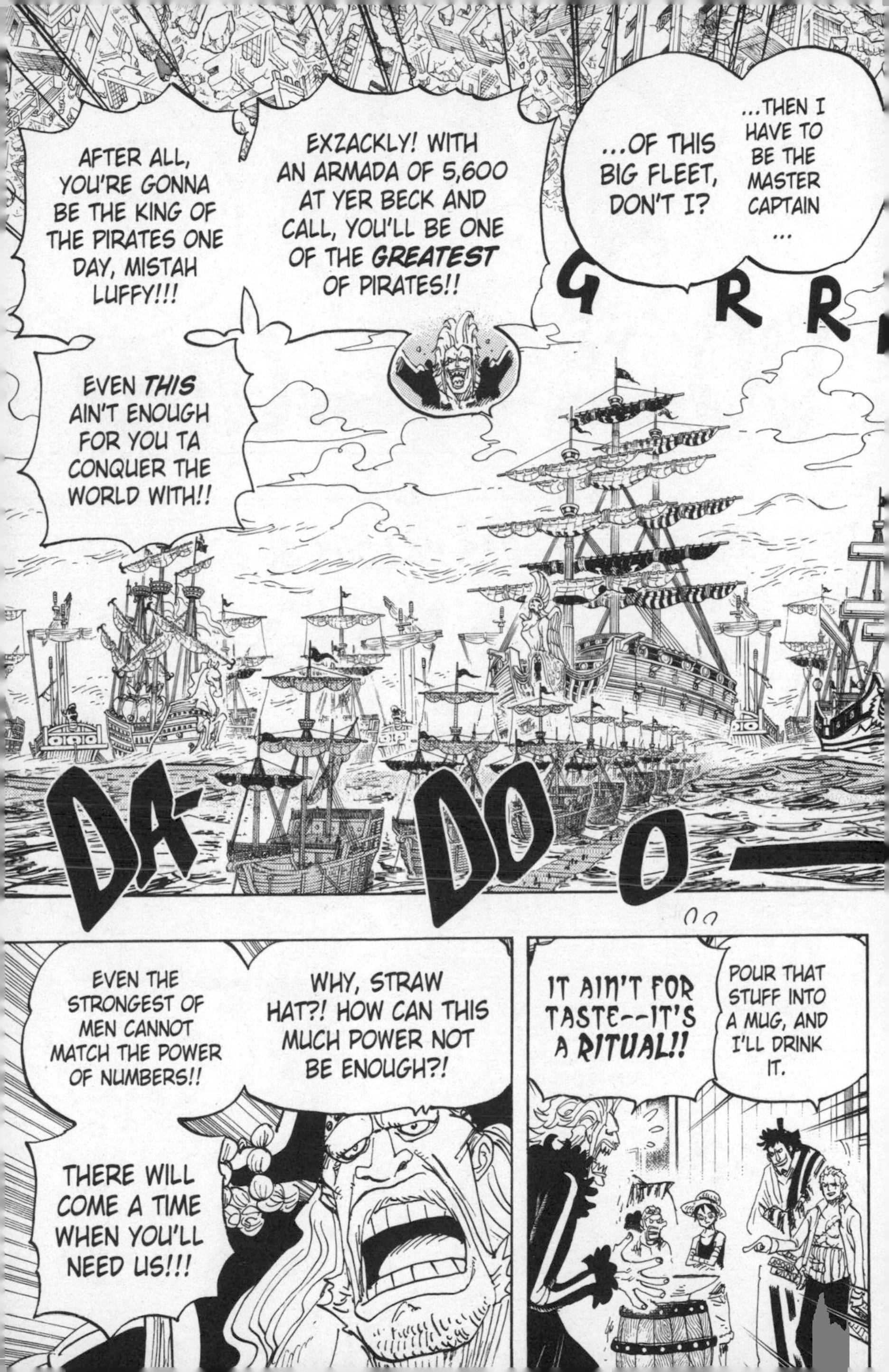

...THEN I HAVE TO BE THE MASTER CAPTAIN ...
...OF THIS BIG FLEET, DON'T I?
GRRR
EXZACKLY! WITH AN ARMADA OF 5,600 AT YER BECK AND CALL, YOU'LL BE ONE OF THE GREATEST OF PIRATES!!
AFTER ALL, YOU'RE GONNA BE THE KING OF THE PIRATES ONE DAY, MISTAH LUFFY!!!
EVEN THIS AIN'T ENOUGH FOR YOU TA CONQUER THE WORLD WITH!!
DA-DO O—
POUR THAT STUFF INTO A MUG, AND I'LL DRINK IT.
IT AIN'T FOR TASTE--IT'S A RITUAL!!
WHY, STRAW HAT?! HOW CAN THIS MUCH POWER NOT BE ENOUGH?!
EVEN THE STRONGEST OF MEN CANNOT MATCH THE POWER OF NUMBERS!!
THERE WILL COME A TIME WHEN YOU'LL NEED US!!!

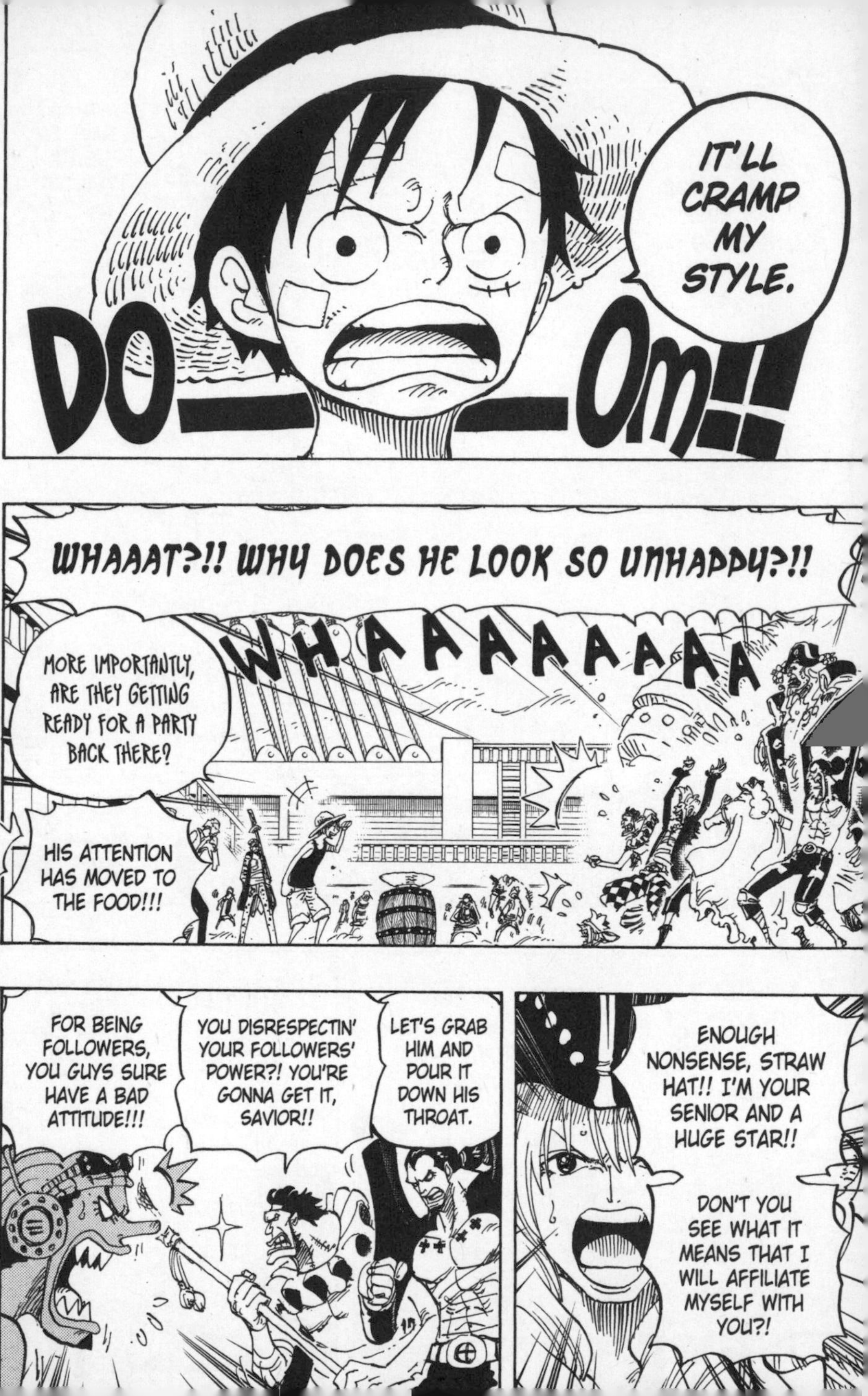
IT'LL CRAMP MY STYLE.
DO—OM!!
WHAAAT?!! WHY DOES HE LOOK SO UNHAPPY?!!
WHAAAAAAAA
MORE IMPORTANTLY, ARE THEY GETTING READY FOR A PARTY BACK THERE?
HIS ATTENTION HAS MOVED TO THE FOOD!!!
ENOUGH NONSENSE, STRAW HAT!! I'M YOUR SENIOR AND A HUGE STAR!!
DON'T YOU SEE WHAT IT MEANS THAT I WILL AFFILIATE MYSELF WITH YOU?!
LET'S GRAB HIM AND POUR IT DOWN HIS THROAT.
YOU DISRESPECTIN' YOUR FOLLOWERS' POWER?! YOU'RE GONNA GET IT, SAVIOR!!
FOR BEING FOLLOWERS, YOU GUYS SURE HAVE A BAD ATTITUDE!!!

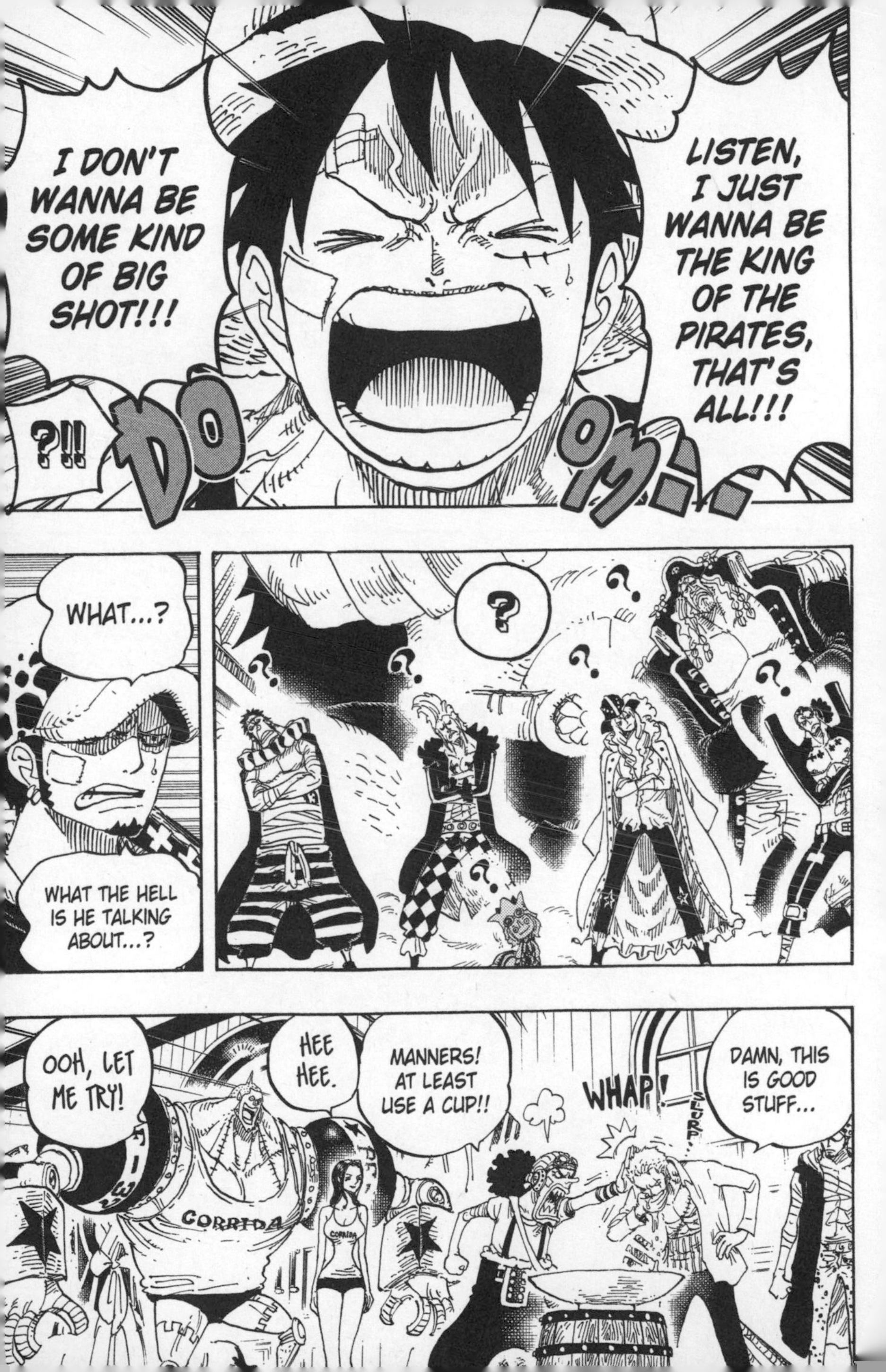
LISTEN, I JUST WANNA BE THE KING OF THE PIRATES, THAT'S ALL!!!
I DON'T WANNA BE SOME KIND OF BIG SHOT!!!
?!!
DOOM...
?
WHAT...?
WHAT THE HELL IS HE TALKING ABOUT...?
DAMN, THIS IS GOOD STUFF...
SLURP...
WHAP!
MANNERS! AT LEAST USE A CUP!!
HEE HEE.
OOH, LET ME TRY!
CORRIDA

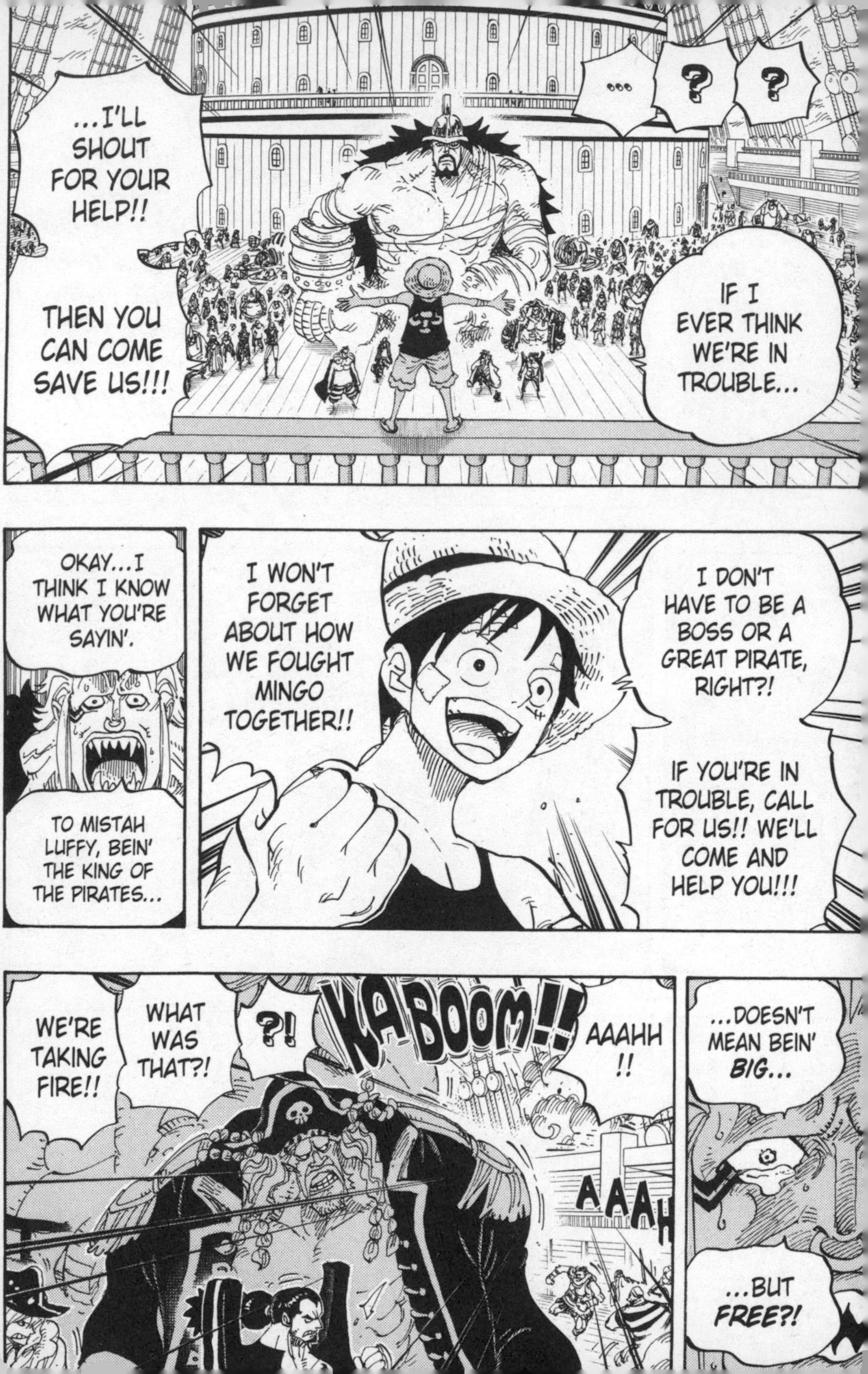
?
?
...
IF I EVER THINK WE'RE IN TROUBLE...
...I'LL SHOUT FOR YOUR HELP!!
THEN YOU CAN COME SAVE US!!!
I DON'T HAVE TO BE A BOSS OR A GREAT PIRATE, RIGHT?!
I WON'T FORGET ABOUT HOW WE FOUGHT MINGO TOGETHER!!
IF YOU'RE IN TROUBLE, CALL FOR US!! WE'LL COME AND HELP YOU!!!
OKAY...I THINK I KNOW WHAT YOU'RE SAYIN'.
TO MISTAH LUFFY, BEIN' THE KING OF THE PIRATES...
...DOESN'T MEAN BEIN' *BIG*...
...BUT *FREE*?!
AAAHH!!
KABOOM!!
AAAH
?!
WHAT WAS THAT?!
WE'RE TAKING FIRE!!

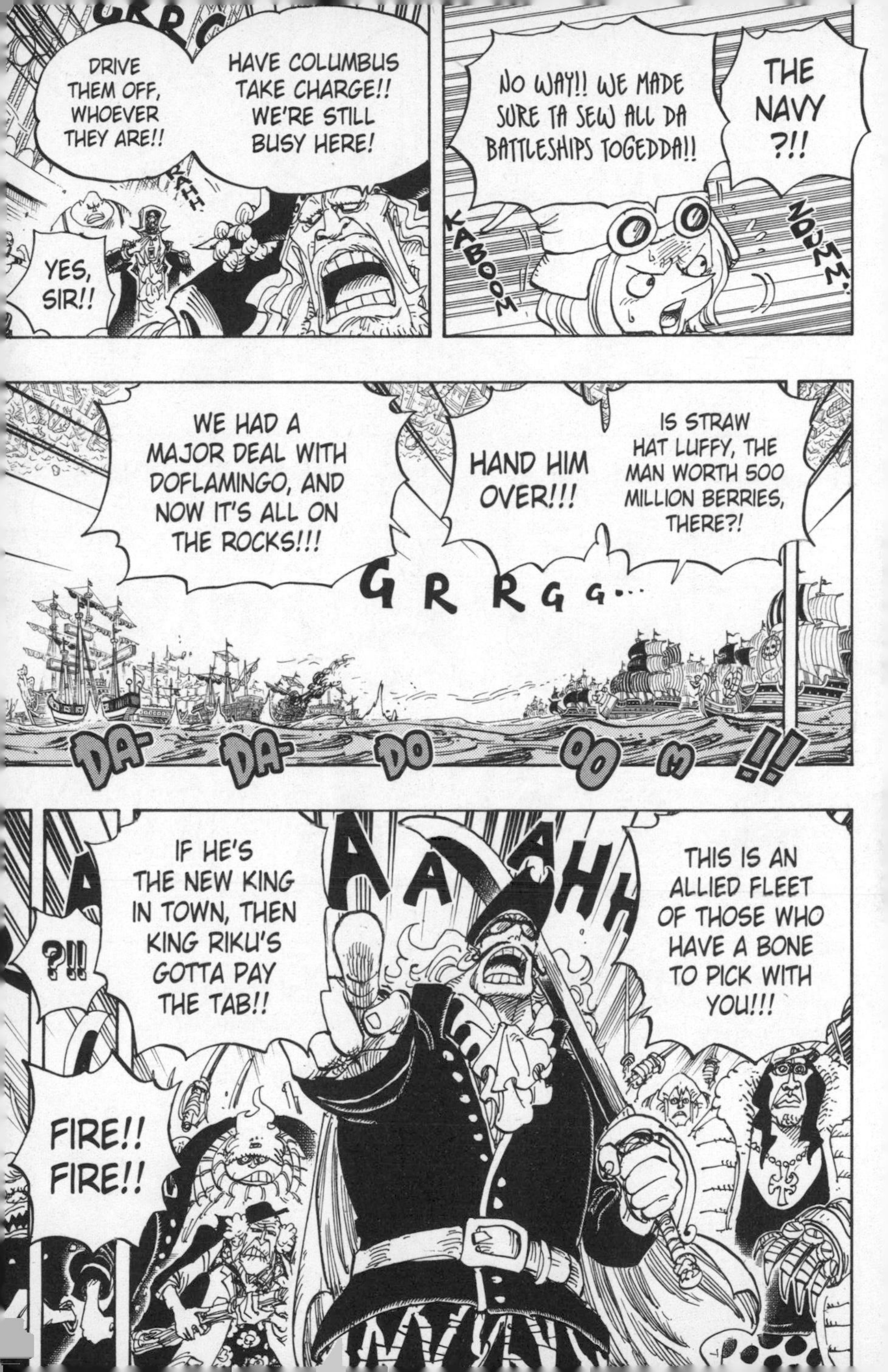
THE NAVY ?!!
NO WAY!! WE MADE SURE TA SEW ALL DA BATTLESHIPS TOGEDDA!!
KABOOM
ZDUMM
HAVE COLUMBUS TAKE CHARGE!! WE'RE STILL BUSY HERE!
DRIVE THEM OFF, WHOEVER THEY ARE!!
YES, SIR!!
IS STRAW HAT LUFFY, THE MAN WORTH 500 MILLION BERRIES, THERE?!
HAND HIM OVER!!!
WE HAD A MAJOR DEAL WITH DOFLAMINGO, AND NOW IT'S ALL ON THE ROCKS!!!
GRRGG...
DA-DA-DOOOM!!!
THIS IS AN ALLIED FLEET OF THOSE WHO HAVE A BONE TO PICK WITH YOU!!!
AAAHH
IF HE'S THE NEW KING IN TOWN, THEN KING RIKU'S GOTTA PAY THE TAB!!
?!!
FIRE!! FIRE!!

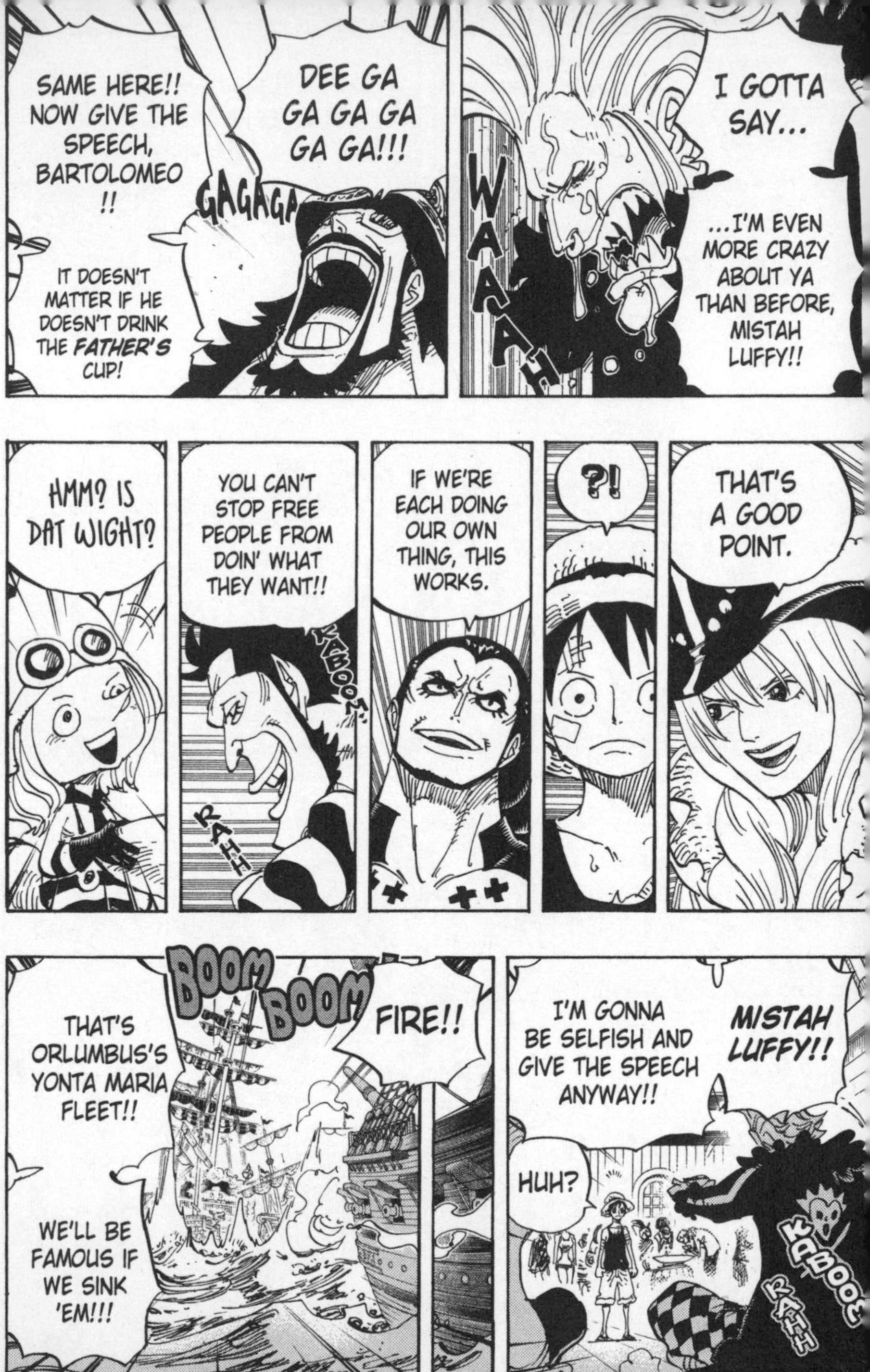
I GOTTA SAY...
WAAAH
...I'M EVEN MORE CRAZY ABOUT YA THAN BEFORE, MISTAH LUFFY!!
DEE GA GA GA GA GA GA!!!
GAGAGA
SAME HERE!! NOW GIVE THE SPEECH, BARTOLOMEO!!
IT DOESN'T MATTER IF HE DOESN'T DRINK THE FATHER'S CUP!
THAT'S A GOOD POINT.
?!
IF WE'RE EACH DOING OUR OWN THING, THIS WORKS.
YOU CAN'T STOP FREE PEOPLE FROM DOIN' WHAT THEY WANT!!
KABOOM
RAHH
HMM? IS DAT WIGHT?
MISTAH LUFFY!!
I'M GONNA BE SELFISH AND GIVE THE SPEECH ANYWAY!!
HUH?
KABOOM
RAHH
FIRE!!
BOOM BOOM
THAT'S ORLUMBUS'S YONTA MARIA FLEET!!
WE'LL BE FAMOUS IF WE SINK 'EM!!!

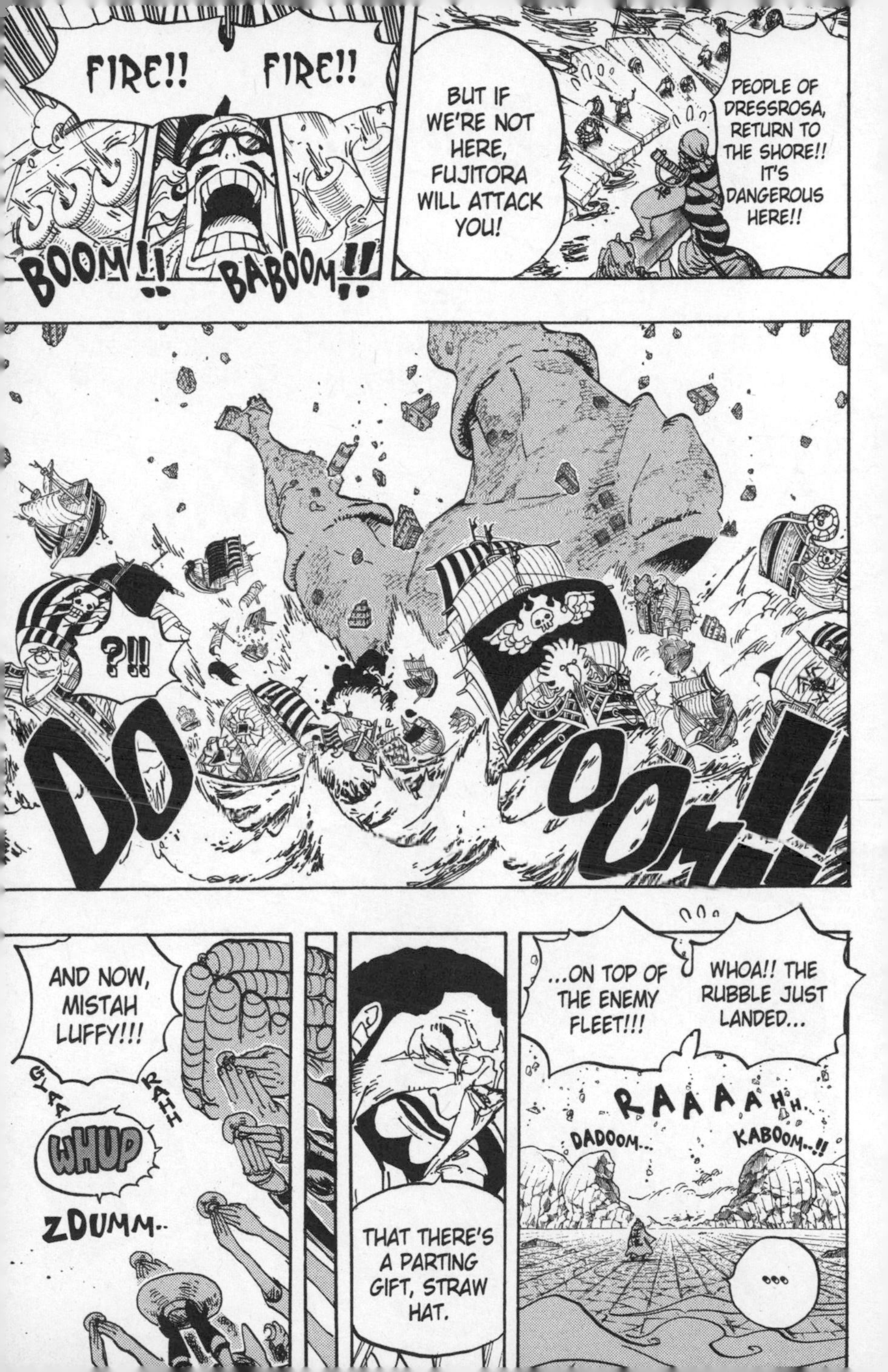
PEOPLE OF DRESSROSA, RETURN TO THE SHORE!! IT'S DANGEROUS HERE!!
BUT IF WE'RE NOT HERE, FUJITORA WILL ATTACK YOU!
FIRE!!
FIRE!!
BOOM!!
BABOOM!!
?!!
DOOOM!!
WHOA!! THE RUBBLE JUST LANDED...
...ON TOP OF THE ENEMY FLEET!!!
RAAAAHH..
KABOOM..!!
DADOOM...
...
THAT THERE'S A PARTING GIFT, STRAW HAT.
AND NOW, MISTAH LUFFY!!!!
GYAA
RAHH
WHUP
ZDUMM..

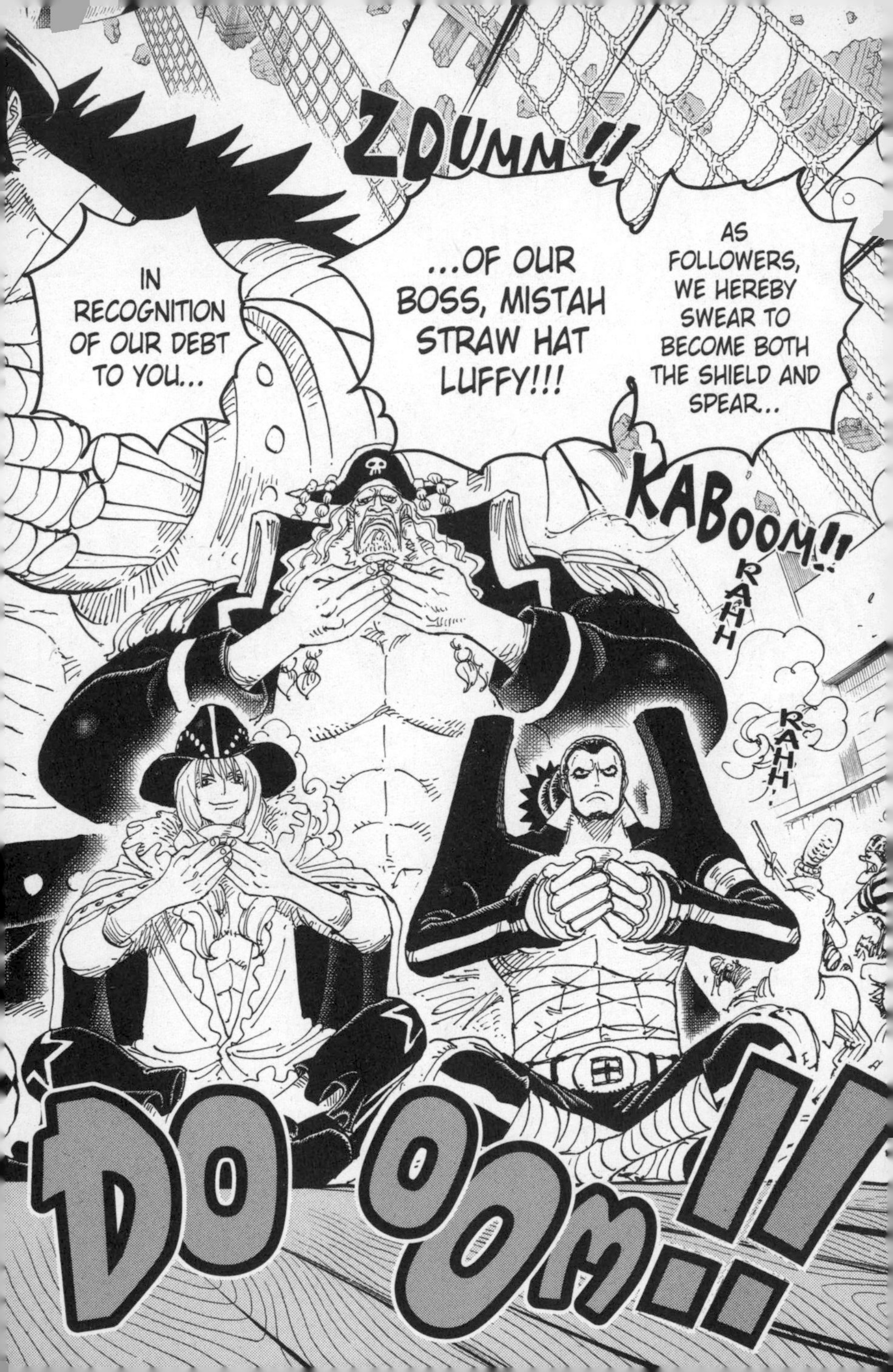
ZDUMM!!
AS FOLLOWERS, WE HEREBY SWEAR TO BECOME BOTH THE SHIELD AND SPEAR...
...OF OUR BOSS, MISTAH STRAW HAT LUFFY!!!
IN RECOGNITION OF OUR DEBT TO YOU...
KABOOM!!
RAHH
RAHH
DOOOM..!!

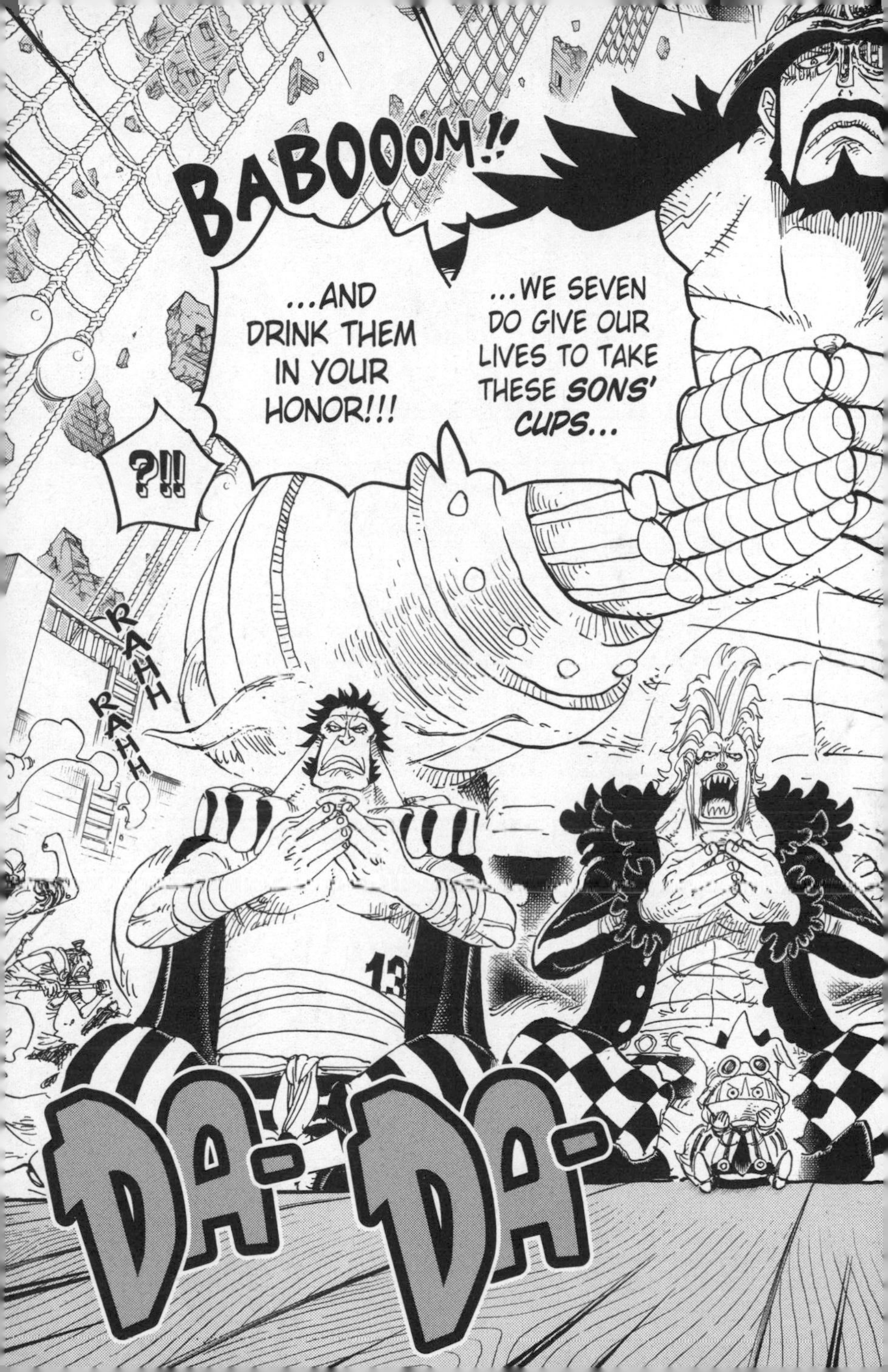
BABOOOM!!
...WE SEVEN DO GIVE OUR LIVES TO TAKE THESE SONS' CUPS...
...AND DRINK THEM IN YOUR HONOR!!!
?!!
RAHH
RAHH
DA-DA-

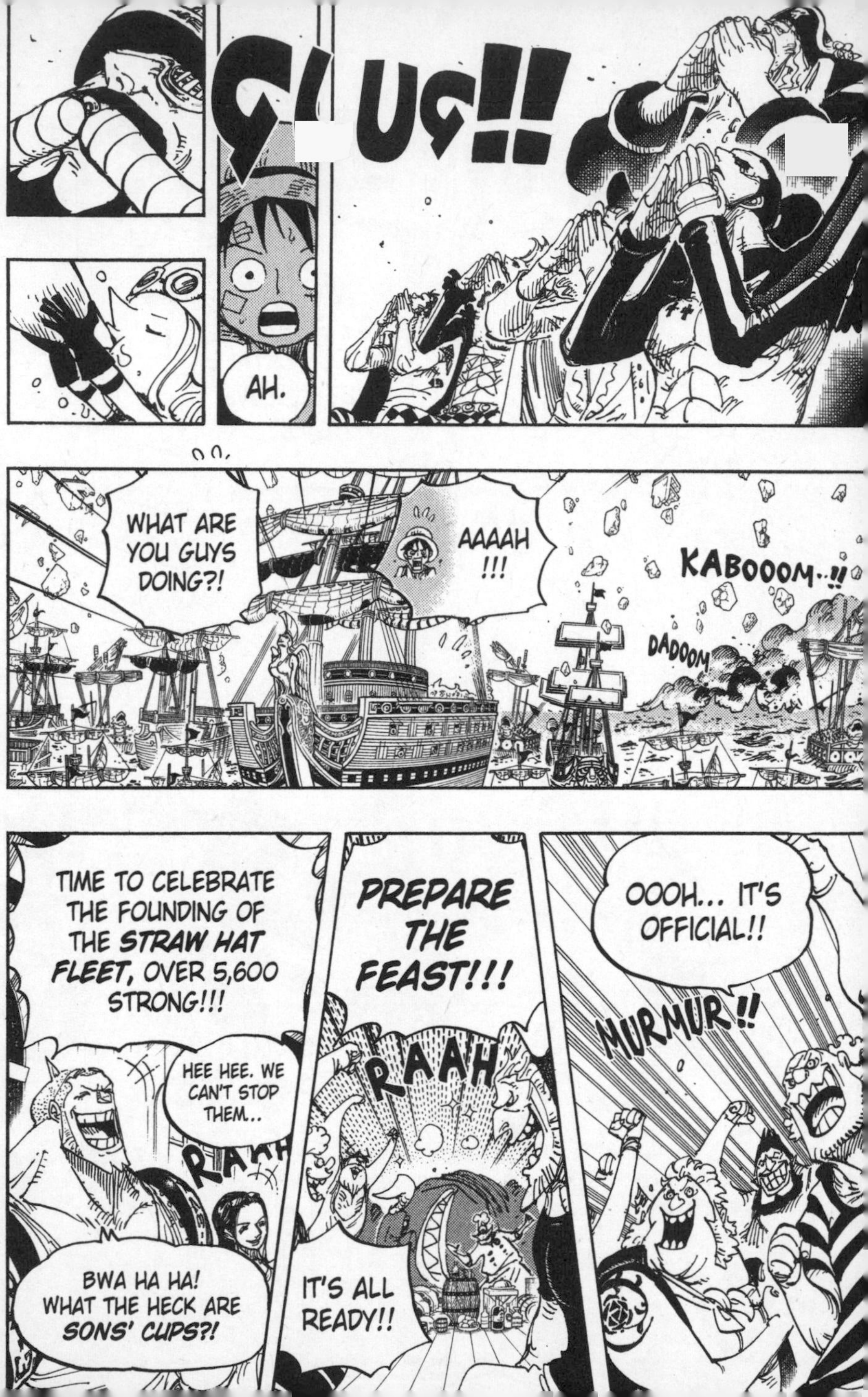
GLUG!!
AH.
KABOOOM..!!
DADOOM
AAAAH!!!
WHAT ARE YOU GUYS DOING?!
OOOH... IT'S OFFICIAL!!
MURMUR!!
PREPARE THE FEAST!!!
RAAH
IT'S ALL READY!!
TIME TO CELEBRATE THE FOUNDING OF THE STRAW HAT FLEET, OVER 5,600 STRONG!!!
HEE HEE. WE CAN'T STOP THEM...
RAAH
BWA HA HA! WHAT THE HECK ARE SONS' CUPS?!

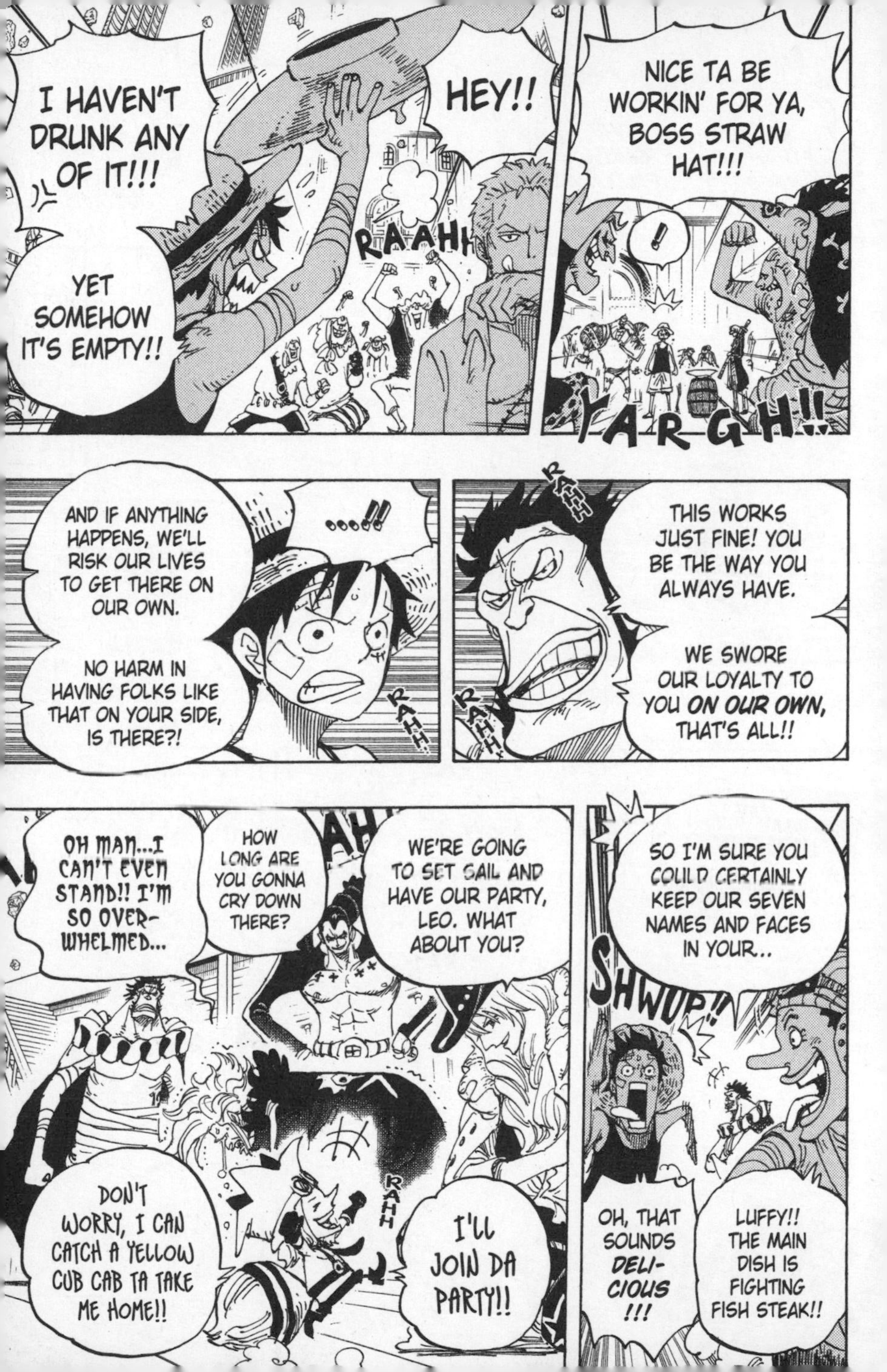
NICE TA BE WORKIN' FOR YA, BOSS STRAW HAT!!!
!
YARGH!!
HEY!!
I HAVEN'T DRUNK ANY OF IT!!!
RAAHH
YET SOMEHOW IT'S EMPTY!!
RAHH
THIS WORKS JUST FINE! YOU BE THE WAY YOU ALWAYS HAVE.
WE SWORE OUR LOYALTY TO YOU ON OUR OWN, THAT'S ALL!!
RAHH
...!!
AND IF ANYTHING HAPPENS, WE'LL RISK OUR LIVES TO GET THERE ON OUR OWN.
NO HARM IN HAVING FOLKS LIKE THAT ON YOUR SIDE, IS THERE?!
RAHH
SO I'M SURE YOU COULD CERTAINLY KEEP OUR SEVEN NAMES AND FACES IN YOUR...
SHWUP!!
LUFFY!! THE MAIN DISH IS FIGHTING FISH STEAK!!
OH, THAT SOUNDS DELICIOUS!!!
WE'RE GOING TO SET SAIL AND HAVE OUR PARTY, LEO. WHAT ABOUT YOU?
HOW LONG ARE YOU GONNA CRY DOWN THERE?
OH MAN...I CAN'T EVEN STAND!! I'M SO OVER-WHELMED...
I'LL JOIN DA PARTY!!
RAHH
DON'T WORRY, I CAN CATCH A YELLOW CUB CAB TA TAKE ME HOME!!

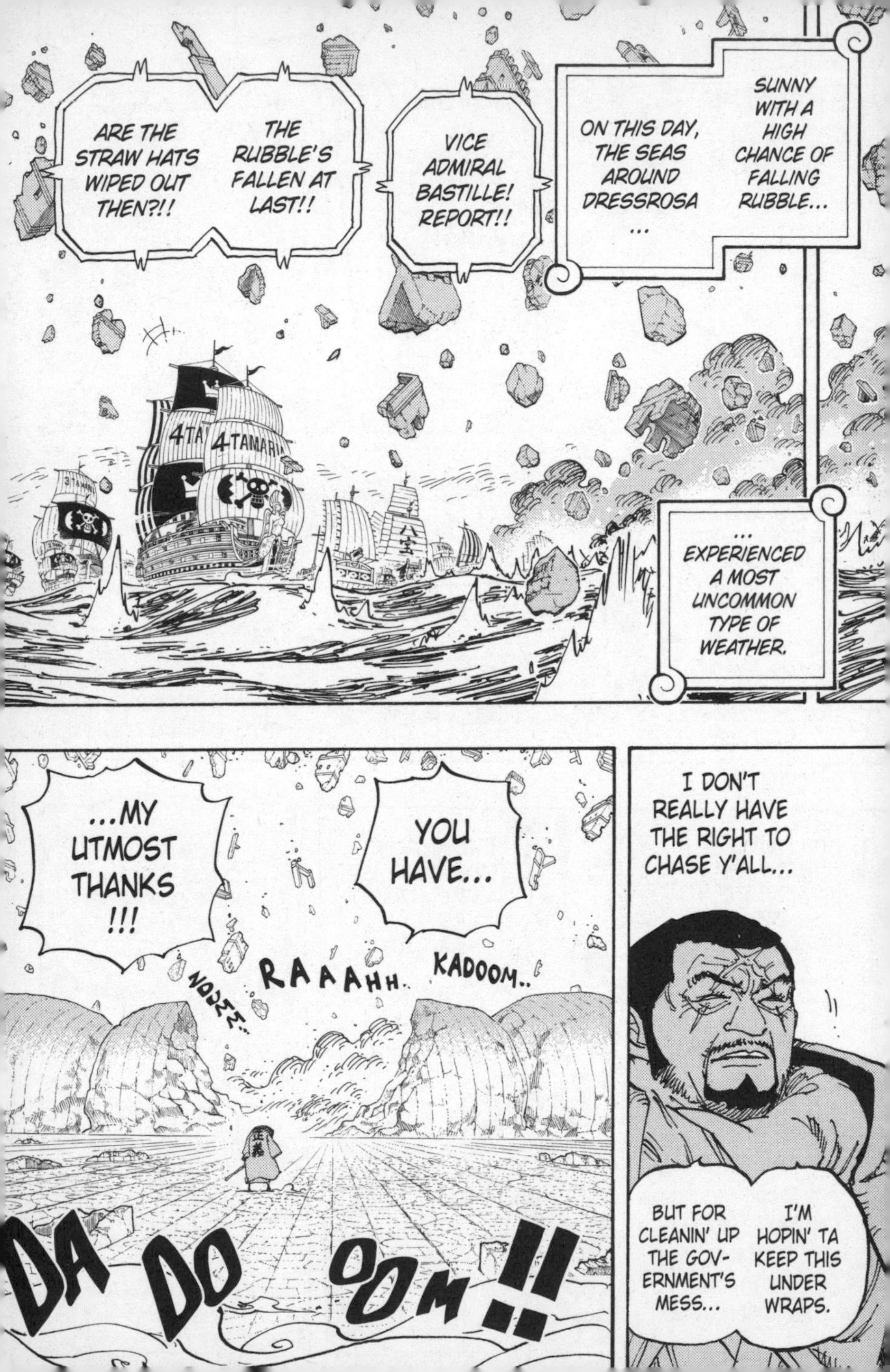
SUNNY WITH A HIGH CHANCE OF FALLING RUBBLE...
ON THIS DAY, THE SEAS AROUND DRESSROSA ...
VICE ADMIRAL BASTILLE! REPORT!!
THE RUBBLE'S FALLEN AT LAST!!
ARE THE STRAW HATS WIPED OUT THEN?!!
... EXPERIENCED A MOST UNCOMMON TYPE OF WEATHER.
I DON'T REALLY HAVE THE RIGHT TO CHASE Y'ALL...
I'M HOPIN' TA KEEP THIS UNDER WRAPS.
BUT FOR CLEANIN' UP THE GOV-ERNMENT'S MESS...
YOU HAVE...
...MY UTMOST THANKS!!!
KADOOM..
RAAAHH..
DA DO OOM!!

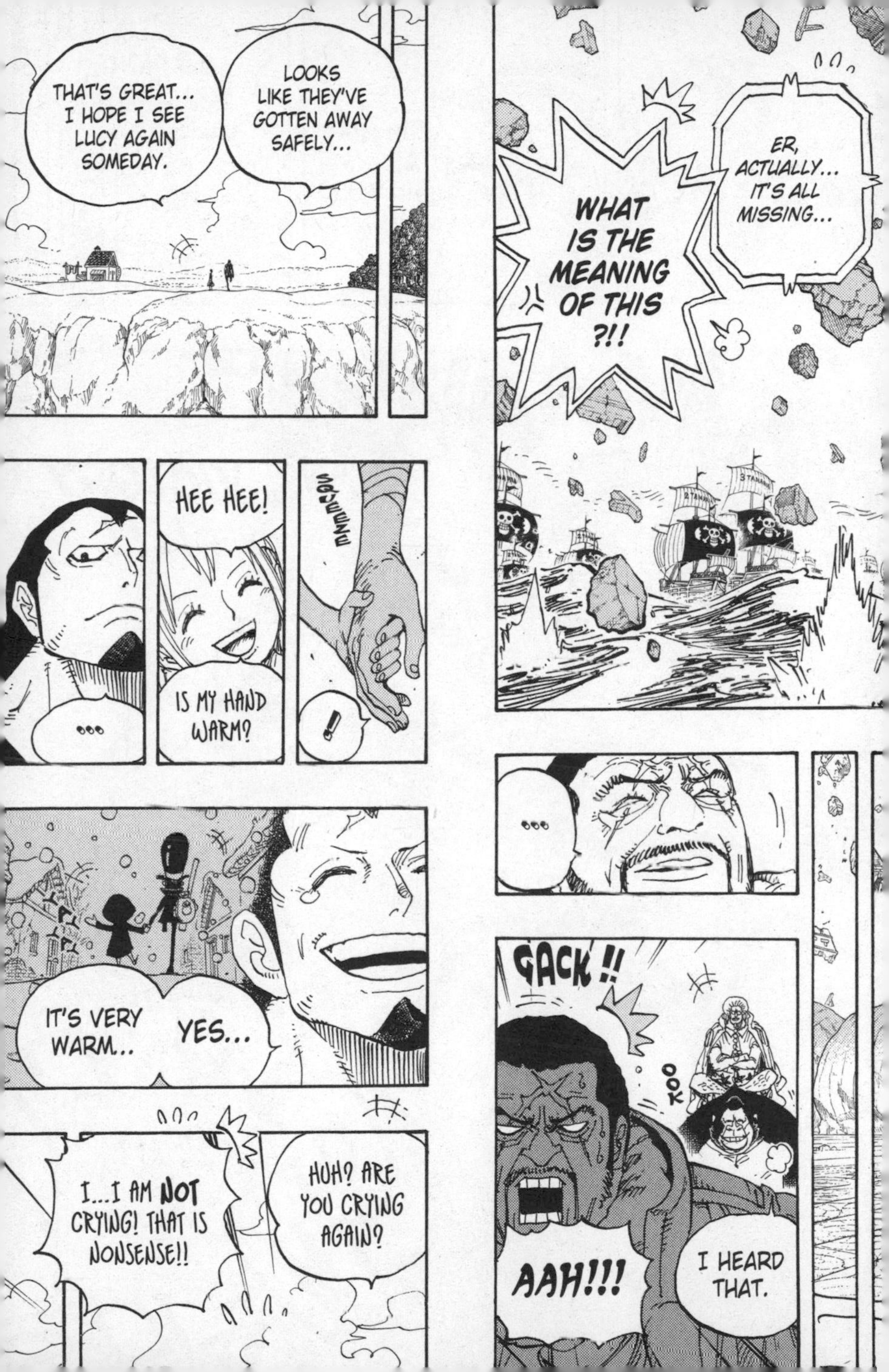
ER, ACTUALLY... IT'S ALL MISSING...
WHAT IS THE MEANING OF THIS?!!
...
GACK!!
OOK
I HEARD THAT.
AAH!!!
LOOKS LIKE THEY'VE GOTTEN AWAY SAFELY...
THAT'S GREAT... I HOPE I SEE LUCY AGAIN SOMEDAY.
SQUEEZE
!
HEE HEE!
IS MY HAND WARM?
...
YES...
IT'S VERY WARM...
HUH? ARE YOU CRYING AGAIN?
I...I AM **NOT** CRYING! THAT IS NONSENSE!!

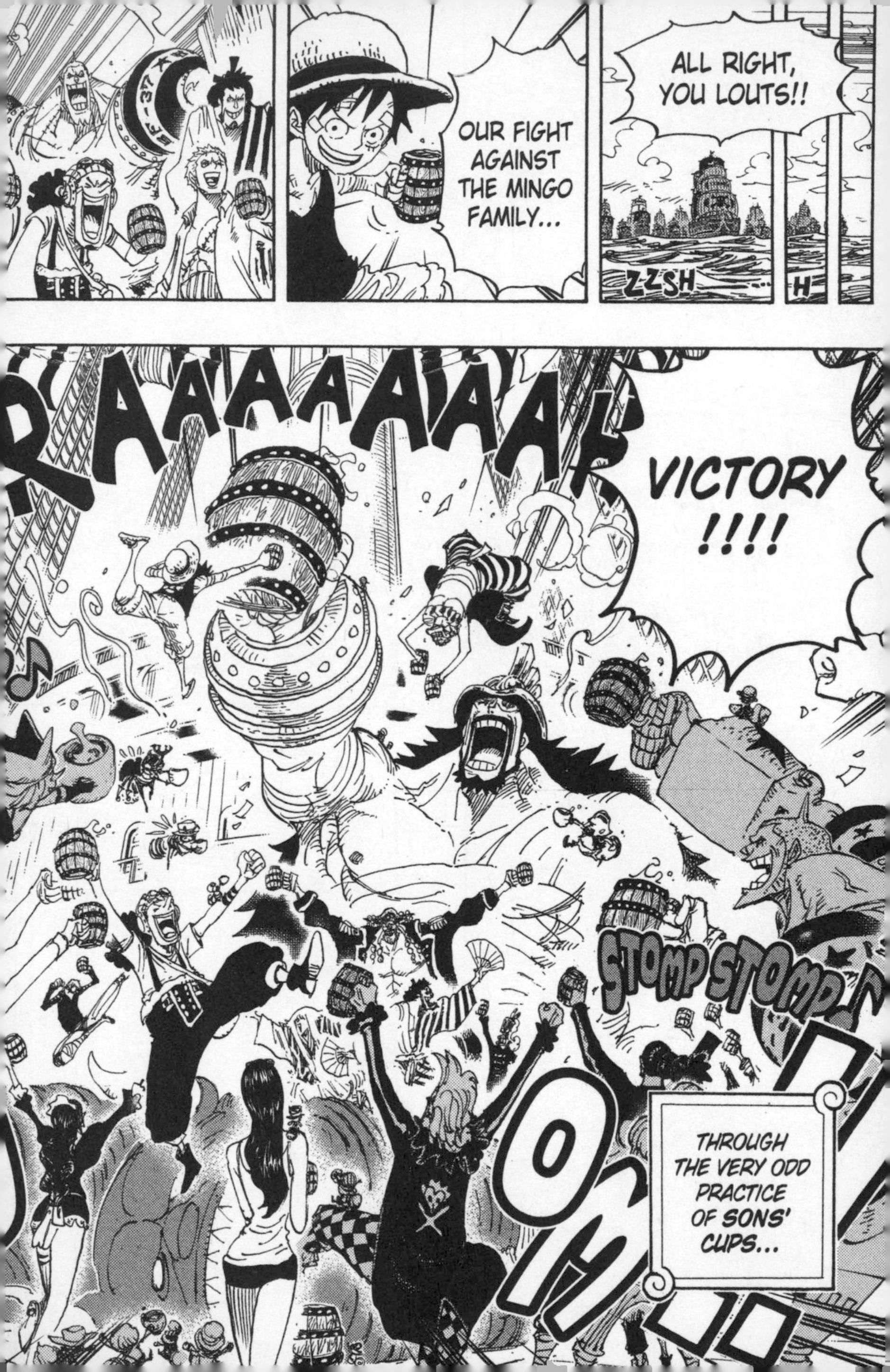

ALL RIGHT, YOU LOUTS!!
ZZSH
H
OUR FIGHT AGAINST THE MINGO FAMILY...
VICTORY !!!!
RAAAAAAAH
STOMP STOMP
THROUGH THE VERY ODD PRACTICE OF SONS' CUPS...

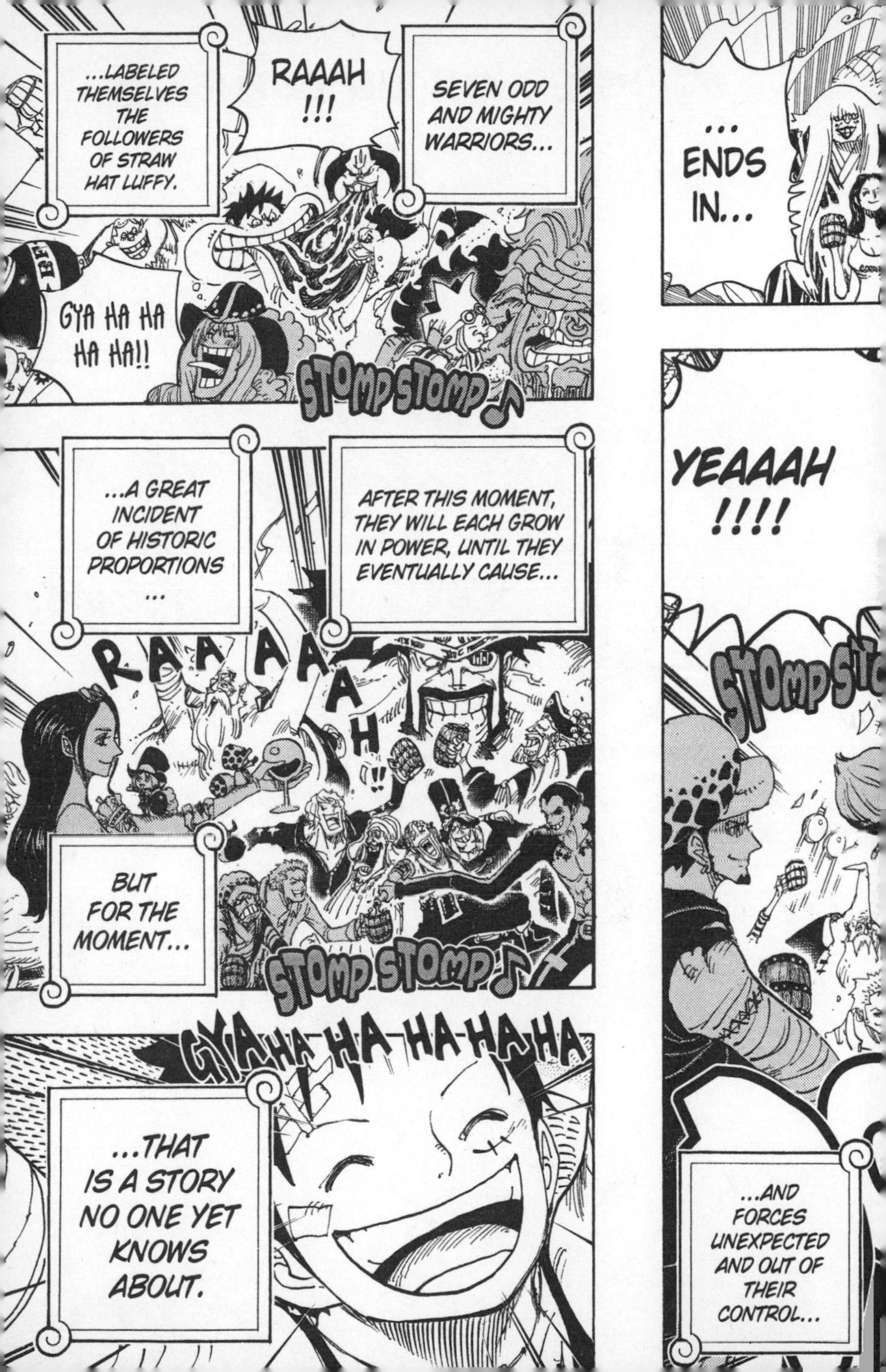
...ENDS IN...
YEAAAH !!!!
STOMP STO
...AND FORCES UNEXPECTED AND OUT OF THEIR CONTROL...
SEVEN ODD AND MIGHTY WARRIORS...
RAAAH !!!
...LABELED THEMSELVES THE FOLLOWERS OF STRAW HAT LUFFY.
GYA HA HA HA HA!!
STOMP STOMP
AFTER THIS MOMENT, THEY WILL EACH GROW IN POWER, UNTIL THEY EVENTUALLY CAUSE...
...A GREAT INCIDENT OF HISTORIC PROPORTIONS...
RAAAAAH!!
BUT FOR THE MOMENT...
STOMP STOMP
GYAHA HA HA HA HA
...THAT IS A STORY NO ONE YET KNOWS ABOUT.

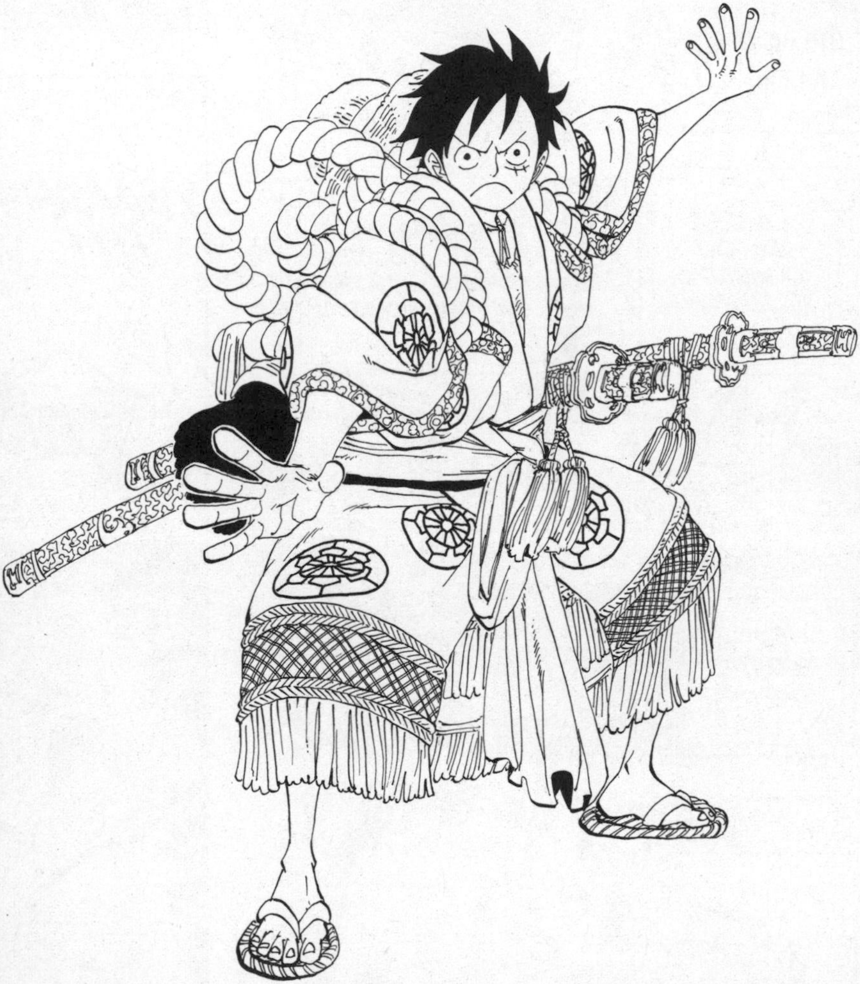

# Chapter 801: OPENING SPEECH

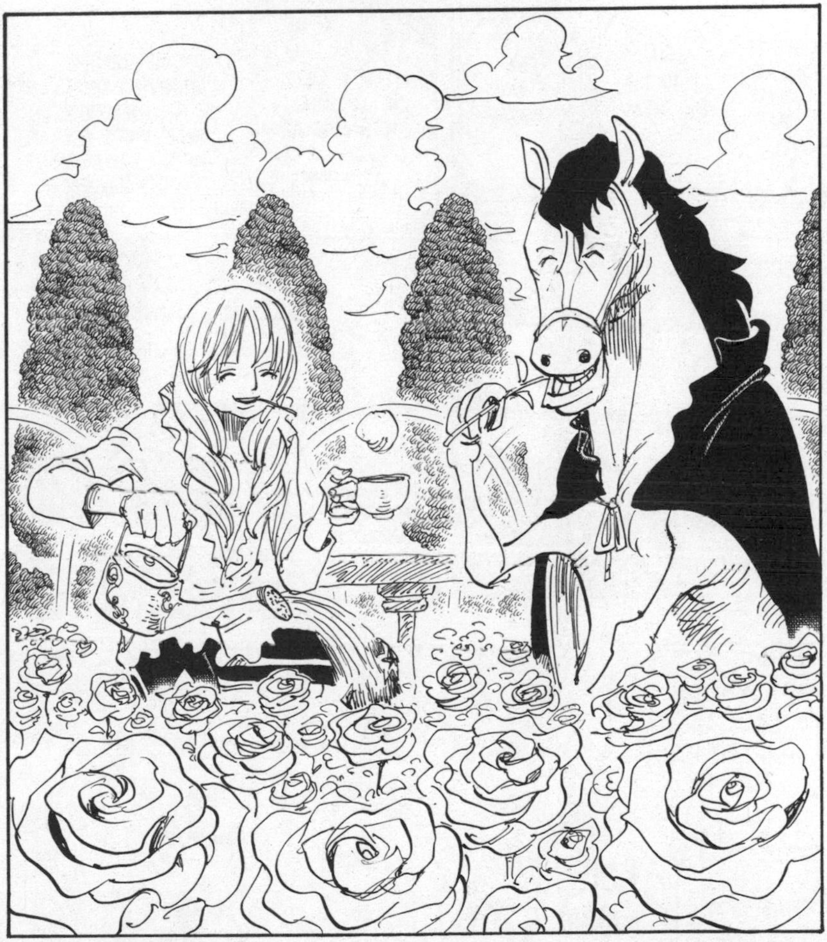

REQUEST: "CAVENDISH AND HIS HORSE FARUL CULTIVATING ROSES" BY SAKURA FROM CHIBA

THE PALACE OF DRESS-ROSA
NOT FINDING A LIST OF SMUGGLERS.
BUT THERE WERE OBVIOUS SIGNS IT WAS ALL STOLEN...
AS I SUSPECTED ...
ALL OF THE MILITARY WEAPONS LEFT IN THE UNDERGROUND PORT WERE STOLEN AFTER THE INCIDENT CONCLUDED.
THAT'S A LOT OF MATERIAL-- THIS WAS AN ORGANIZATION AT WORK.
THE NAVY WAS ALARMED ABOUT IT TOO.
CIPHER POL "AIGIS" 0
THE REVOLUTIONARIES ?
YEAH... HAD TO BE THEM.
WE'RE DONE HERE. COME BACK.
CLICK!
THEY'RE AN OBNOXIOUS BUNCH...
YES! YOU'RE EXACTLY RIGHT, BOSS!!
JUST LIKE YOU.
KOO-KAROO
DOOM!!
YOWZA! TALK ABOUT HARSH! HA HA HA...HA...
THIS IS A LAND OF TRAGEDY.

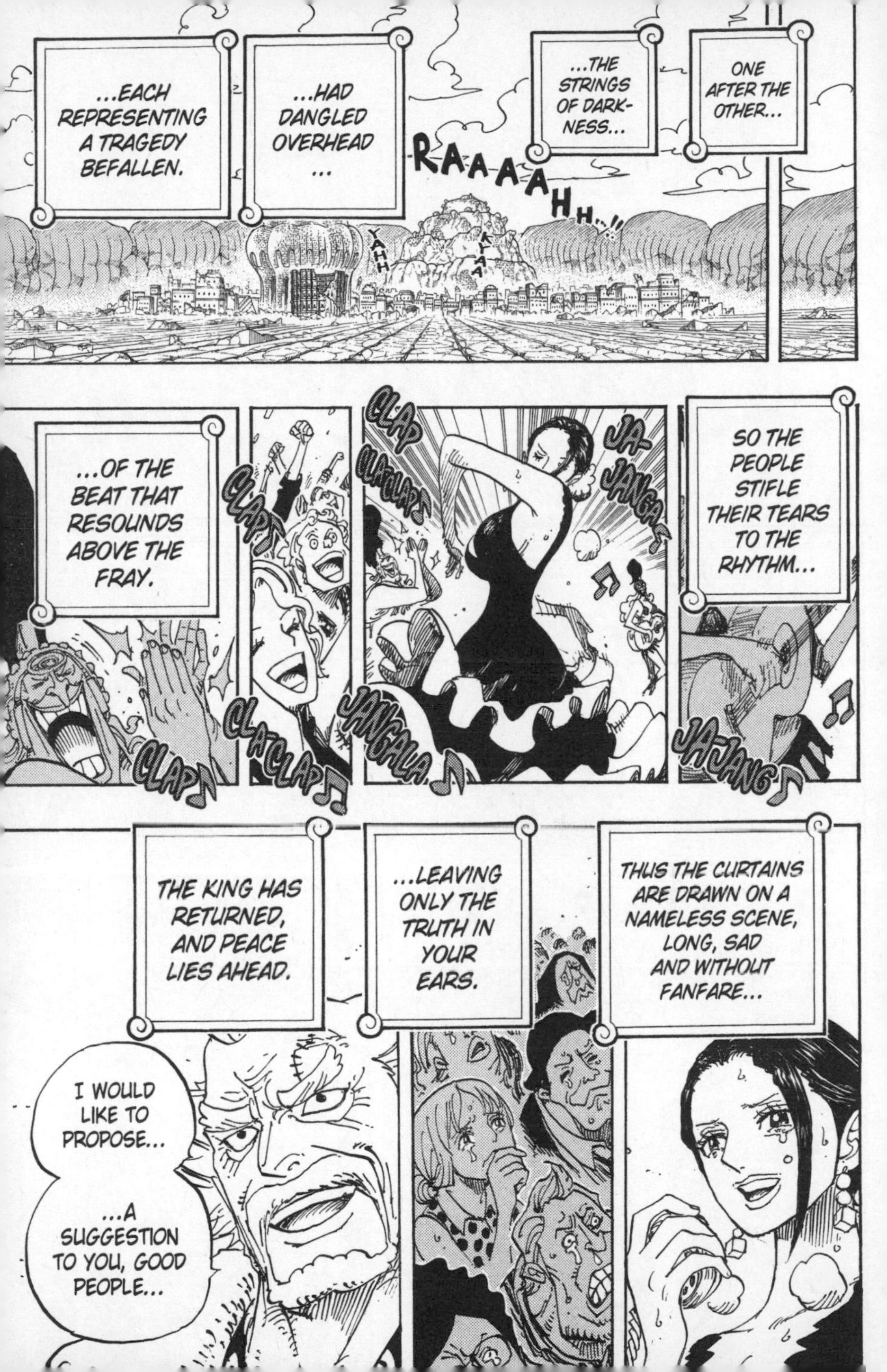
ONE AFTER THE OTHER...
...THE STRINGS OF DARK-NESS...
RAAAAAHH...!!
KYAA
YAHH
...HAD DANGLED OVERHEAD ...
...EACH REPRESENTING A TRAGEDY BEFALLEN.
SO THE PEOPLE STIFLE THEIR TEARS TO THE RHYTHM...
JA-JANG
JA-JANGA
CLAP
CLAPCLAP
JANGALA
CLAP
CLA-CLAP
...OF THE BEAT THAT RESOUNDS ABOVE THE FRAY.
CLAP
THUS THE CURTAINS ARE DRAWN ON A NAMELESS SCENE, LONG, SAD AND WITHOUT FANFARE...
...LEAVING ONLY THE TRUTH IN YOUR EARS.
THE KING HAS RETURNED, AND PEACE LIES AHEAD.
I WOULD LIKE TO PROPOSE...
...A SUGGESTION TO YOU, GOOD PEOPLE...

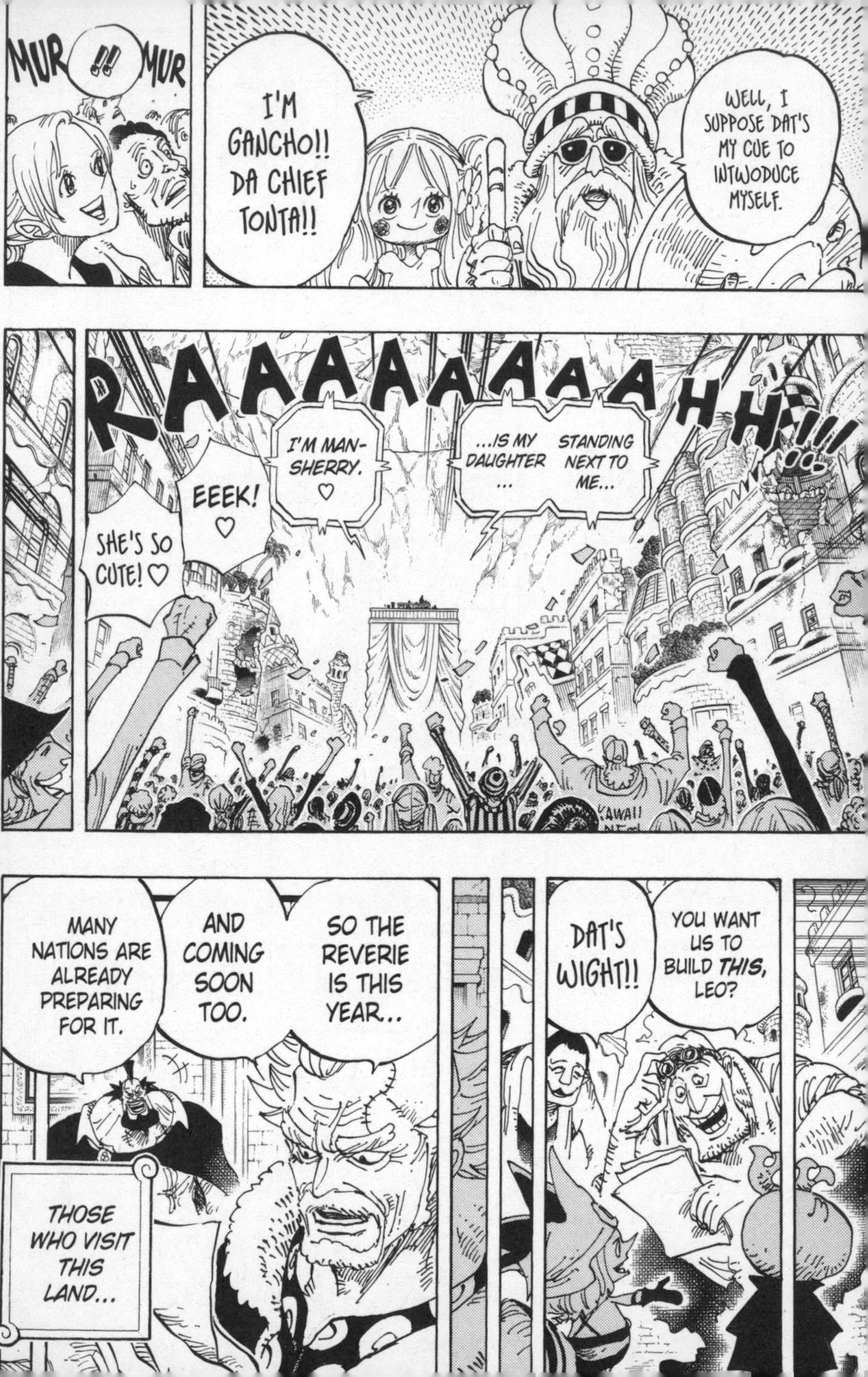
WELL, I SUPPOSE DAT'S MY CUE TO INTWODUCE MYSELF.
I'M GANCHO!! DA CHIEF TONTA!!
MUR !! MUR
RAAAAAAAAHH!!!!
STANDING NEXT TO ME...
...IS MY DAUGHTER...
I'M MAN-SHERRY. ♡
EEEK! ♡
SHE'S SO CUTE! ♡
KAWAII
YOU WANT US TO BUILD THIS, LEO?
DAT'S WIGHT!!
SO THE REVERIE IS THIS YEAR...
AND COMING SOON TOO.
MANY NATIONS ARE ALREADY PREPARING FOR IT.
THOSE WHO VISIT THIS LAND...

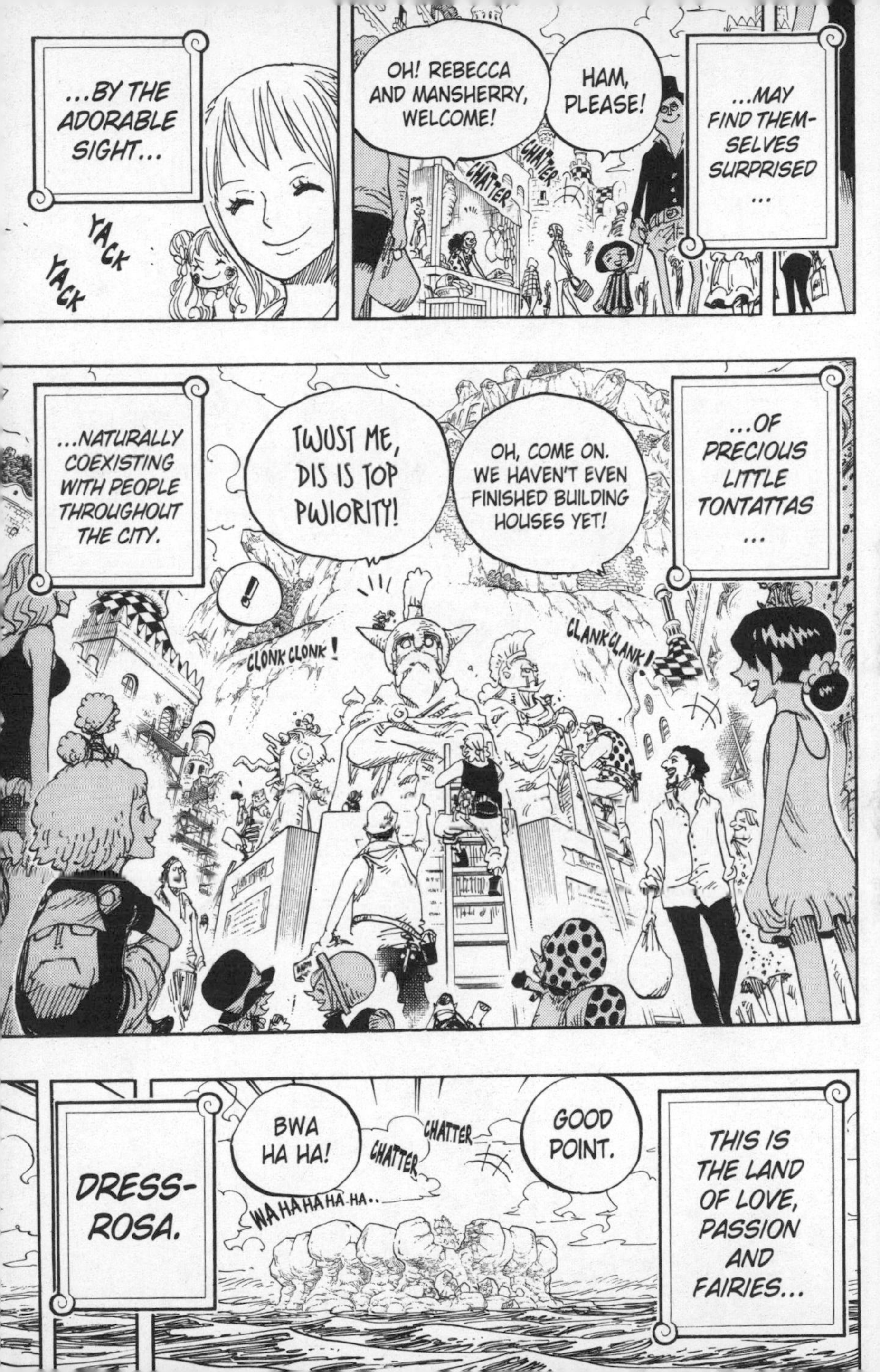
...MAY FIND THEMSELVES SURPRISED...
HAM, PLEASE!
OH! REBECCA AND MANSHERRY, WELCOME!
CHATTER
CHATTER
...BY THE ADORABLE SIGHT...
YACK
YACK
...OF PRECIOUS LITTLE TONTATTAS...
OH, COME ON. WE HAVEN'T EVEN FINISHED BUILDING HOUSES YET!
TWUST ME, DIS IS TOP PWIORITY!
...NATURALLY COEXISTING WITH PEOPLE THROUGHOUT THE CITY.
!
CLANK CLANK!
CLONK CLONK!
THIS IS THE LAND OF LOVE, PASSION AND FAIRIES...
GOOD POINT.
CHATTER
CHATTER
BWA HA HA!
WA HA HA HA-HA..
DRESS-ROSA.

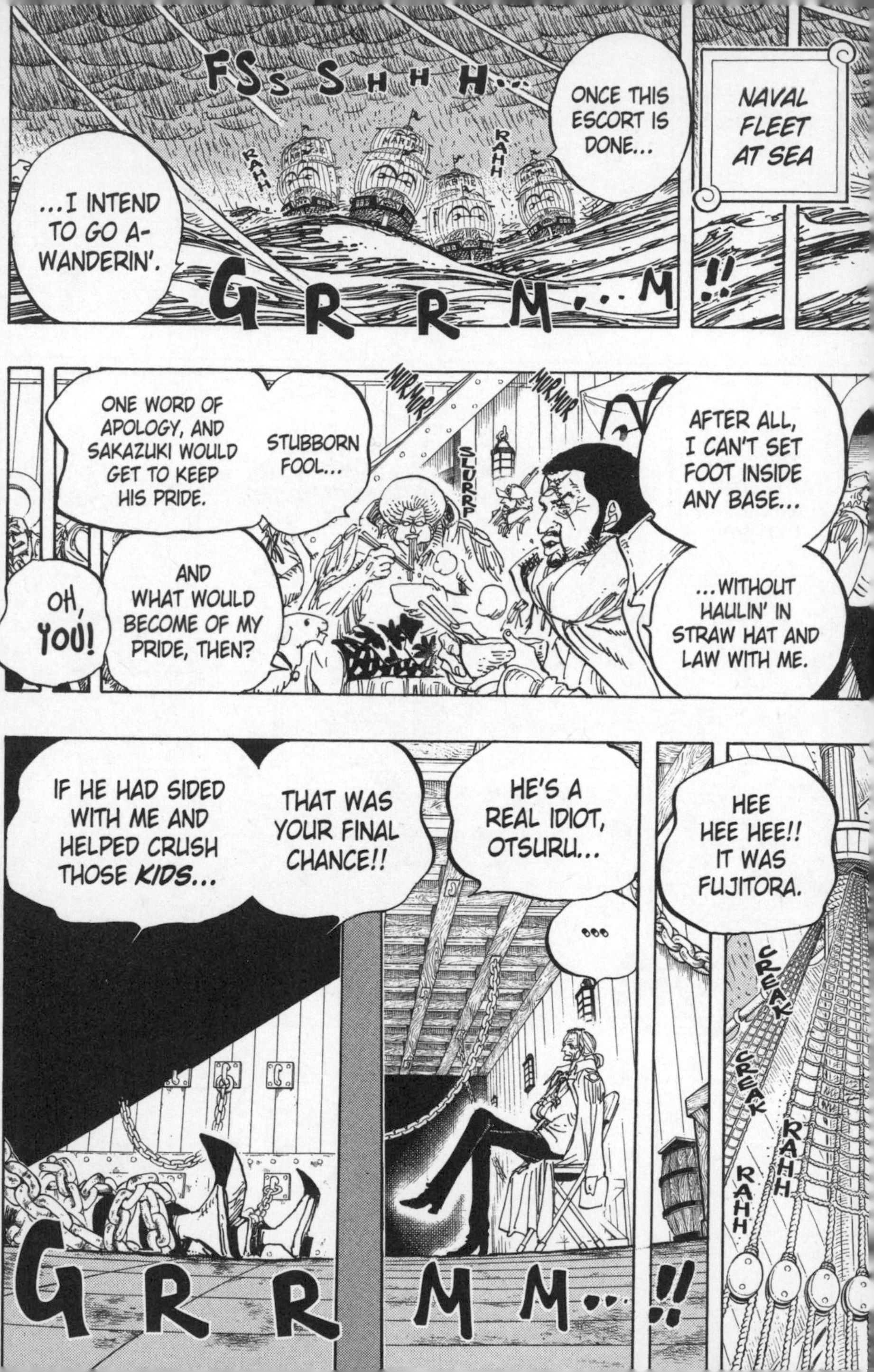

NAVAL FLEET AT SEA
FSSSHHH...
RAHH
RAHH
ONCE THIS ESCORT IS DONE...
...I INTEND TO GO A-WANDERIN'.
GRRM...M!!
AFTER ALL, I CAN'T SET FOOT INSIDE ANY BASE...
...WITHOUT HAULIN' IN STRAW HAT AND LAW WITH ME.
MURMUR
MURMUR
SLURRP
STUBBORN FOOL...
ONE WORD OF APOLOGY, AND SAKAZUKI WOULD GET TO KEEP HIS PRIDE.
AND WHAT WOULD BECOME OF MY PRIDE, THEN?
OH, YOU!
HEE HEE HEE!! IT WAS FUJITORA.
CREAK
CREAK
RAHH
RAHH
HE'S A REAL IDIOT, OTSURU...
...
THAT WAS YOUR FINAL CHANCE!!
IF HE HAD SIDED WITH ME AND HELPED CRUSH THOSE *KIDS*...
GRRMM...!!

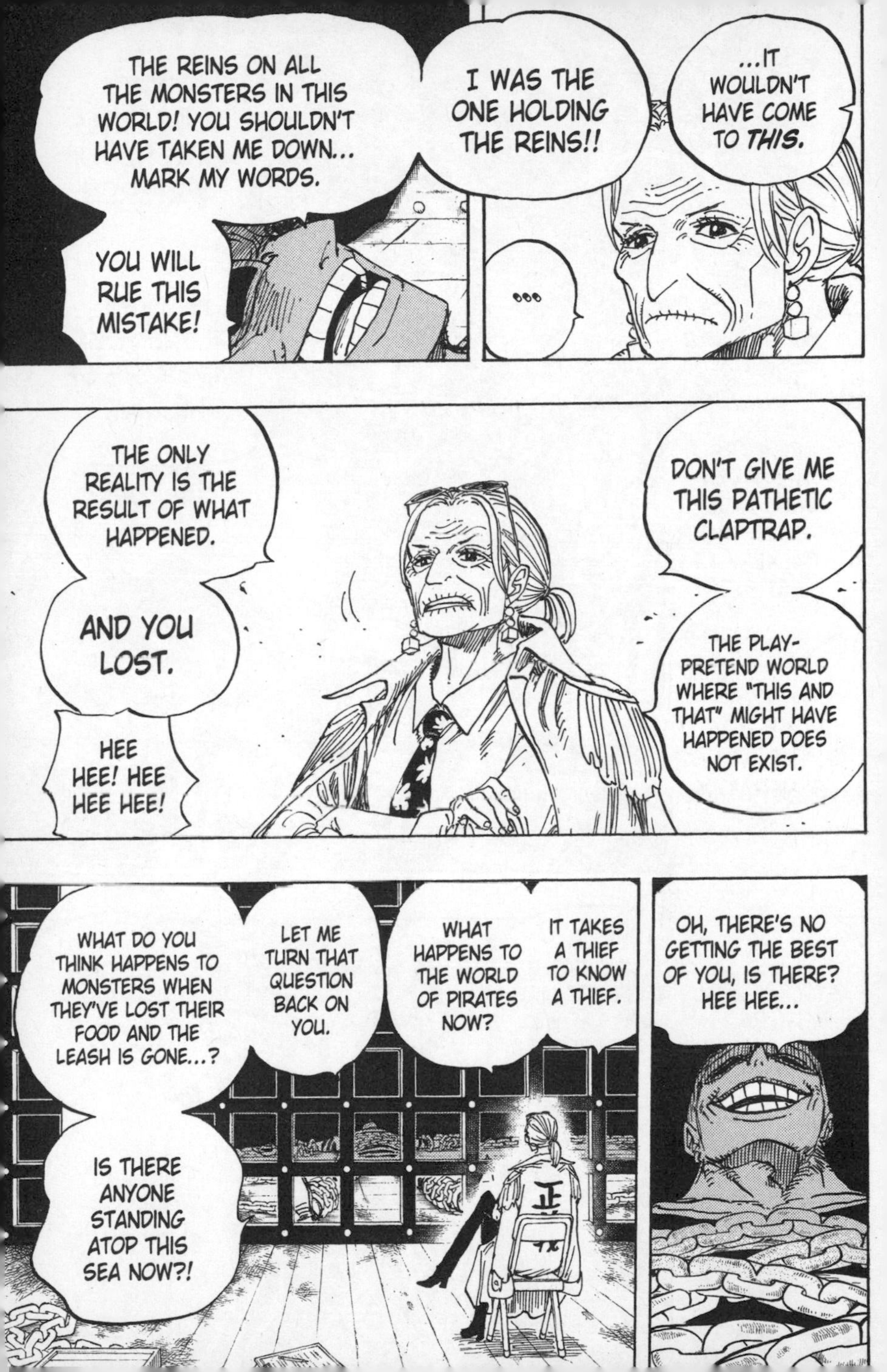
...IT WOULDN'T HAVE COME TO *THIS.*
...
I WAS THE ONE HOLDING THE REINS!!
THE REINS ON ALL THE MONSTERS IN THIS WORLD! YOU SHOULDN'T HAVE TAKEN ME DOWN... MARK MY WORDS.
YOU WILL RUE THIS MISTAKE!
DON'T GIVE ME THIS PATHETIC CLAPTRAP.
THE PLAY-PRETEND WORLD WHERE "THIS AND THAT" MIGHT HAVE HAPPENED DOES NOT EXIST.
THE ONLY REALITY IS THE RESULT OF WHAT HAPPENED.
AND YOU LOST.
HEE HEE! HEE HEE HEE!
OH, THERE'S NO GETTING THE BEST OF YOU, IS THERE? HEE HEE...
IT TAKES A THIEF TO KNOW A THIEF.
WHAT HAPPENS TO THE WORLD OF PIRATES NOW?
LET ME TURN THAT QUESTION BACK ON YOU.
WHAT DO YOU THINK HAPPENS TO MONSTERS WHEN THEY'VE LOST THEIR FOOD AND THE LEASH IS GONE...?
IS THERE ANYONE STANDING ATOP THIS SEA NOW?!

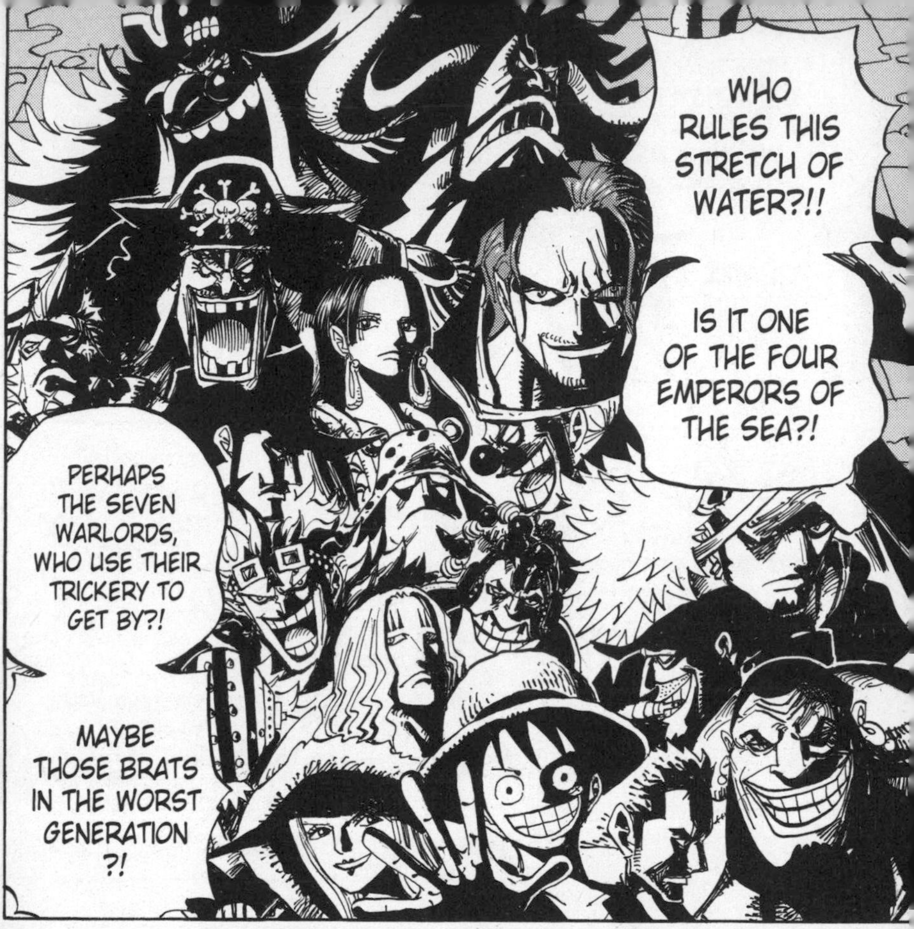
WHO RULES THIS STRETCH OF WATER?!!
IS IT ONE OF THE FOUR EMPERORS OF THE SEA?!
PERHAPS THE SEVEN WARLORDS, WHO USE THEIR TRICKERY TO GET BY?!
MAYBE THOSE BRATS IN THE WORST GENERATION ?!

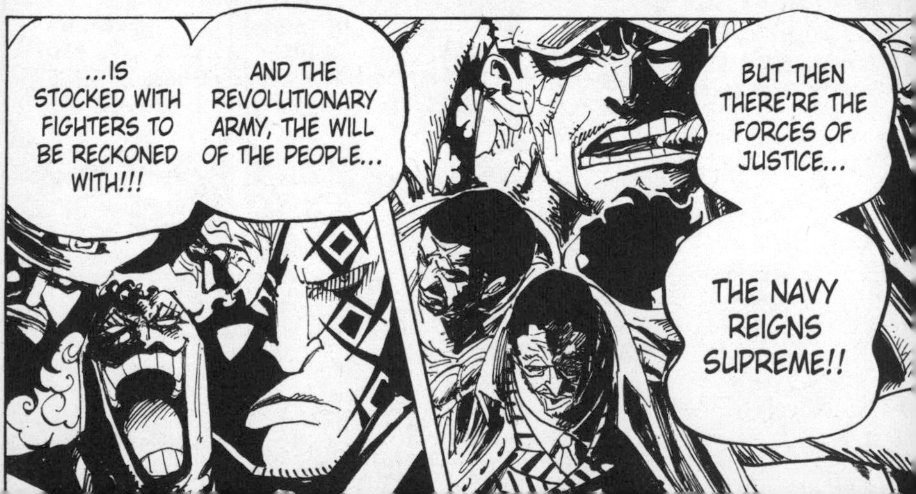
BUT THEN THERE'RE THE FORCES OF JUSTICE...
THE NAVY REIGNS SUPREME!!
AND THE REVOLUTIONARY ARMY, THE WILL OF THE PEOPLE...
...IS STOCKED WITH FIGHTERS TO BE RECKONED WITH!!!

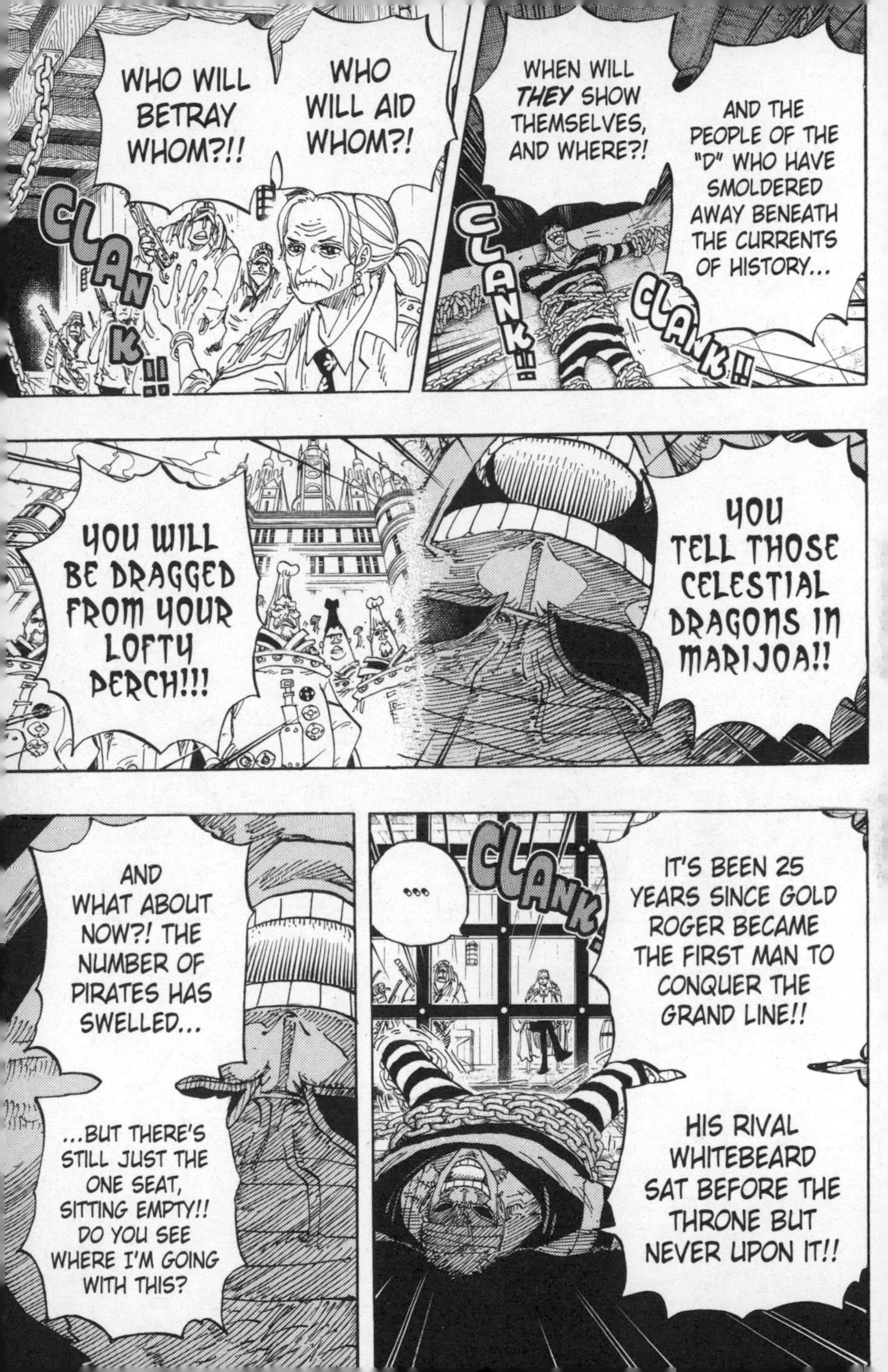
AND THE PEOPLE OF THE "D" WHO HAVE SMOLDERED AWAY BENEATH THE CURRENTS OF HISTORY...
WHEN WILL *THEY* SHOW THEMSELVES, AND WHERE?!
CLANK!!
CLANK!!
WHO WILL AID WHOM?!
WHO WILL BETRAY WHOM?!!
CLANK!!
YOU TELL THOSE CELESTIAL DRAGONS IN MARIJOA!!
YOU WILL BE DRAGGED FROM YOUR LOFTY PERCH!!!
IT'S BEEN 25 YEARS SINCE GOLD ROGER BECAME THE FIRST MAN TO CONQUER THE GRAND LINE!!
CLANK
...
HIS RIVAL WHITEBEARD SAT BEFORE THE THRONE BUT NEVER UPON IT!!
AND WHAT ABOUT NOW?! THE NUMBER OF PIRATES HAS SWELLED...
...BUT THERE'S STILL JUST THE ONE SEAT, SITTING EMPTY!! DO YOU SEE WHERE I'M GOING WITH THIS?

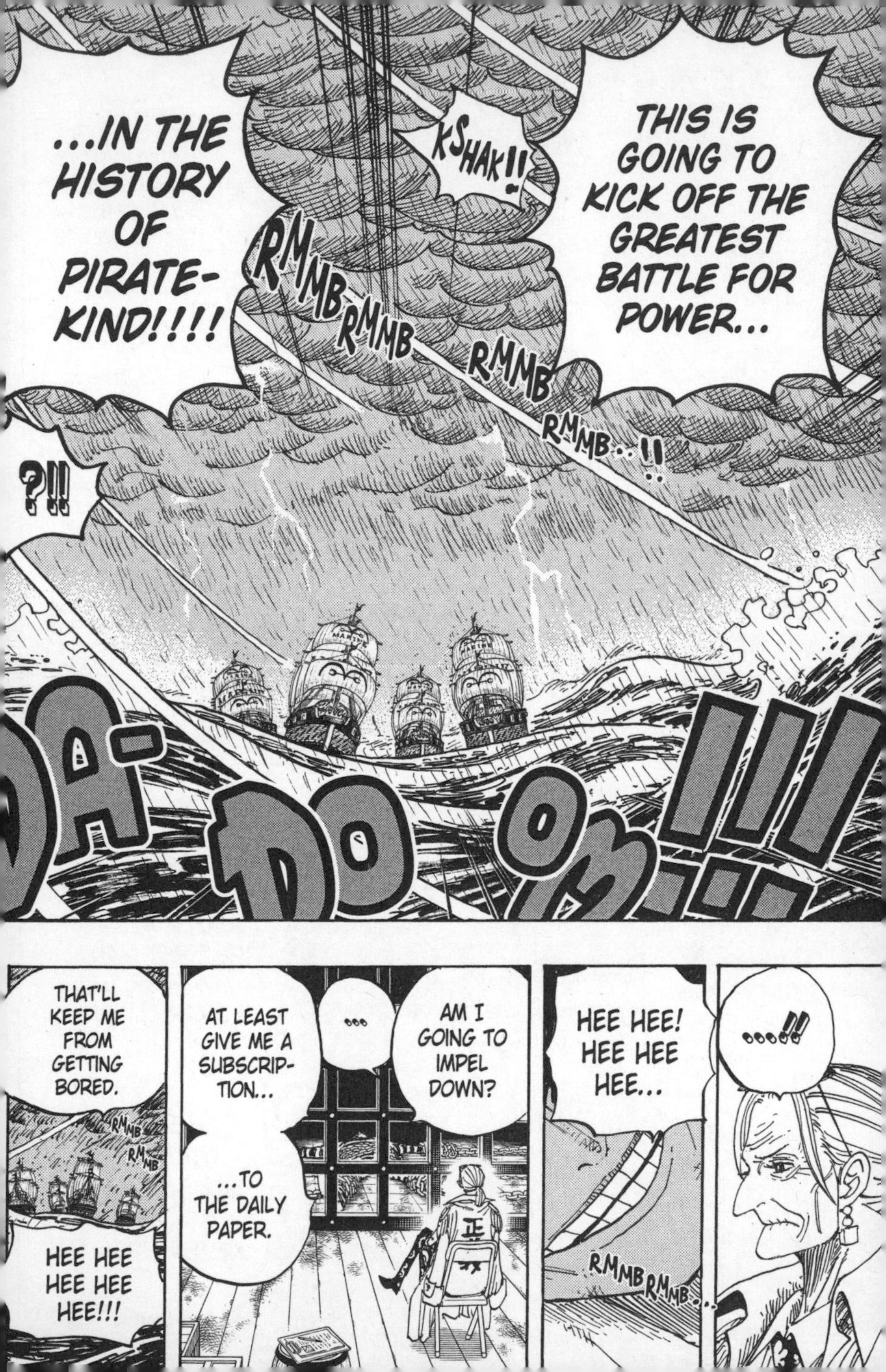
THIS IS GOING TO KICK OFF THE GREATEST BATTLE FOR POWER...
...IN THE HISTORY OF PIRATE-KIND!!!!
KSHAK!!
RMMB RMMB
RMMB
RMMB..!!
?!!
DA-DO-OM!!!!
...!!
HEE HEE! HEE HEE HEE...
RMMB RMMB...
AM I GOING TO IMPEL DOWN?
...
AT LEAST GIVE ME A SUBSCRIP-TION...
...TO THE DAILY PAPER.
THAT'LL KEEP ME FROM GETTING BORED.
RMMB
RMMB
HEE HEE HEE HEE HEE!!!

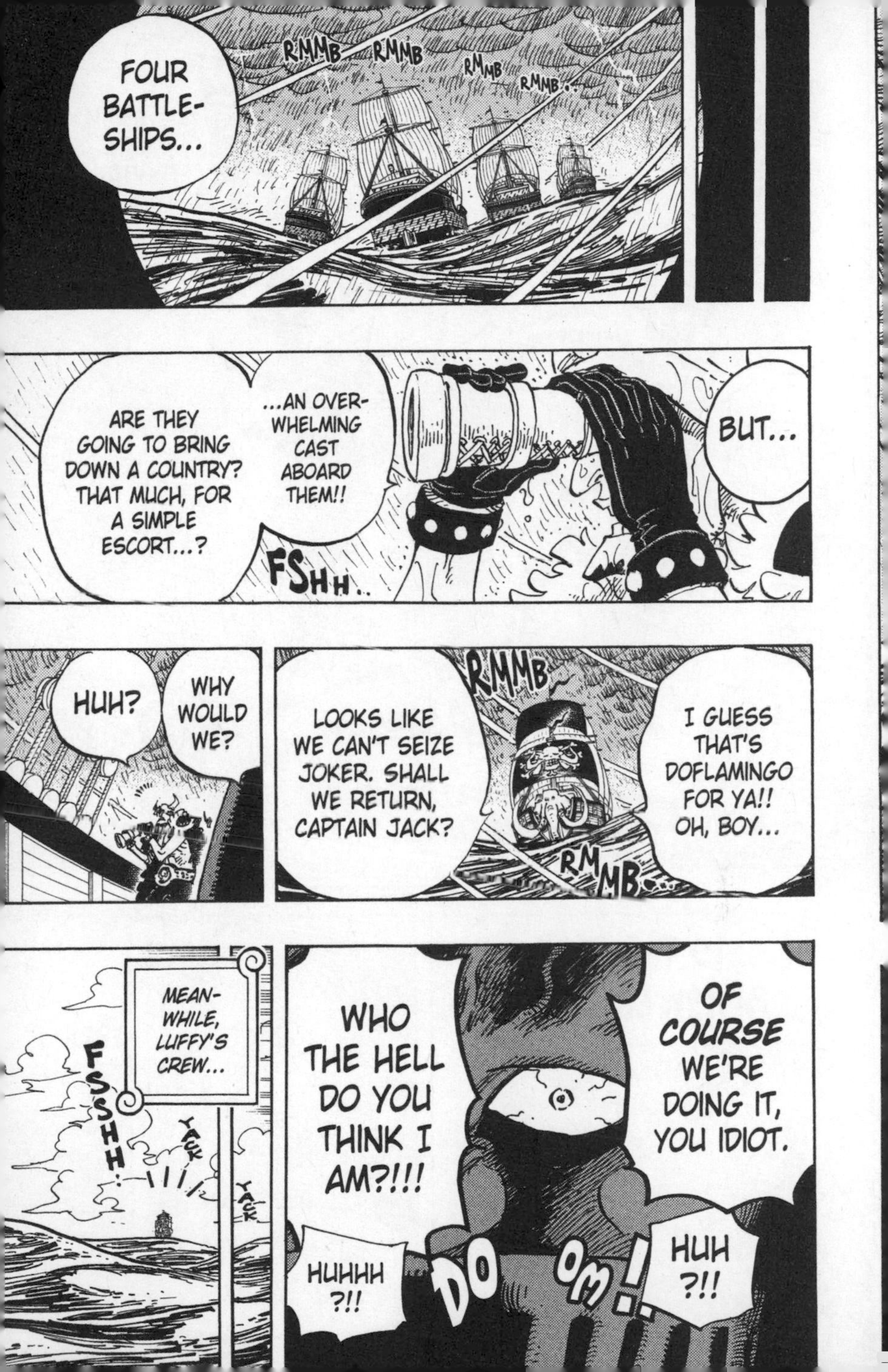
RMMB RMMB
RMMB RMMB..
FOUR BATTLE-SHIPS...
BUT...
...AN OVER-WHELMING CAST ABOARD THEM!!
ARE THEY GOING TO BRING DOWN A COUNTRY? THAT MUCH, FOR A SIMPLE ESCORT...?
FSHH..
I GUESS THAT'S DOFLAMINGO FOR YA!! OH, BOY...
RMMB
LOOKS LIKE WE CAN'T SEIZE JOKER. SHALL WE RETURN, CAPTAIN JACK?
RMMB...
WHY WOULD WE?
HUH?
OF COURSE WE'RE DOING IT, YOU IDIOT.
WHO THE HELL DO YOU THINK I AM?!!!
HUH ?!!
DOOM!!
HUHHH ?!!
MEAN-WHILE, LUFFY'S CREW...
YACK
YACK
FSSHH!

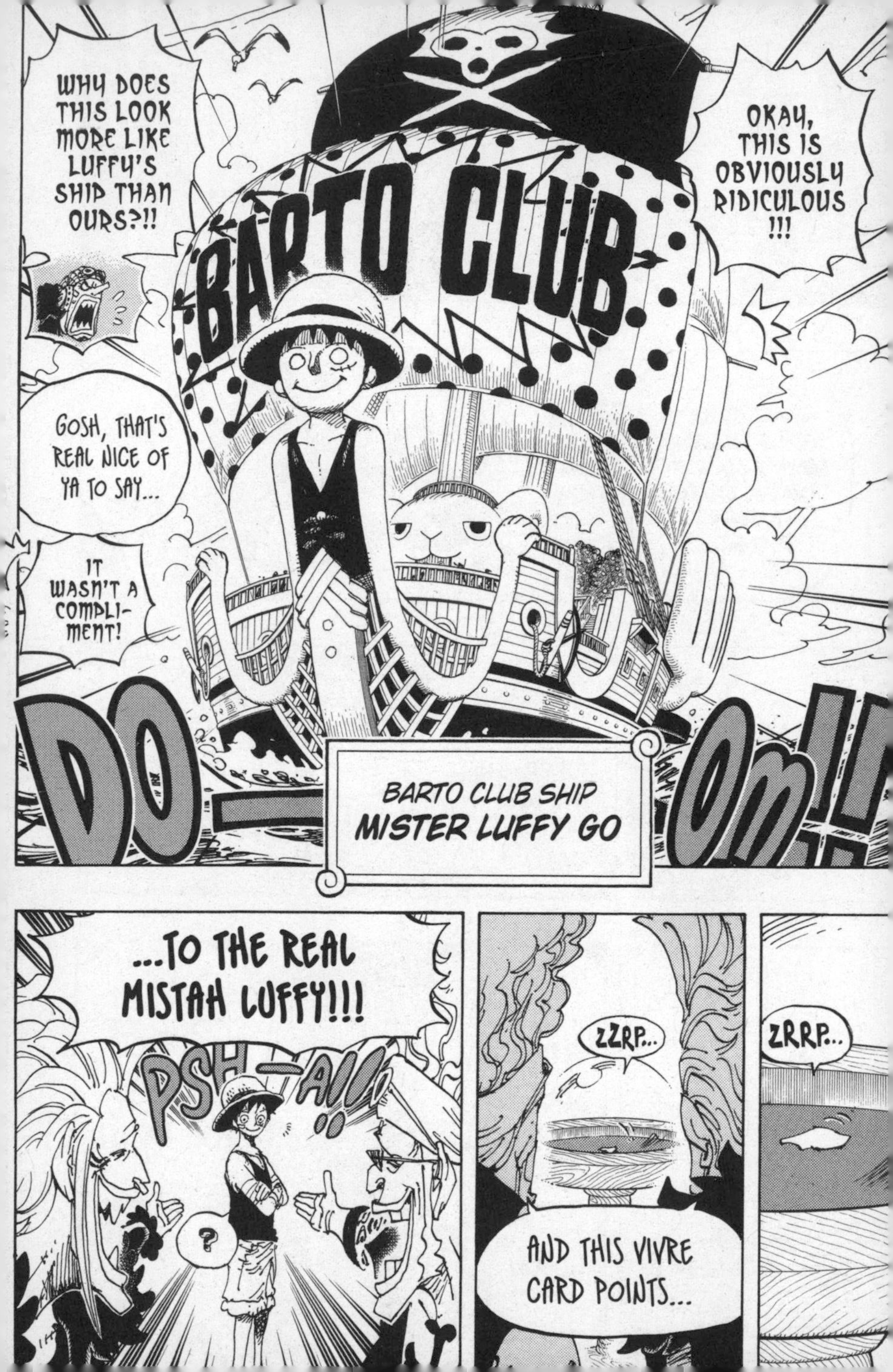
OKAY, THIS IS OBVIOUSLY RIDICULOUS!!!
WHY DOES THIS LOOK MORE LIKE LUFFY'S SHIP THAN OURS?!!
BARTO CLUB
GOSH, THAT'S REAL NICE OF YA TO SAY...
IT WASN'T A COMPLI-MENT!
DO—OM!!
BARTO CLUB SHIP
MISTER LUFFY GO
ZRRP...
ZZRP...
AND THIS VIVRE CARD POINTS...
...TO THE REAL MISTAH LUFFY!!!
PSH—A!!
?

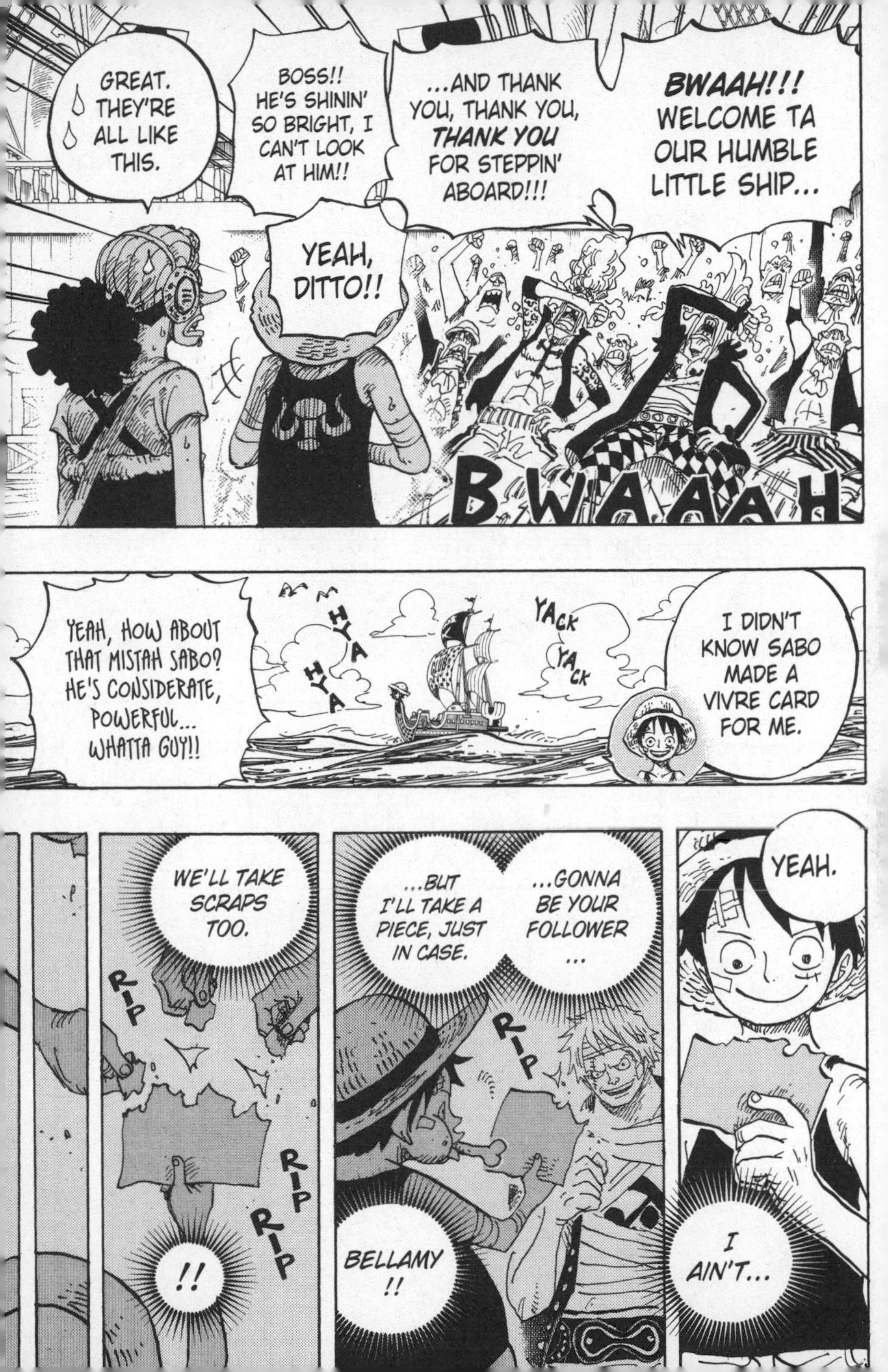
BWAAH!!! WELCOME TA OUR HUMBLE LITTLE SHIP...
...AND THANK YOU, THANK YOU, THANK YOU FOR STEPPIN' ABOARD!!!
BOSS!! HE'S SHININ' SO BRIGHT, I CAN'T LOOK AT HIM!!
YEAH, DITTO!!
GREAT. THEY'RE ALL LIKE THIS.
BWAAAH
I DIDN'T KNOW SABO MADE A VIVRE CARD FOR ME.
YACK
YACK
HYA
HYA
YEAH, HOW ABOUT THAT MISTAH SABO? HE'S CONSIDERATE, POWERFUL... WHATTA GUY!!
YEAH.
I AIN'T...
...GONNA BE YOUR FOLLOWER ...
...BUT I'LL TAKE A PIECE, JUST IN CASE.
RIP
BELLAMY !!
WE'LL TAKE SCRAPS TOO.
RIP
RIP
RIP
!!

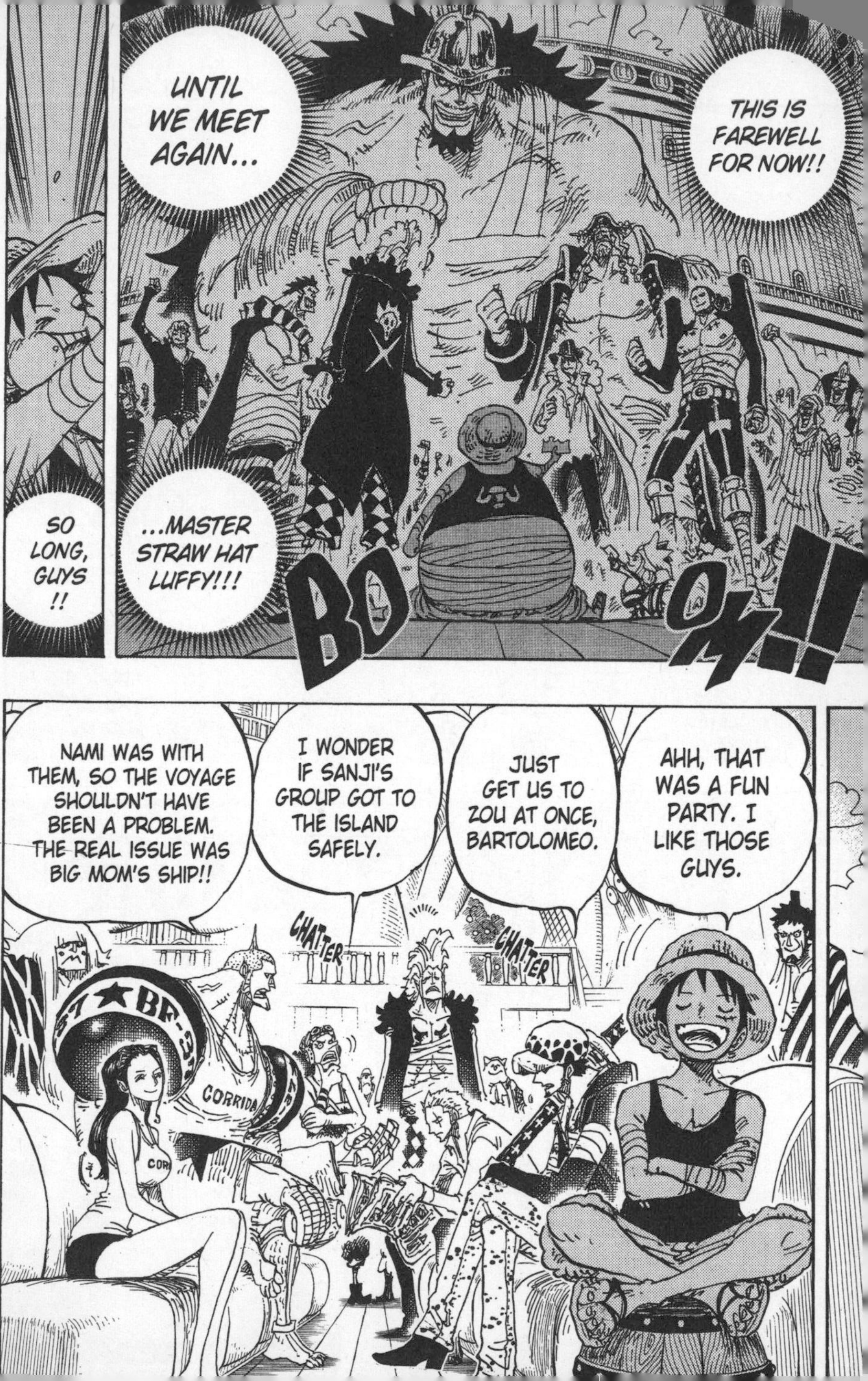
THIS IS FAREWELL FOR NOW!!
UNTIL WE MEET AGAIN...
...MASTER STRAW HAT LUFFY!!!
BOOM!!
SO LONG, GUYS !!
AHH, THAT WAS A FUN PARTY. I LIKE THOSE GUYS.
JUST GET US TO ZOU AT ONCE, BARTOLOMEO.
CHATTER
I WONDER IF SANJI'S GROUP GOT TO THE ISLAND SAFELY.
CHATTER
NAMI WAS WITH THEM, SO THE VOYAGE SHOULDN'T HAVE BEEN A PROBLEM. THE REAL ISSUE WAS BIG MOM'S SHIP!!
CORRIDA

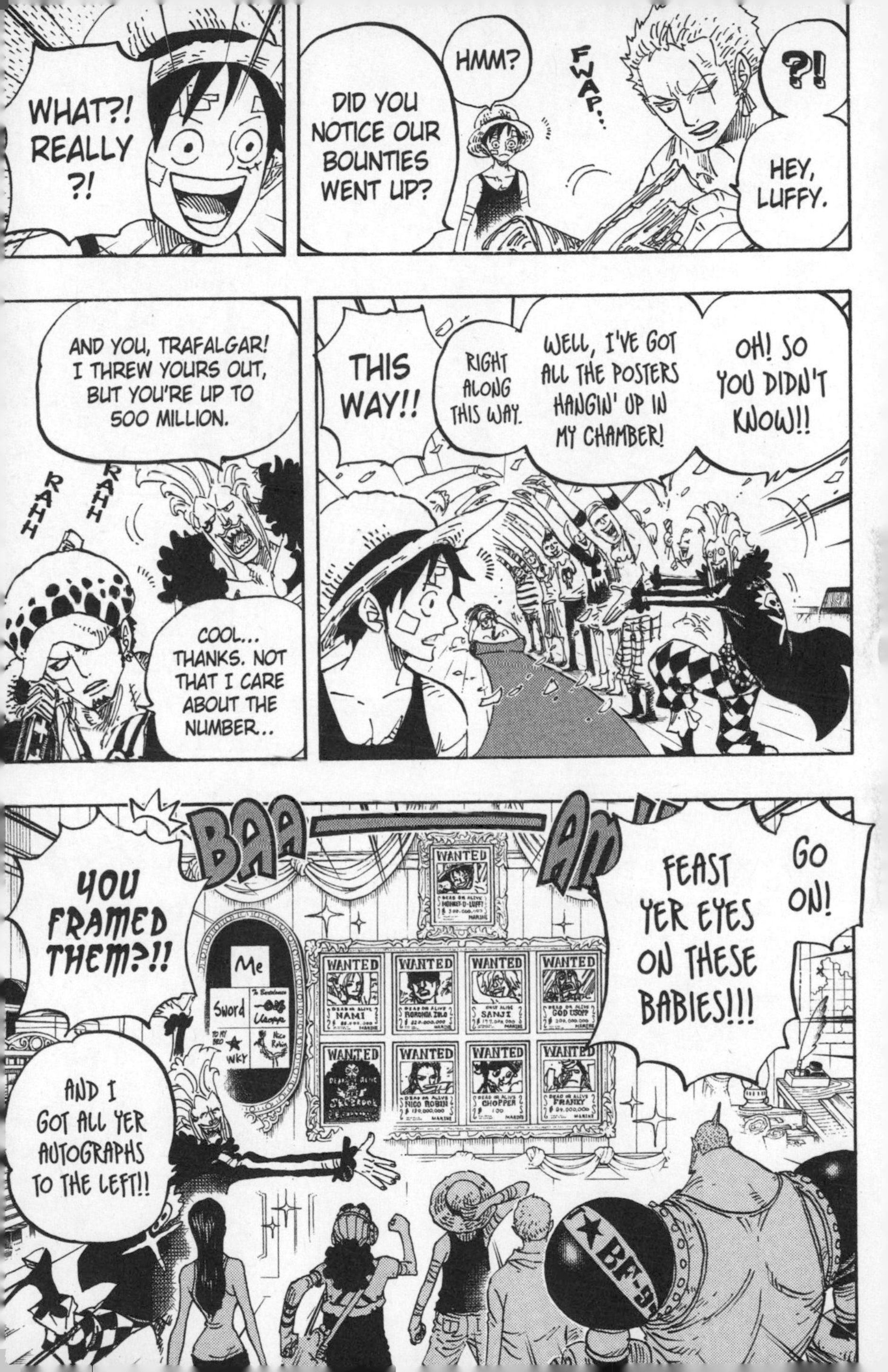
HEY, LUFFY.
?!
FWAP...
HMM?
DID YOU NOTICE OUR BOUNTIES WENT UP?
WHAT?! REALLY ?!
OH! SO YOU DIDN'T KNOW!!
WELL, I'VE GOT ALL THE POSTERS HANGIN' UP IN MY CHAMBER!
RIGHT ALONG THIS WAY.
THIS WAY!!
AND YOU, TRAFALGAR! I THREW YOURS OUT, BUT YOU'RE UP TO 500 MILLION.
RAHH
RAHH
COOL... THANKS. NOT THAT I CARE ABOUT THE NUMBER...
GO ON!
FEAST YER EYES ON THESE BABIES!!!
BAA———AM
YOU FRAMED THEM?!!
WANTED
WANTED
NAMI
WANTED
RORONOA ZORO
WANTED
SANJI
WANTED
GOD USOPP
WANTED
WANTED
NICO ROBIN
WANTED
CHOPPER
WANTED
FRANKY
Me
Sword
AND I GOT ALL YER AUTOGRAPHS TO THE LEFT!!

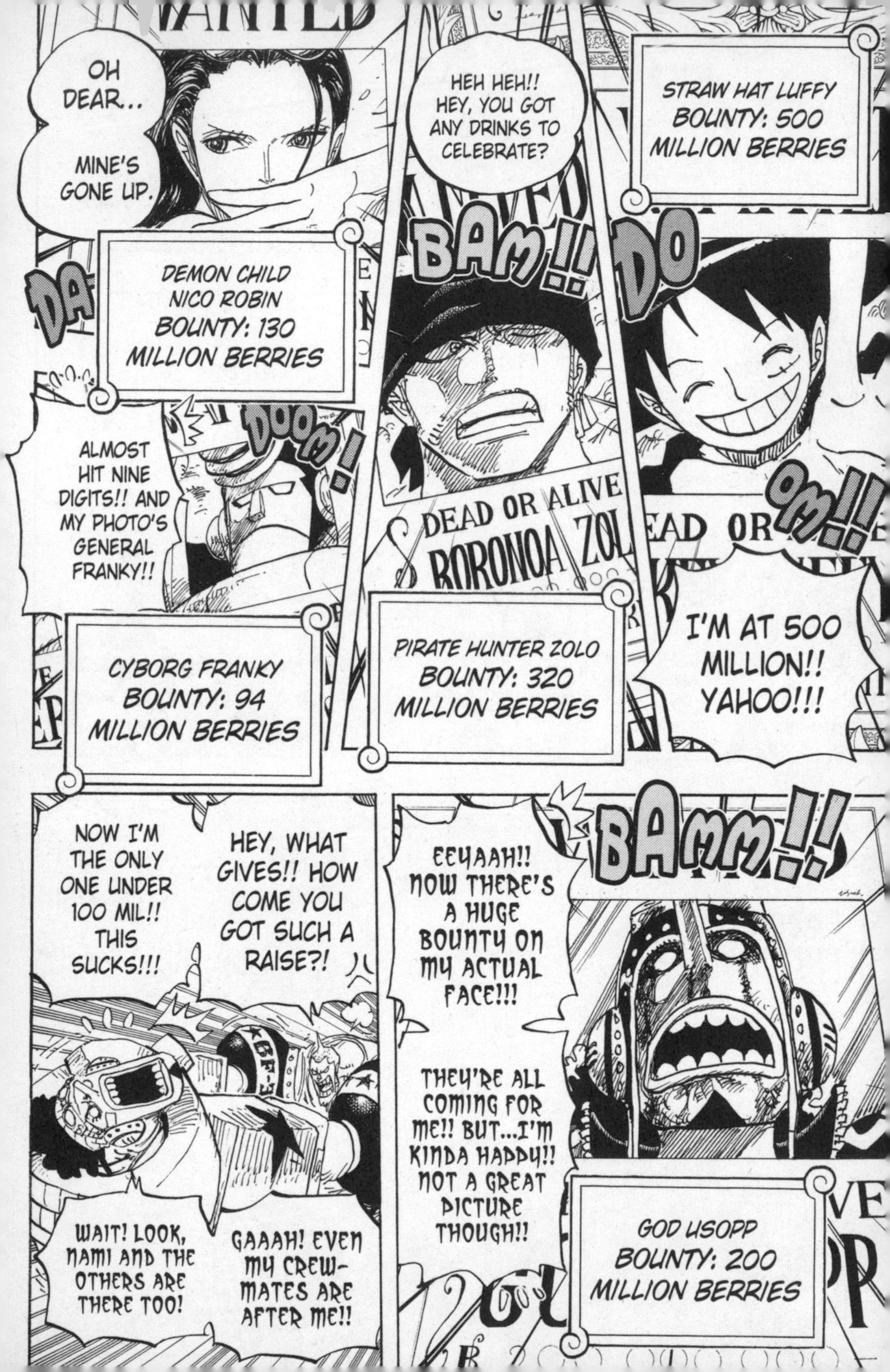

STRAW HAT LUFFY BOUNTY: 500 MILLION BERRIES
DO
OM!!
I'M AT 500 MILLION!! YAHOO!!!
HEH HEH!! HEY, YOU GOT ANY DRINKS TO CELEBRATE?
BAM!!
DEAD OR ALIVE
PIRATE HUNTER ZOLO BOUNTY: 320 MILLION BERRIES
OH DEAR...
MINE'S GONE UP.
DA
DEMON CHILD NICO ROBIN BOUNTY: 130 MILLION BERRIES
DOOM!
ALMOST HIT NINE DIGITS!! AND MY PHOTO'S GENERAL FRANKY!!
CYBORG FRANKY BOUNTY: 94 MILLION BERRIES
BAMM!!
EEYAAH!! NOW THERE'S A HUGE BOUNTY ON MY ACTUAL FACE!!!
THEY'RE ALL COMING FOR ME!! BUT...I'M KINDA HAPPY!! NOT A GREAT PICTURE THOUGH!!
GOD USOPP BOUNTY: 200 MILLION BERRIES
HEY, WHAT GIVES!! HOW COME YOU GOT SUCH A RAISE?!
NOW I'M THE ONLY ONE UNDER 100 MIL!! THIS SUCKS!!!
GAAAH! EVEN MY CREW-MATES ARE AFTER ME!!
WAIT! LOOK, NAMI AND THE OTHERS ARE THERE TOO!

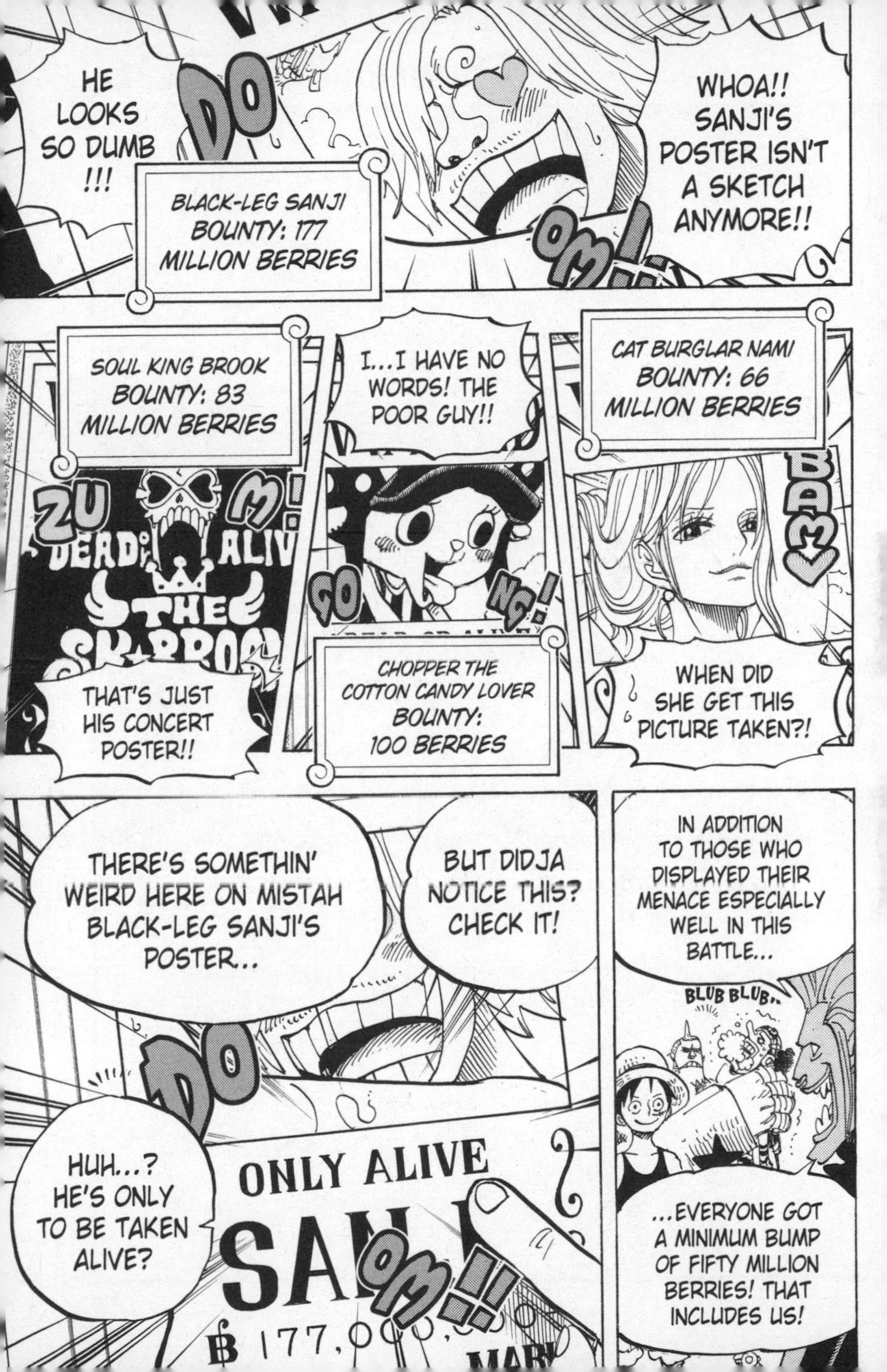
WHOA!! SANJI'S POSTER ISN'T A SKETCH ANYMORE!!
DO
OM!!
BLACK-LEG SANJI BOUNTY: 177 MILLION BERRIES
HE LOOKS SO DUMB!!!
CAT BURGLAR NAMI BOUNTY: 66 MILLION BERRIES
BAM
WHEN DID SHE GET THIS PICTURE TAKEN?!
I...I HAVE NO WORDS! THE POOR GUY!!
GO
NG!
CHOPPER THE COTTON CANDY LOVER BOUNTY: 100 BERRIES
SOUL KING BROOK BOUNTY: 83 MILLION BERRIES
ZU
M!
THAT'S JUST HIS CONCERT POSTER!!
IN ADDITION TO THOSE WHO DISPLAYED THEIR MENACE ESPECIALLY WELL IN THIS BATTLE...
BLUB BLUB..
...EVERYONE GOT A MINIMUM BUMP OF FIFTY MILLION BERRIES! THAT INCLUDES US!
BUT DIDJA NOTICE THIS? CHECK IT!
THERE'S SOMETHIN' WEIRD HERE ON MISTAH BLACK-LEG SANJI'S POSTER...
DO
OM!!
HUH...? HE'S ONLY TO BE TAKEN ALIVE?
ONLY ALIVE

# Chapter 802: ZOU

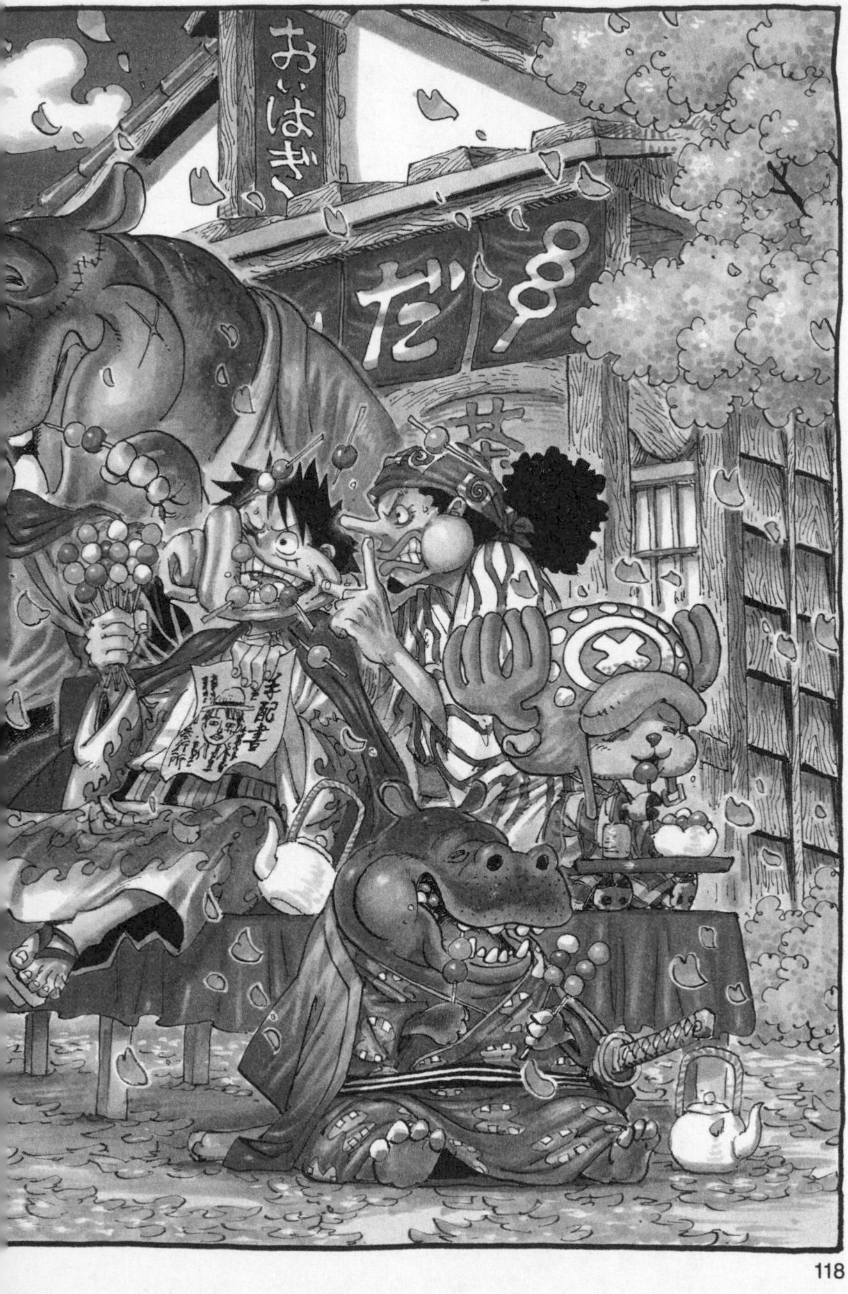
おいはぎ
手配書

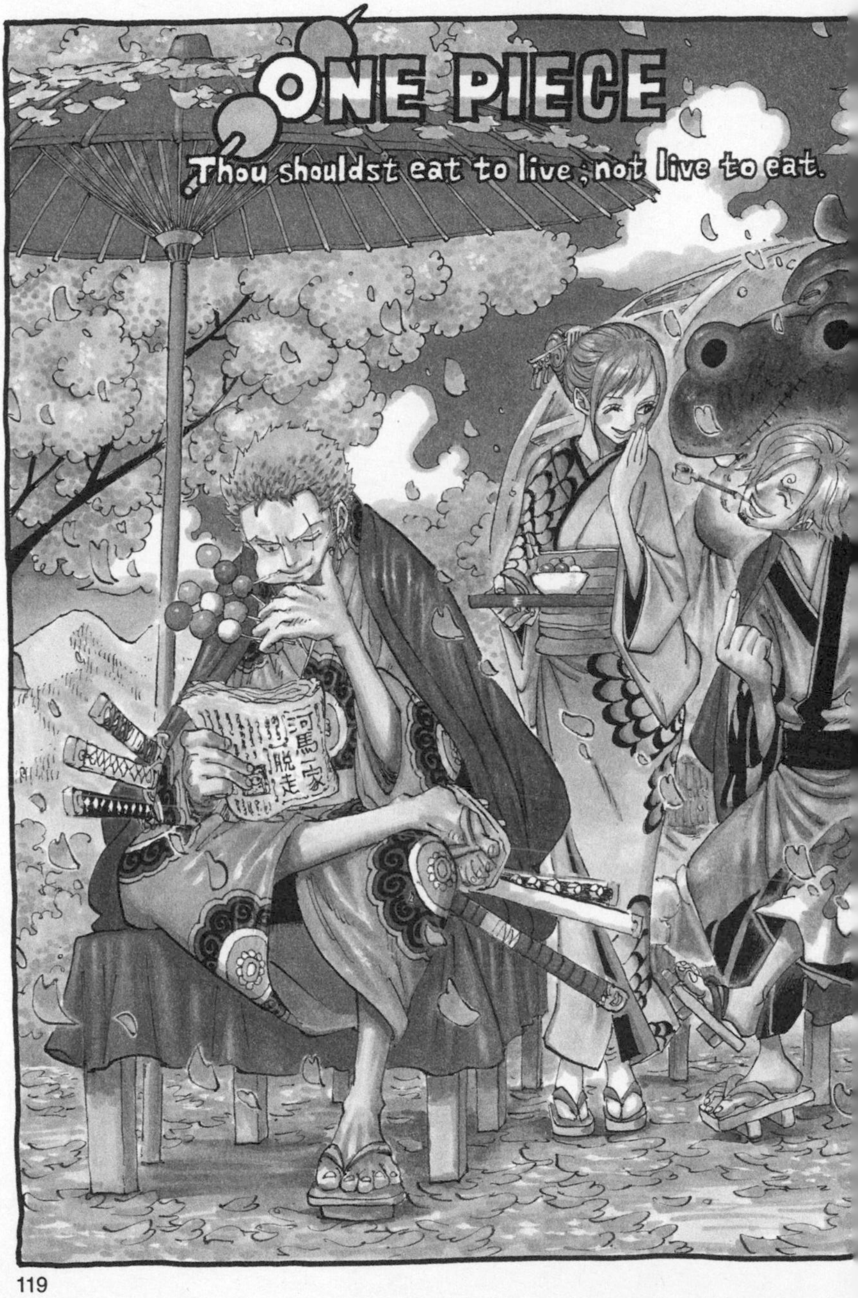
ONE PIECE
Thou shouldst eat to live; not live to eat.
河馬一家
脱走

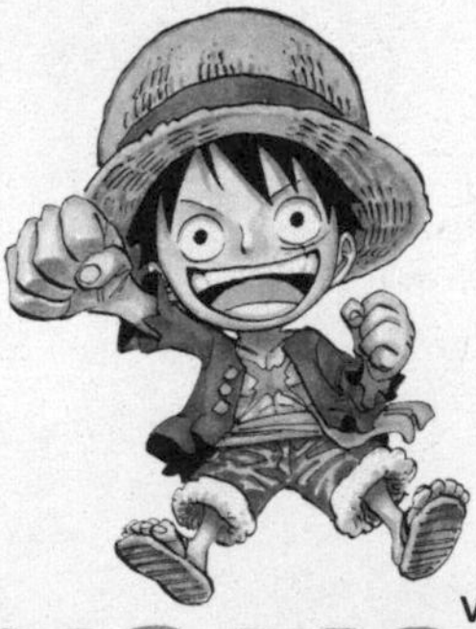

vol.80

ONE PIECE

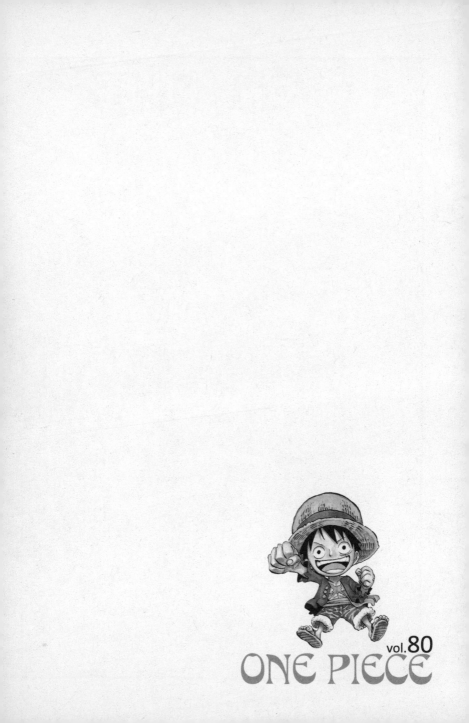

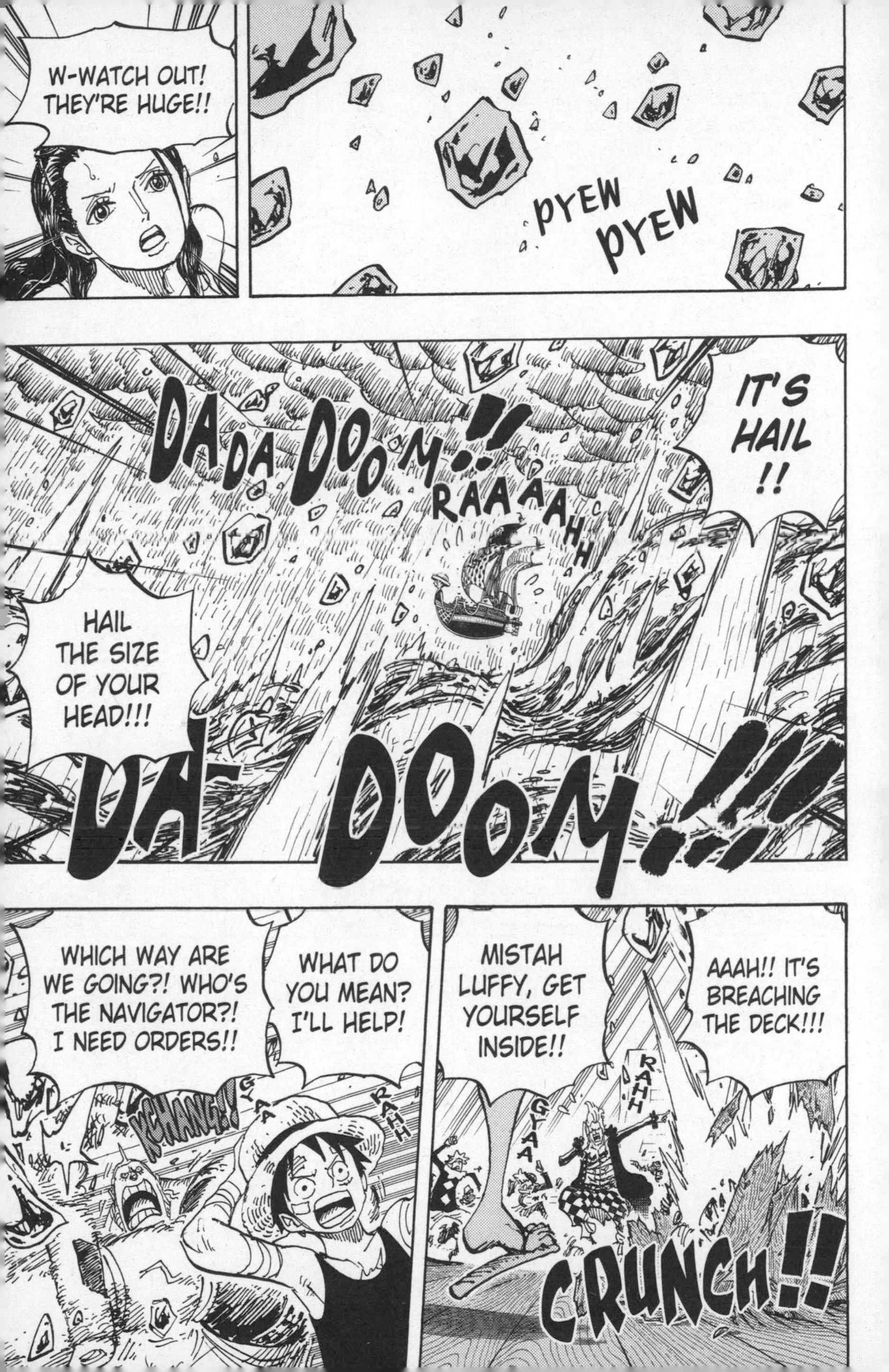
PYEW PYEW
W-WATCH OUT! THEY'RE HUGE!!
IT'S HAIL!!
DADA DOOM!!
RAAAAHH
HAIL THE SIZE OF YOUR HEAD!!!
DA DOOM!!!
AAAH!! IT'S BREACHING THE DECK!!!
MISTAH LUFFY, GET YOURSELF INSIDE!!
RAHH
GYAA
CRUNCH!!
WHAT DO YOU MEAN? I'LL HELP!
WHICH WAY ARE WE GOING?! WHO'S THE NAVIGATOR?! I NEED ORDERS!!
RAHH
GYA
KCHANG!!

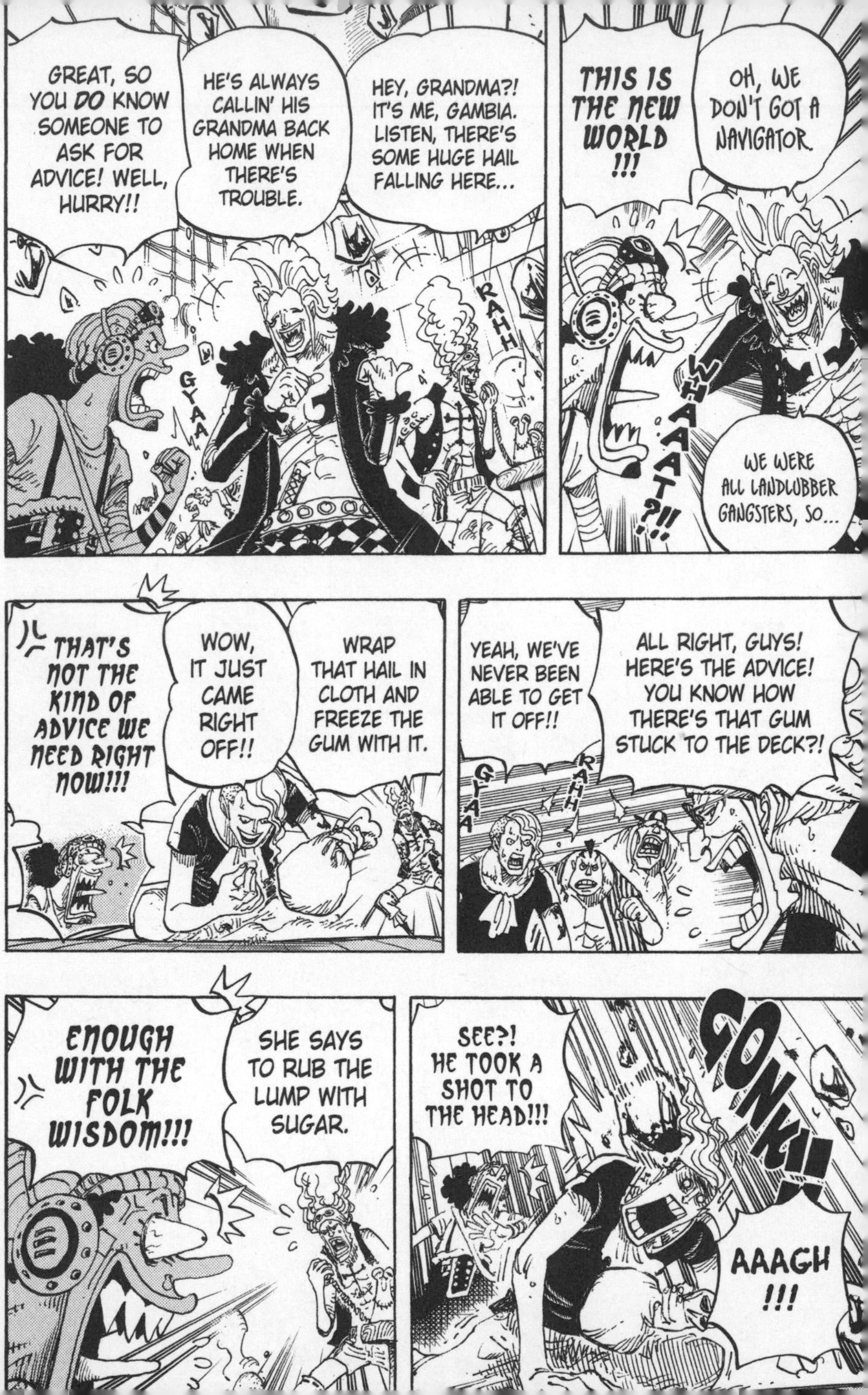

OH, WE DON'T GOT A NAVIGATOR.
THIS IS THE NEW WORLD!!!
WHAAAAT?!!
WE WERE ALL LANDLUBBER GANGSTERS, SO...
HEY, GRANDMA?! IT'S ME, GAMBIA. LISTEN, THERE'S SOME HUGE HAIL FALLING HERE...
RAHH
HE'S ALWAYS CALLIN' HIS GRANDMA BACK HOME WHEN THERE'S TROUBLE.
GREAT, SO YOU DO KNOW SOMEONE TO ASK FOR ADVICE! WELL, HURRY!!
GYAA
ALL RIGHT, GUYS! HERE'S THE ADVICE! YOU KNOW HOW THERE'S THAT GUM STUCK TO THE DECK?!
YEAH, WE'VE NEVER BEEN ABLE TO GET IT OFF!!
RAHH
GYAA
WRAP THAT HAIL IN CLOTH AND FREEZE THE GUM WITH IT.
WOW, IT JUST CAME RIGHT OFF!!
THAT'S NOT THE KIND OF ADVICE WE NEED RIGHT NOW!!!
GONK!!
SEE?! HE TOOK A SHOT TO THE HEAD!!!
AAAGH!!!
SHE SAYS TO RUB THE LUMP WITH SUGAR.
ENOUGH WITH THE FOLK WISDOM!!!

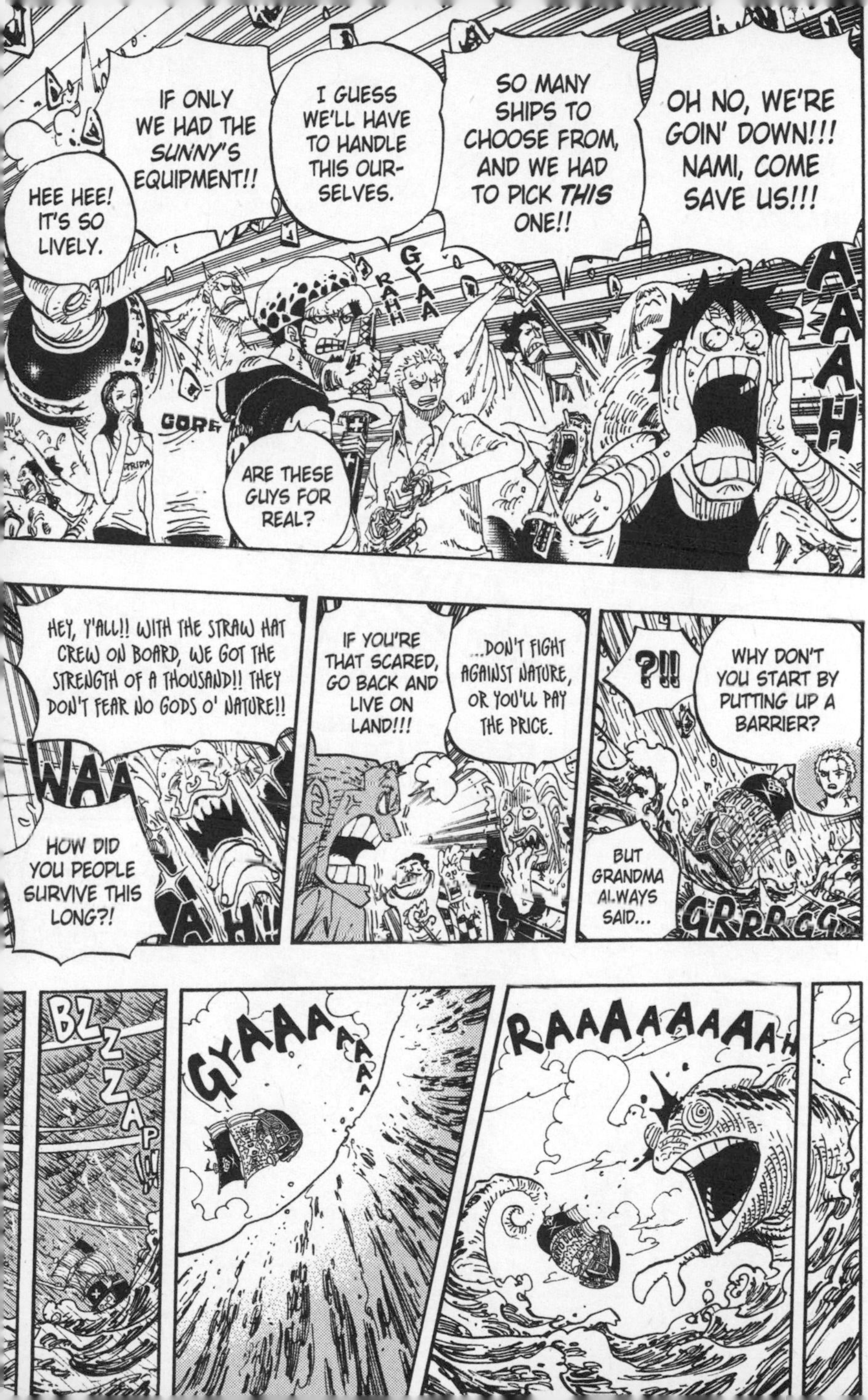
OH NO, WE'RE GOIN' DOWN!!! NAMI, COME SAVE US!!!
AAAAH
SO MANY SHIPS TO CHOOSE FROM, AND WE HAD TO PICK THIS ONE!!
GYAA
RAHH
I GUESS WE'LL HAVE TO HANDLE THIS OURSELVES.
IF ONLY WE HAD THE SUNNY'S EQUIPMENT!!
HEE HEE! IT'S SO LIVELY.
ARE THESE GUYS FOR REAL?
WHY DON'T YOU START BY PUTTING UP A BARRIER?
?!!
BUT GRANDMA ALWAYS SAID...
GRRRGG
...DON'T FIGHT AGAINST NATURE, OR YOU'LL PAY THE PRICE.
IF YOU'RE THAT SCARED, GO BACK AND LIVE ON LAND!!!
HEY, Y'ALL!! WITH THE STRAW HAT CREW ON BOARD, WE GOT THE STRENGTH OF A THOUSAND!! THEY DON'T FEAR NO GODS O' NATURE!!
WAAAH!!
HOW DID YOU PEOPLE SURVIVE THIS LONG?!
RAAAAAAAAAH
GYAAAAAAA
BZZZAP!!

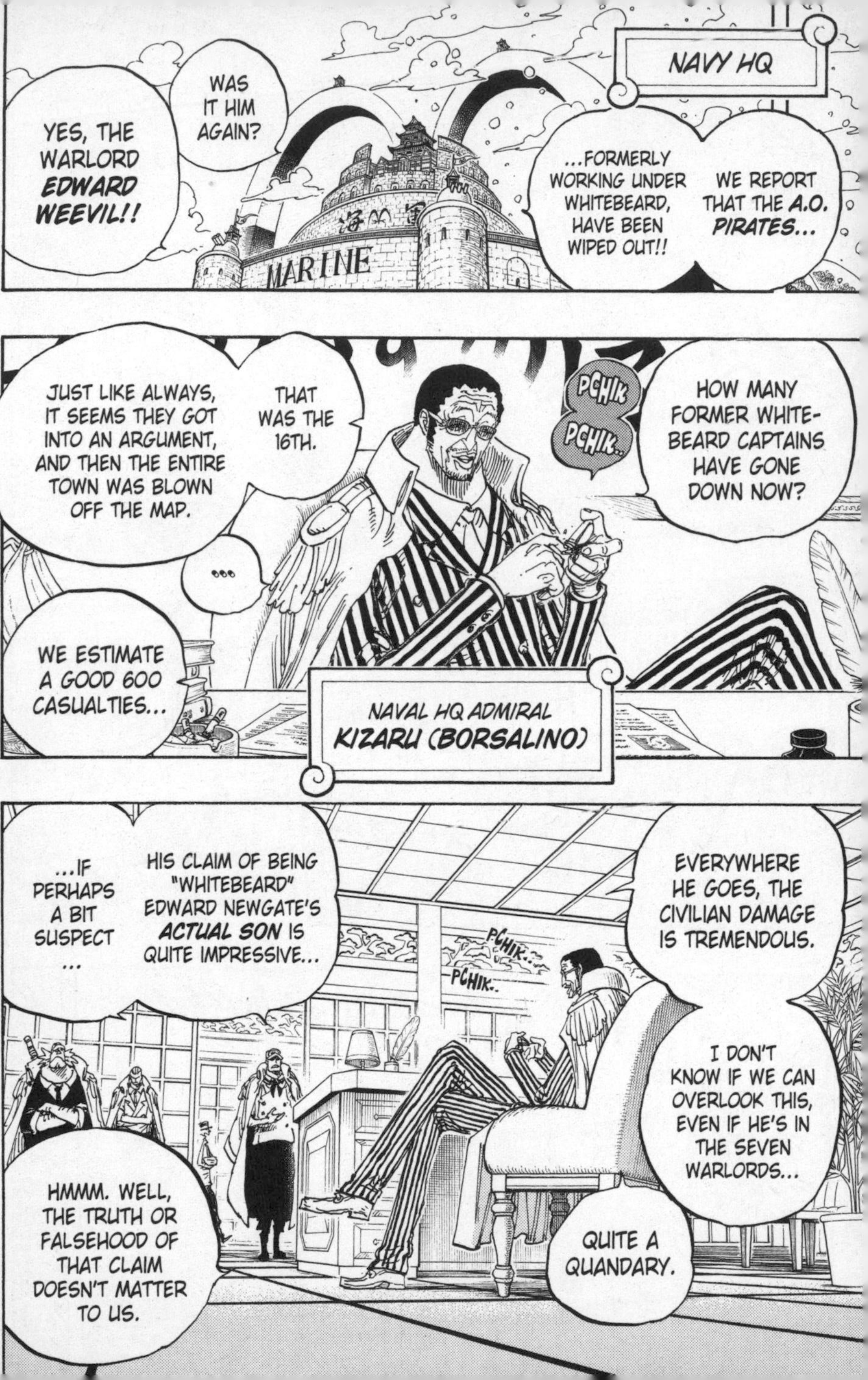
NAVY HQ
WE REPORT THAT THE A.O. PIRATES...
...FORMERLY WORKING UNDER WHITEBEARD, HAVE BEEN WIPED OUT!!
WAS IT HIM AGAIN?
YES, THE WARLORD EDWARD WEEVIL!!
MARINE
HOW MANY FORMER WHITE-BEARD CAPTAINS HAVE GONE DOWN NOW?
PCHIK
PCHIK..
THAT WAS THE 16TH.
JUST LIKE ALWAYS, IT SEEMS THEY GOT INTO AN ARGUMENT, AND THEN THE ENTIRE TOWN WAS BLOWN OFF THE MAP.
...
NAVAL HQ ADMIRAL KIZARU (BORSALINO)
WE ESTIMATE A GOOD 600 CASUALTIES...
EVERYWHERE HE GOES, THE CIVILIAN DAMAGE IS TREMENDOUS.
I DON'T KNOW IF WE CAN OVERLOOK THIS, EVEN IF HE'S IN THE SEVEN WARLORDS...
HIS CLAIM OF BEING "WHITEBEARD" EDWARD NEWGATE'S ACTUAL SON IS QUITE IMPRESSIVE...
...IF PERHAPS A BIT SUSPECT...
PCHIK..
PCHIK..
QUITE A QUANDARY.
HMMM. WELL, THE TRUTH OR FALSEHOOD OF THAT CLAIM DOESN'T MATTER TO US.

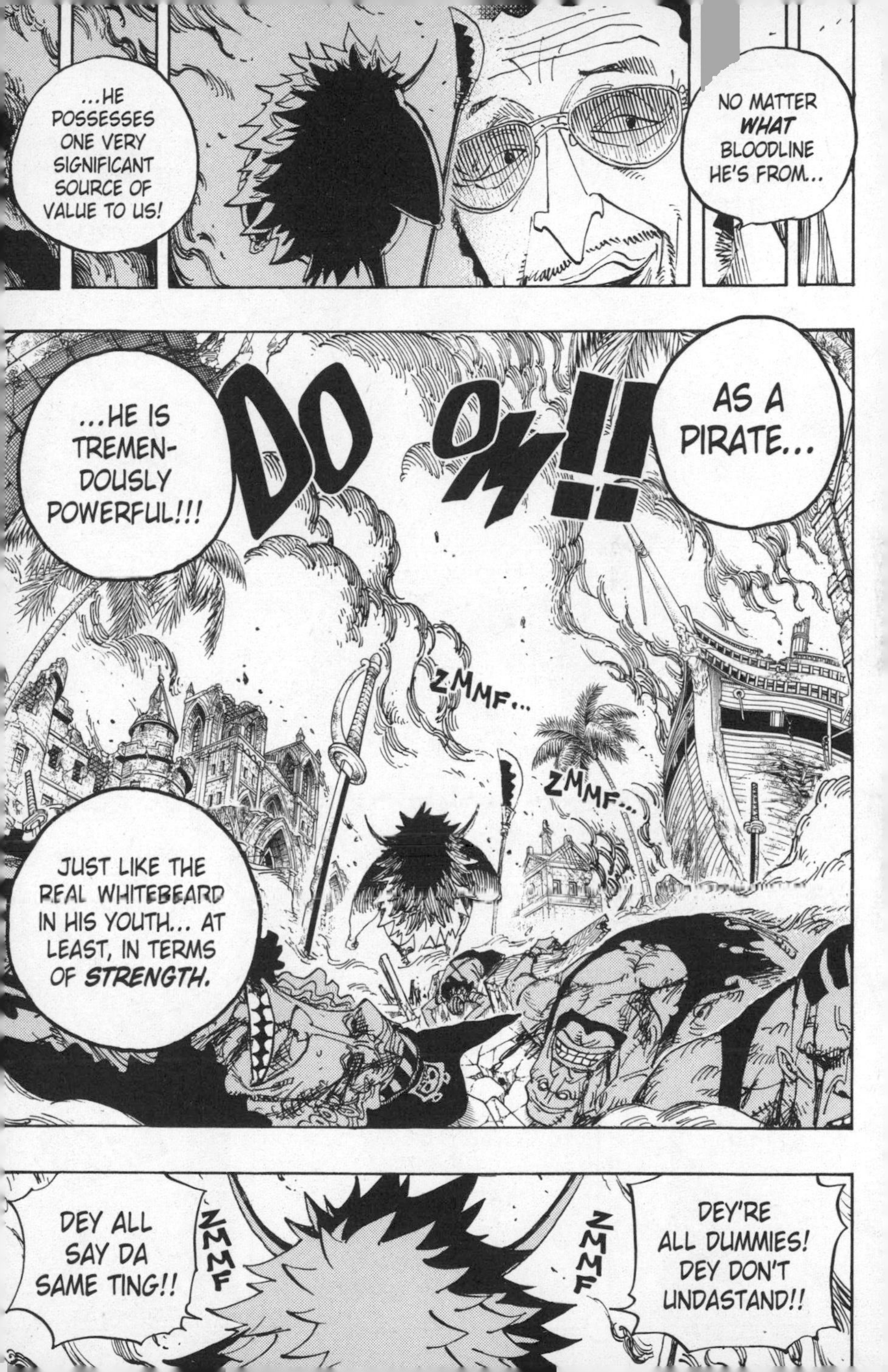
NO MATTER WHAT BLOODLINE HE'S FROM...
...HE POSSESSES ONE VERY SIGNIFICANT SOURCE OF VALUE TO US!
AS A PIRATE...
DOOM!!
...HE IS TREMEN-DOUSLY POWERFUL!!!
ZMMF...
ZMMF...
JUST LIKE THE REAL WHITEBEARD IN HIS YOUTH... AT LEAST, IN TERMS OF STRENGTH.
DEY'RE ALL DUMMIES! DEY DON'T UNDASTAND!!
ZMMF
ZMMF
DEY ALL SAY DA SAME TING!!

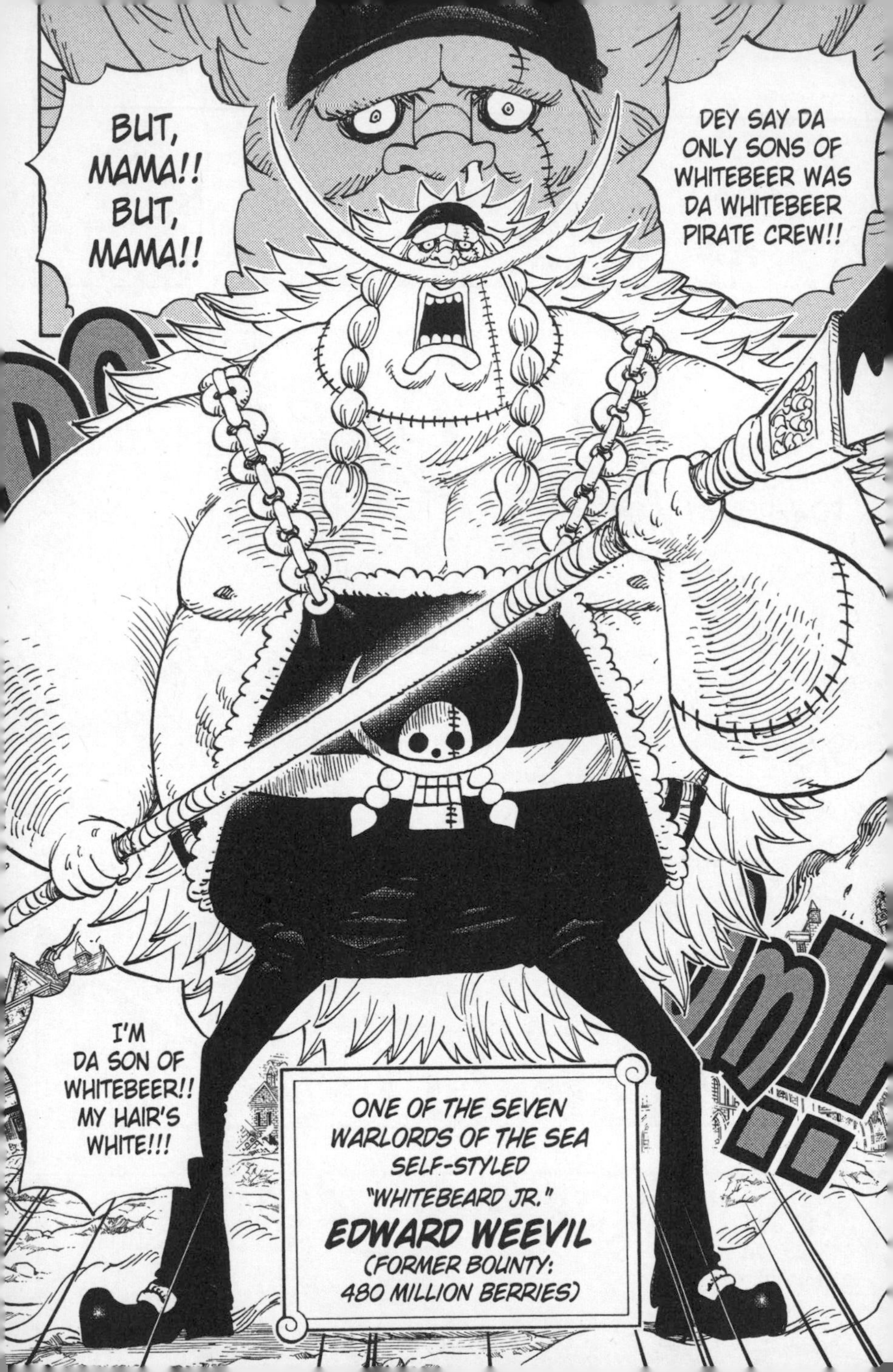
DEY SAY DA ONLY SONS OF WHITEBEER WAS DA WHITEBEER PIRATE CREW!!
BUT, MAMA!! BUT, MAMA!!
ONE OF THE SEVEN WARLORDS OF THE SEA
SELF-STYLED "WHITEBEARD JR."
EDWARD WEEVIL
(FORMER BOUNTY: 480 MILLION BERRIES)
I'M DA SON OF WHITEBEER!! MY HAIR'S WHITE!!!

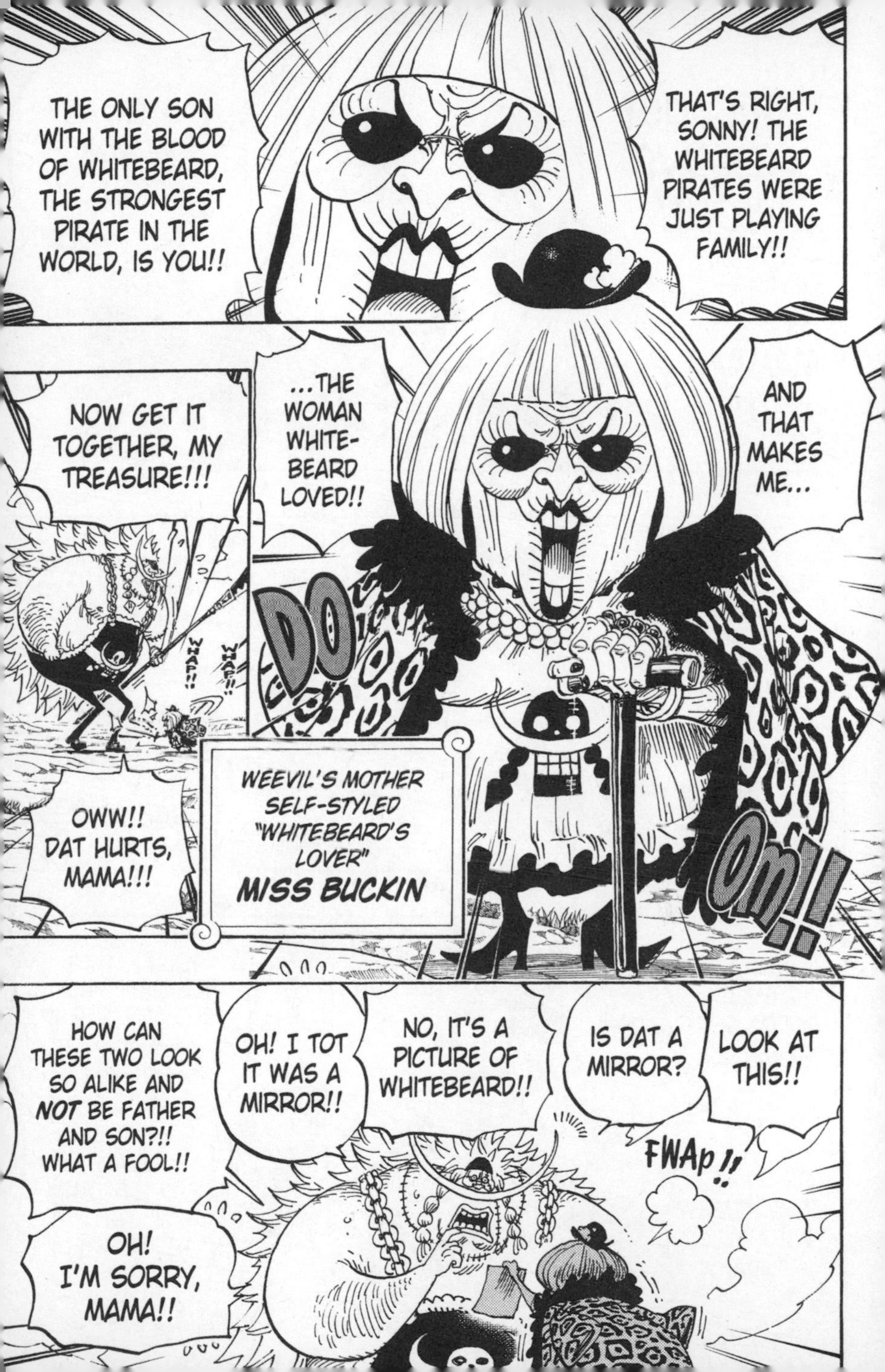
THAT'S RIGHT, SONNY! THE WHITEBEARD PIRATES WERE JUST PLAYING FAMILY!!
THE ONLY SON WITH THE BLOOD OF WHITEBEARD, THE STRONGEST PIRATE IN THE WORLD, IS YOU!!
AND THAT MAKES ME...
...THE WOMAN WHITEBEARD LOVED!!
DOOM!!
WEEVIL'S MOTHER SELF-STYLED "WHITEBEARD'S LOVER" MISS BUCKIN
NOW GET IT TOGETHER, MY TREASURE!!!
WHAP!!
WHAP!!
OWW!! DAT HURTS, MAMA!!!
LOOK AT THIS!!
FWAp!!
IS DAT A MIRROR?
NO, IT'S A PICTURE OF WHITEBEARD!!
OH! I TOT IT WAS A MIRROR!!
HOW CAN THESE TWO LOOK SO ALIKE AND NOT BE FATHER AND SON?!! WHAT A FOOL!!
OH! I'M SORRY, MAMA!!

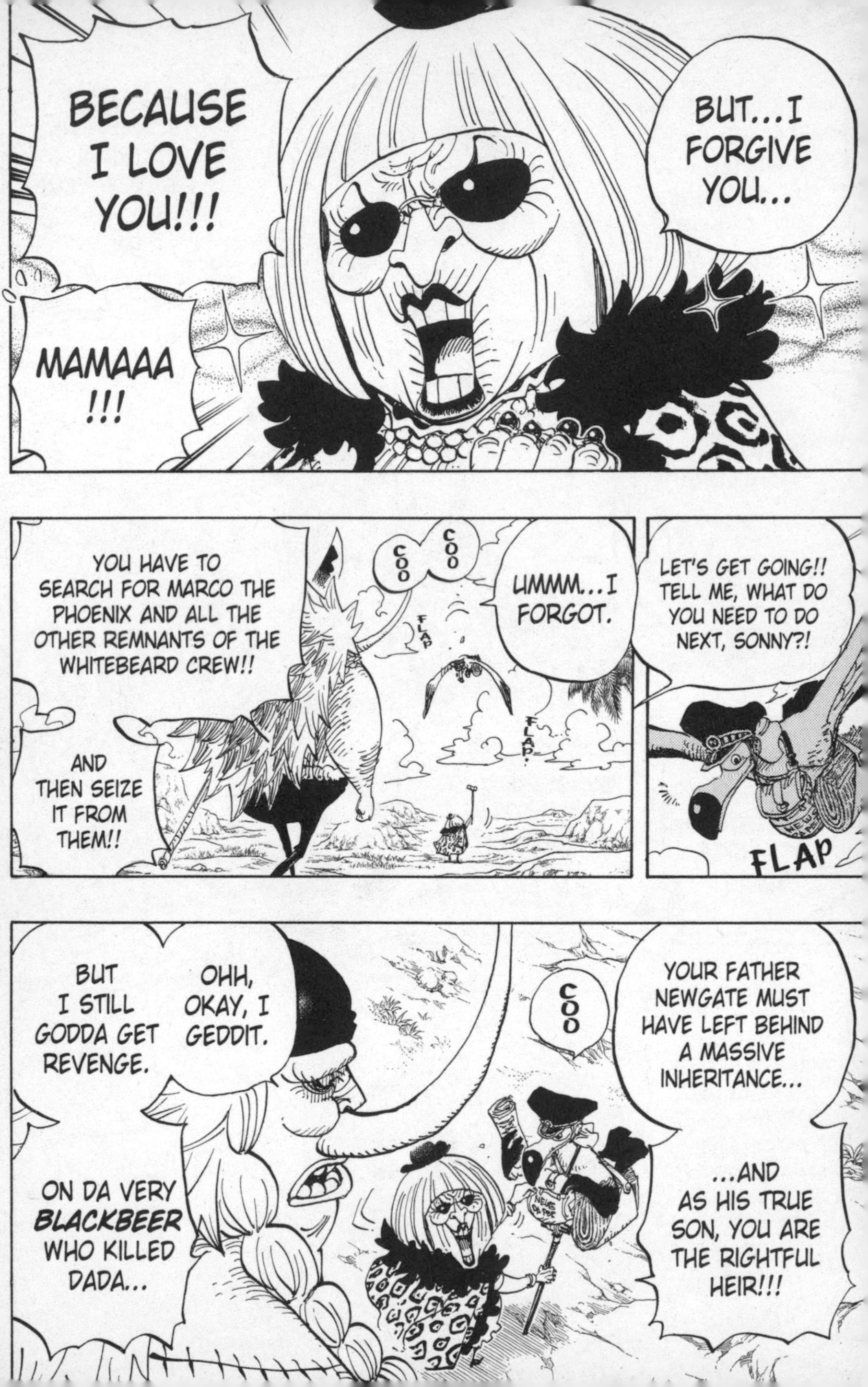
BUT...I FORGIVE YOU...
BECAUSE I LOVE YOU!!!
MAMAAA!!!
LET'S GET GOING!! TELL ME, WHAT DO YOU NEED TO DO NEXT, SONNY?!
FLAP
UMMM...I FORGOT.
COO
COO
FLAP
FLAP
YOU HAVE TO SEARCH FOR MARCO THE PHOENIX AND ALL THE OTHER REMNANTS OF THE WHITEBEARD CREW!!
AND THEN SEIZE IT FROM THEM!!
YOUR FATHER NEWGATE MUST HAVE LEFT BEHIND A MASSIVE INHERITANCE...
...AND AS HIS TRUE SON, YOU ARE THE RIGHTFUL HEIR!!!
COO
OHH, OKAY, I GEDDIT.
BUT I STILL GODDA GET REVENGE.
ON DA VERY *BLACKBEER* WHO KILLED DADA...

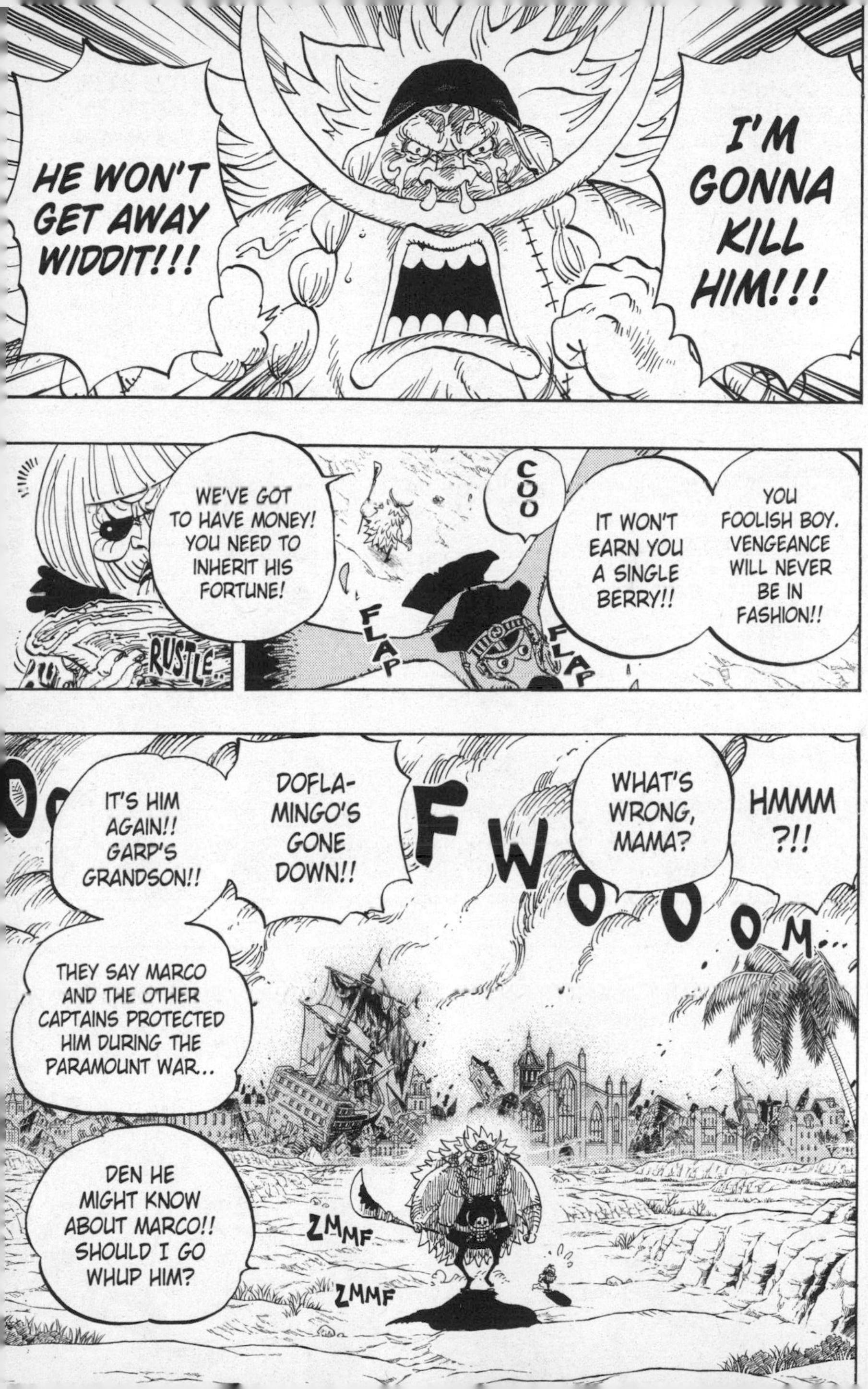
I'M GONNA KILL HIM!!!
HE WON'T GET AWAY WIDDIT!!!
YOU FOOLISH BOY. VENGEANCE WILL NEVER BE IN FASHION!!
IT WON'T EARN YOU A SINGLE BERRY!!
COO
FLAP
FLAP
WE'VE GOT TO HAVE MONEY! YOU NEED TO INHERIT HIS FORTUNE!
RUSTLE..
HMMM ?!!
WHAT'S WRONG, MAMA?
FWOOOOM...
DOFLA-MINGO'S GONE DOWN!!
IT'S HIM AGAIN!! GARP'S GRANDSON!!
THEY SAY MARCO AND THE OTHER CAPTAINS PROTECTED HIM DURING THE PARAMOUNT WAR..
DEN HE MIGHT KNOW ABOUT MARCO!! SHOULD I GO WHUP HIM?
ZMMF
ZMMF

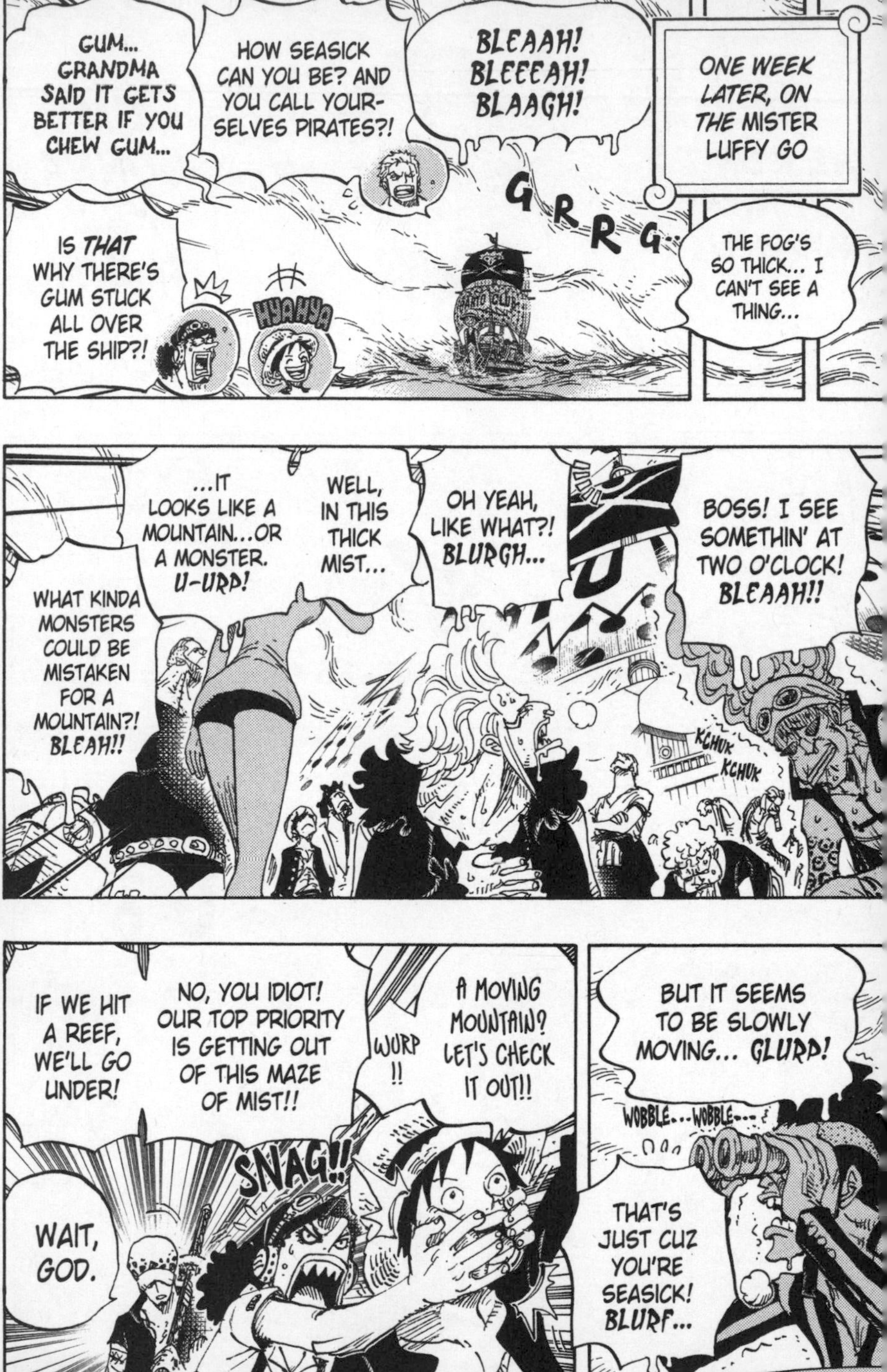
ONE WEEK LATER, ON THE MISTER LUFFY GO
THE FOG'S SO THICK... I CAN'T SEE A THING...
GRRRG
BLEAAH! BLEEEAH! BLAAGH!
HOW SEASICK CAN YOU BE? AND YOU CALL YOURSELVES PIRATES?!
GUM... GRANDMA SAID IT GETS BETTER IF YOU CHEW GUM...
IS THAT WHY THERE'S GUM STUCK ALL OVER THE SHIP?!
HYAHYA
BOSS! I SEE SOMETHIN' AT TWO O'CLOCK! BLEAAH!!
OH YEAH, LIKE WHAT?! BLURGH...
WELL, IN THIS THICK MIST...
...IT LOOKS LIKE A MOUNTAIN...OR A MONSTER. U-URP!
WHAT KINDA MONSTERS COULD BE MISTAKEN FOR A MOUNTAIN?! BLEAH!!
KCHUK KCHUK
BUT IT SEEMS TO BE SLOWLY MOVING... GLURP!
WOBBLE... WOBBLE...
THAT'S JUST CUZ YOU'RE SEASICK! BLURF...
A MOVING MOUNTAIN? LET'S CHECK IT OUT!!
WURP !!
NO, YOU IDIOT! OUR TOP PRIORITY IS GETTING OUT OF THIS MAZE OF MIST!!
IF WE HIT A REEF, WE'LL GO UNDER!
SNAG!!
WAIT, GOD.

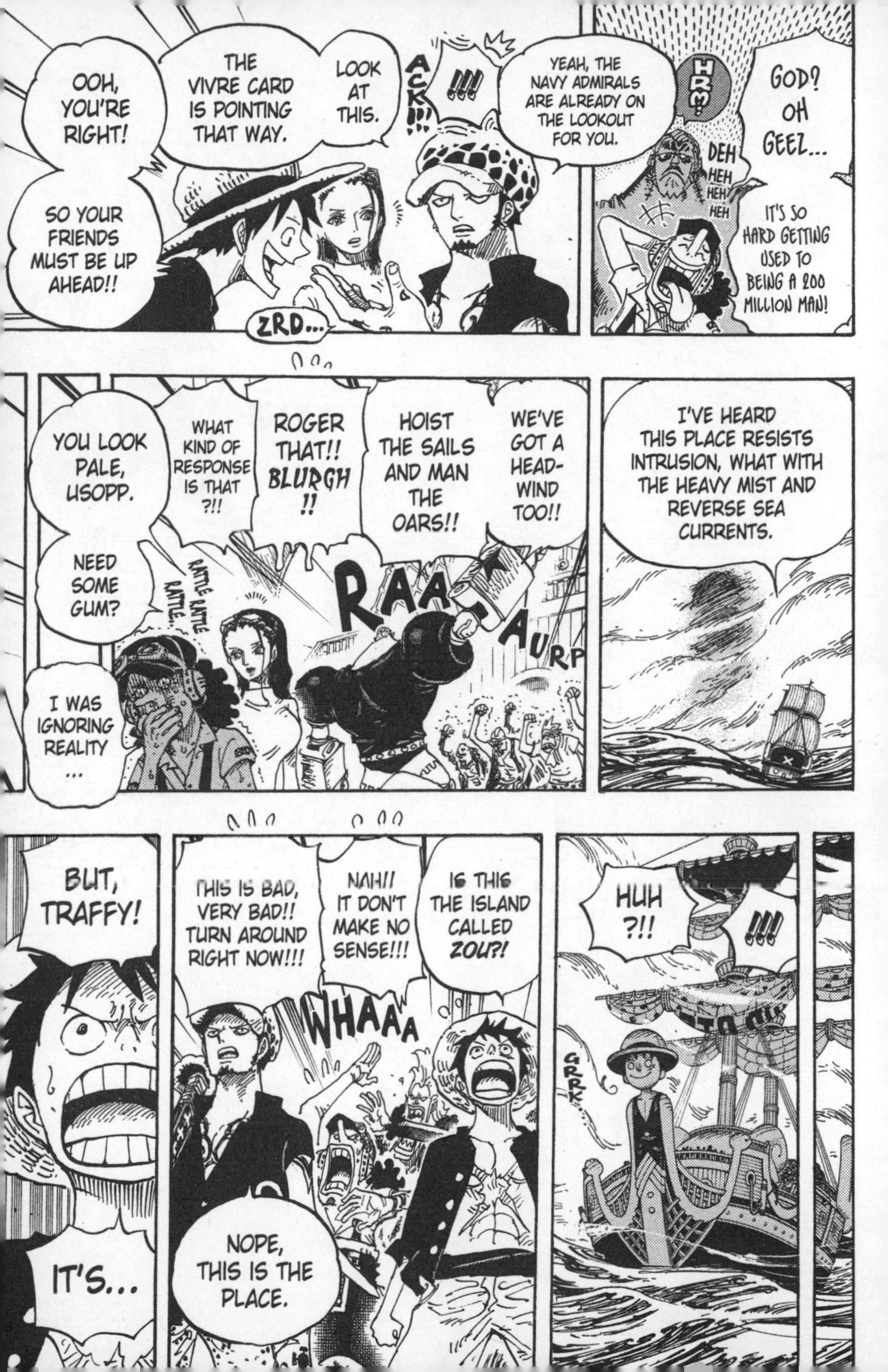
GOD? OH GEEZ...
HRM
DEH HEH HEH HEH
IT'S SO HARD GETTING USED TO BEING A 200 MILLION MAN!
YEAH, THE NAVY ADMIRALS ARE ALREADY ON THE LOOKOUT FOR YOU.
!!!
ACK!!!
LOOK AT THIS.
THE VIVRE CARD IS POINTING THAT WAY.
OOH, YOU'RE RIGHT!
SO YOUR FRIENDS MUST BE UP AHEAD!!
ZRD...
I'VE HEARD THIS PLACE RESISTS INTRUSION, WHAT WITH THE HEAVY MIST AND REVERSE SEA CURRENTS.
WE'VE GOT A HEAD-WIND TOO!!
HOIST THE SAILS AND MAN THE OARS!!
ROGER THAT!! BLURGH !!
WHAT KIND OF RESPONSE IS THAT ?!!
RAA
AURP
YOU LOOK PALE, USOPP.
RATTLE RATTLE...
NEED SOME GUM?
I WAS IGNORING REALITY ...
!!!
HUH ?!!
GRRK...
IS THIS THE ISLAND CALLED ZOU?!
NAH!! IT DON'T MAKE NO SENSE!!!
THIS IS BAD, VERY BAD!! TURN AROUND RIGHT NOW!!!
WHAAAA
NOPE, THIS IS THE PLACE.
BUT, TRAFFY!
IT'S...

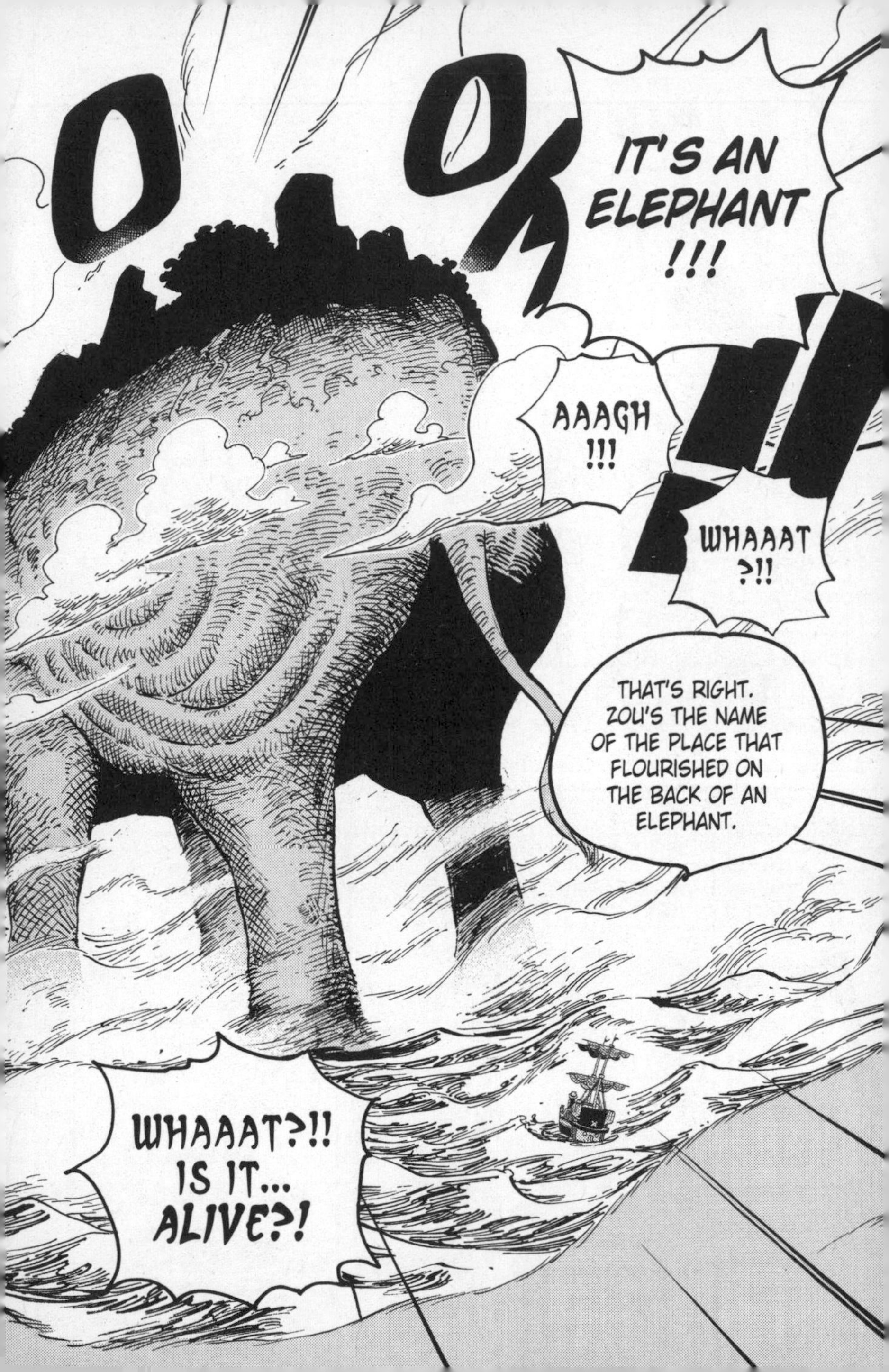
IT'S AN ELEPHANT !!!
AAAGH !!!
WHAAAT ?!!
THAT'S RIGHT. ZOU'S THE NAME OF THE PLACE THAT FLOURISHED ON THE BACK OF AN ELEPHANT.
WHAAAT?!! IS IT... ALIVE?!

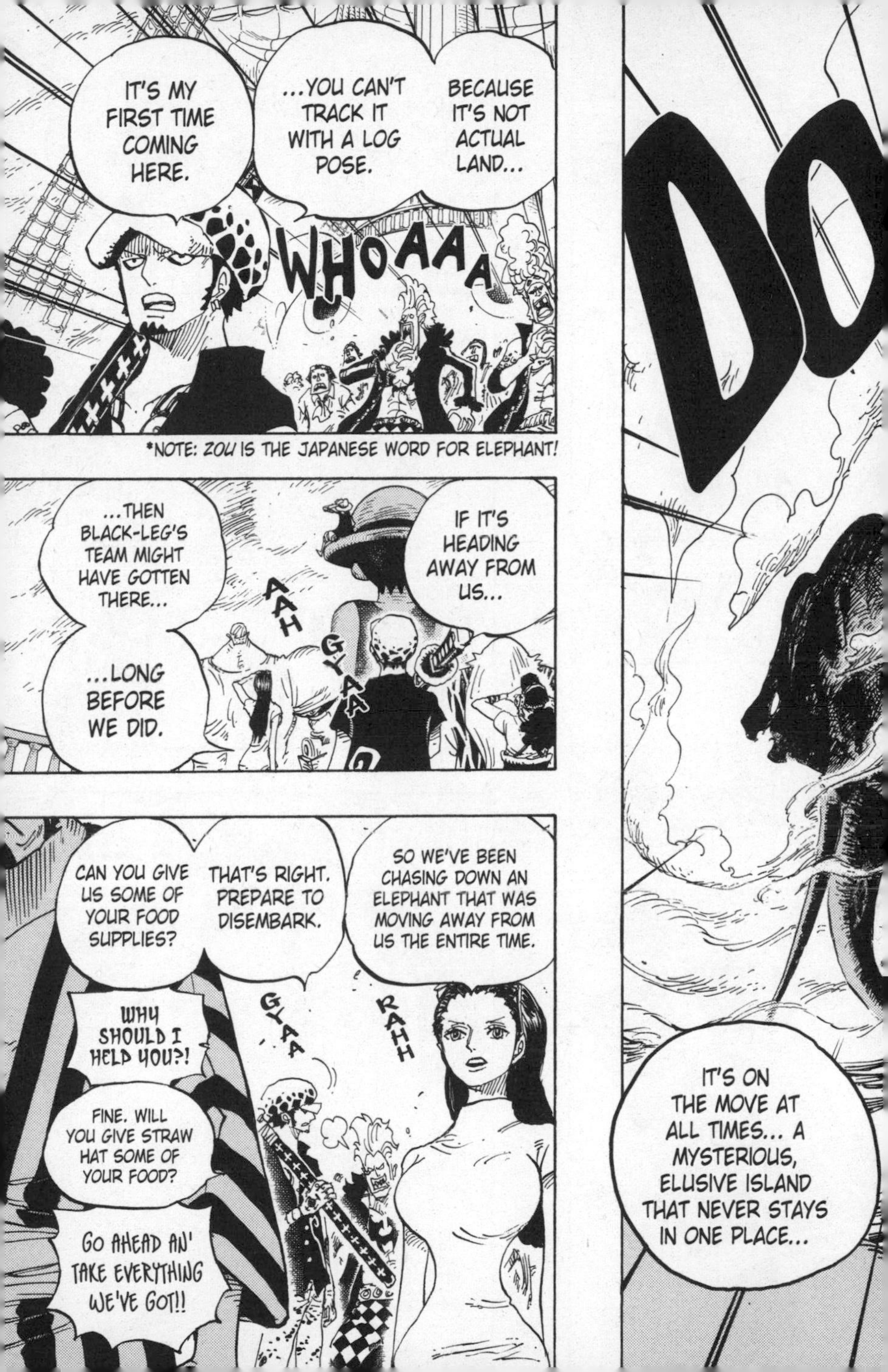
DO
IT'S ON THE MOVE AT ALL TIMES... A MYSTERIOUS, ELUSIVE ISLAND THAT NEVER STAYS IN ONE PLACE...
BECAUSE IT'S NOT ACTUAL LAND...
...YOU CAN'T TRACK IT WITH A LOG POSE.
IT'S MY FIRST TIME COMING HERE.
WHOAAA
*NOTE: *ZOU* IS THE JAPANESE WORD FOR ELEPHANT!
IF IT'S HEADING AWAY FROM US...
GYAA
AAH
...THEN BLACK-LEG'S TEAM MIGHT HAVE GOTTEN THERE...
...LONG BEFORE WE DID.
SO WE'VE BEEN CHASING DOWN AN ELEPHANT THAT WAS MOVING AWAY FROM US THE ENTIRE TIME.
RAHH
GYAA
THAT'S RIGHT. PREPARE TO DISEMBARK.
CAN YOU GIVE US SOME OF YOUR FOOD SUPPLIES?
WHY SHOULD I HELP YOU?!
FINE. WILL YOU GIVE STRAW HAT SOME OF YOUR FOOD?
GO AHEAD AN' TAKE EVERYTHING WE'VE GOT!!

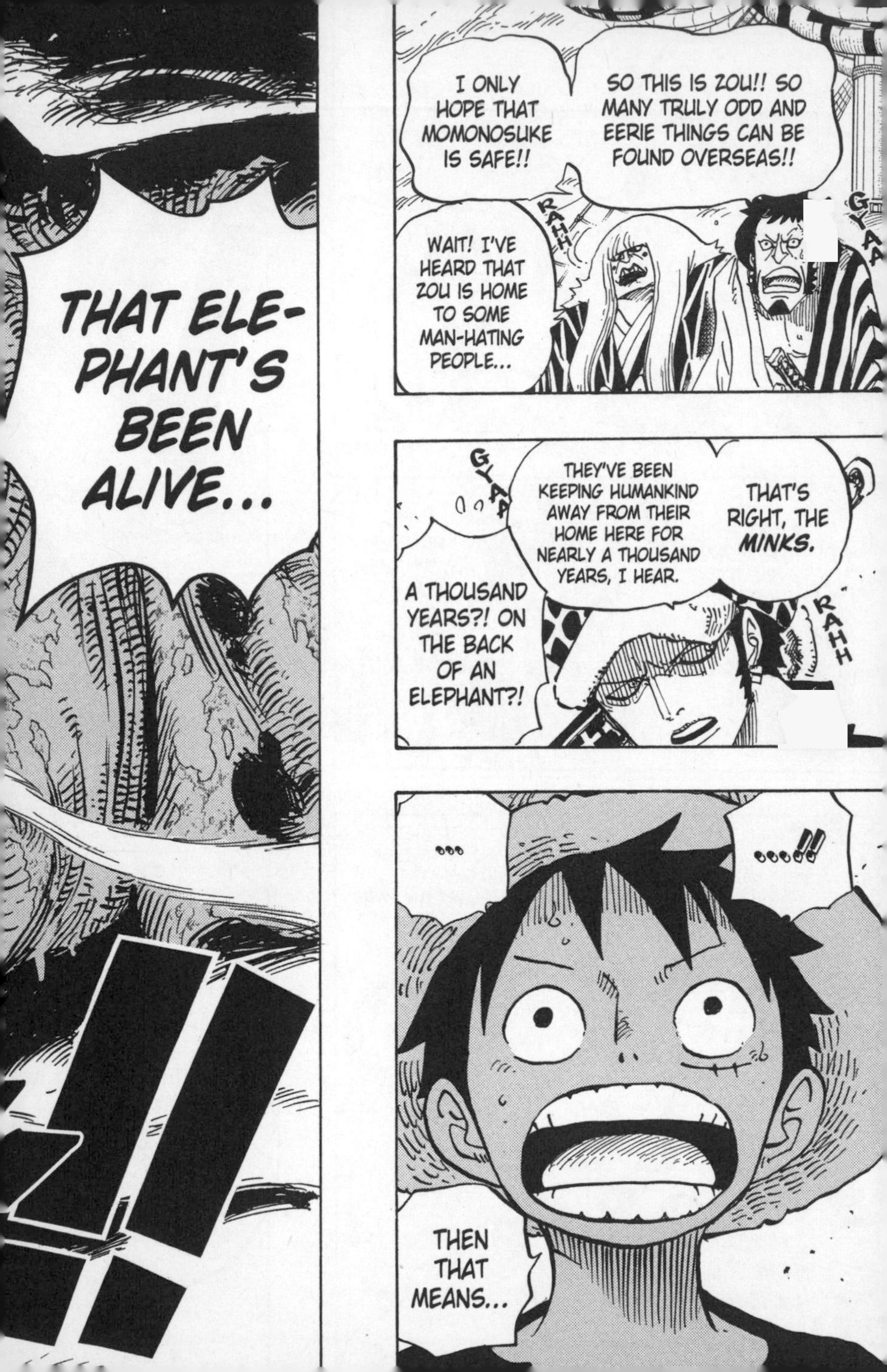
GYAA
SO THIS IS ZOU!! SO MANY TRULY ODD AND EERIE THINGS CAN BE FOUND OVERSEAS!!
I ONLY HOPE THAT MOMONOSUKE IS SAFE!!
RAHH
WAIT! I'VE HEARD THAT ZOU IS HOME TO SOME MAN-HATING PEOPLE...
RAHH
THAT'S RIGHT, THE *MINKS.*
THEY'VE BEEN KEEPING HUMANKIND AWAY FROM THEIR HOME HERE FOR NEARLY A THOUSAND YEARS, I HEAR.
GYAA
A THOUSAND YEARS?! ON THE BACK OF AN ELEPHANT?!
......!!
...
THEN THAT MEANS...
THAT ELE-PHANT'S BEEN ALIVE...
!!

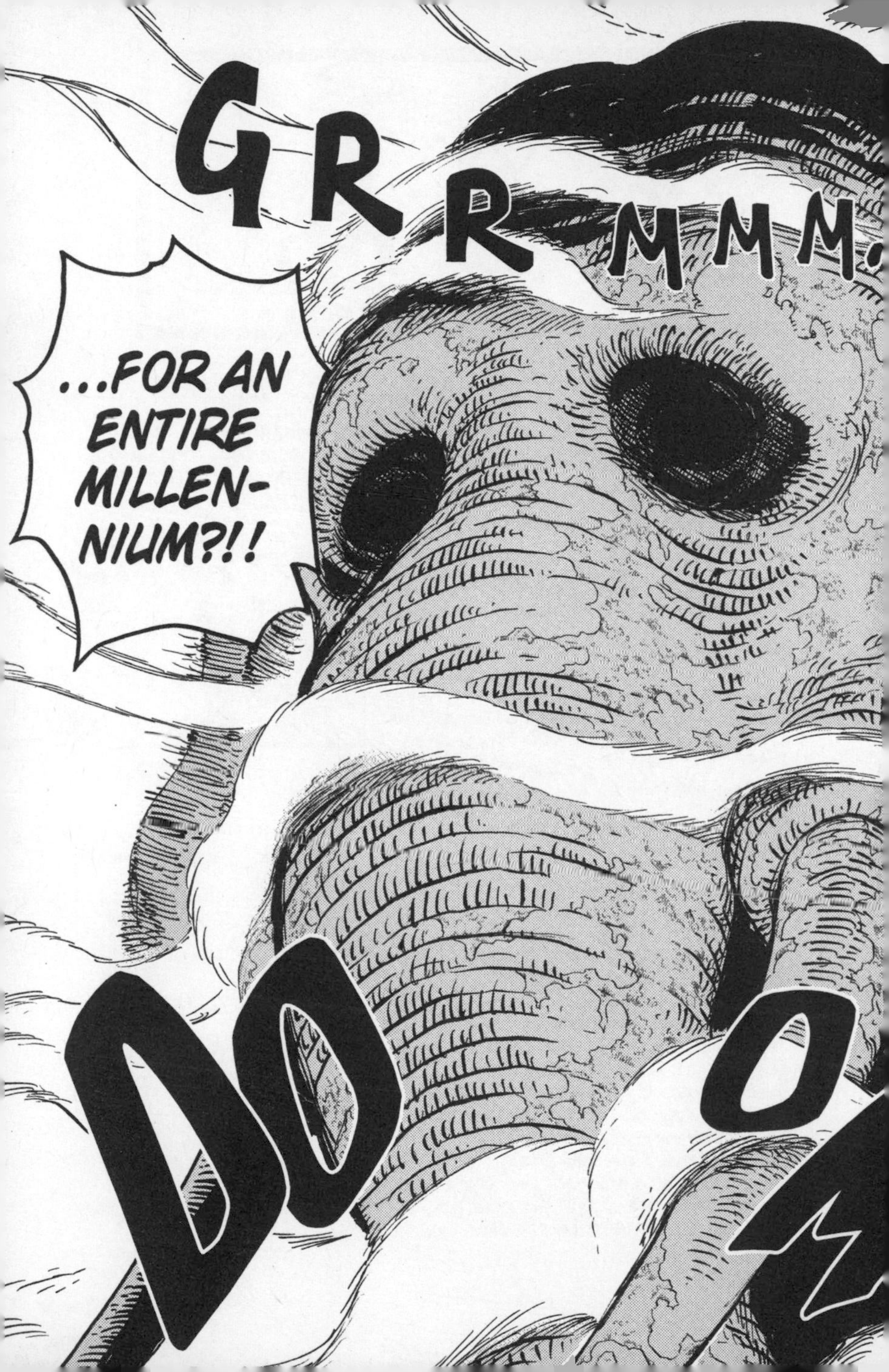
GRRMMM...
...FOR AN ENTIRE MILLEN-NIUM?!!
DOO

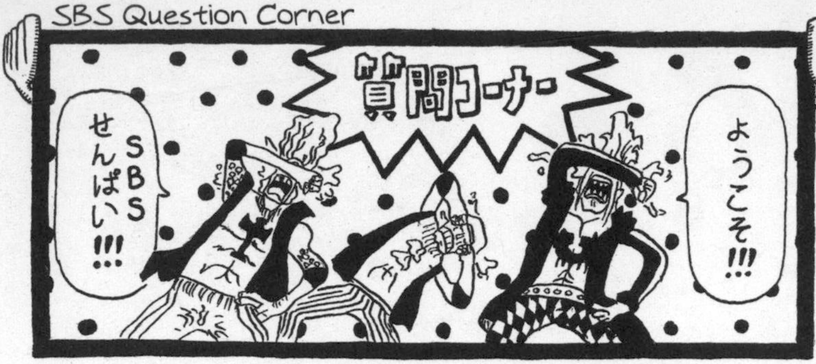
質問コーナー
ようこそ!!!
SBSせんぱい!!!

(Snir, Australia)

Q: In the flashback to the Corrida Coliseum in Chapter 794, Luffy says, "Bwat hadda gug thod yuza deah!!! Whah kuh bom da flubba ahh ga ueaahh!!" What exactly is he trying to say? If I could interpret, it would be "What the hell, I wanted to spend so much more time with you!!! Man…Odacchi's obsession with big boobs is crazy, right?" Is that correct?

--Shuntamu from Kumamoto

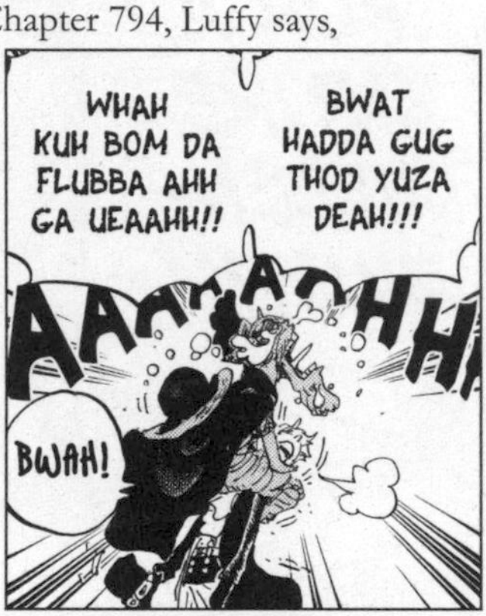
BWAT HADDA GUG THOD YUZA DEAH!!!
WHAH KUH BOM DA FLUBBA AHH GA UEAAHH!!
BWAH!

A: Bzzt, wrong. The latter part was so wrong, it practically defies belief. The correct answer is this: "What the hell, where have you been all this time?!! I was so sure you were dead. I'm so glad. By the way, Odacchi's obsession with big boobs is crazy, right?"

Q: Mr. Oda! Heso! I noticed that the ruined island Balloon Terminal that Urouge was on recently had a ton of balloons stuck to it... Is it floating with the power of the balloons?!

--Kamiki

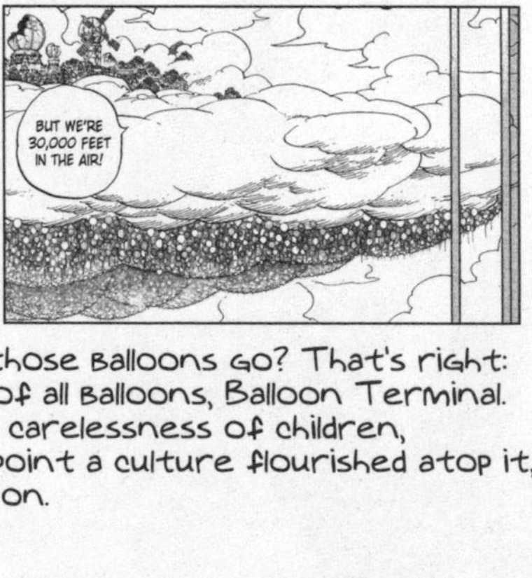
BUT WE'RE 30,000 FEET IN THE AIR!

A: You were looking very closely (^ ^). That's right! Balloons are packed full of helium gas, the very personification of the "desire to fly." We've all seen what happens when a child lets go of a balloon and it flies away to much crying and screaming. So where do those balloons go? That's right: to this, the final destination of all balloons, Balloon Terminal. It's a sky island born from the carelessness of children, wandering the skies. At one point a culture flourished atop it, then died out, but it still flies on.

# Chapter 803: ELEPHANT CLIMBING

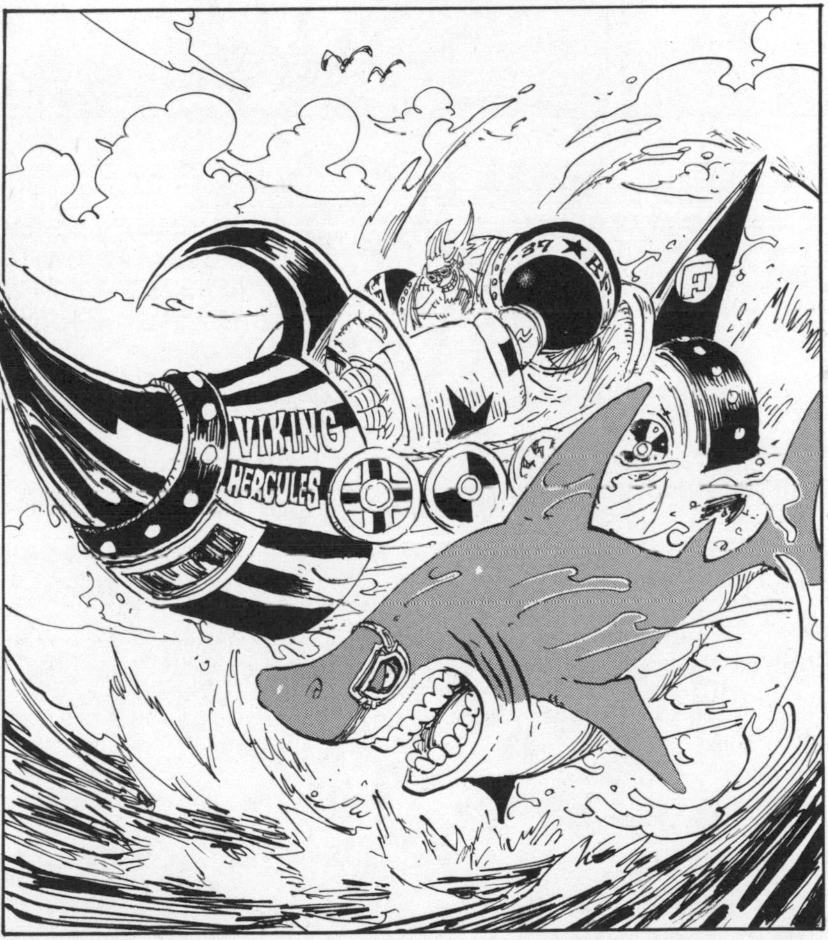
VIKING
HERCULES

REQUEST: "FRANKY RACING A SHARK IN A SHIP DESIGNED BY USOPP" BY GEZIO FROM FUKUSHIMA

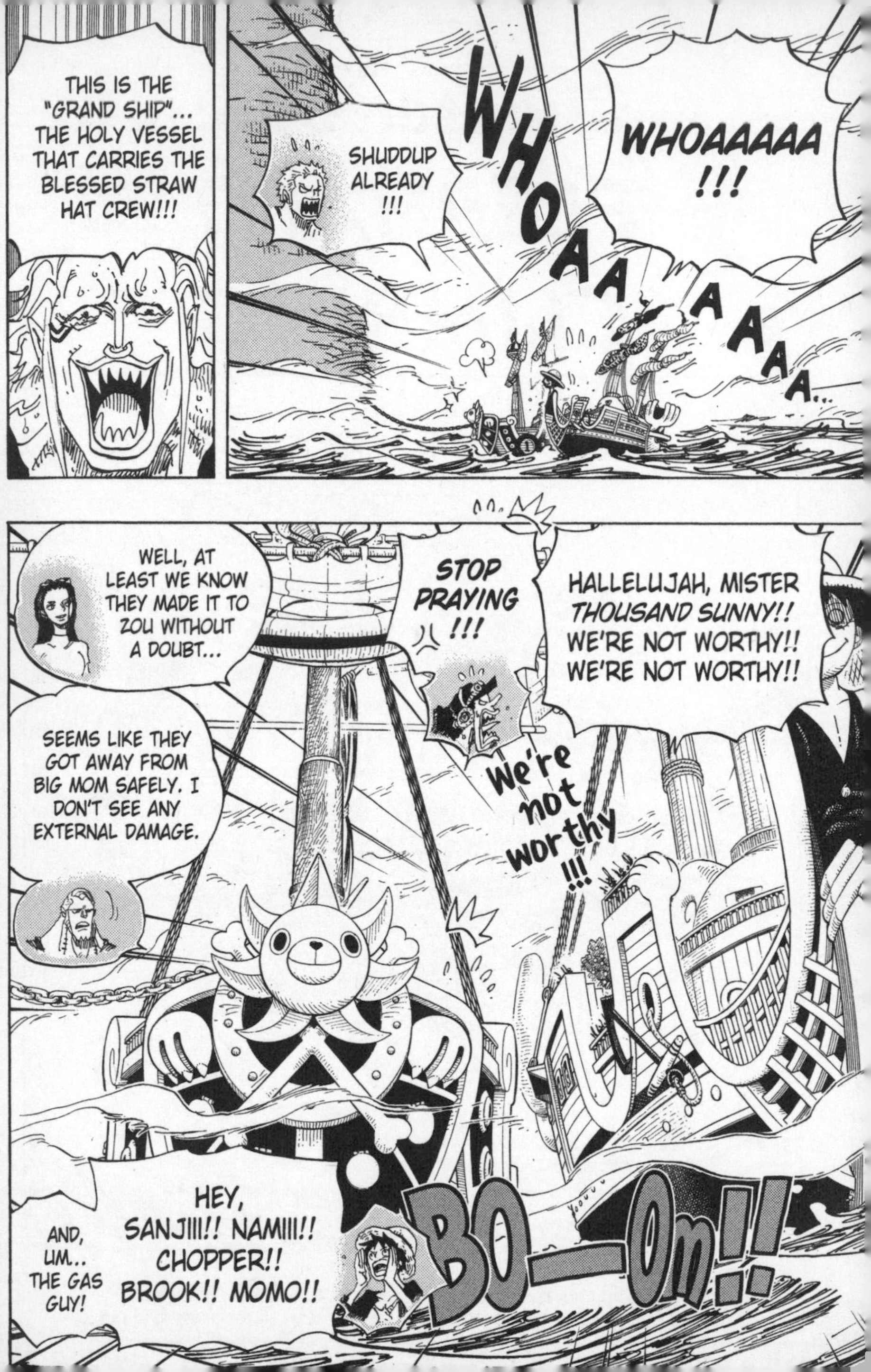
WHOAAAAA !!!
WHOAAAAAA...
SHUDDUP ALREADY !!!
THIS IS THE "GRAND SHIP"... THE HOLY VESSEL THAT CARRIES THE BLESSED STRAW HAT CREW!!!
HALLELUJAH, MISTER *THOUSAND SUNNY*!! WE'RE NOT WORTHY!! WE'RE NOT WORTHY!!
STOP PRAYING !!!
We're not worthy !!!
WELL, AT LEAST WE KNOW THEY MADE IT TO ZOU WITHOUT A DOUBT...
SEEMS LIKE THEY GOT AWAY FROM BIG MOM SAFELY. I DON'T SEE ANY EXTERNAL DAMAGE.
BO-OM!!
HEY, SANJIII!! NAMIII!! CHOPPER!! BROOK!! MOMO!!
AND, UM... THE GAS GUY!

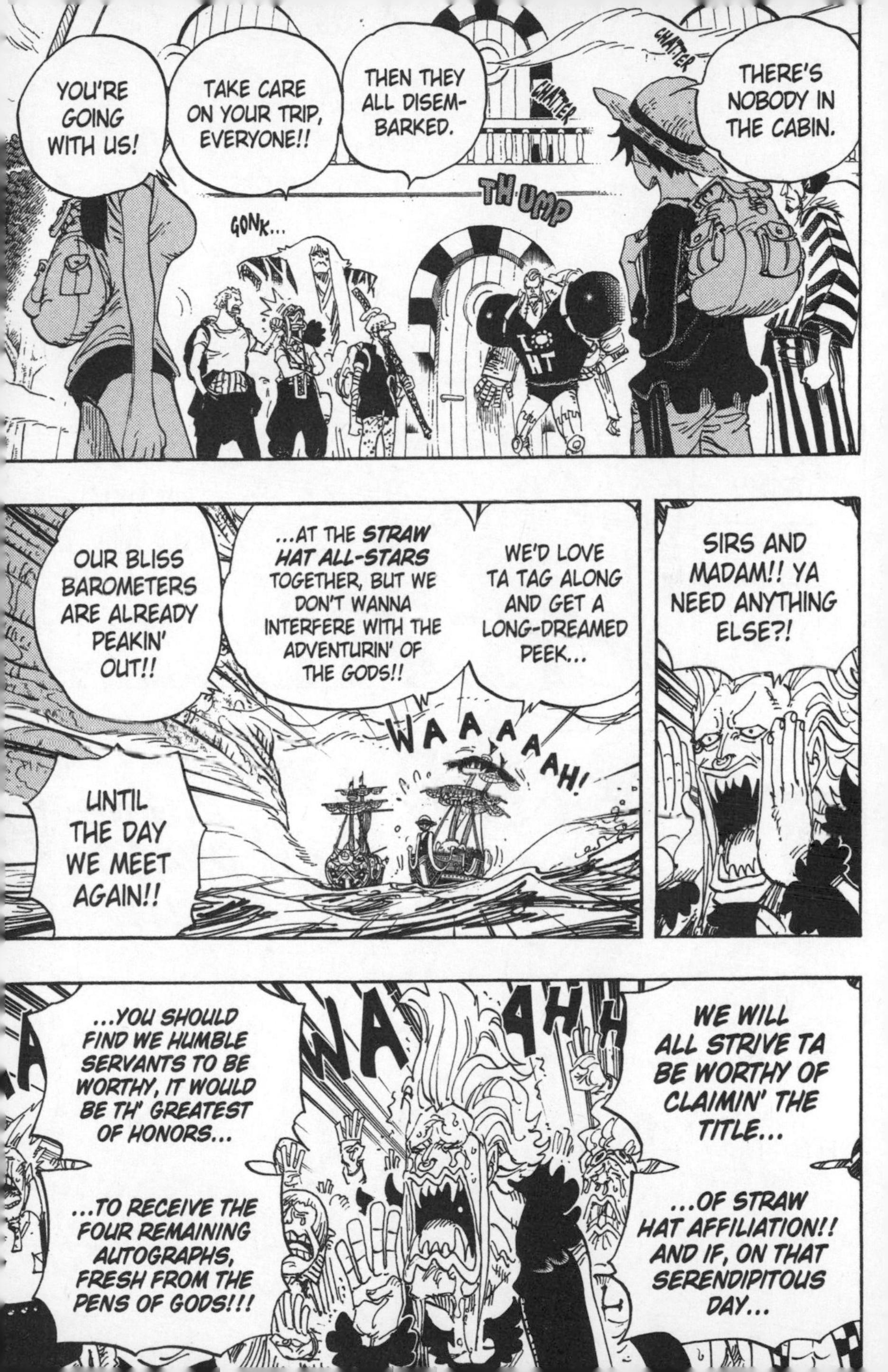
CHATTER
CHATTER
THERE'S NOBODY IN THE CABIN.
THEN THEY ALL DISEMBARKED.
THUMP
TAKE CARE ON YOUR TRIP, EVERYONE!!
YOU'RE GOING WITH US!
GONK...
SIRS AND MADAM!! YA NEED ANYTHING ELSE?!
WE'D LOVE TA TAG ALONG AND GET A LONG-DREAMED PEEK...
...AT THE STRAW HAT ALL-STARS TOGETHER, BUT WE DON'T WANNA INTERFERE WITH THE ADVENTURIN' OF THE GODS!!
OUR BLISS BAROMETERS ARE ALREADY PEAKIN' OUT!!
WAAAAAH!
UNTIL THE DAY WE MEET AGAIN!!
WE WILL ALL STRIVE TA BE WORTHY OF CLAIMIN' THE TITLE...
...OF STRAW HAT AFFILIATION!! AND IF, ON THAT SERENDIPITOUS DAY...
WAAHH
...YOU SHOULD FIND WE HUMBLE SERVANTS TO BE WORTHY, IT WOULD BE TH' GREATEST OF HONORS...
...TO RECEIVE THE FOUR REMAINING AUTOGRAPHS, FRESH FROM THE PENS OF GODS!!!

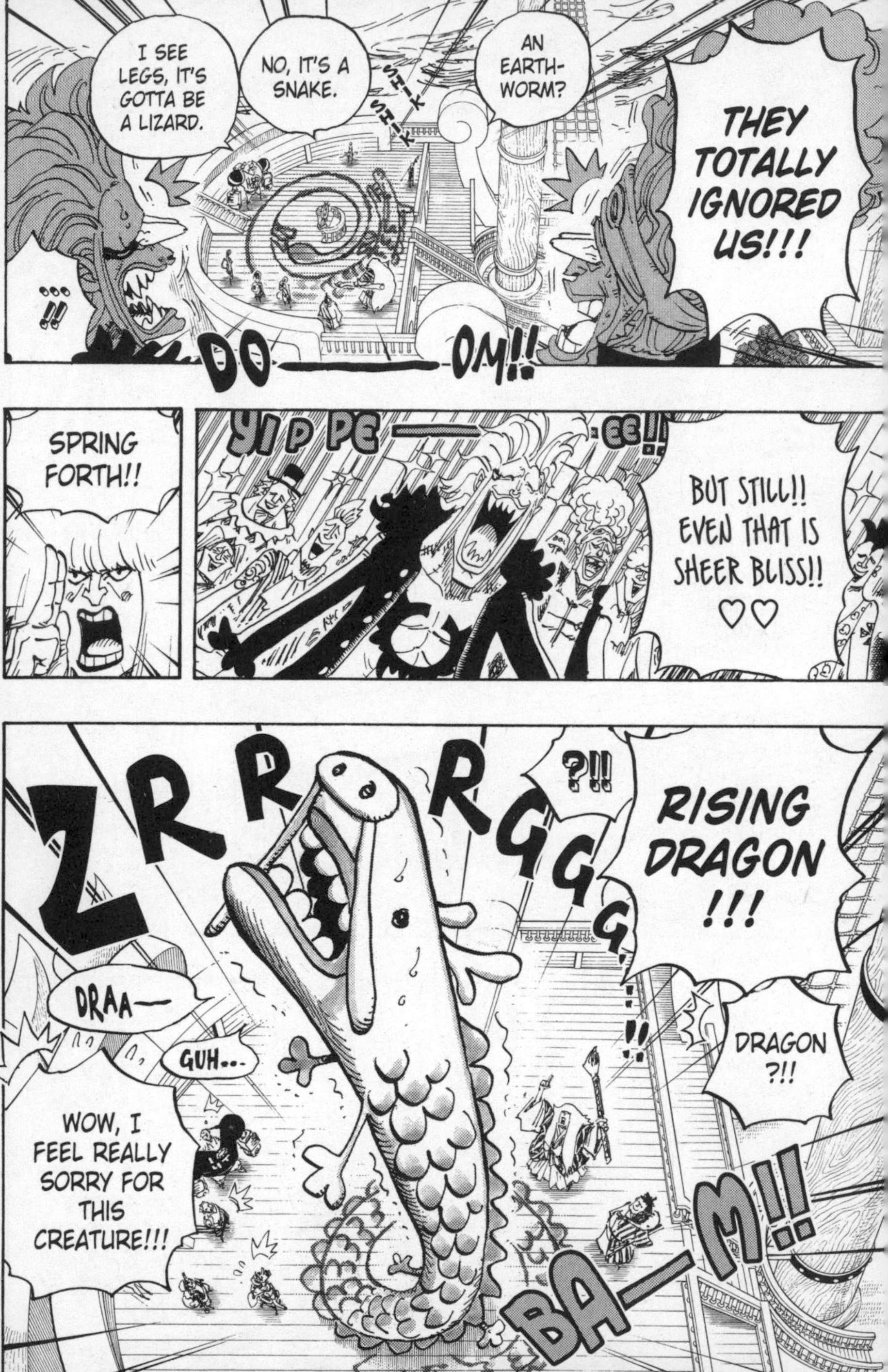
THEY TOTALLY IGNORED US!!!
AN EARTH-WORM?
SHI-K SHI-K
NO, IT'S A SNAKE.
I SEE LEGS, IT'S GOTTA BE A LIZARD.
...!!
DO—OM!!
BUT STILL!! EVEN THAT IS SHEER BLISS!! ♡♡
YIPPE—EE!!
SPRING FORTH!!
?!!
RISING DRAGON!!!
ZRRRGGGG..!!
DRAGON?!!
BA—M!!
DRAA—
GUH...
WOW, I FEEL REALLY SORRY FOR THIS CREATURE!!!

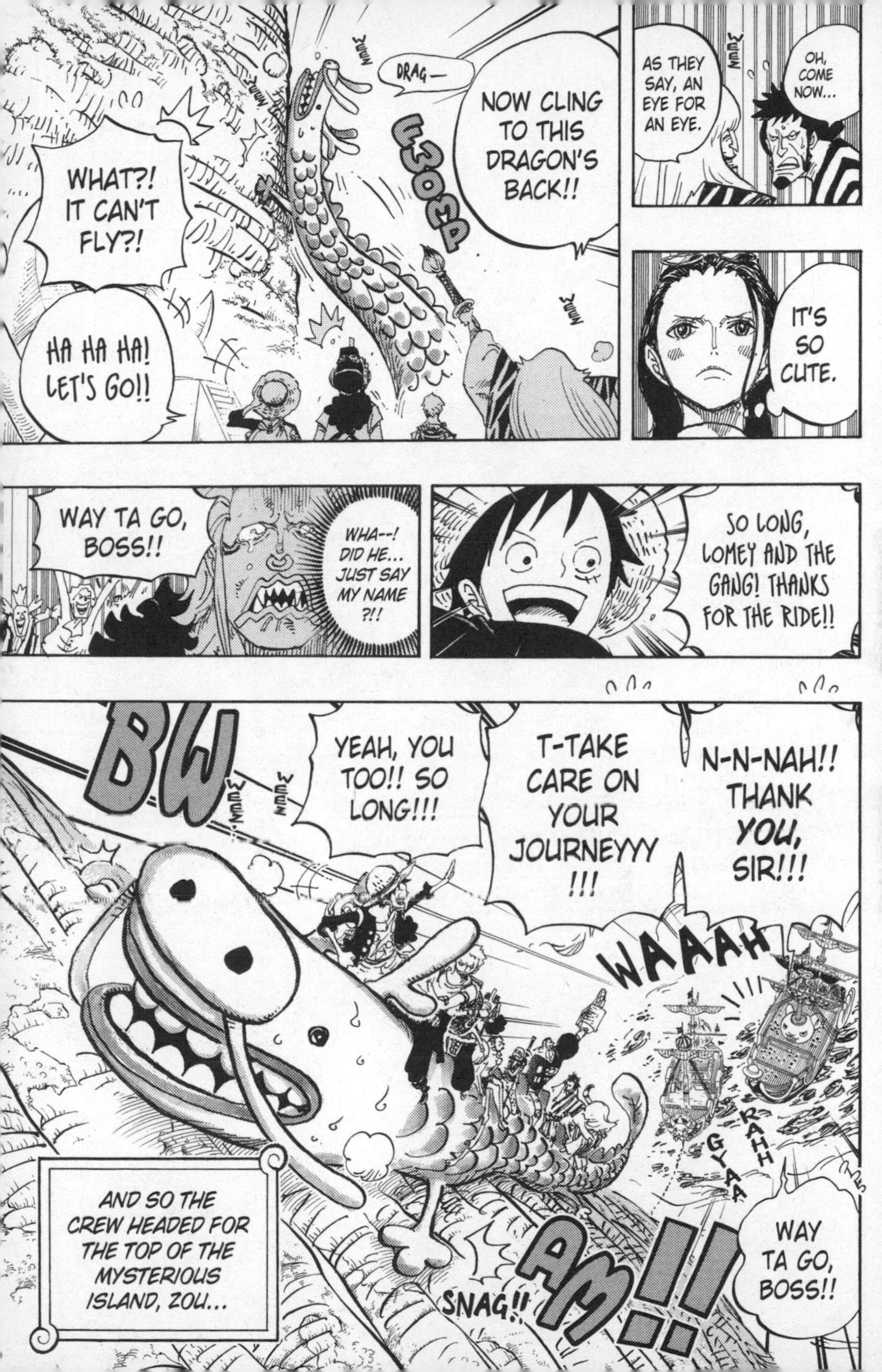
OH, COME NOW...
AS THEY SAY, AN EYE FOR AN EYE.
IT'S SO CUTE.
NOW CLING TO THIS DRAGON'S BACK!!
DRAG—
FWOMP
WHAT?! IT CAN'T FLY?!
HA HA HA! LET'S GO!!
SO LONG, LOMEY AND THE GANG! THANKS FOR THE RIDE!!
WHA--! DID HE... JUST SAY MY NAME ?!!
WAY TA GO, BOSS!!
N-N-NAH!! THANK YOU, SIR!!!
T-TAKE CARE ON YOUR JOURNEYYY !!!
YEAH, YOU TOO!! SO LONG!!!
BWAM!!
WAAAH
RAHH
GYAA
WAY TA GO, BOSS!!
SNAG!!
AND SO THE CREW HEADED FOR THE TOP OF THE MYSTERIOUS ISLAND, ZOU...

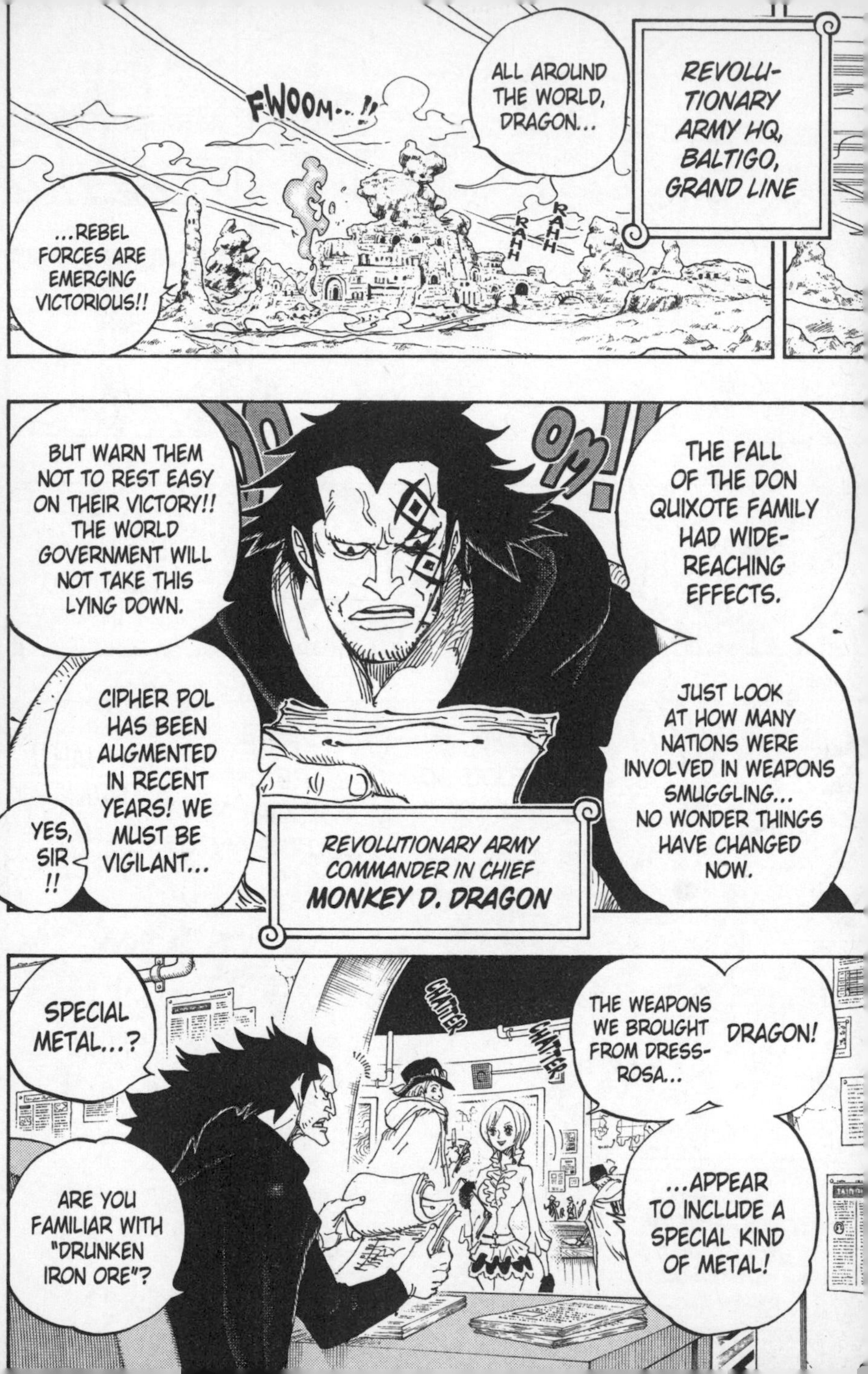
REVOLUTIONARY ARMY HQ, BALTIGO, GRAND LINE
ALL AROUND THE WORLD, DRAGON...
FWOOM...!!
RAHH RAHH
...REBEL FORCES ARE EMERGING VICTORIOUS!!
THE FALL OF THE DON QUIXOTE FAMILY HAD WIDE-REACHING EFFECTS.
JUST LOOK AT HOW MANY NATIONS WERE INVOLVED IN WEAPONS SMUGGLING... NO WONDER THINGS HAVE CHANGED NOW.
OM!!
BUT WARN THEM NOT TO REST EASY ON THEIR VICTORY!! THE WORLD GOVERNMENT WILL NOT TAKE THIS LYING DOWN.
REVOLUTIONARY ARMY COMMANDER IN CHIEF MONKEY D. DRAGON
CIPHER POL HAS BEEN AUGMENTED IN RECENT YEARS! WE MUST BE VIGILANT...
YES, SIR!!
DRAGON!
THE WEAPONS WE BROUGHT FROM DRESS-ROSA...
...APPEAR TO INCLUDE A SPECIAL KIND OF METAL!
CHATTER
CHATTER
SPECIAL METAL...?
ARE YOU FAMILIAR WITH "DRUNKEN IRON ORE"?

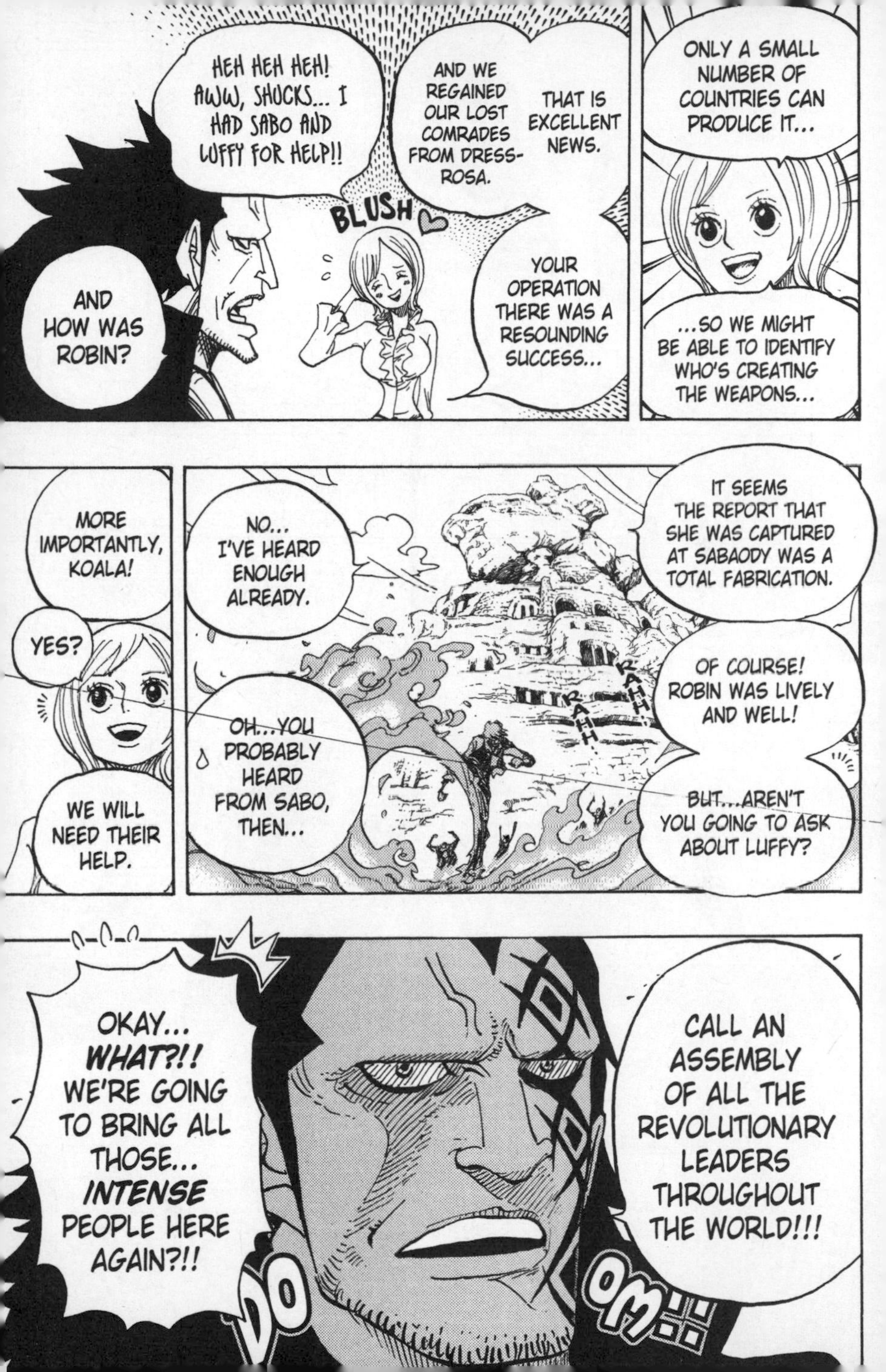
ONLY A SMALL NUMBER OF COUNTRIES CAN PRODUCE IT...
...SO WE MIGHT BE ABLE TO IDENTIFY WHO'S CREATING THE WEAPONS...
AND WE REGAINED OUR LOST COMRADES FROM DRESS-ROSA.
THAT IS EXCELLENT NEWS.
YOUR OPERATION THERE WAS A RESOUNDING SUCCESS...
HEH HEH HEH! AWW, SHUCKS... I HAD SABO AND LUFFY FOR HELP!!
BLUSH
AND HOW WAS ROBIN?
IT SEEMS THE REPORT THAT SHE WAS CAPTURED AT SABAODY WAS A TOTAL FABRICATION.
OF COURSE! ROBIN WAS LIVELY AND WELL!
RAHH...
RAHH...
BUT...AREN'T YOU GOING TO ASK ABOUT LUFFY?
NO... I'VE HEARD ENOUGH ALREADY.
OH...YOU PROBABLY HEARD FROM SABO, THEN...
MORE IMPORTANTLY, KOALA!
YES?
WE WILL NEED THEIR HELP.
CALL AN ASSEMBLY OF ALL THE REVOLUTIONARY LEADERS THROUGHOUT THE WORLD!!!
DOOM!!
OKAY... WHAT?!! WE'RE GOING TO BRING ALL THOSE... INTENSE PEOPLE HERE AGAIN?!!

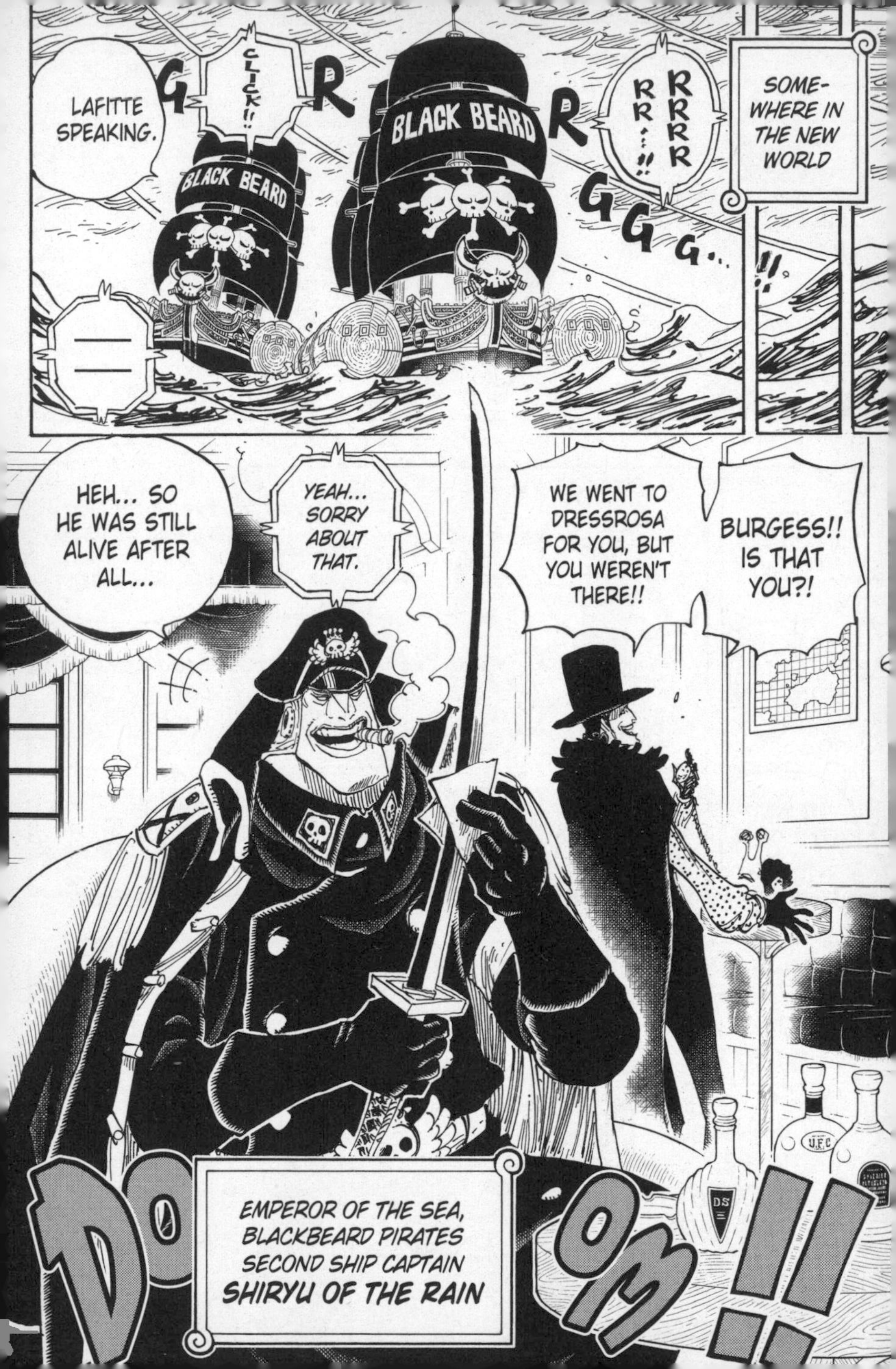
SOMEWHERE IN THE NEW WORLD
RRRR RR...!!
GRRGGG...!!
CLICK!!
LAFITTE SPEAKING.
———
BURGESS!! IS THAT YOU?!
WE WENT TO DRESSROSA FOR YOU, BUT YOU WEREN'T THERE!!
YEAH... SORRY ABOUT THAT.
HEH... SO HE WAS STILL ALIVE AFTER ALL...
DOOM!!
EMPEROR OF THE SEA, BLACKBEARD PIRATES SECOND SHIP CAPTAIN
SHIRYU OF THE RAIN

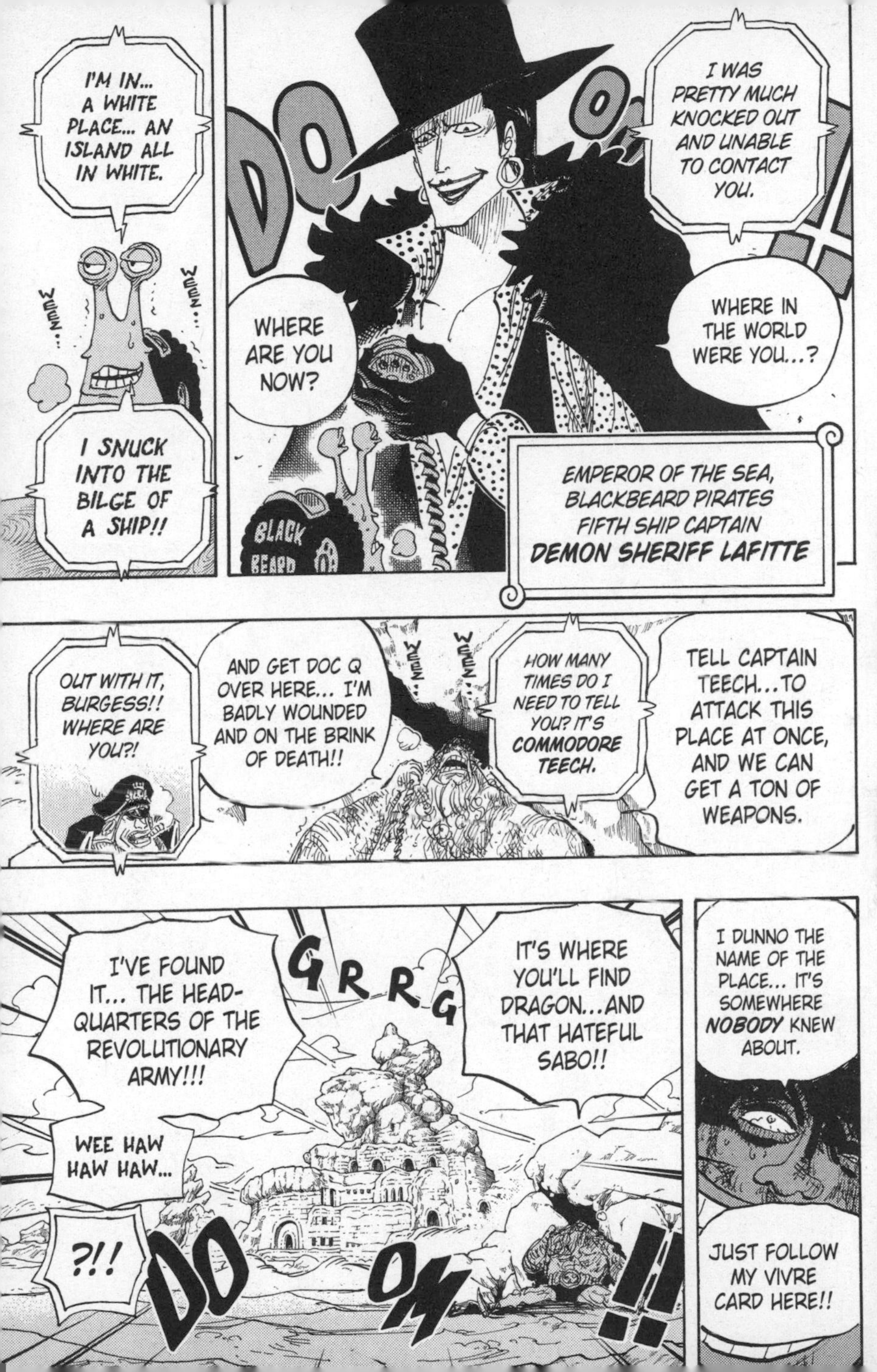
I WAS PRETTY MUCH KNOCKED OUT AND UNABLE TO CONTACT YOU.
WHERE IN THE WORLD WERE YOU...?
WHERE ARE YOU NOW?
EMPEROR OF THE SEA, BLACKBEARD PIRATES FIFTH SHIP CAPTAIN
DEMON SHERIFF LAFITTE
BLACK BEARD
I'M IN... A WHITE PLACE... AN ISLAND ALL IN WHITE.
WEEZ
WEEZ
I SNUCK INTO THE BILGE OF A SHIP!!
TELL CAPTAIN TEECH...TO ATTACK THIS PLACE AT ONCE, AND WE CAN GET A TON OF WEAPONS.
HOW MANY TIMES DO I NEED TO TELL YOU? IT'S COMMODORE TEECH.
WEEZ
WEEZ
AND GET DOC Q OVER HERE... I'M BADLY WOUNDED AND ON THE BRINK OF DEATH!!
OUT WITH IT, BURGESS!! WHERE ARE YOU?!
I DUNNO THE NAME OF THE PLACE... IT'S SOMEWHERE NOBODY KNEW ABOUT.
JUST FOLLOW MY VIVRE CARD HERE!!
IT'S WHERE YOU'LL FIND DRAGON...AND THAT HATEFUL SABO!!
GRRG
I'VE FOUND IT... THE HEAD-QUARTERS OF THE REVOLUTIONARY ARMY!!!
WEE HAW HAW HAW...
DOOM!!
?!!

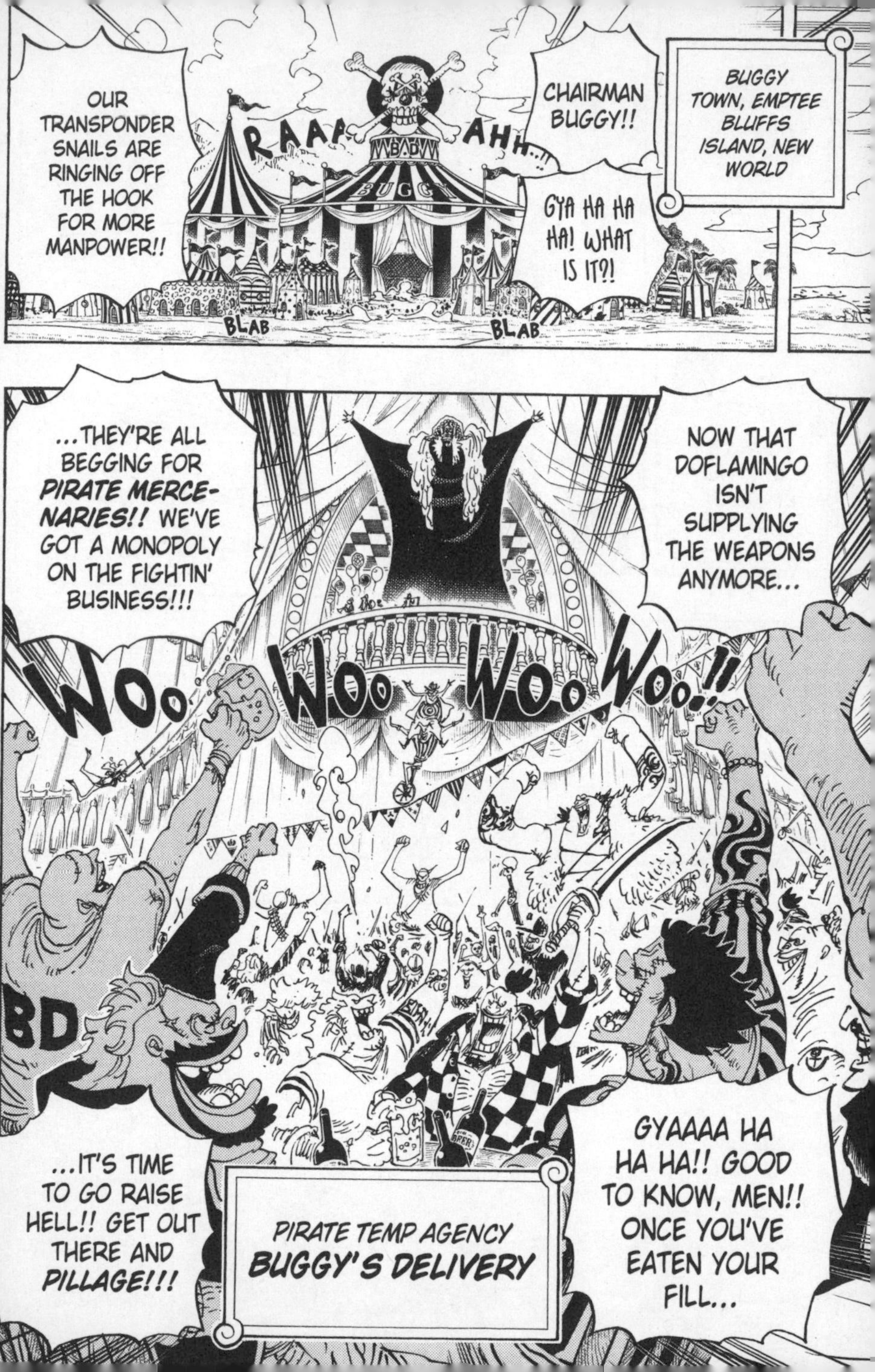
BUGGY TOWN, EMPTEE BLUFFS ISLAND, NEW WORLD
CHAIRMAN BUGGY!!
GYA HA HA HA! WHAT IS IT?!
RAAP AHH..!!
BUGGY
OUR TRANSPONDER SNAILS ARE RINGING OFF THE HOOK FOR MORE MANPOWER!!
BLAB
BLAB
NOW THAT DOFLAMINGO ISN'T SUPPLYING THE WEAPONS ANYMORE...
...THEY'RE ALL BEGGING FOR *PIRATE MERCE-NARIES!!* WE'VE GOT A MONOPOLY ON THE FIGHTIN' BUSINESS!!!
WOO WOO WOO WOO..!!
BD
GYAAAA HA HA HA!! GOOD TO KNOW, MEN!! ONCE YOU'VE EATEN YOUR FILL...
PIRATE TEMP AGENCY
**BUGGY'S DELIVERY**
...IT'S TIME TO GO RAISE HELL!! GET OUT THERE AND *PILLAGE!!!*

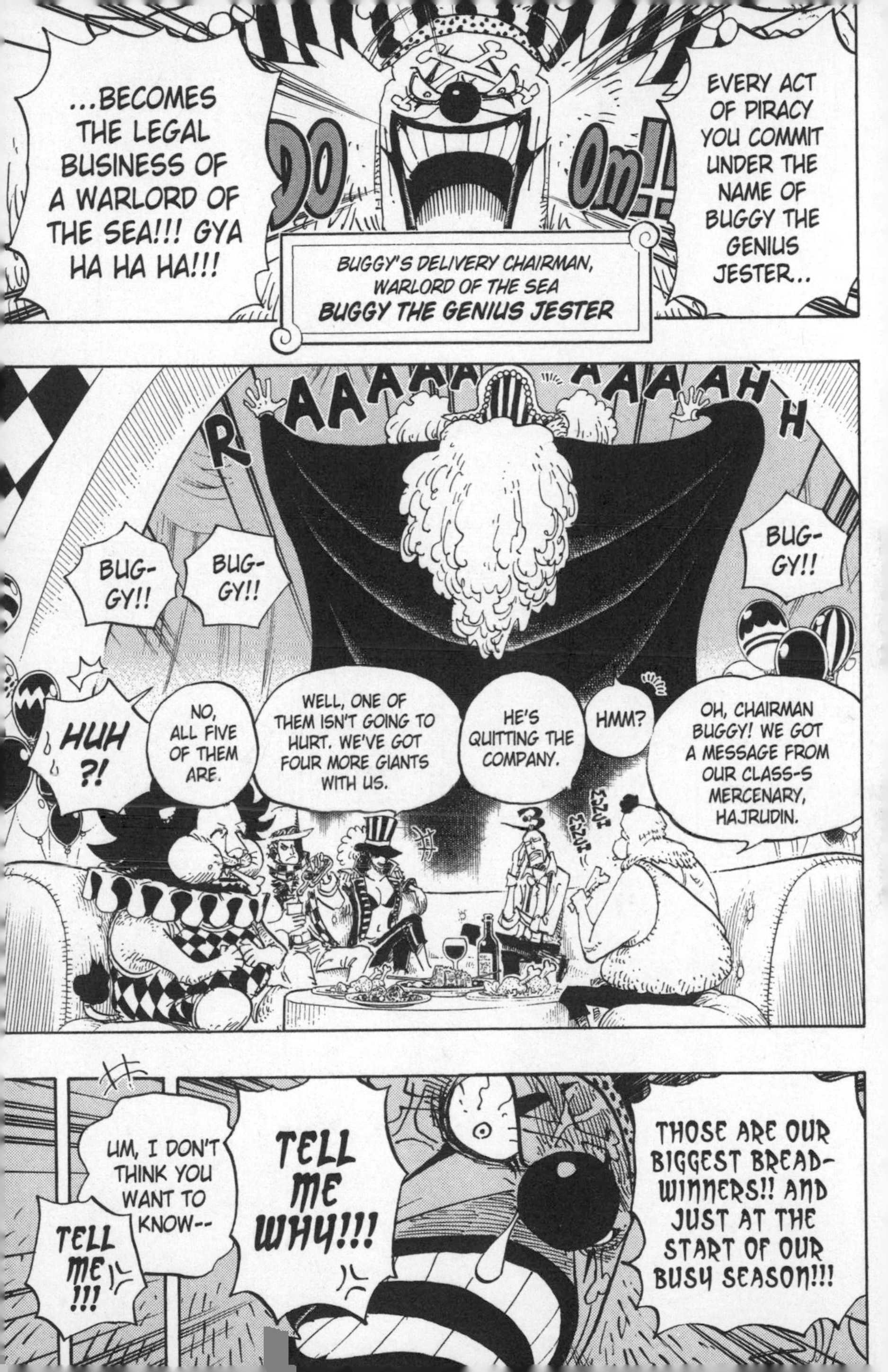
EVERY ACT OF PIRACY YOU COMMIT UNDER THE NAME OF BUGGY THE GENIUS JESTER...
...BECOMES THE LEGAL BUSINESS OF A WARLORD OF THE SEA!!! GYA HA HA HA!!!
DOOm!!
BUGGY'S DELIVERY CHAIRMAN, WARLORD OF THE SEA
BUGGY THE GENIUS JESTER
RAAAAAAAAAH
BUG-GY!!
BUG-GY!!
BUG-GY!!
OH, CHAIRMAN BUGGY! WE GOT A MESSAGE FROM OUR CLASS-S MERCENARY, HAJRUDIN.
HMM?
HE'S QUITTING THE COMPANY.
WELL, ONE OF THEM ISN'T GOING TO HURT. WE'VE GOT FOUR MORE GIANTS WITH US.
NO, ALL FIVE OF THEM ARE.
HUH ?!
THOSE ARE OUR BIGGEST BREAD-WINNERS!! AND JUST AT THE START OF OUR BUSY SEASON!!!
TELL ME WHY!!!
UM, I DON'T THINK YOU WANT TO KNOW--
TELL ME!!!

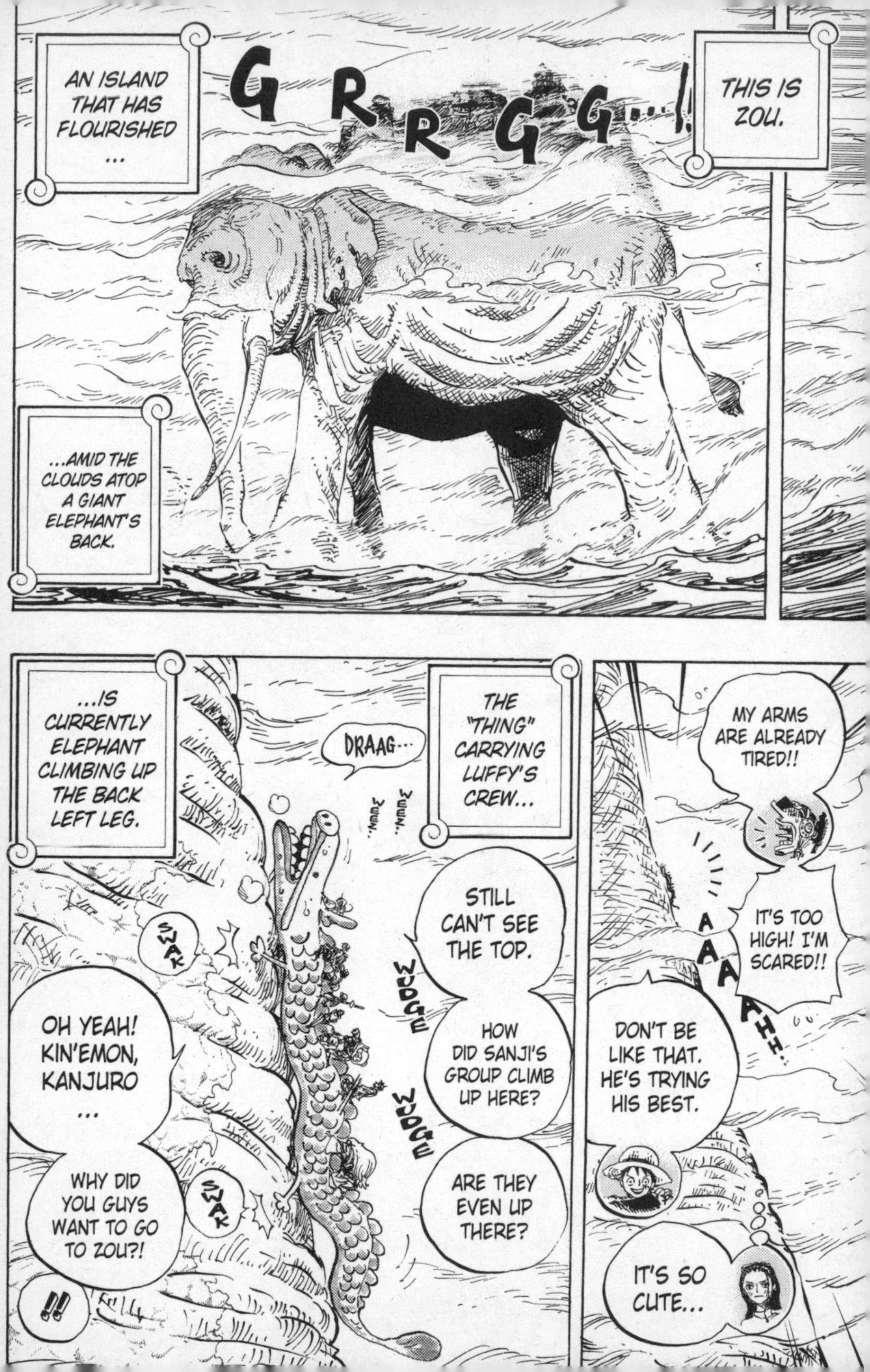
THIS IS ZOU.
GRRRGGG...!!
AN ISLAND THAT HAS FLOURISHED ...
...AMID THE CLOUDS ATOP A GIANT ELEPHANT'S BACK.
MY ARMS ARE ALREADY TIRED!!
IT'S TOO HIGH! I'M SCARED!!
AAAAHH...
DON'T BE LIKE THAT. HE'S TRYING HIS BEST.
IT'S SO CUTE...
THE "THING" CARRYING LUFFY'S CREW...
...IS CURRENTLY ELEPHANT CLIMBING UP THE BACK LEFT LEG.
DRAAG...
WEEN... WEEN...
STILL CAN'T SEE THE TOP.
HOW DID SANJI'S GROUP CLIMB UP HERE?
ARE THEY EVEN UP THERE?
WUDGE
WUDGE
SWAK
OH YEAH! KIN'EMON, KANJURO ...
WHY DID YOU GUYS WANT TO GO TO ZOU?!
SWAK
!!

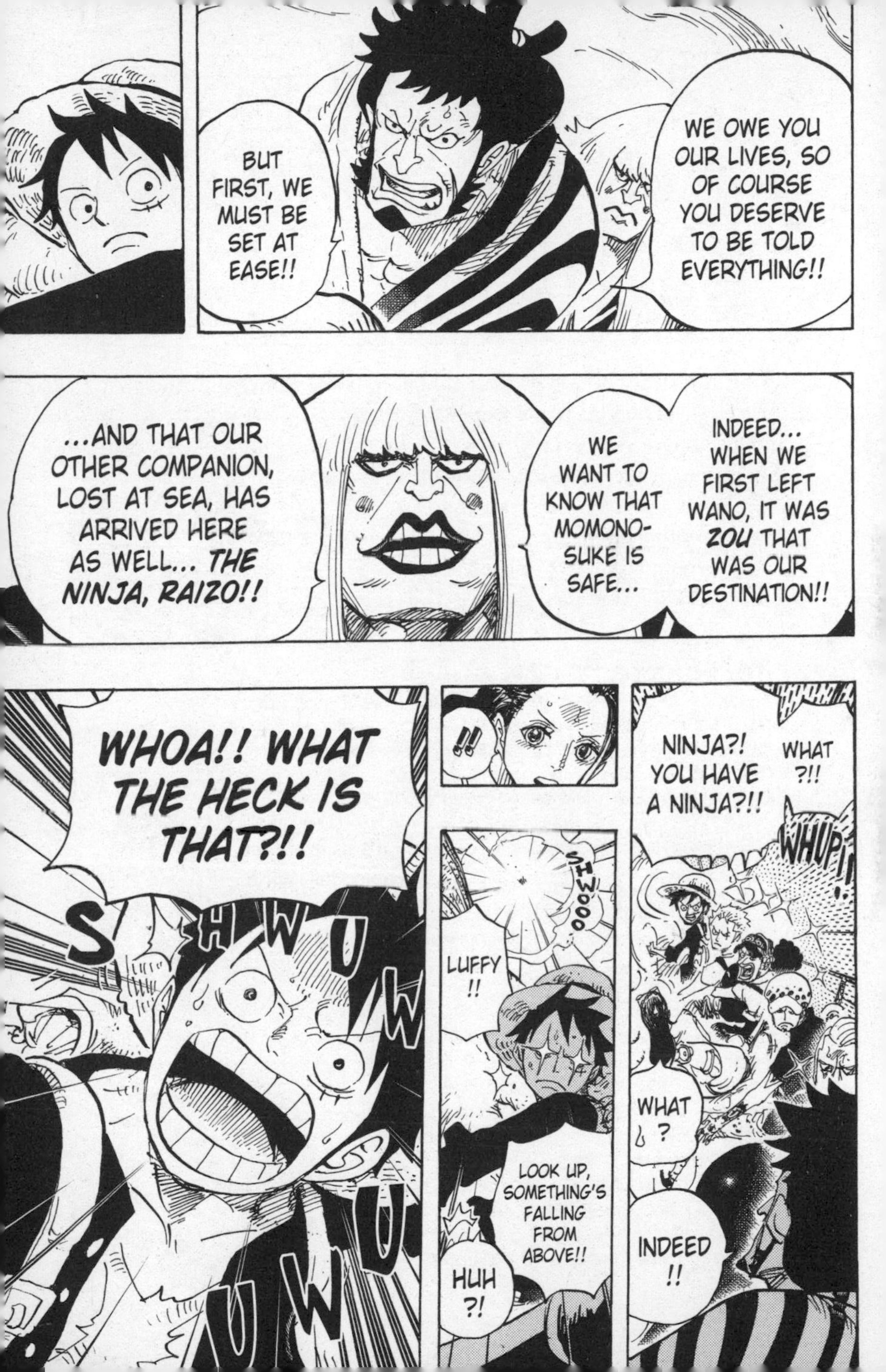
WE OWE YOU OUR LIVES, SO OF COURSE YOU DESERVE TO BE TOLD EVERYTHING!!
BUT FIRST, WE MUST BE SET AT EASE!!
INDEED... WHEN WE FIRST LEFT WANO, IT WAS ZOU THAT WAS OUR DESTINATION!!
WE WANT TO KNOW THAT MOMONO-SUKE IS SAFE...
...AND THAT OUR OTHER COMPANION, LOST AT SEA, HAS ARRIVED HERE AS WELL... THE NINJA, RAIZO!!
WHAT ?!!
NINJA?! YOU HAVE A NINJA?!!
WHUP!!
WHAT ?
INDEED !!
!!
SHWOOO
LUFFY !!
LOOK UP, SOMETHING'S FALLING FROM ABOVE!!
HUH ?!
WHOA!! WHAT THE HECK IS THAT?!!

SBS Question Corner

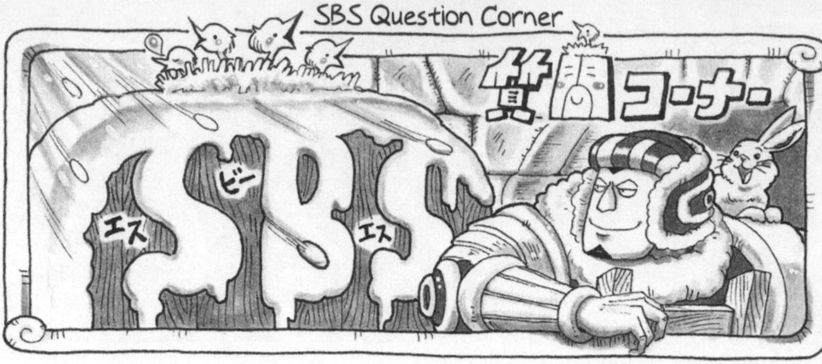
質問コーナー
SBS
エス
ビー
エス

(Hippo Iron, Saitama)

Q: So why do all the nobles of Goa Kingdom (aside from Sabo) and the Celestial Dragons (aside from Dofy and his family) look so ugly? Is it because they're so ugly on the inside? Knowing you, there's a verrrry deep reason, so I would love to hear it.

--Neverending Summer Vacation Homework (cry)

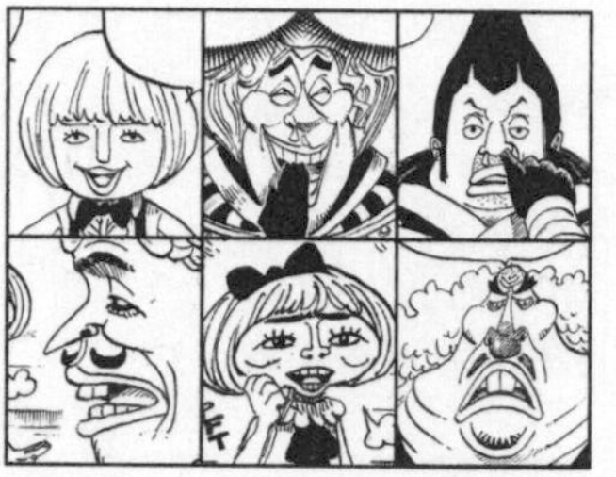

A: Well, you see,

I really hate those guys!!

The way they abuse their power like that! I don't understand what makes them so special. Well, if they're not going to have a shred of kindness and decency, then I'm gonna draw 'em with weird faces!!! ...Oh! Sorry. I got carried away there.

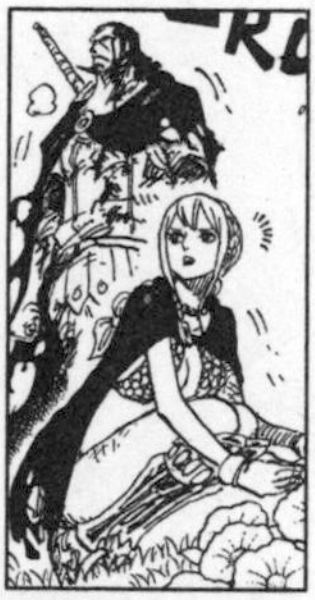

Q: After the fight with Diamante, I thought it was odd that Rebecca's cape was so torn, given that Robin was keeping her safe. Upon closer look, it seems that she ripped it up to tend to Kyros's wounds. Aren't you worried this might be a little too sexy?

--Peko

A: I am in admiration of your imagination and observation! That's right. Rebecca used her cape to staunch the bleeding for Kyros. At first, I was going to have her use a lot more of her cape for first aid, but it was really getting much too sexy! So I held back and only ripped half as much of her cape!! Whew, that's better!! Rebecca really needs that cape!!

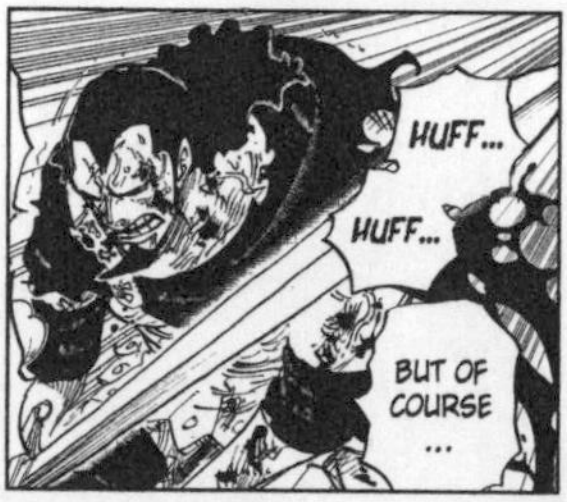
HUFF...
HUFF...
BUT OF COURSE
...

# Chapter 804:
# ADVENTURE IN THE LAND ATOP THE ELEPHANT'S BACK

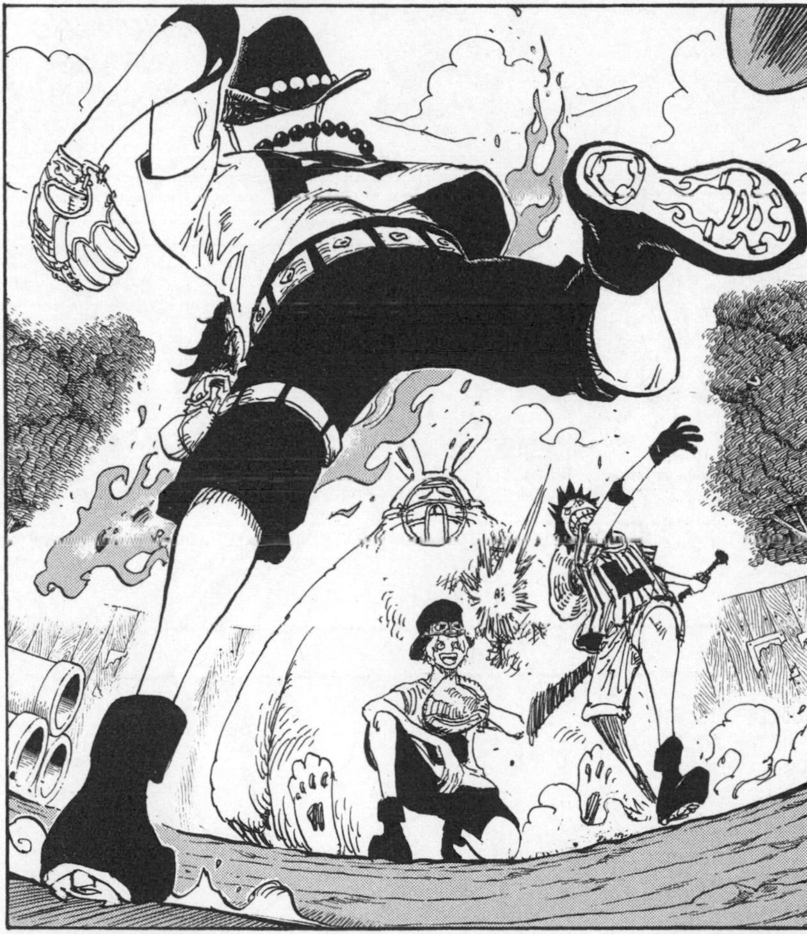

REQUEST: "ACE THE PITCHER AND SABO THE CATCHER PLAYING BASEBALL WITH A LAPIN" BY CHIETH FROM NISHINOMIYA

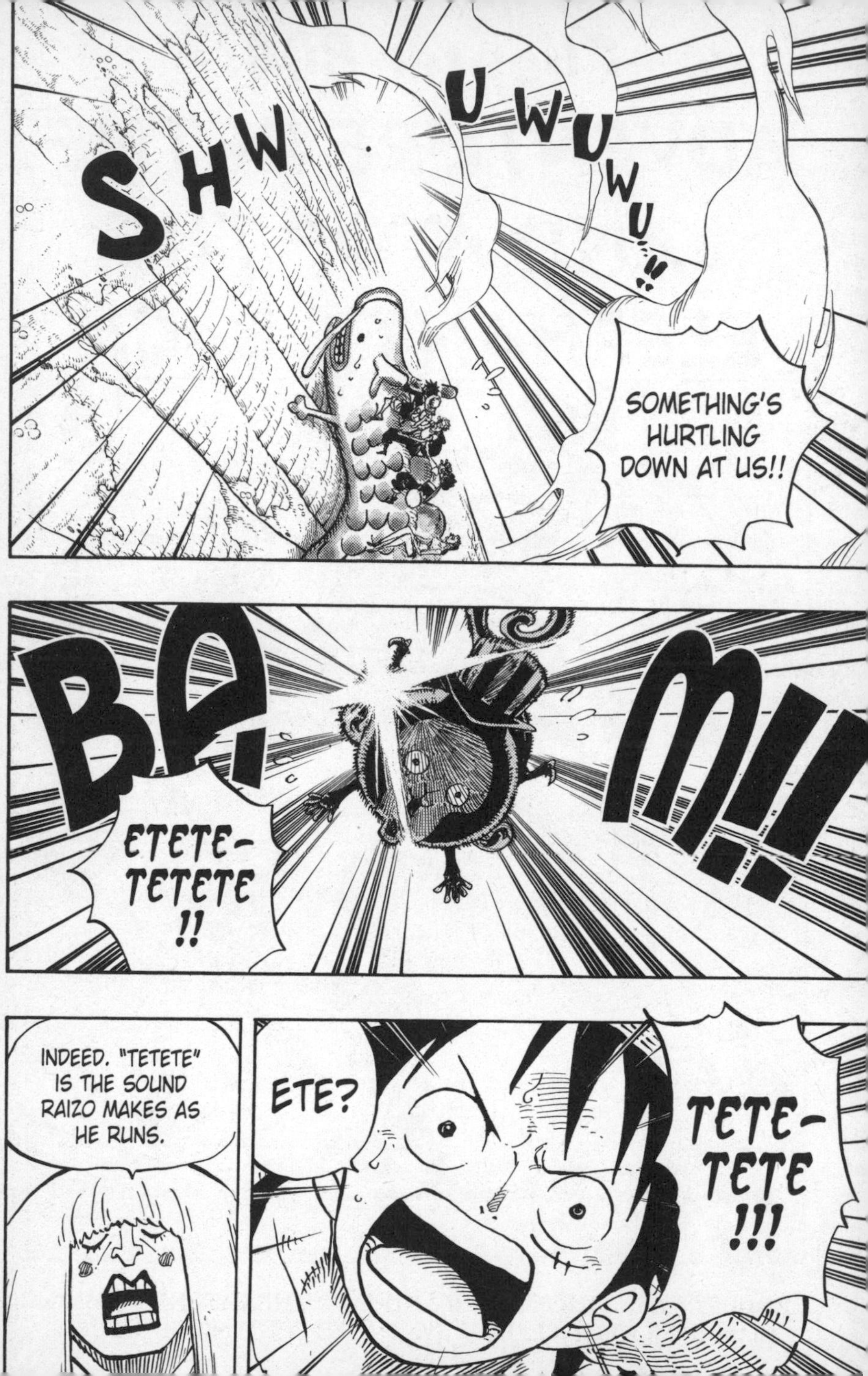
SOMETHING'S HURTLING DOWN AT US!!
SHW...UWUWUWU...!!
BEM!!!
ETETE-TETETE!!
TETE-TETE!!!
ETE?
INDEED. "TETETE" IS THE SOUND RAIZO MAKES AS HE RUNS.

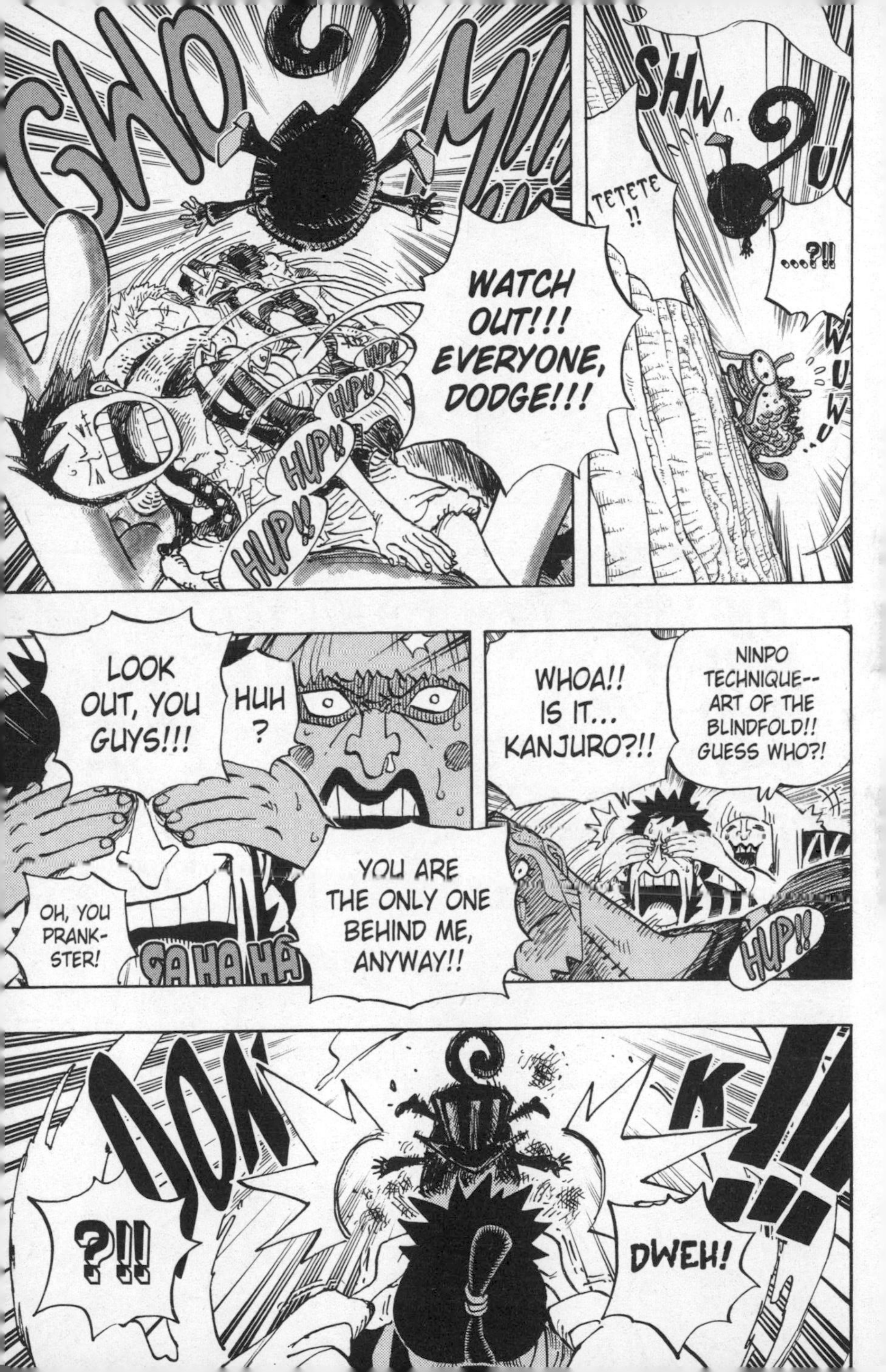
TETETE!!
...?!!
WATCH OUT!!! EVERYONE, DODGE!!!
HUP!!
HUP!!
HUP!!
HUP!!
HUP!!
NINPO TECHNIQUE-- ART OF THE BLINDFOLD!! GUESS WHO?!
WHOA!! IS IT... KANJURO?!!
HUP!!
HUH?
LOOK OUT, YOU GUYS!!!
YOU ARE THE ONLY ONE BEHIND ME, ANYWAY!!
OH, YOU PRANKSTER!
GAHAHA
DWEH!
?!!

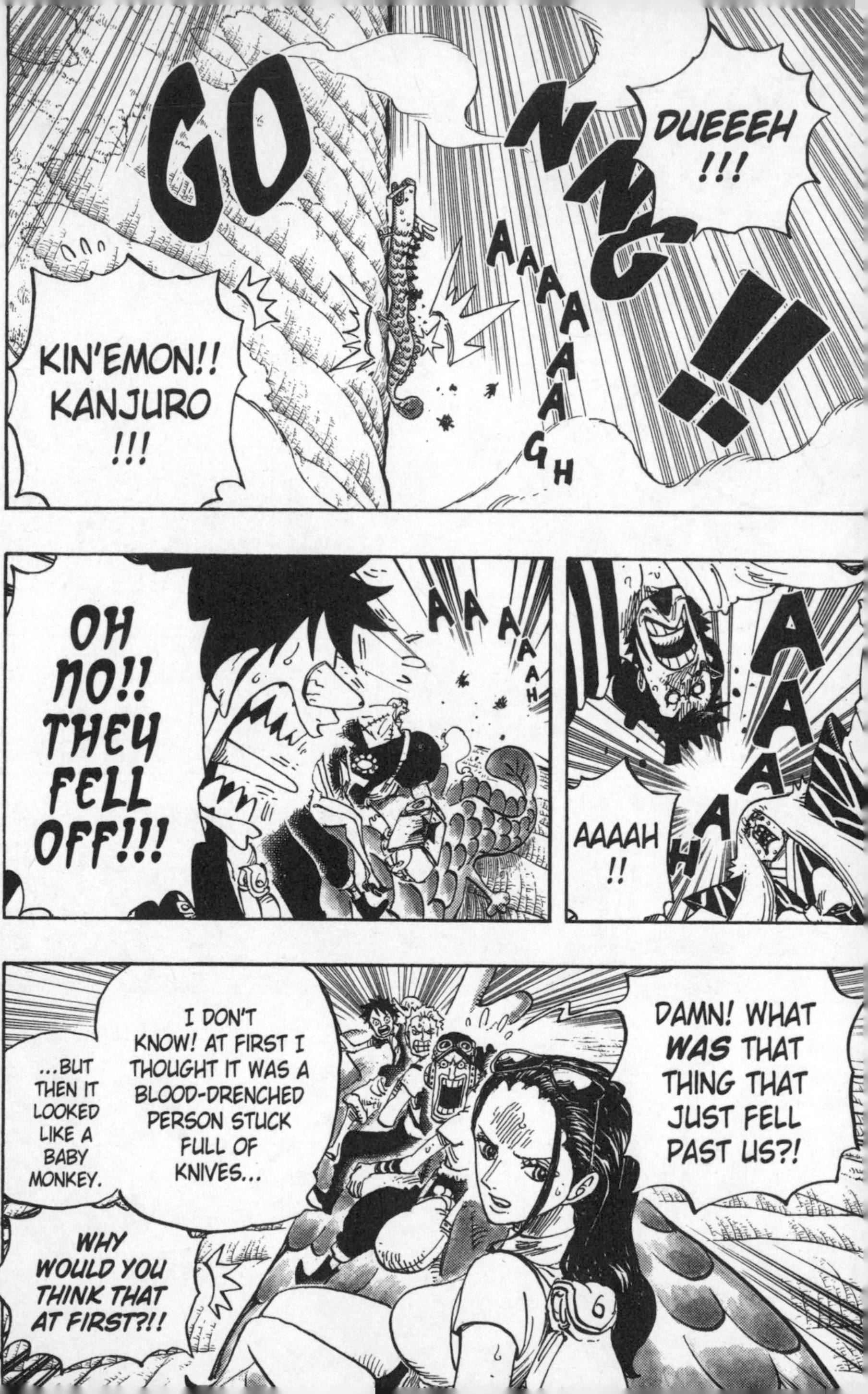
DUEEEH!!!
GONNG!!
AAAAAAAGH
KIN'EMON!! KANJURO!!!
AAAAH
AAAAH!!
AAAAAH
OH NO!! THEY FELL OFF!!!
DAMN! WHAT **WAS** THAT THING THAT JUST FELL PAST US?!
I DON'T KNOW! AT FIRST I THOUGHT IT WAS A BLOOD-DRENCHED PERSON STUCK FULL OF KNIVES...
...BUT THEN IT LOOKED LIKE A BABY MONKEY.
*WHY WOULD YOU THINK THAT AT FIRST?!!*

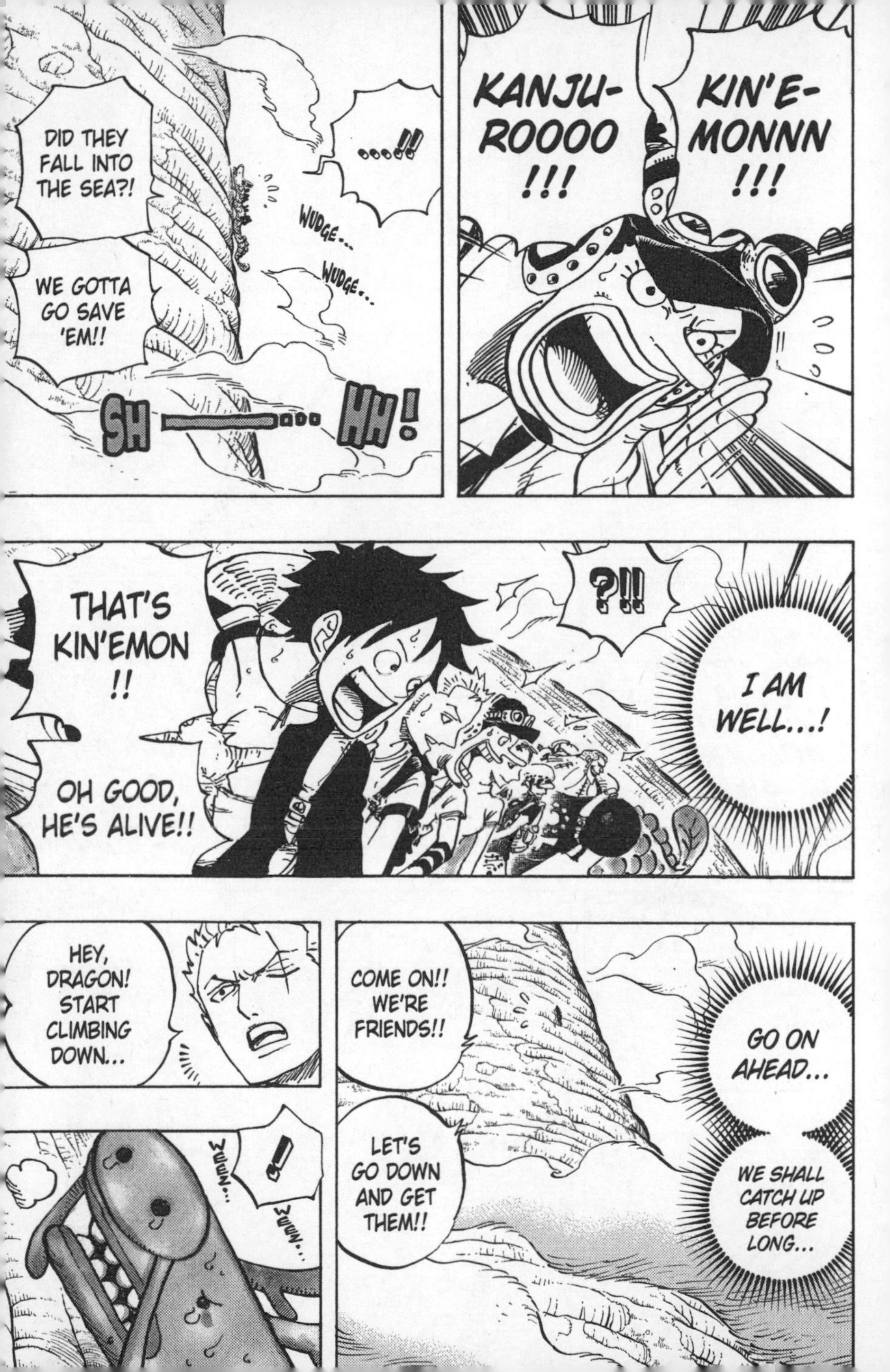
KIN'E-MONNN!!!
KANJU-ROOOO!!!
....!!
DID THEY FALL INTO THE SEA?!
WUDGE...
WUDGE...
WE GOTTA GO SAVE 'EM!!
SH———...HH!
?!!
I AM WELL...!
THAT'S KIN'EMON!!
OH GOOD, HE'S ALIVE!!
GO ON AHEAD...
WE SHALL CATCH UP BEFORE LONG...
COME ON!! WE'RE FRIENDS!!
LET'S GO DOWN AND GET THEM!!
HEY, DRAGON! START CLIMBING DOWN...
!
WEEN...
WEEN...

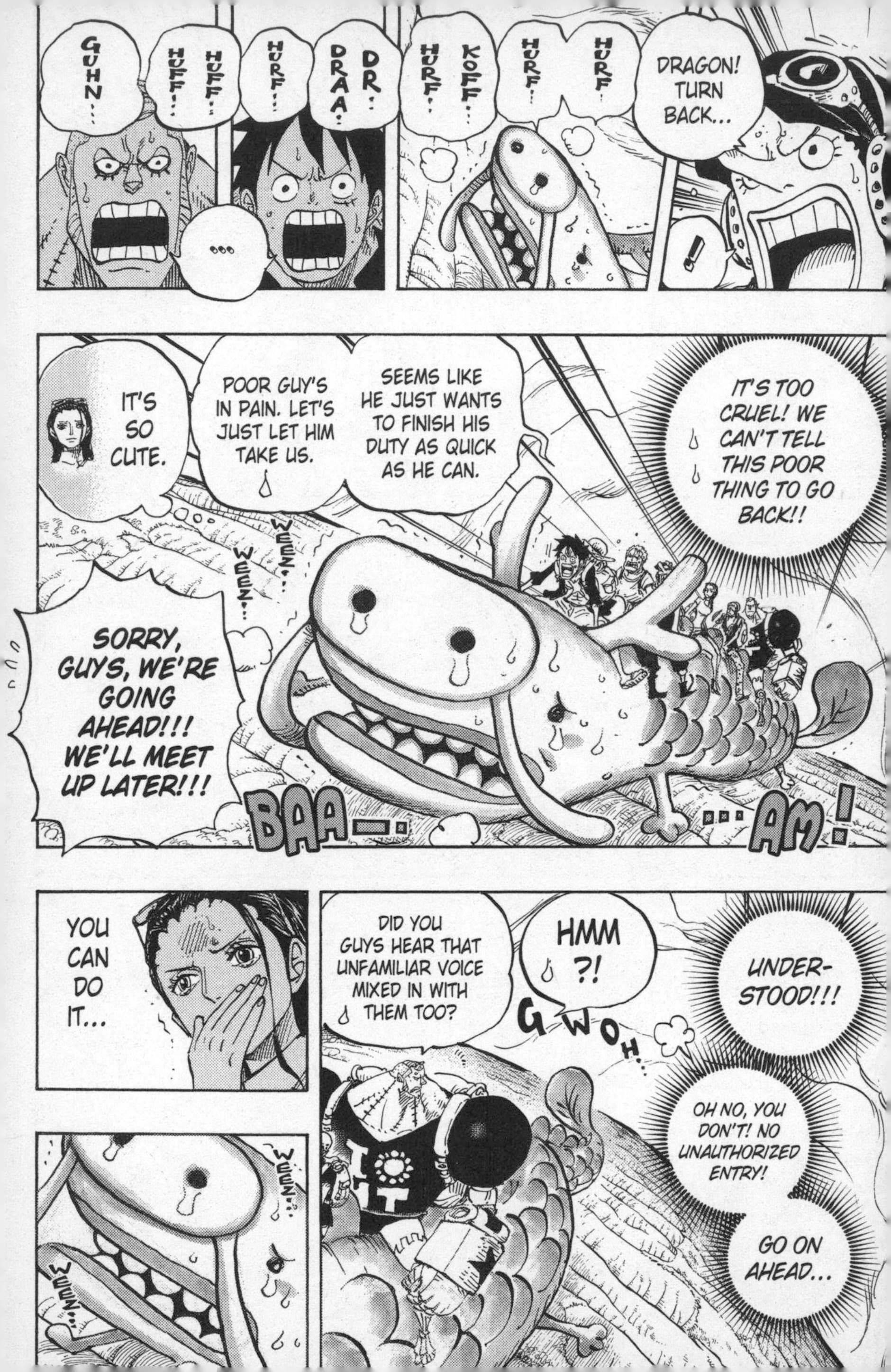
DRAGON! TURN BACK...
!
HURF
HURF...
KOFF...
HURF...
DR...
DRAAA...
HURF...
HUFF...
HUFF...
GUHN...
...
IT'S TOO CRUEL! WE CAN'T TELL THIS POOR THING TO GO BACK!!
SEEMS LIKE HE JUST WANTS TO FINISH HIS DUTY AS QUICK AS HE CAN.
POOR GUY'S IN PAIN. LET'S JUST LET HIM TAKE US.
IT'S SO CUTE.
WEEZ...
WEEZ...
SORRY, GUYS, WE'RE GOING AHEAD!!! WE'LL MEET UP LATER!!!
BAA...
...AM!
UNDER-STOOD!!!
HMM ?!
DID YOU GUYS HEAR THAT UNFAMILIAR VOICE MIXED IN WITH THEM TOO?
GWOH...
OH NO, YOU DON'T! NO UNAUTHORIZED ENTRY!
GO ON AHEAD...
YOU CAN DO IT...
WEEZ...
WEEZ...

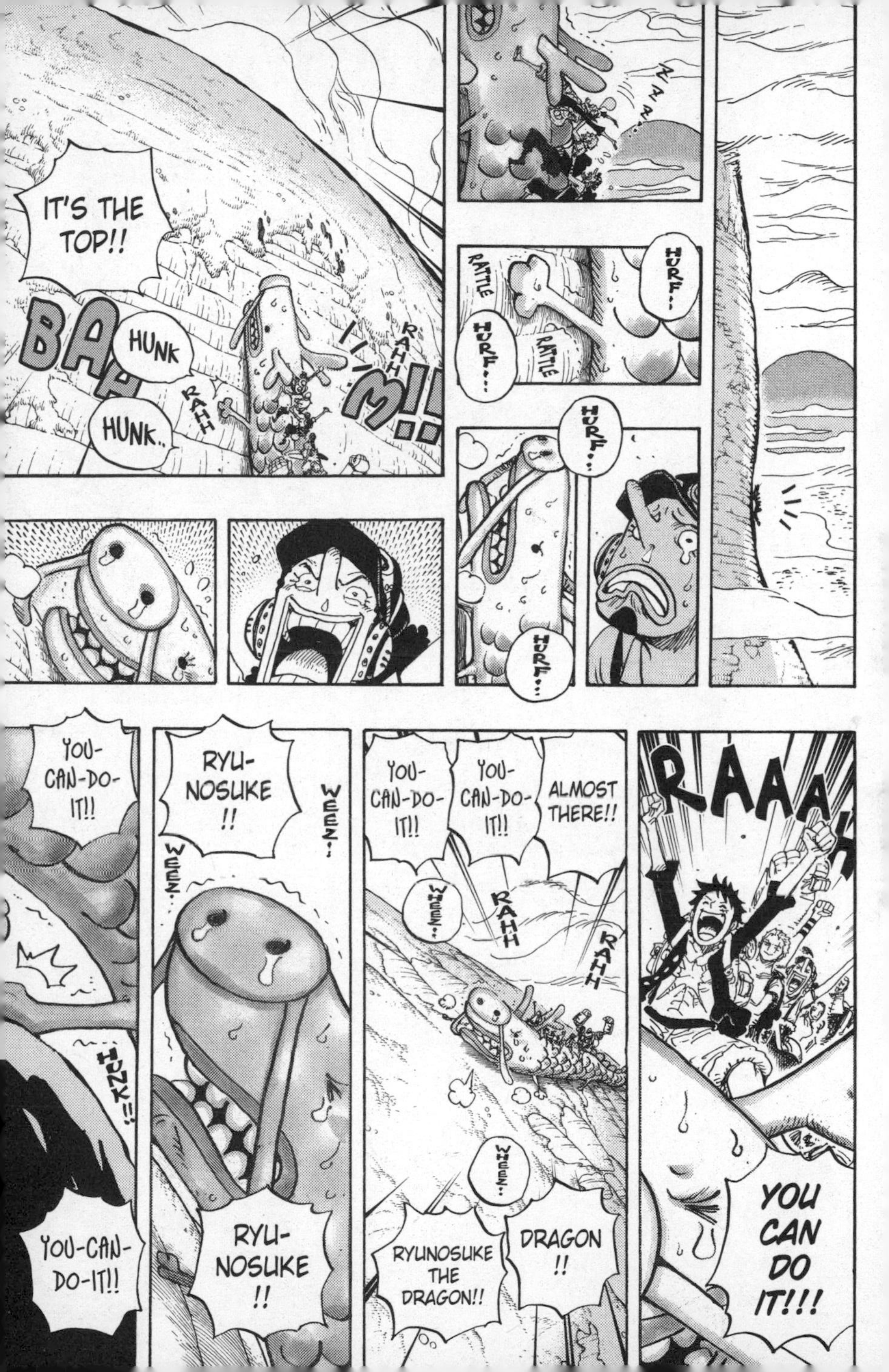
ZRRR...
HURF...
RATTLE
HURF...
RATTLE
IT'S THE TOP!!
BAM!!
RAHH
HUNK
RAHH
HUNK..
HURF...
HURF...
RAAAH
YOU CAN DO IT!!!
ALMOST THERE!!
YOU-CAN-DO-IT!!
YOU-CAN-DO-IT!!
WHEEZ..
RAHH
RAHH
WHEEZ..
DRAGON!!
RYUNOSUKE THE DRAGON!!
RYU-NOSUKE!!
WEEZ..
WEEZ..
RYU-NOSUKE!!
YOU-CAN-DO-IT!!
HUNK!!
YOU-CAN-DO-IT!!

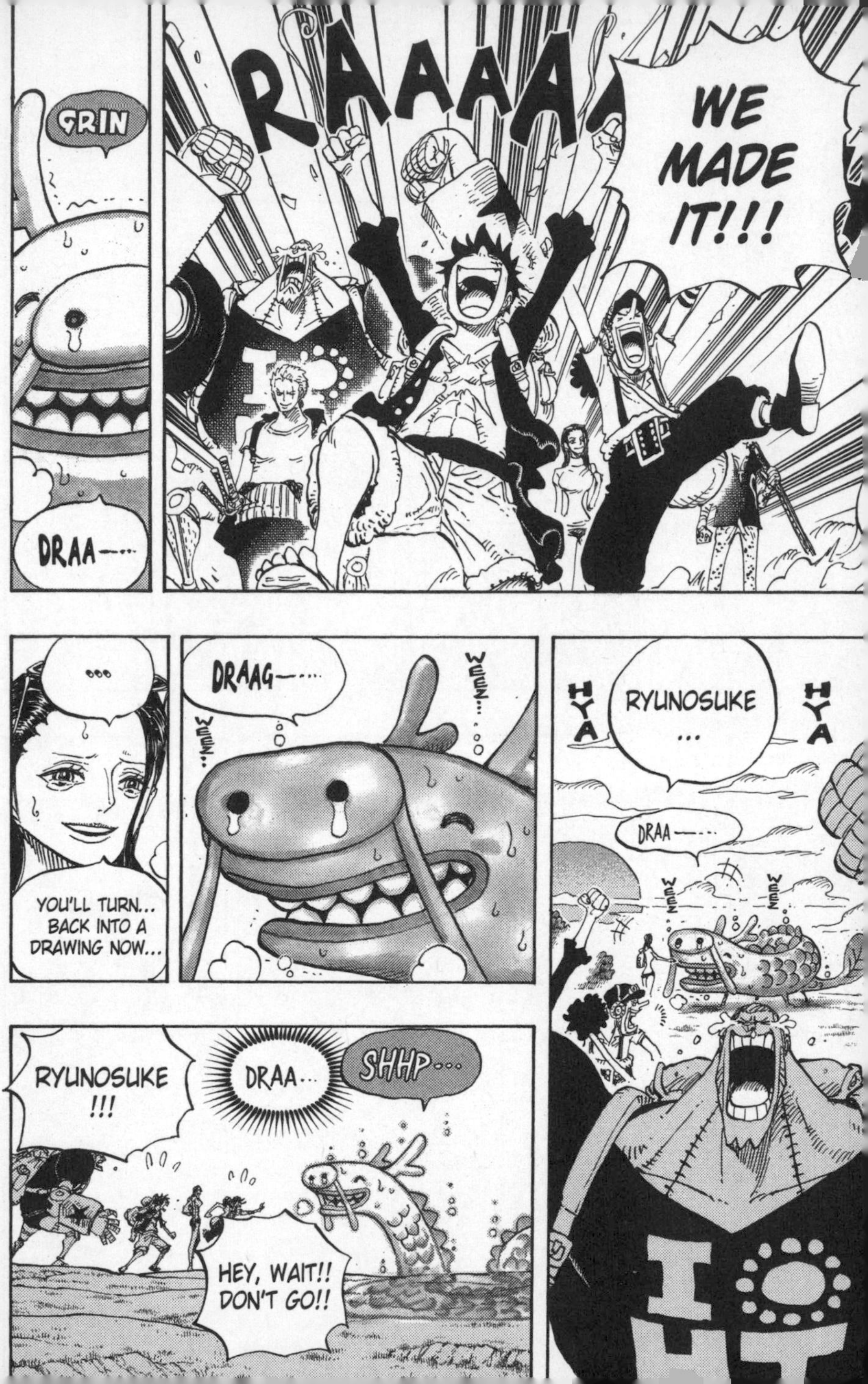
WE MADE IT!!!
RAAAAA
GRIN
DRAA----
HYA
RYUNOSUKE ...
HYA
DRAA----
WEEZ
WEEZ
WEEZ...
DRAAG----
WEEZ...
...
YOU'LL TURN... BACK INTO A DRAWING NOW...
SHHP...
DRAA...
RYUNOSUKE !!!
HEY, WAIT!! DON'T GO!!

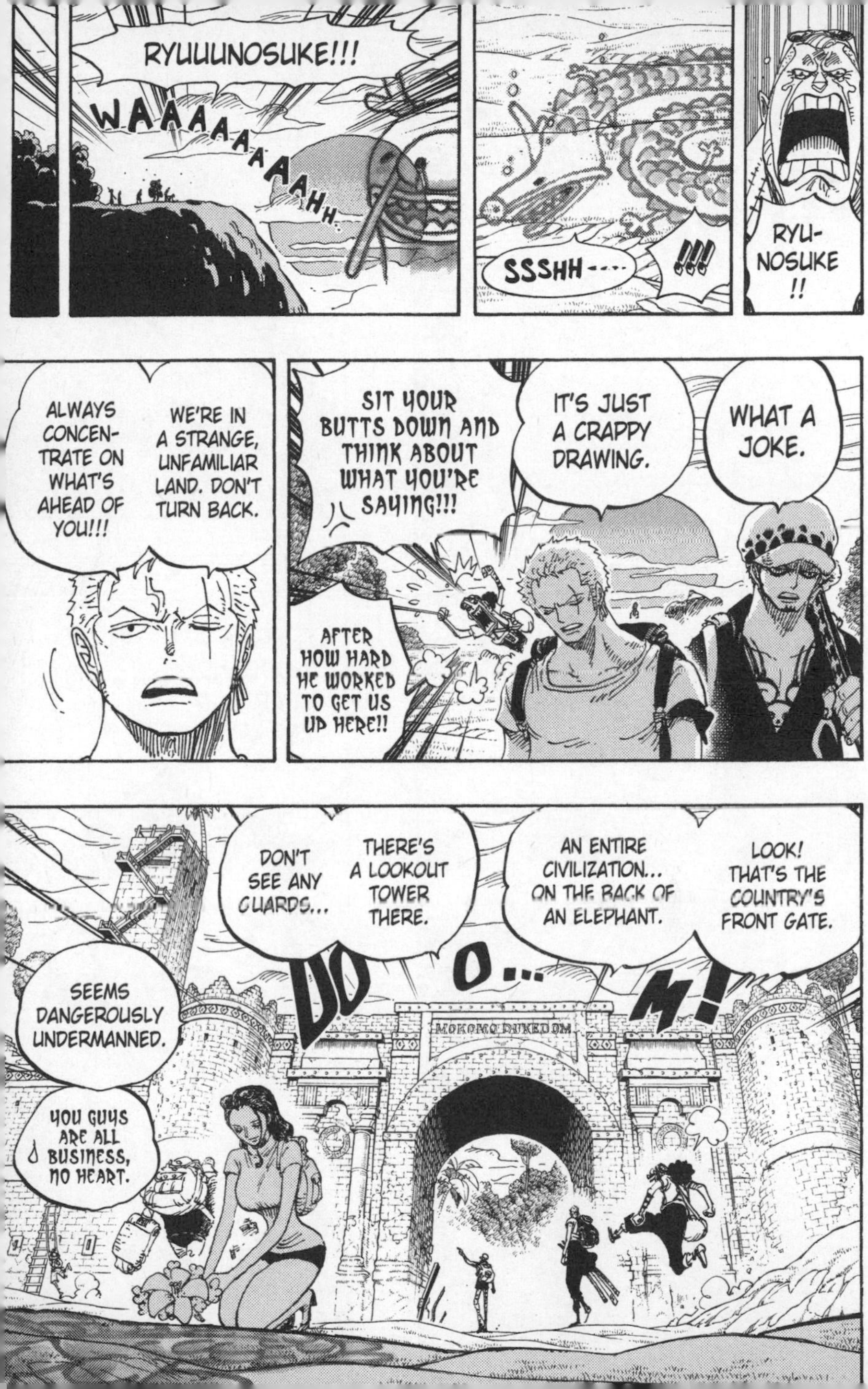
RYU-NOSUKE !!
SSSHH----
!!!
RYUUUNOSUKE!!!
WAAAAAAAAAHH
WHAT A JOKE.
IT'S JUST A CRAPPY DRAWING.
SIT YOUR BUTTS DOWN AND THINK ABOUT WHAT YOU'RE SAYING!!!
AFTER HOW HARD HE WORKED TO GET US UP HERE!!
WE'RE IN A STRANGE, UNFAMILIAR LAND. DON'T TURN BACK.
ALWAYS CONCEN-TRATE ON WHAT'S AHEAD OF YOU!!!
LOOK! THAT'S THE COUNTRY'S FRONT GATE.
AN ENTIRE CIVILIZATION... ON THE BACK OF AN ELEPHANT.
THERE'S A LOOKOUT TOWER THERE.
DON'T SEE ANY GUARDS...
DO O... M!
MOKOMO DUKEDOM
SEEMS DANGEROUSLY UNDERMANNED.
YOU GUYS ARE ALL BUSINESS, NO HEART.

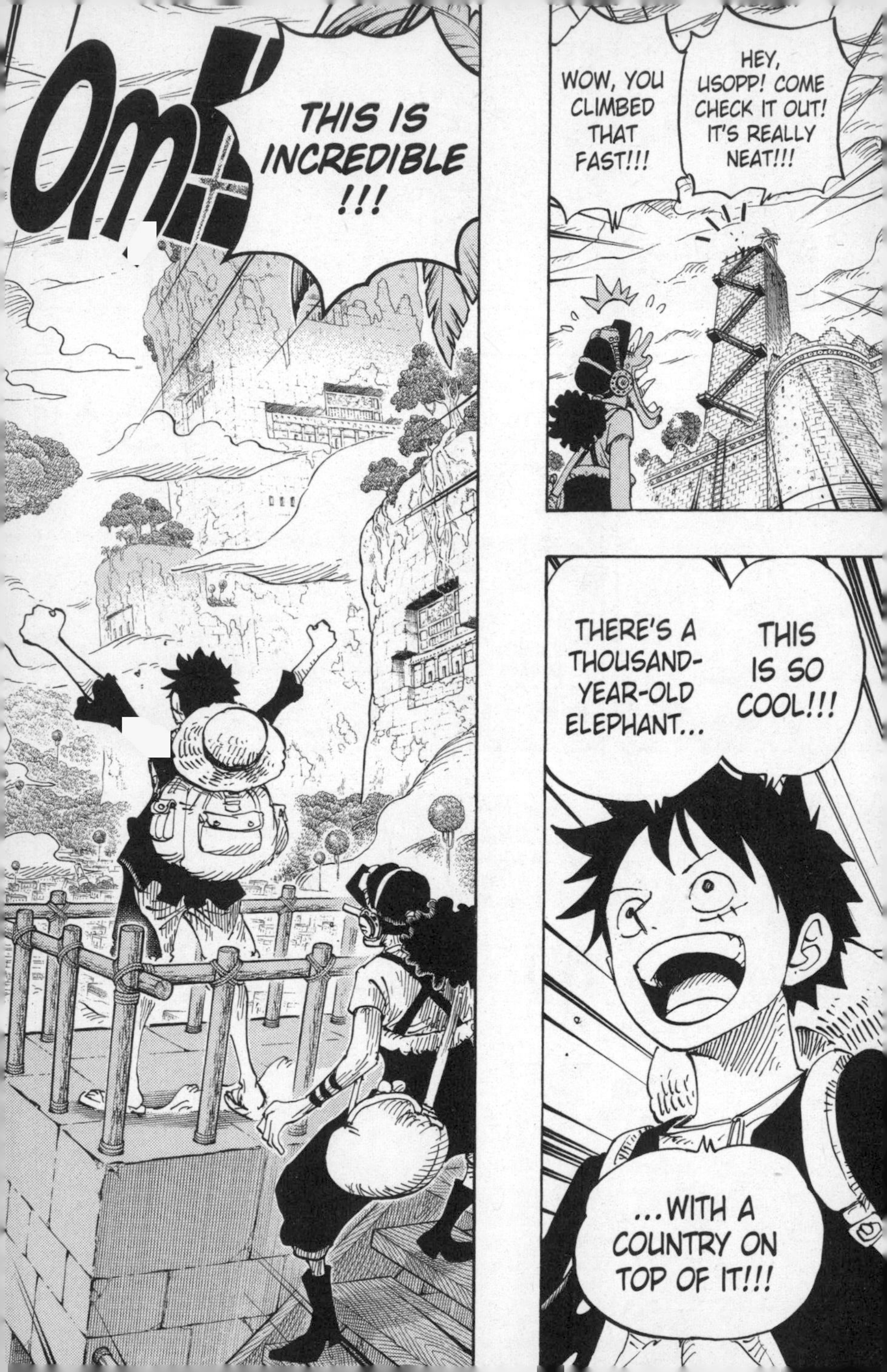
HEY, USOPP! COME CHECK IT OUT! IT'S REALLY NEAT!!!
WOW, YOU CLIMBED THAT FAST!!!
THIS IS SO COOL!!!
THERE'S A THOUSAND-YEAR-OLD ELEPHANT...
...WITH A COUNTRY ON TOP OF IT!!!
THIS IS INCREDIBLE!!!

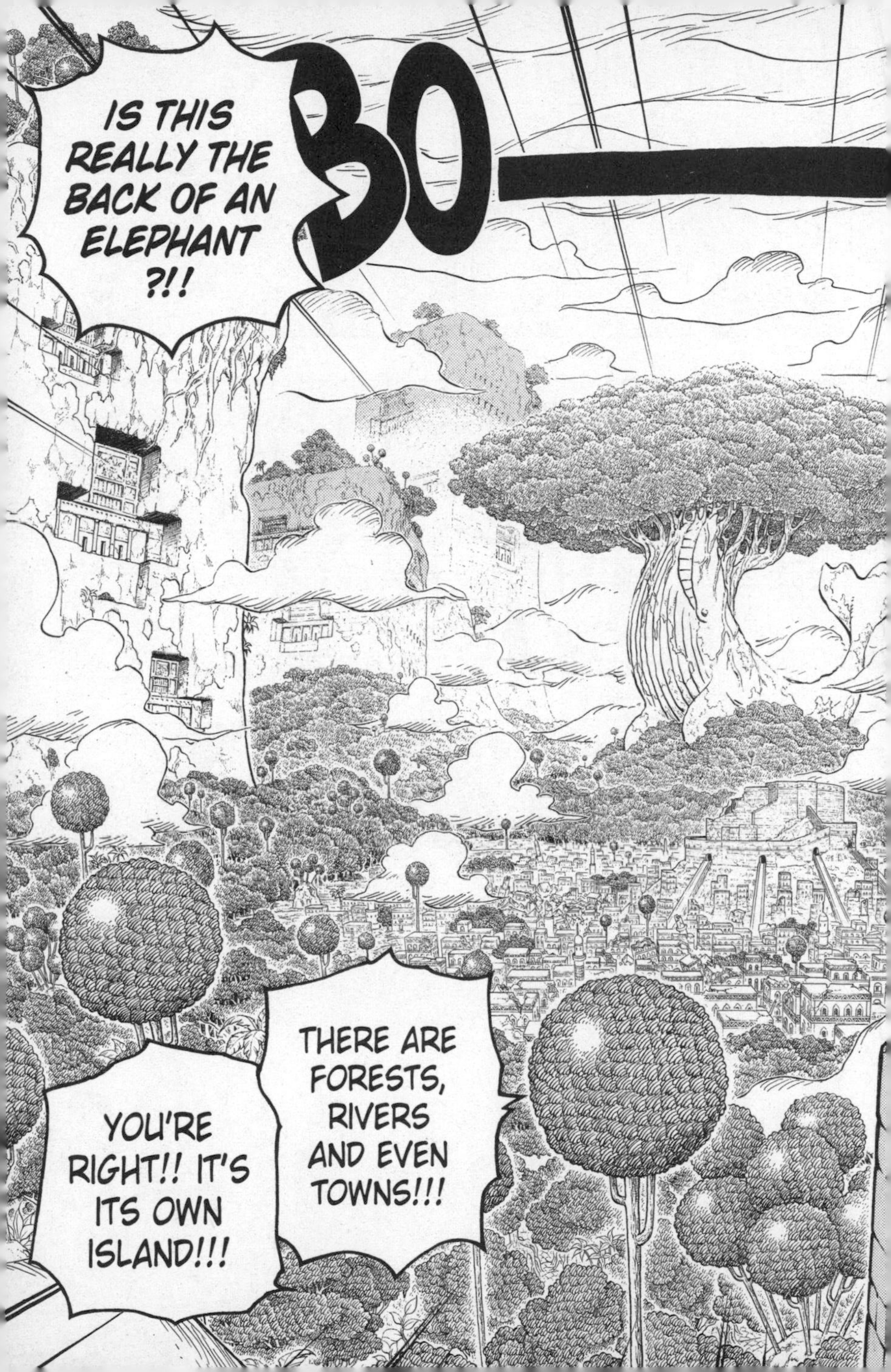
BO—
IS THIS REALLY THE BACK OF AN ELEPHANT ?!!
THERE ARE FORESTS, RIVERS AND EVEN TOWNS!!!
YOU'RE RIGHT!! IT'S ITS OWN ISLAND!!!

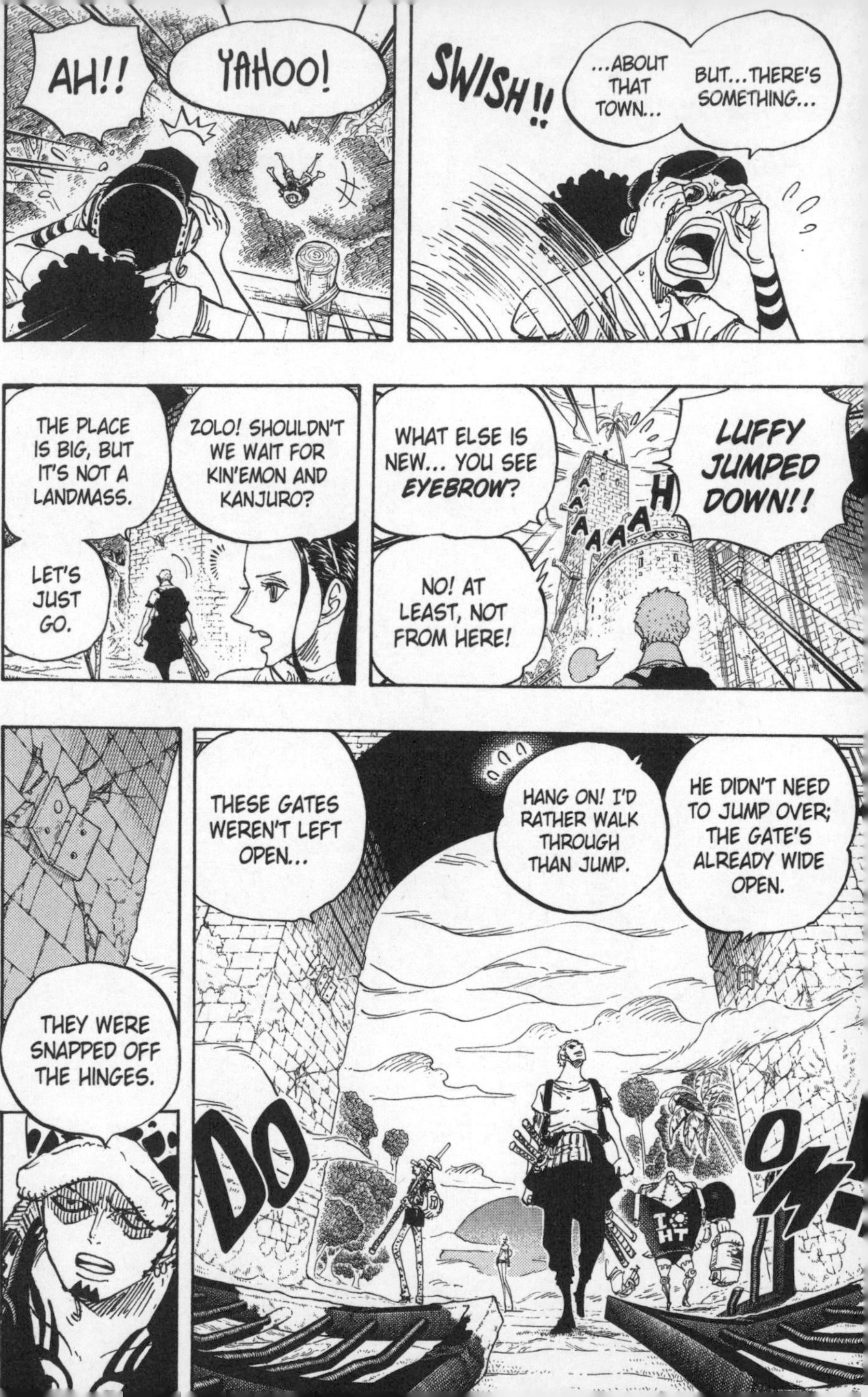
BUT...THERE'S SOMETHING...
...ABOUT THAT TOWN...
SWISH!!
YAHOO!
AH!!
LUFFY JUMPED DOWN!!
AAAAAH
WHAT ELSE IS NEW... YOU SEE EYEBROW?
NO! AT LEAST, NOT FROM HERE!
ZOLO! SHOULDN'T WE WAIT FOR KIN'EMON AND KANJURO?
THE PLACE IS BIG, BUT IT'S NOT A LANDMASS.
LET'S JUST GO.
HE DIDN'T NEED TO JUMP OVER; THE GATE'S ALREADY WIDE OPEN.
HANG ON! I'D RATHER WALK THROUGH THAN JUMP.
THESE GATES WEREN'T LEFT OPEN...
DO
THEY WERE SNAPPED OFF THE HINGES.

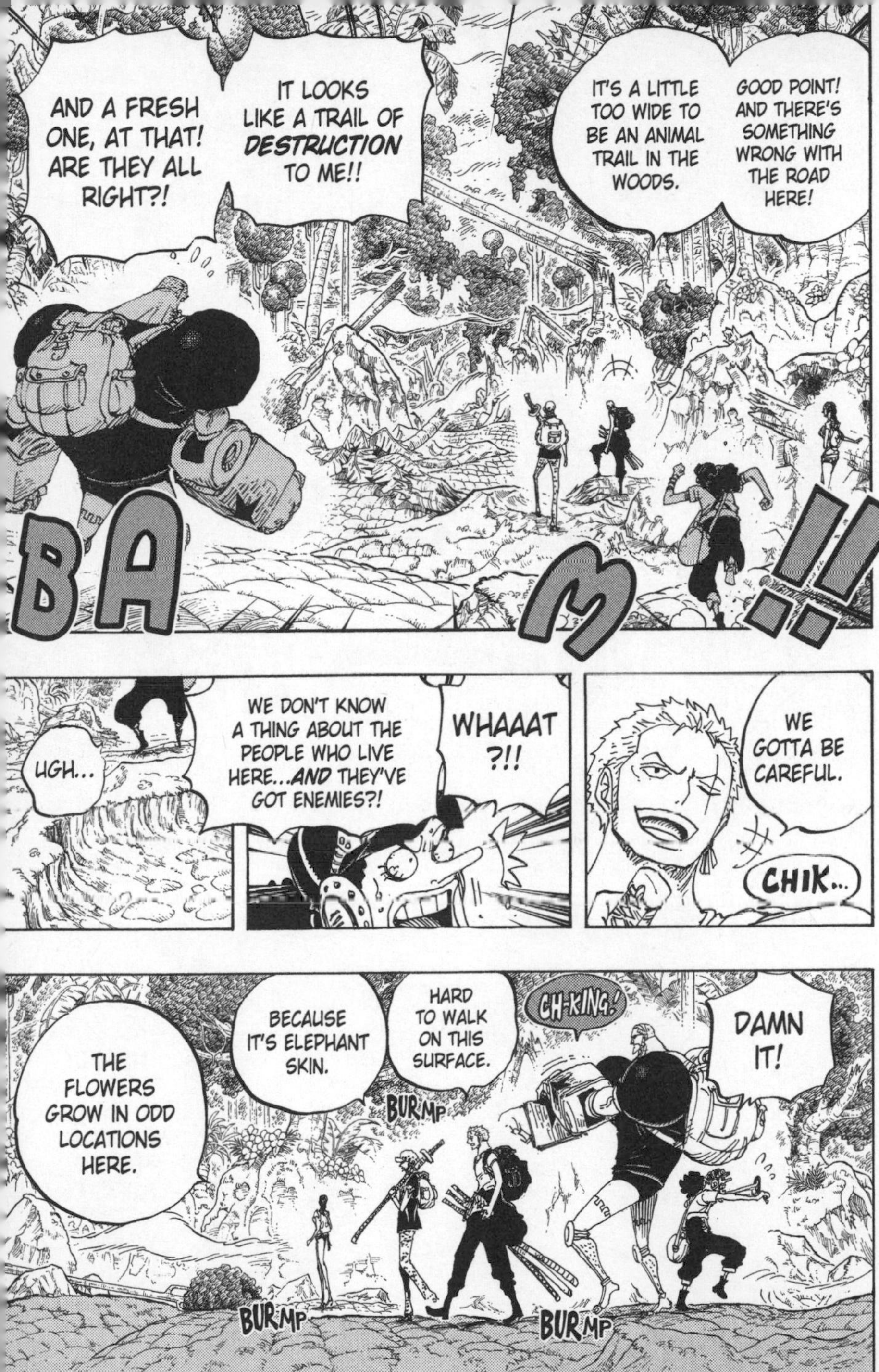
GOOD POINT! AND THERE'S SOMETHING WRONG WITH THE ROAD HERE!
IT'S A LITTLE TOO WIDE TO BE AN ANIMAL TRAIL IN THE WOODS.
IT LOOKS LIKE A TRAIL OF *DESTRUCTION* TO ME!!
AND A FRESH ONE, AT THAT! ARE THEY ALL RIGHT?!
BAM!!
WE GOTTA BE CAREFUL.
CHIK...
WHAAAT?!!
WE DON'T KNOW A THING ABOUT THE PEOPLE WHO LIVE HERE...*AND* THEY'VE GOT ENEMIES?!
UGH...
DAMN IT!
CH-KING!
HARD TO WALK ON THIS SURFACE.
BECAUSE IT'S ELEPHANT SKIN.
BURMP
THE FLOWERS GROW IN ODD LOCATIONS HERE.
BURMP
BURMP

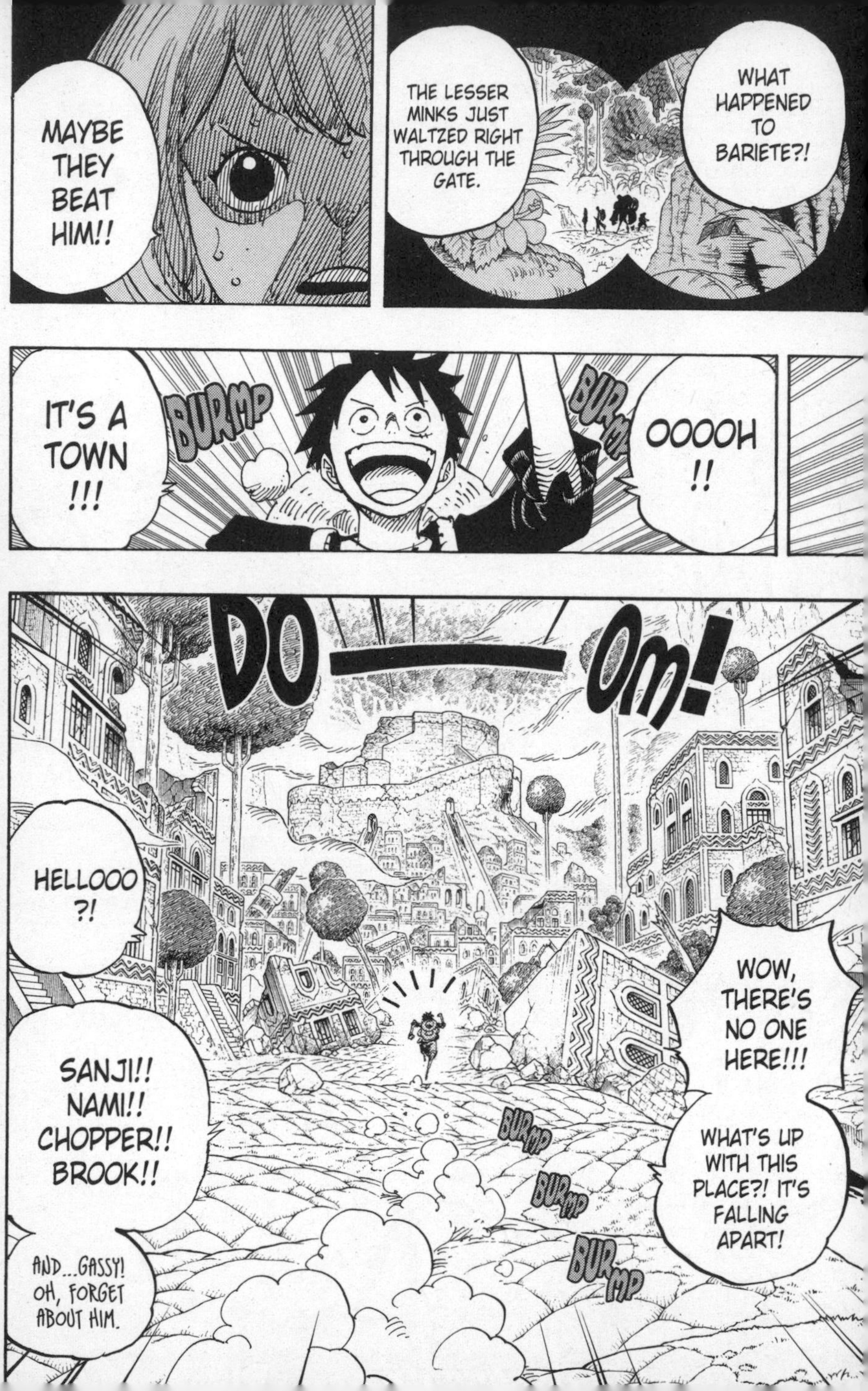
WHAT HAPPENED TO BARIETE?!
THE LESSER MINKS JUST WALTZED RIGHT THROUGH THE GATE.
MAYBE THEY BEAT HIM!!
OOOOH!!
BURMP
BURMP
IT'S A TOWN!!!
DO—OM!
WOW, THERE'S NO ONE HERE!!!
HELLOOO?!
WHAT'S UP WITH THIS PLACE?! IT'S FALLING APART!
SANJI!! NAMI!! CHOPPER!! BROOK!!
BURMP
BURMP
BURMP
AND...GASSY! OH, FORGET ABOUT HIM.

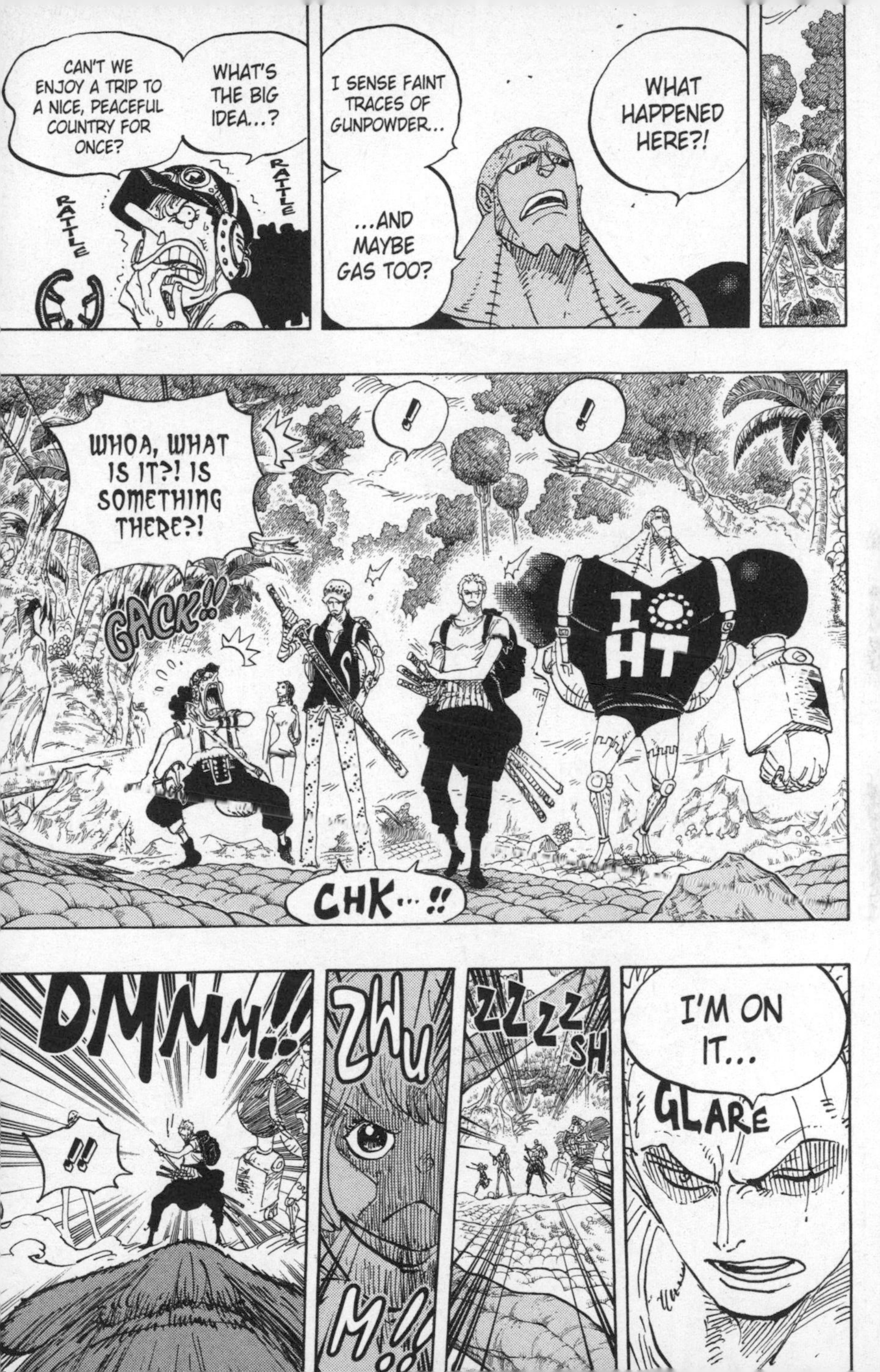
WHAT HAPPENED HERE?!
I SENSE FAINT TRACES OF GUNPOWDER...
...AND MAYBE GAS TOO?
WHAT'S THE BIG IDEA...?
CAN'T WE ENJOY A TRIP TO A NICE, PEACEFUL COUNTRY FOR ONCE?
RATTLE
RATTLE
!
!
WHOA, WHAT IS IT?! IS SOMETHING THERE?!
GACK!!
CHK...!!
I'M ON IT...
GLARE
ZZZZSH
ZHUM!!
DMMM!!
!!

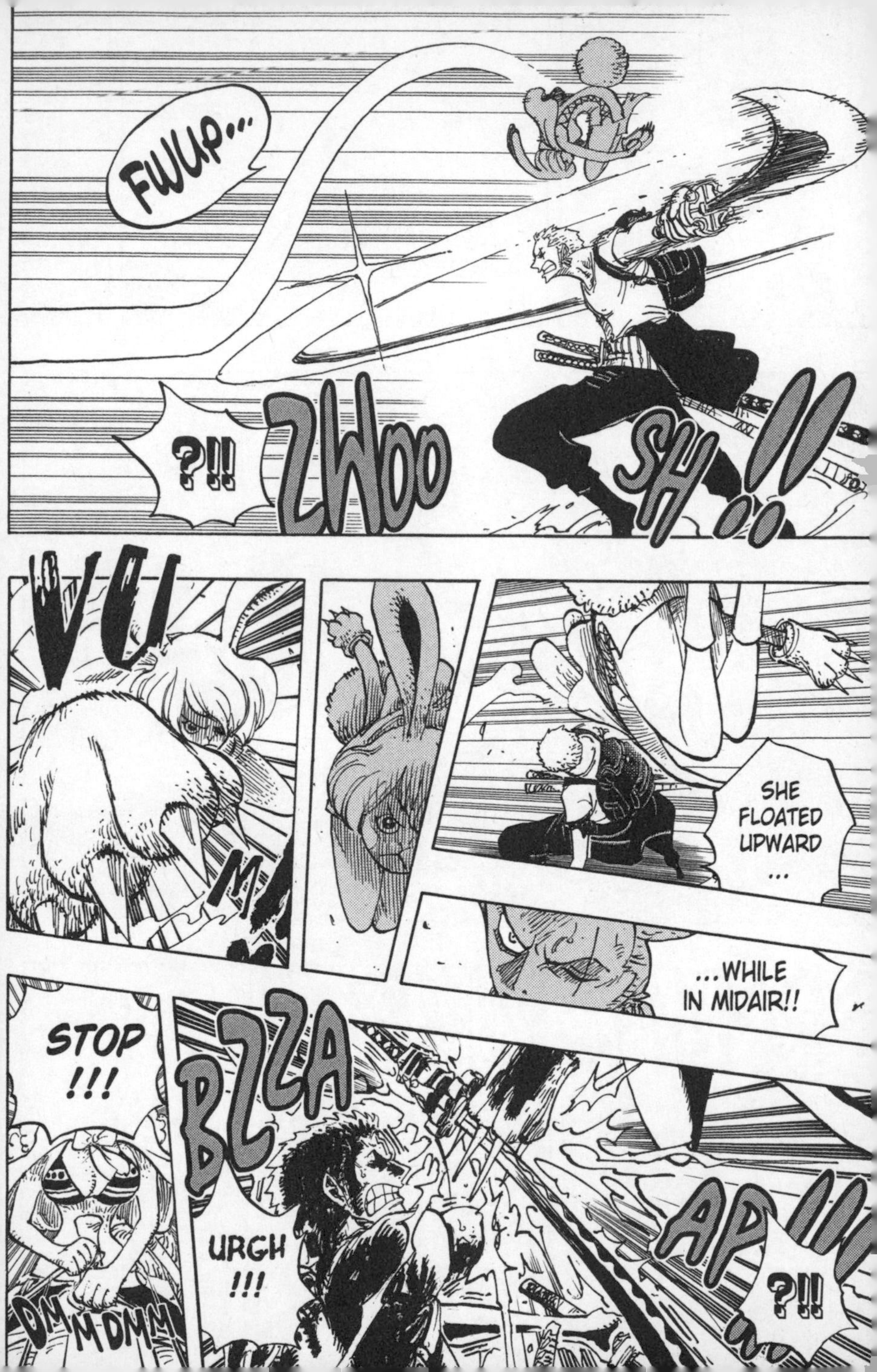
FWUP...
ZWOOSH!!
?!!
SHE FLOATED UPWARD ...
...WHILE IN MIDAIR!!
VUM
BZZAP!!!
?!!
URGH !!!
STOP !!!
DMMDMM

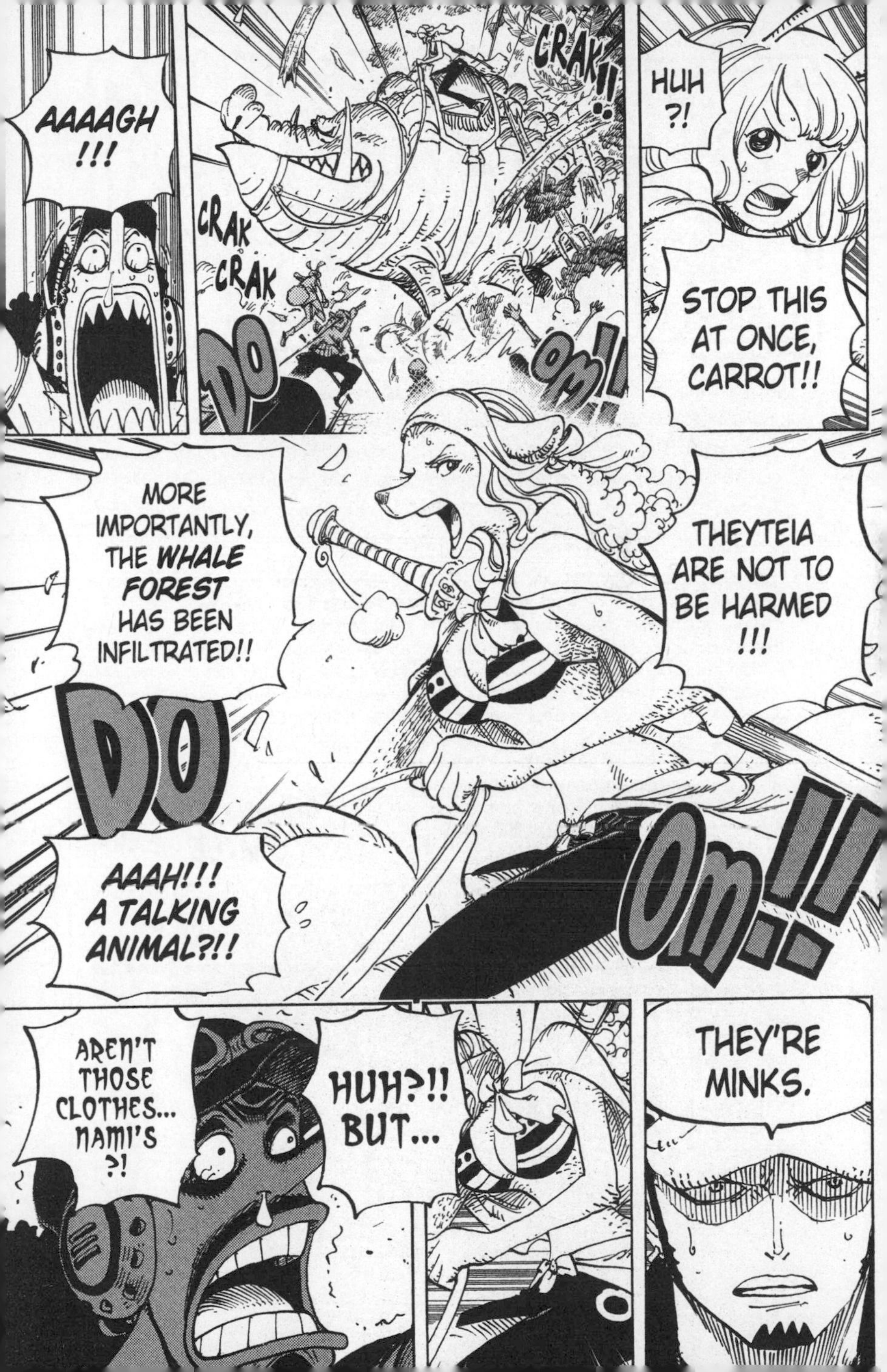
HUH ?!
STOP THIS AT ONCE, CARROT!!
CRAK!!
CRAK CRAK
DO OM!!
AAAAGH !!!
THEYTEIA ARE NOT TO BE HARMED !!!
MORE IMPORTANTLY, THE WHALE FOREST HAS BEEN INFILTRATED!!
DO OM!!
AAAH!!! A TALKING ANIMAL?!!
THEY'RE MINKS.
HUH?!! BUT...
AREN'T THOSE CLOTHES... NAMI'S ?!

SBS Question Corner

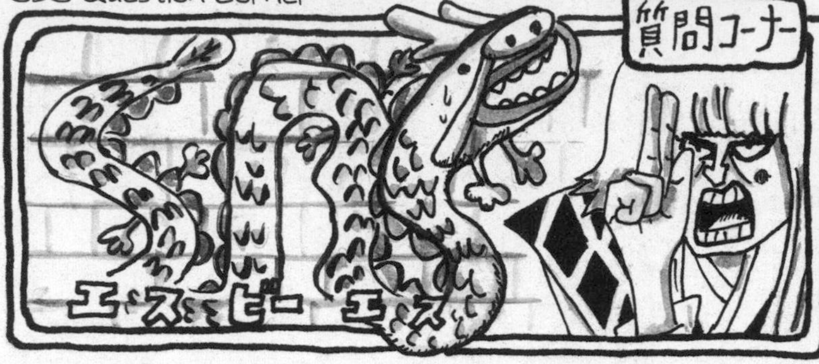
質問コーナー
エスビーエス

(HayatoAsami, Kanagawa)

Q: Hello, Oda Sensei. I noticed that on the cover page of Chapter 766, if you read the top character on each menu item from left to right, it spells out (redacted). Also, there's (redacted), (redacted) and (redacted)!! This chapter was in the same issue of *Weekly Shonen Jump* as the final installment of *Naruto*, right? I guess it must have been a very special manga for you.

--Gokira

A: Yes, you're right about that. But it is a "hidden message," you see, and I'm not going to reveal my secret on my own, so I chose to omit the answer from this letter. But I did get many curious questions from people who only read the collected volumes, so I decided I ought to explain the situation and my thoughts on it. Of course, I'm sure everyone knows about the ninja manga named Naruto, which concluded its run after fifteen long years in Shonen Jump. The cover of the One Piece chapter from that final issue was this. ➡ There are a number of messages hidden in it. Many people seem to think that One Piece and Naruto are enemies, but as a matter of fact, I've been a close friend of Masashi Kishimoto, the author, for years (laughs). With how fierce the competition is to stay in the pages of Jump, I was delighted to have company for so long. It also helps that we're the same age. At this moment, Kishimoto has escaped the hell of weekly serialization and is kicking back, doing a bit of work here and there, and generally relaxing and enjoying himself. (^ ^)

**Chapter 766:**
**SMILE**

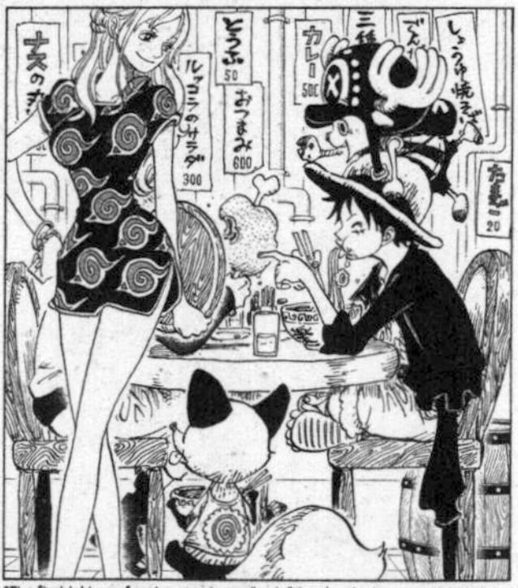

*The first letters of each menu sign spell out "Naruto, otsukare-san deshita" (Thanks for the great run, Naruto!)

# Chapter 805:
# THE MINKS

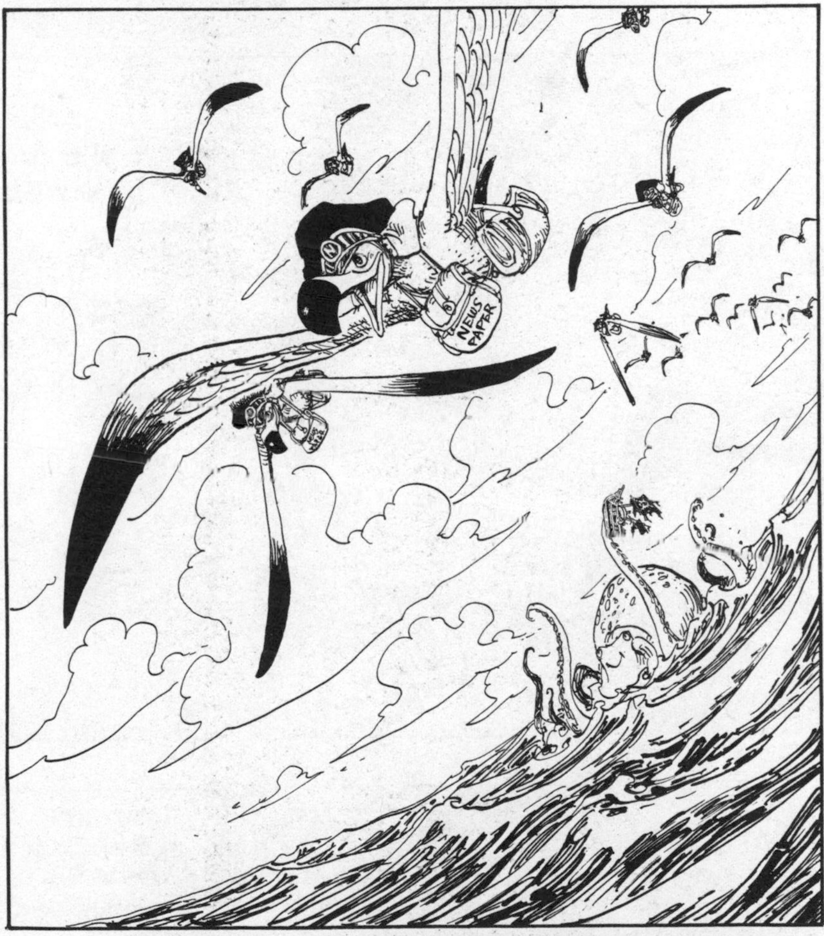
NEWS PAPER

LIMITED COVER SERIES, NO. 22, DECKS OF THE WORLD, 500-MILLION-MAN ARC, VOL. 1: "NEWS COOS TRAVEL TO THE ENDS OF THE SEA"

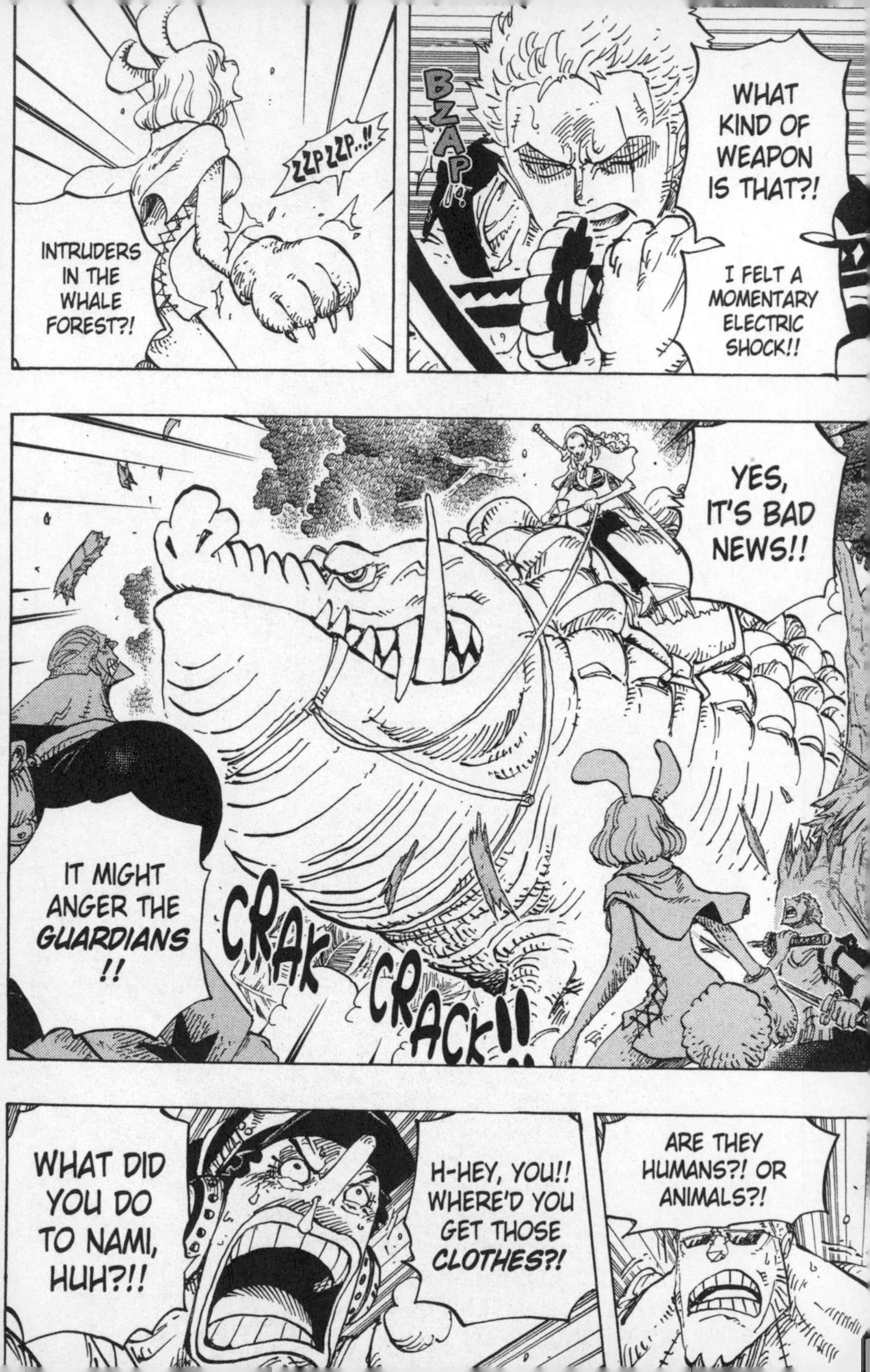
BZAP!!
WHAT KIND OF WEAPON IS THAT?!
I FELT A MOMENTARY ELECTRIC SHOCK!!
ZZP ZZP..!!
INTRUDERS IN THE WHALE FOREST?!
YES, IT'S BAD NEWS!!
IT MIGHT ANGER THE GUARDIANS!!
CRAK
CRACK!!
ARE THEY HUMANS?! OR ANIMALS?!
H-HEY, YOU!! WHERE'D YOU GET THOSE CLOTHES?!
WHAT DID YOU DO TO NAMI, HUH?!!

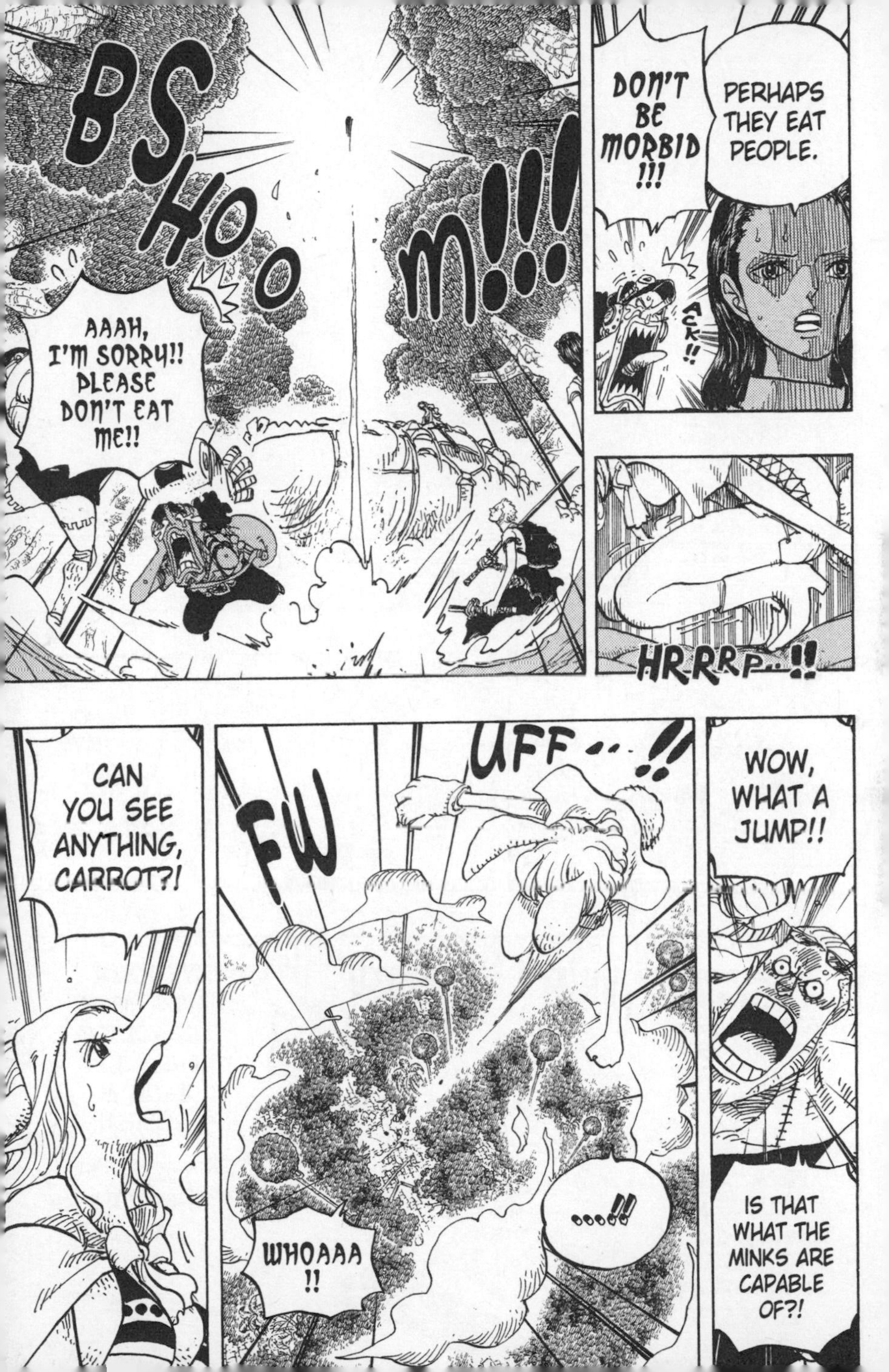
PERHAPS THEY EAT PEOPLE.
DON'T BE MORBID!!!
ACK!!
HR-RRP...!!
BSHOOOM!!!
AAAH, I'M SORRY!! PLEASE DON'T EAT ME!!
WOW, WHAT A JUMP!!
IS THAT WHAT THE MINKS ARE CAPABLE OF?!
FWUFF...!!
.....!!
WHOAAA!!
CAN YOU SEE ANYTHING, CARROT?!

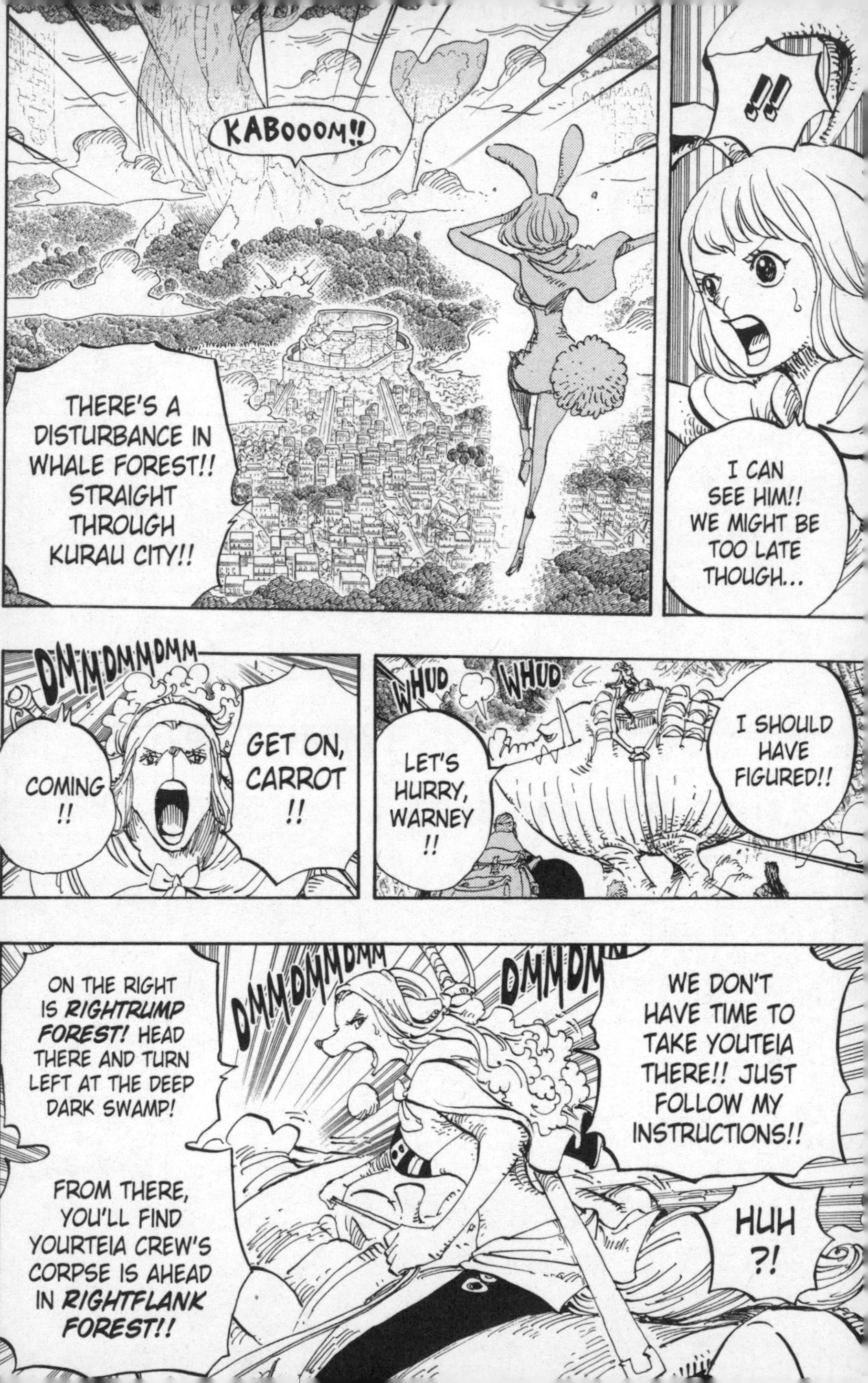
!!
I CAN SEE HIM!! WE MIGHT BE TOO LATE THOUGH...
KABOOOM!!
THERE'S A DISTURBANCE IN WHALE FOREST!! STRAIGHT THROUGH KURAU CITY!!
WHUD
WHUD
I SHOULD HAVE FIGURED!!
LET'S HURRY, WARNEY !!
DMMDMMDMM
GET ON, CARROT !!
COMING !!
DMMDM
WE DON'T HAVE TIME TO TAKE YOUTEIA THERE!! JUST FOLLOW MY INSTRUCTIONS!!
HUH ?!
DMMDMMDMM
ON THE RIGHT IS *RIGHTRUMP FOREST!* HEAD THERE AND TURN LEFT AT THE DEEP DARK SWAMP!
FROM THERE, YOU'LL FIND YOURTEIA CREW'S CORPSE IS AHEAD IN *RIGHTFLANK FOREST!!*

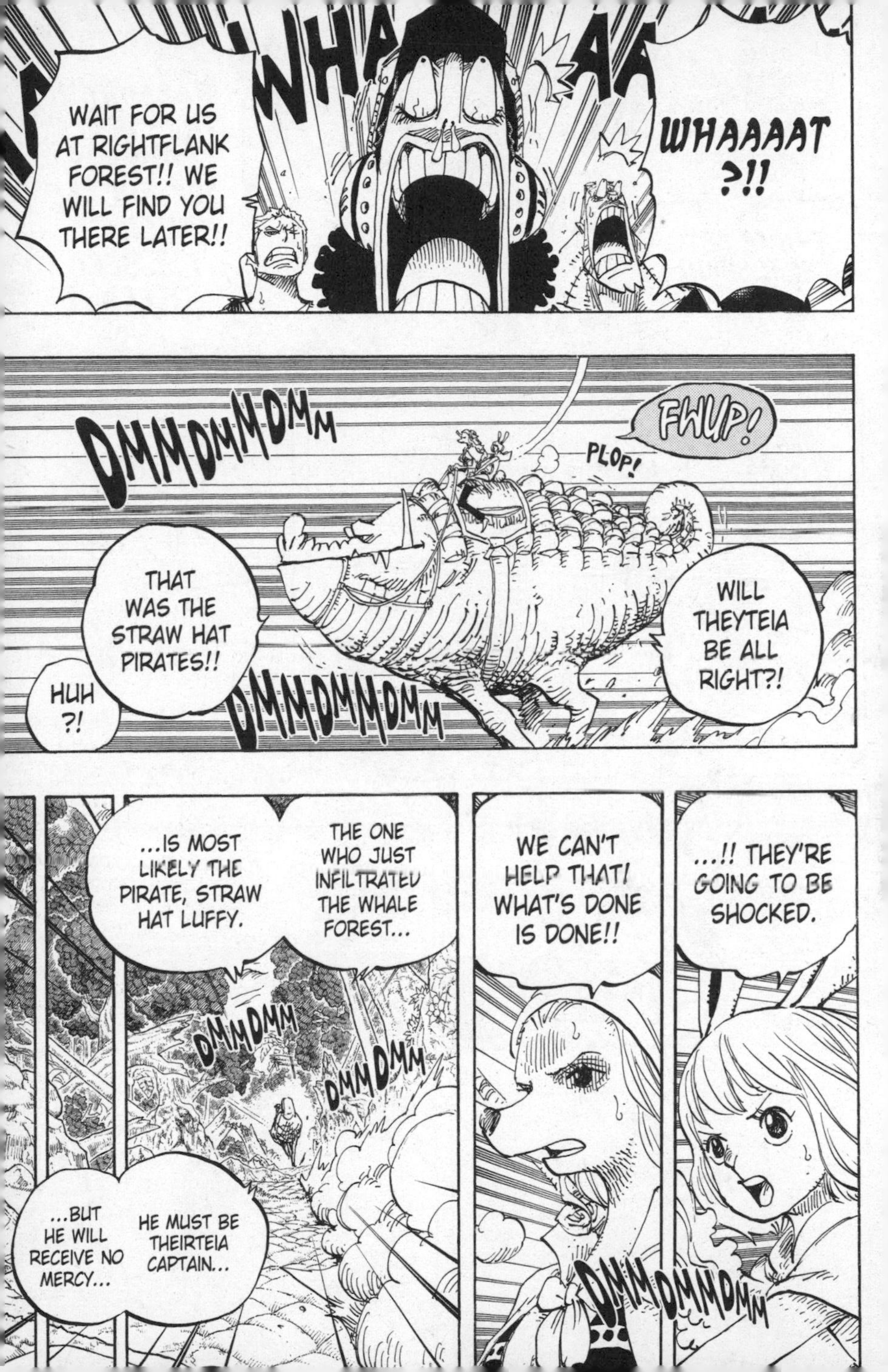
WHAAAAT ?!!
WAIT FOR US AT RIGHTFLANK FOREST!! WE WILL FIND YOU THERE LATER!!
FWUP!
PLOP!
DMMDMMDMM
WILL THEYTEIA BE ALL RIGHT?!
THAT WAS THE STRAW HAT PIRATES!!
HUH ?!
DMMDMMDMM
...!! THEY'RE GOING TO BE SHOCKED.
WE CAN'T HELP THAT! WHAT'S DONE IS DONE!!
DMMDMMDMM
THE ONE WHO JUST INFILTRATED THE WHALE FOREST...
...IS MOST LIKELY THE PIRATE, STRAW HAT LUFFY.
DMMDMM
DMMDMM
HE MUST BE THEIRTEIA CAPTAIN...
...BUT HE WILL RECEIVE NO MERCY...

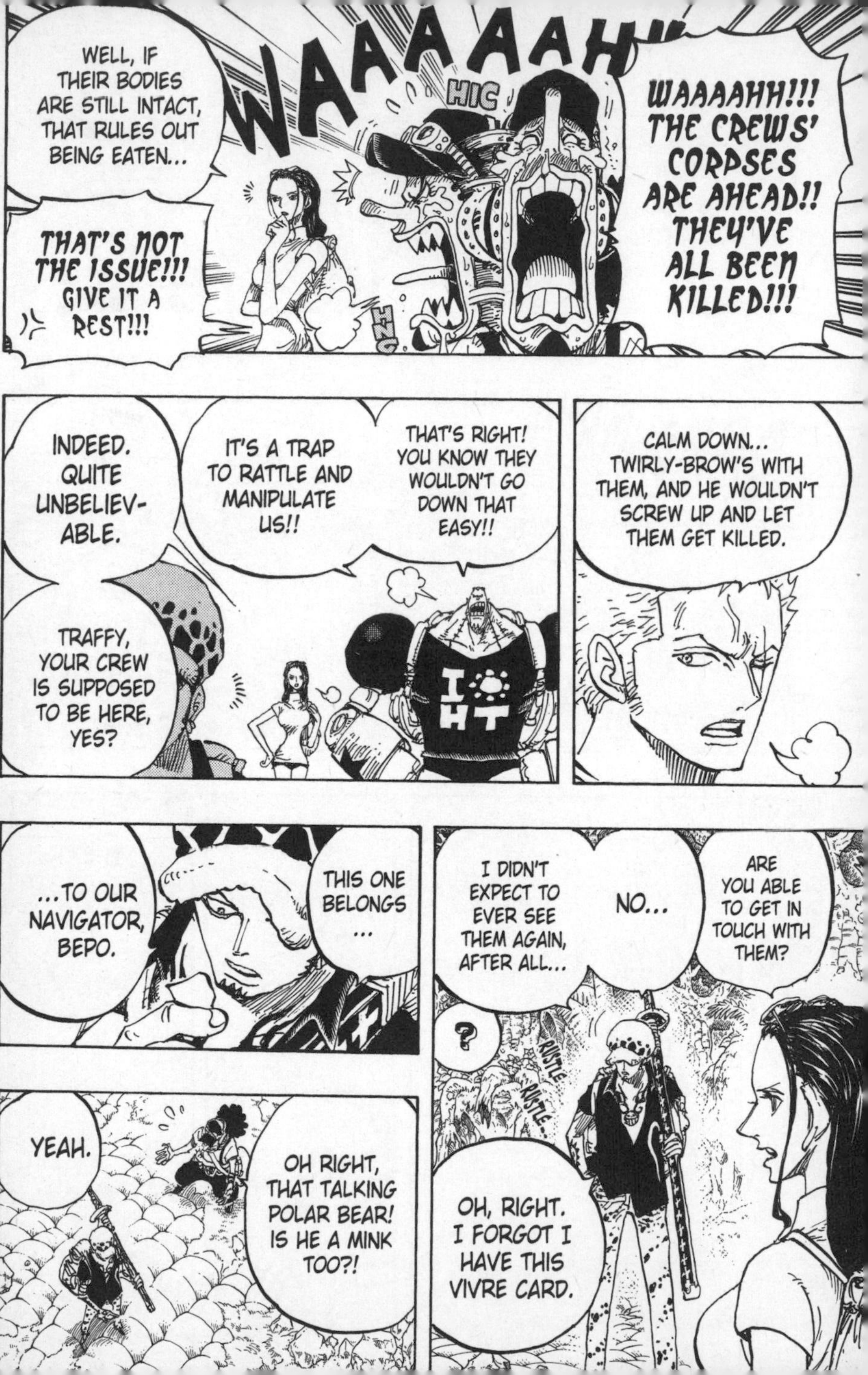
WAAAAAH!!
WAAAAHH!!! THE CREWS' CORPSES ARE AHEAD!! THEY'VE ALL BEEN KILLED!!!
HIC
WELL, IF THEIR BODIES ARE STILL INTACT, THAT RULES OUT BEING EATEN...
THAT'S NOT THE ISSUE!!! GIVE IT A REST!!!
HNG
CALM DOWN... TWIRLY-BROW'S WITH THEM, AND HE WOULDN'T SCREW UP AND LET THEM GET KILLED.
THAT'S RIGHT! YOU KNOW THEY WOULDN'T GO DOWN THAT EASY!!
IT'S A TRAP TO RATTLE AND MANIPULATE US!!
INDEED. QUITE UNBELIEV-ABLE.
TRAFFY, YOUR CREW IS SUPPOSED TO BE HERE, YES?
ARE YOU ABLE TO GET IN TOUCH WITH THEM?
NO...
I DIDN'T EXPECT TO EVER SEE THEM AGAIN, AFTER ALL...
?
RUSTLE
RUSTLE...
OH, RIGHT. I FORGOT I HAVE THIS VIVRE CARD.
THIS ONE BELONGS ...
...TO OUR NAVIGATOR, BEPO.
OH RIGHT, THAT TALKING POLAR BEAR! IS HE A MINK TOO?!
YEAH.

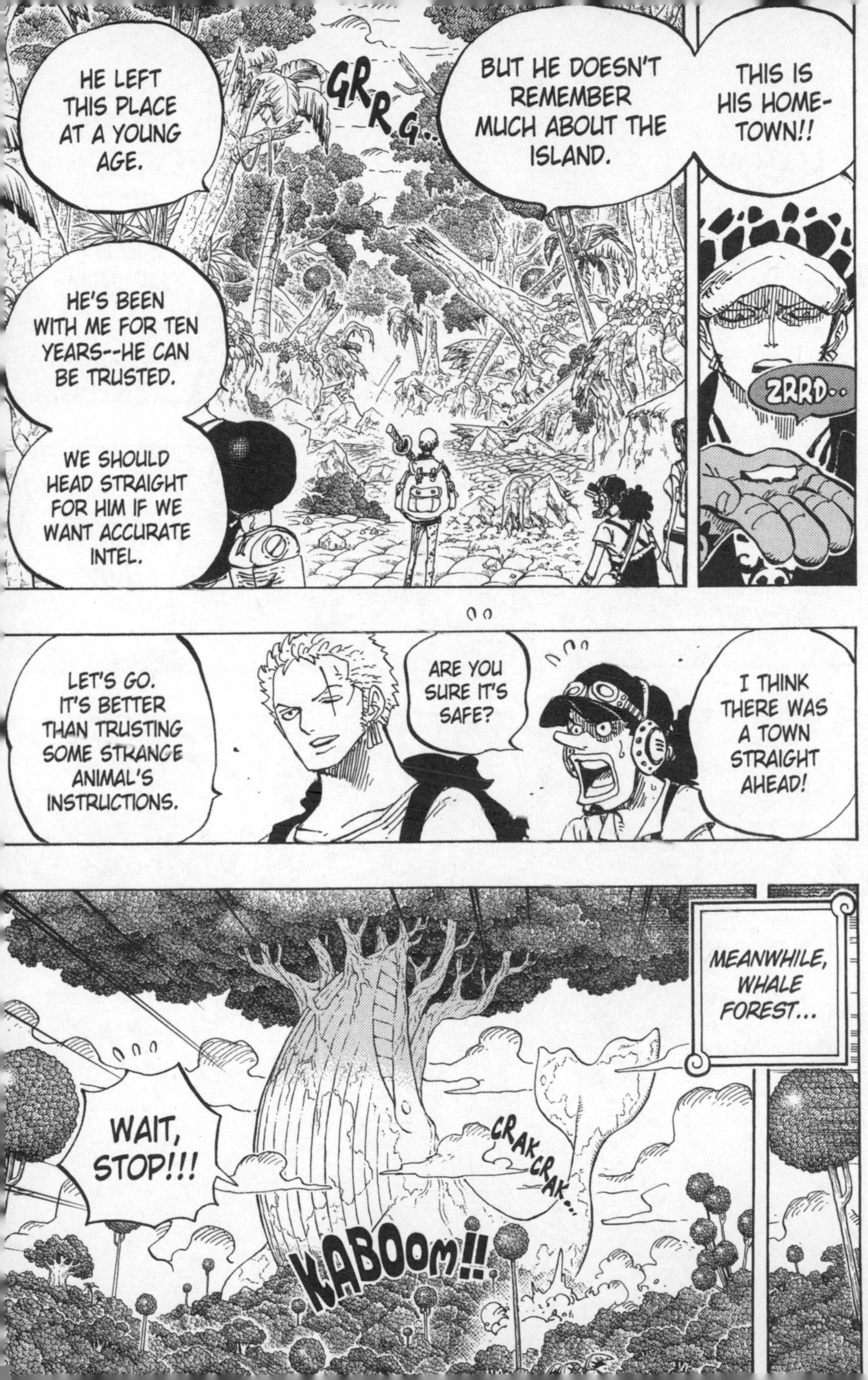
THIS IS HIS HOME-TOWN!!
ZRRD..
BUT HE DOESN'T REMEMBER MUCH ABOUT THE ISLAND.
GRRRG...
HE LEFT THIS PLACE AT A YOUNG AGE.
HE'S BEEN WITH ME FOR TEN YEARS--HE CAN BE TRUSTED.
WE SHOULD HEAD STRAIGHT FOR HIM IF WE WANT ACCURATE INTEL.
I THINK THERE WAS A TOWN STRAIGHT AHEAD!
ARE YOU SURE IT'S SAFE?
LET'S GO. IT'S BETTER THAN TRUSTING SOME STRANGE ANIMAL'S INSTRUCTIONS.
MEANWHILE, WHALE FOREST...
CRAKCRAK...
WAIT, STOP!!!
KABOOM!!

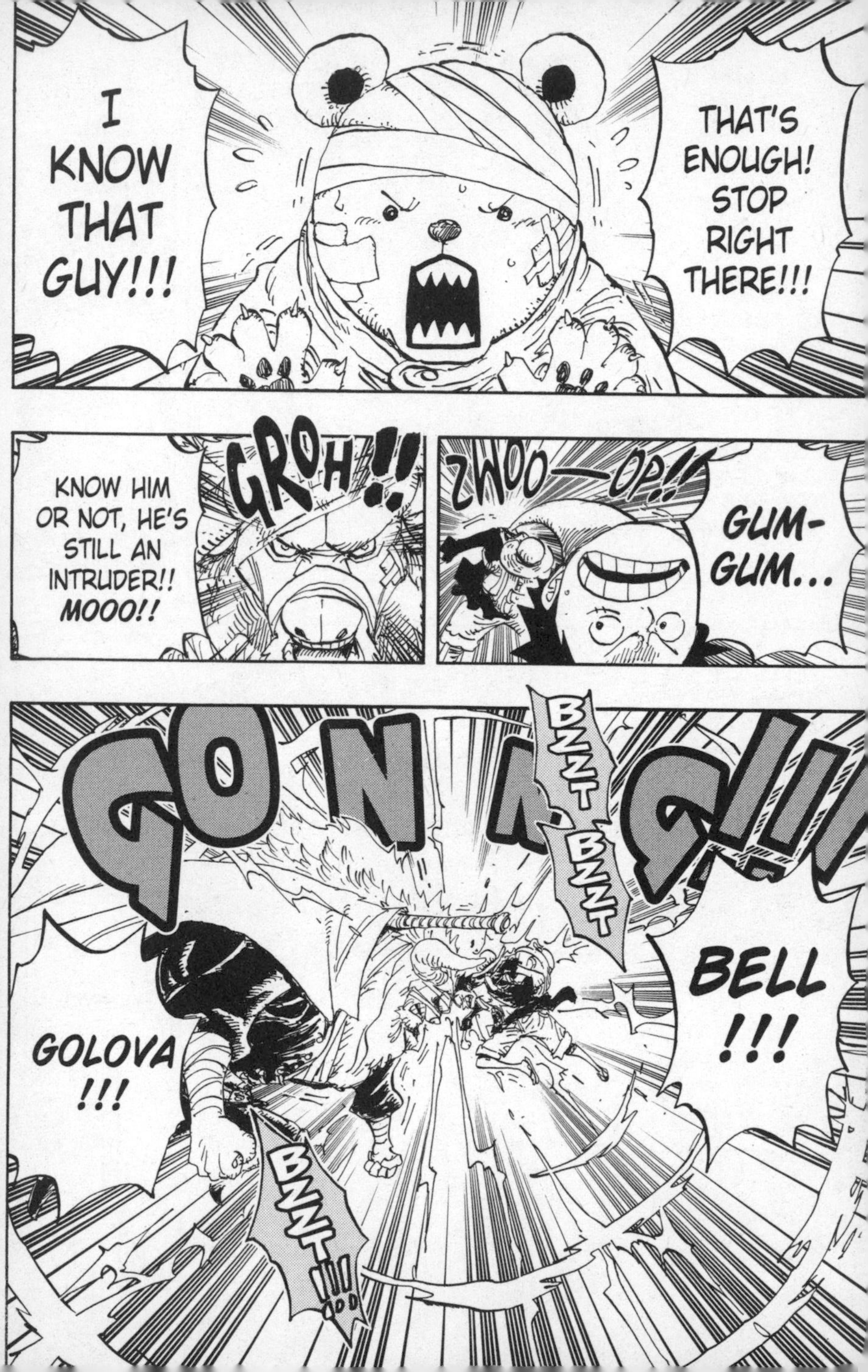
THAT'S ENOUGH! STOP RIGHT THERE!!!
I KNOW THAT GUY!!!
ZWOO—OP!!
GUM-GUM...
GROH!!
KNOW HIM OR NOT, HE'S STILL AN INTRUDER!! MOOO!!
GONNG!!!
BZZT BZZT BZZT
BELL!!!
GOLOVA!!!
BZZT!!!

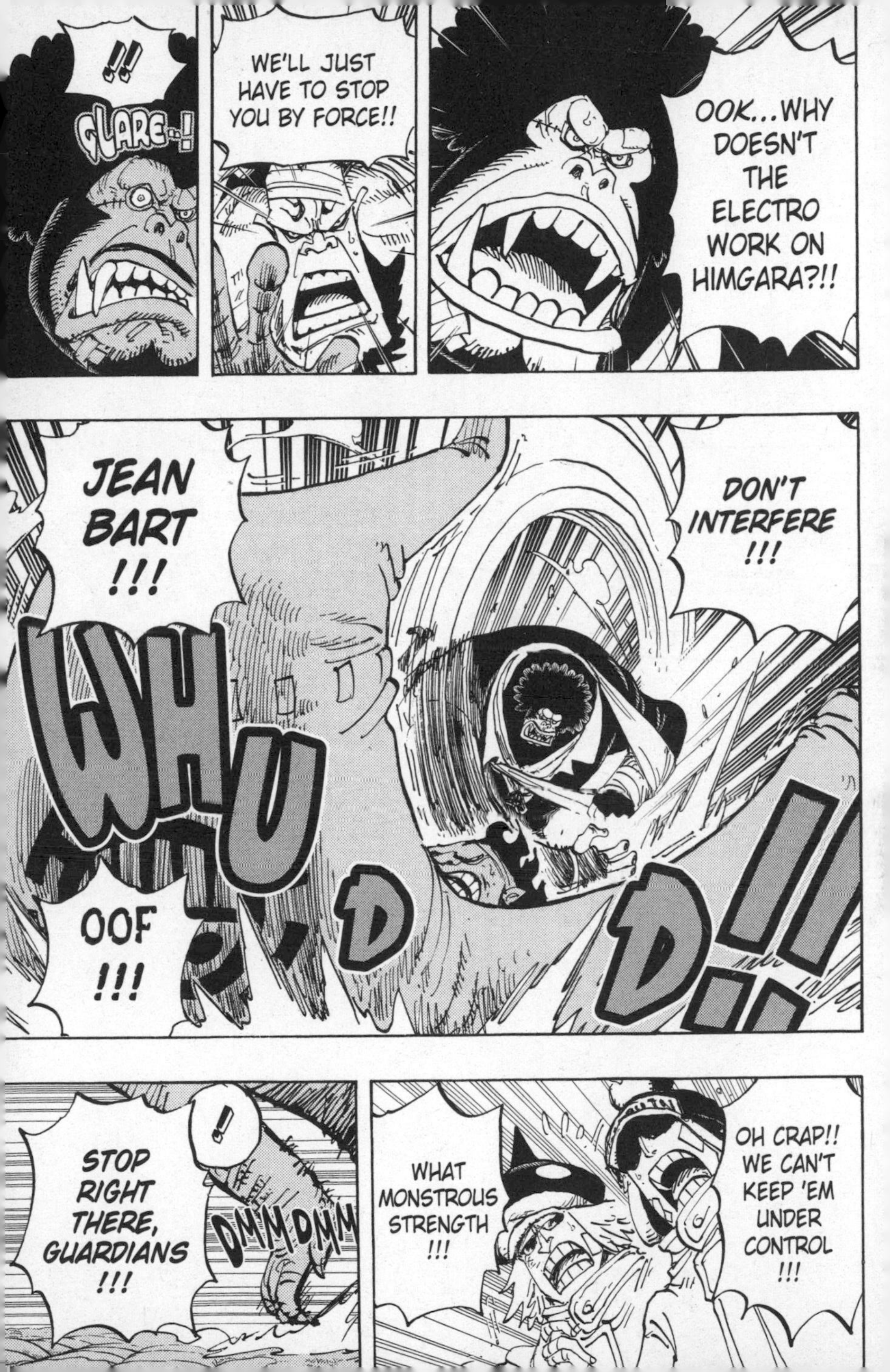
OOK...WHY DOESN'T THE ELECTRO WORK ON HIMGARA?!!
WE'LL JUST HAVE TO STOP YOU BY FORCE!!
!!
GLARE..!
DON'T INTERFERE!!!
JEAN BART!!!
WHUD D D!!
OOF!!!
OH CRAP!! WE CAN'T KEEP 'EM UNDER CONTROL!!!
WHAT MONSTROUS STRENGTH!!!
!
STOP RIGHT THERE, GUARDIANS!!!
DMM DMM

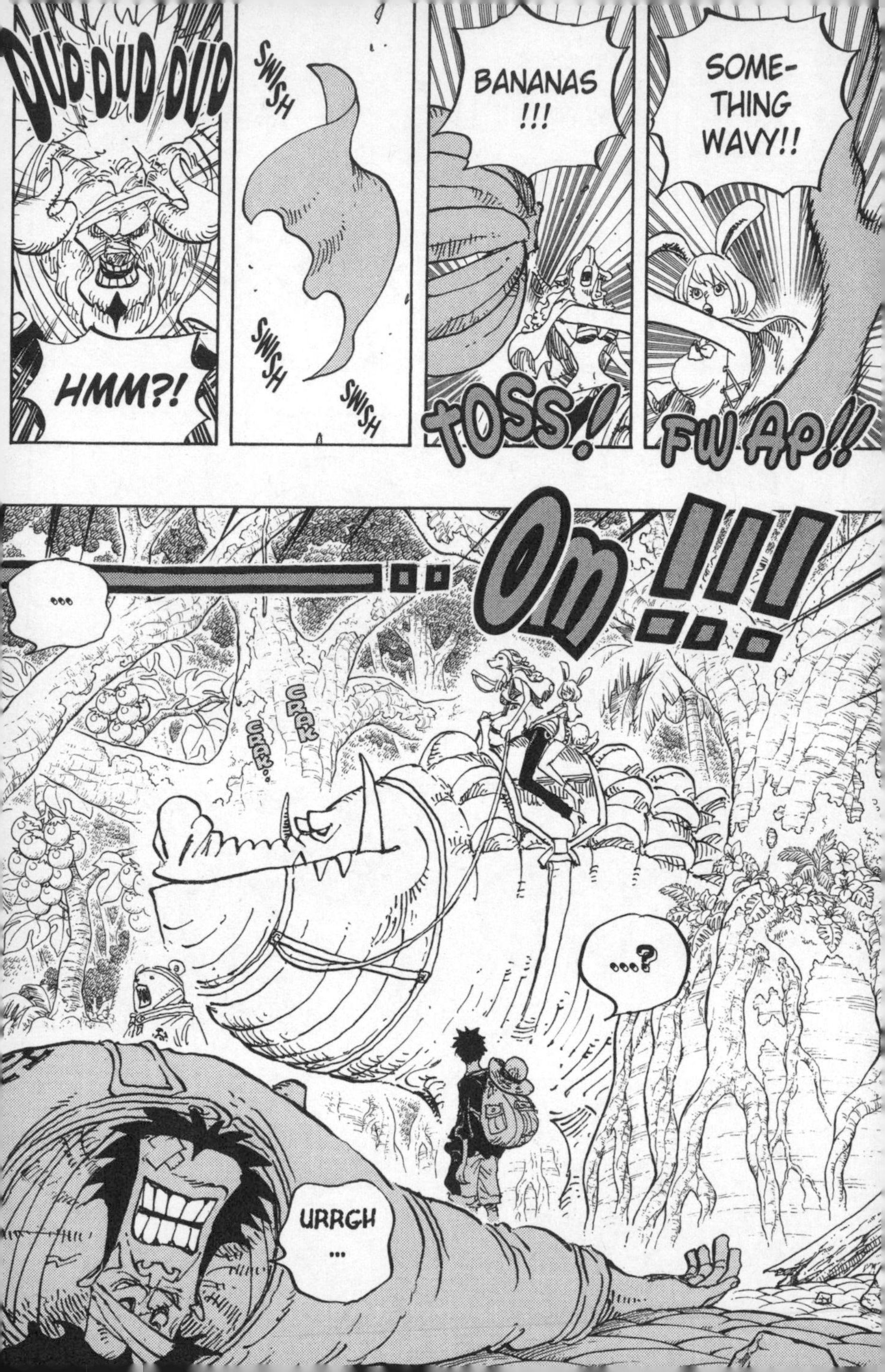
SOME-THING WAVY!!
FWAP!!
BANANAS!!!
TOSS!!
SWISH
SWISH
SWISH
DUD DUD DUD
HMM?!
..OM!!!
...?
CRAK
CRAK..
...
URRGH ...

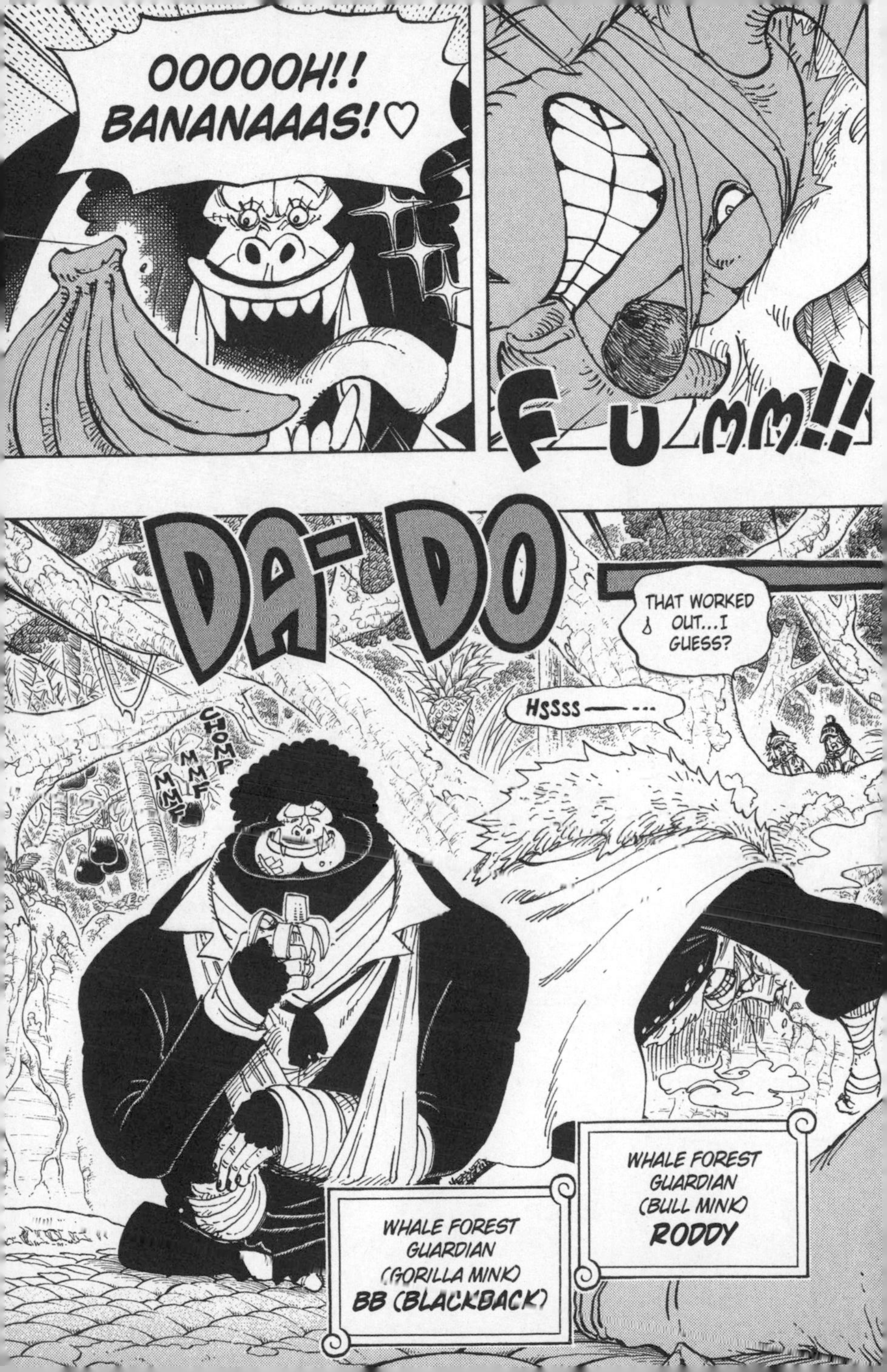
FUMM!!
OOOOOH!! BANANAAAS!♡
DA-DO—
THAT WORKED OUT...I GUESS?
HSSSS——...
CHOMP
MMF
MMF
WHALE FOREST GUARDIAN (BULL MINK) RODDY
WHALE FOREST GUARDIAN (GORILLA MINK) BB (BLACKBACK)

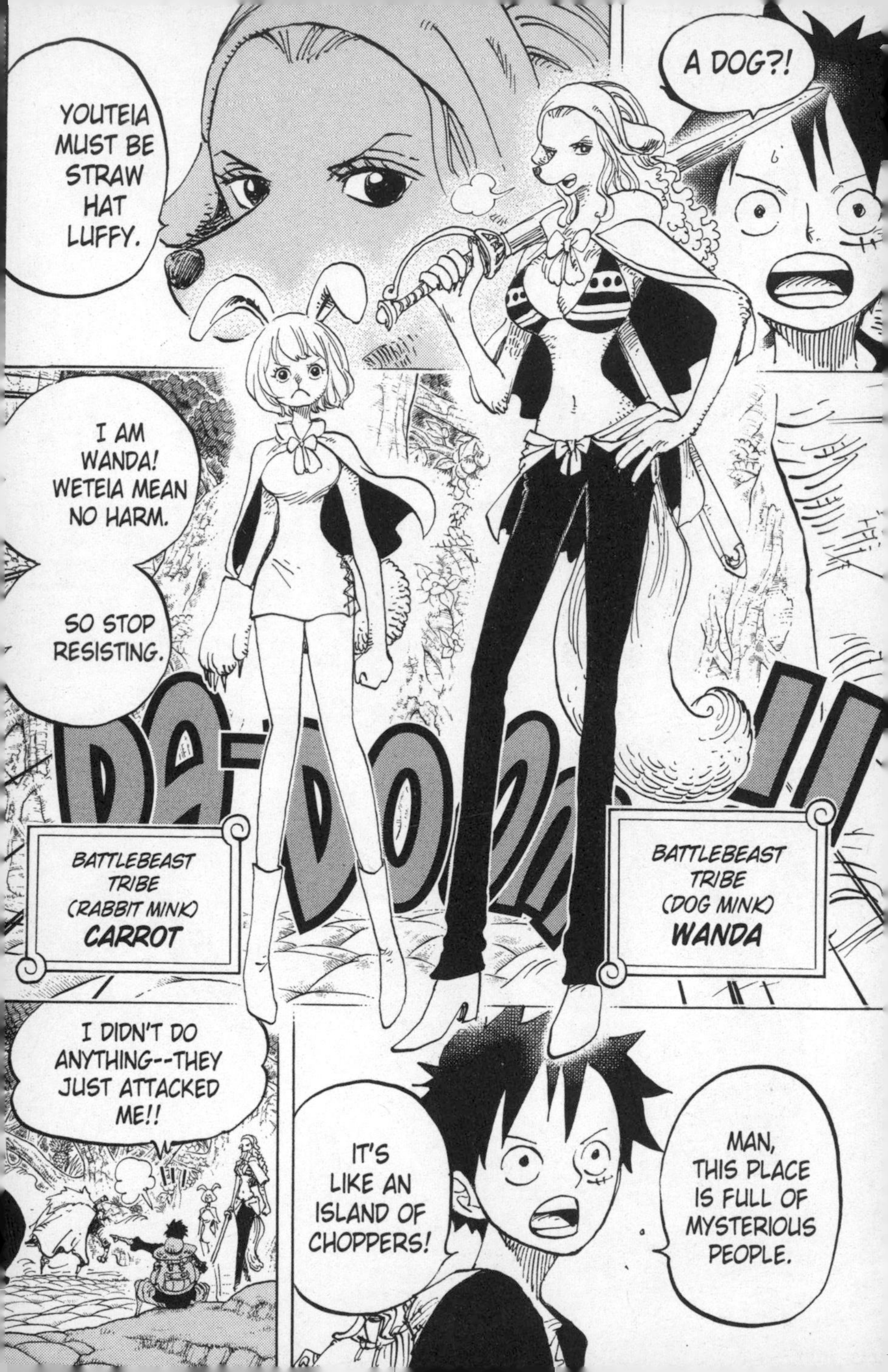
A DOG?!
YOUTEIA MUST BE STRAW HAT LUFFY.
I AM WANDA! WETEIA MEAN NO HARM.
SO STOP RESISTING.
DA-DOOM!!
BATTLEBEAST TRIBE (DOG MINK) WANDA
BATTLEBEAST TRIBE (RABBIT MINK) CARROT
MAN, THIS PLACE IS FULL OF MYSTERIOUS PEOPLE.
IT'S LIKE AN ISLAND OF CHOPPERS!
I DIDN'T DO ANYTHING--THEY JUST ATTACKED ME!!

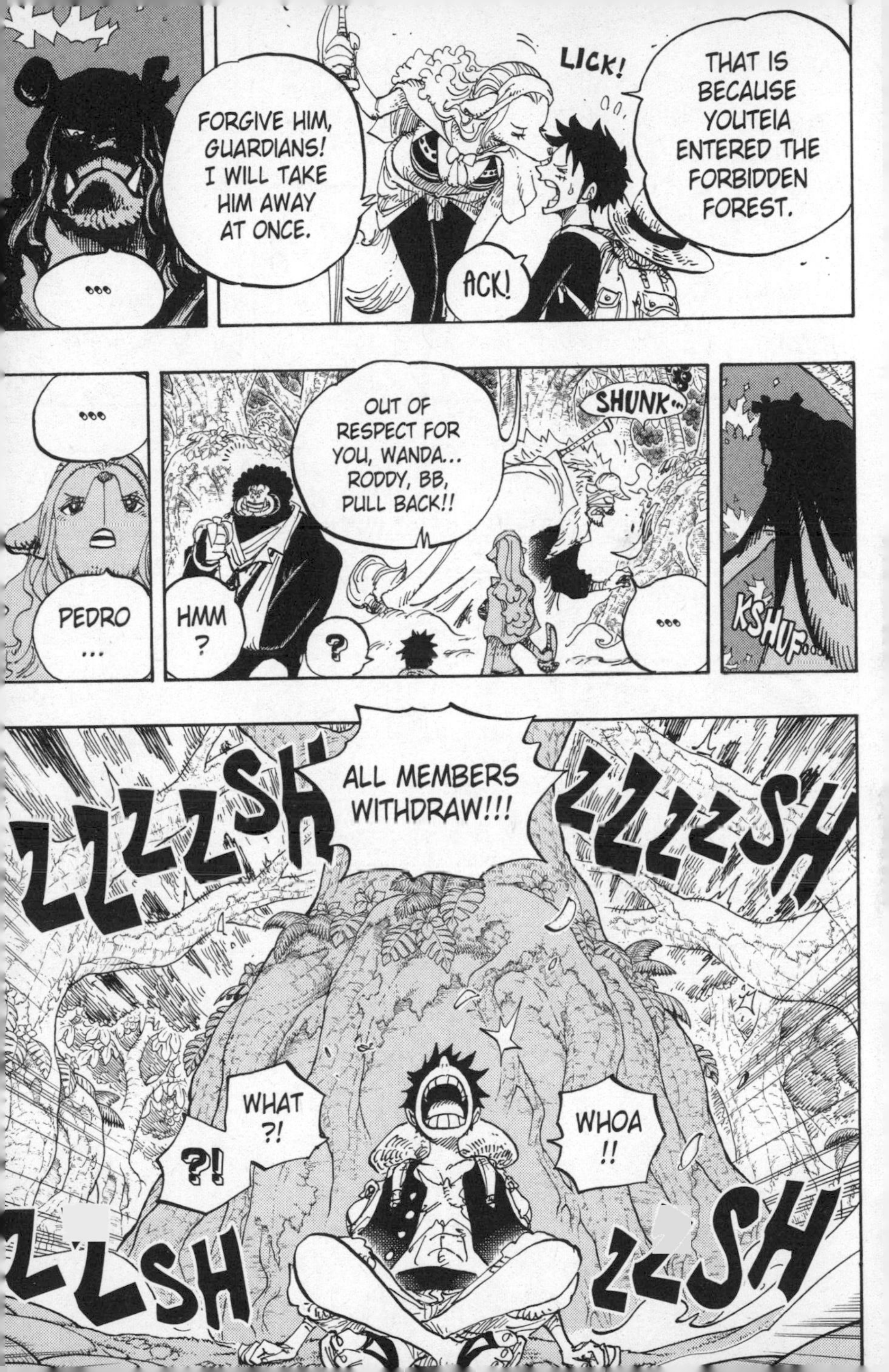
LICK!
THAT IS BECAUSE YOUTEIA ENTERED THE FORBIDDEN FOREST.
FORGIVE HIM, GUARDIANS! I WILL TAKE HIM AWAY AT ONCE.
ACK!
...
KSHUF...
SHUNK...
OUT OF RESPECT FOR YOU, WANDA... RODDY, BB, PULL BACK!!
...
HMM ?
?
...
PEDRO ...
ZZZZSH
ALL MEMBERS WITHDRAW!!!
ZZZZSH
WHOA !!
WHAT ?!
?!
ZZSH
ZZSH

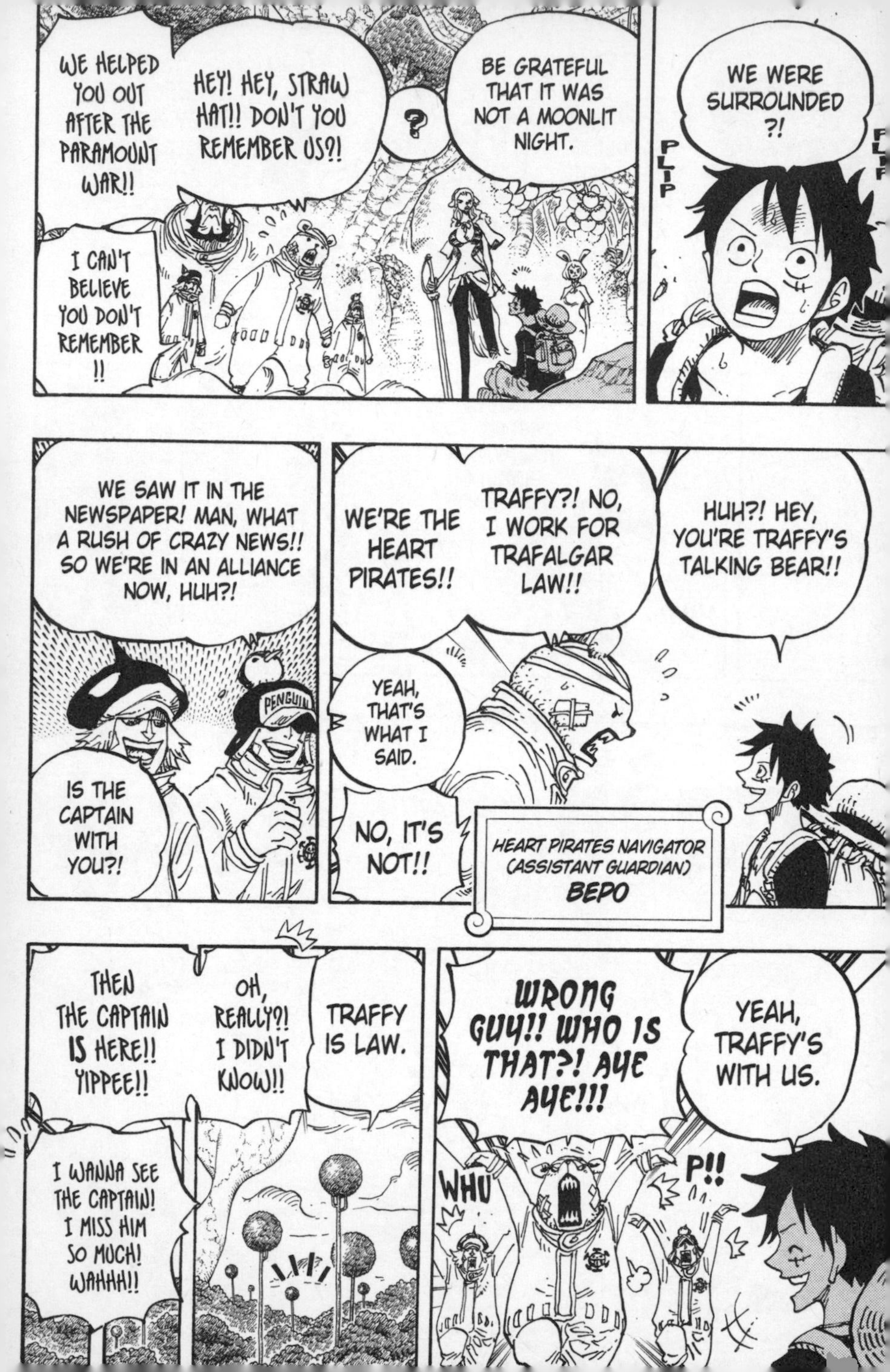
WE WERE SURROUNDED?!
FLIP
FLIP
BE GRATEFUL THAT IT WAS NOT A MOONLIT NIGHT.
?
HEY! HEY, STRAW HAT!! DON'T YOU REMEMBER US?!
WE HELPED YOU OUT AFTER THE PARAMOUNT WAR!!
I CAN'T BELIEVE YOU DON'T REMEMBER!!
HUH?! HEY, YOU'RE TRAFFY'S TALKING BEAR!!
TRAFFY?! NO, I WORK FOR TRAFALGAR LAW!!
WE'RE THE HEART PIRATES!!
YEAH, THAT'S WHAT I SAID.
NO, IT'S NOT!!
HEART PIRATES NAVIGATOR (ASSISTANT GUARDIAN) BEPO
WE SAW IT IN THE NEWSPAPER! MAN, WHAT A RUSH OF CRAZY NEWS!! SO WE'RE IN AN ALLIANCE NOW, HUH?!
IS THE CAPTAIN WITH YOU?!
YEAH, TRAFFY'S WITH US.
WRONG GUY!! WHO IS THAT?! AYE AYE!!!
P!!
WHU
TRAFFY IS LAW.
OH, REALLY?! I DIDN'T KNOW!!
THEN THE CAPTAIN IS HERE!! YIPPEE!!
I WANNA SEE THE CAPTAIN! I MISS HIM SO MUCH! WAHHH!!

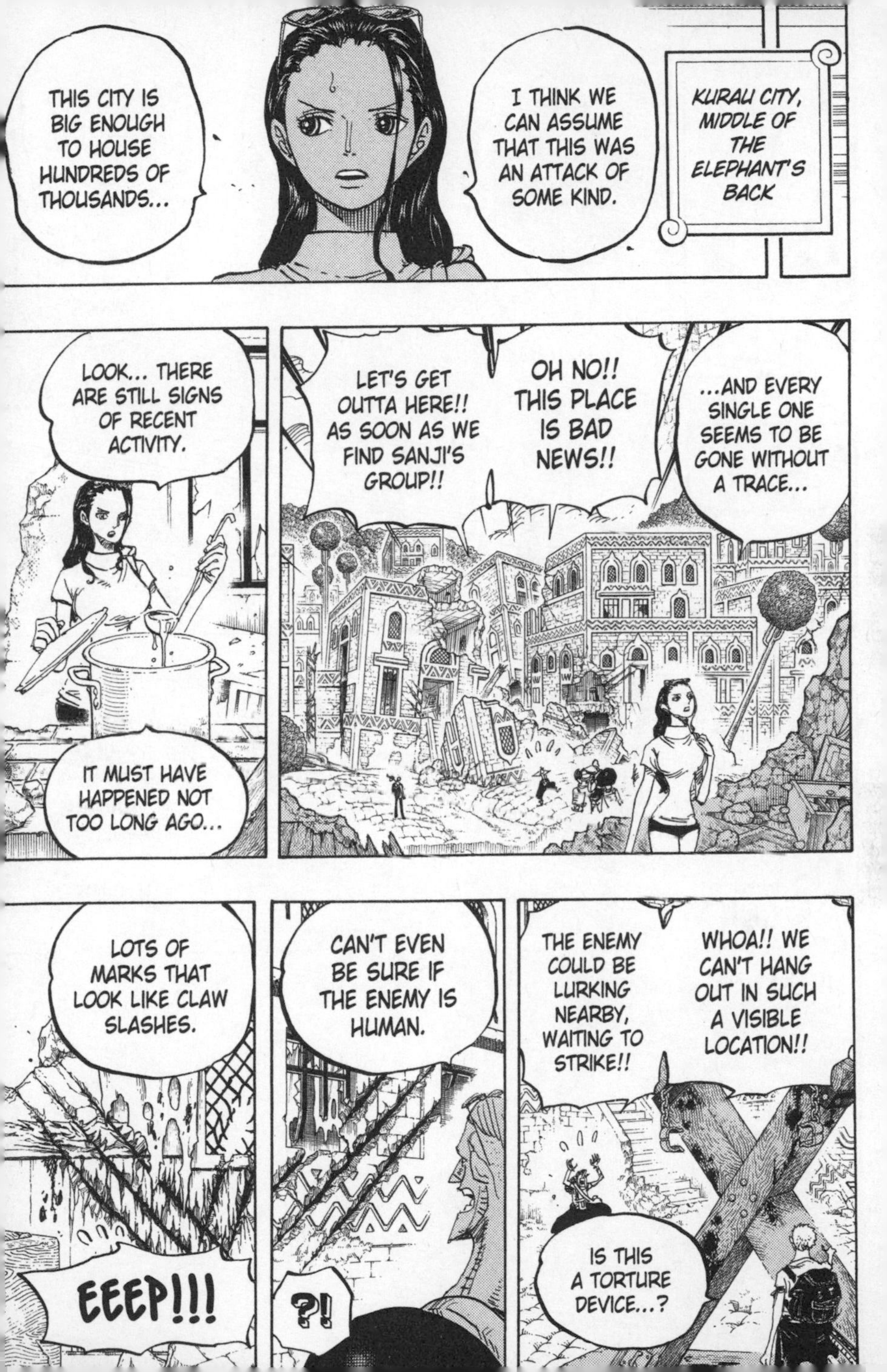
KURAU CITY, MIDDLE OF THE ELEPHANT'S BACK
I THINK WE CAN ASSUME THAT THIS WAS AN ATTACK OF SOME KIND.
THIS CITY IS BIG ENOUGH TO HOUSE HUNDREDS OF THOUSANDS...
...AND EVERY SINGLE ONE SEEMS TO BE GONE WITHOUT A TRACE...
OH NO!! THIS PLACE IS BAD NEWS!!
LET'S GET OUTTA HERE!! AS SOON AS WE FIND SANJI'S GROUP!!
LOOK... THERE ARE STILL SIGNS OF RECENT ACTIVITY.
IT MUST HAVE HAPPENED NOT TOO LONG AGO...
WHOA!! WE CAN'T HANG OUT IN SUCH A VISIBLE LOCATION!!
THE ENEMY COULD BE LURKING NEARBY, WAITING TO STRIKE!!
IS THIS A TORTURE DEVICE...?
CAN'T EVEN BE SURE IF THE ENEMY IS HUMAN.
?!
LOTS OF MARKS THAT LOOK LIKE CLAW SLASHES.
EEEP!!!

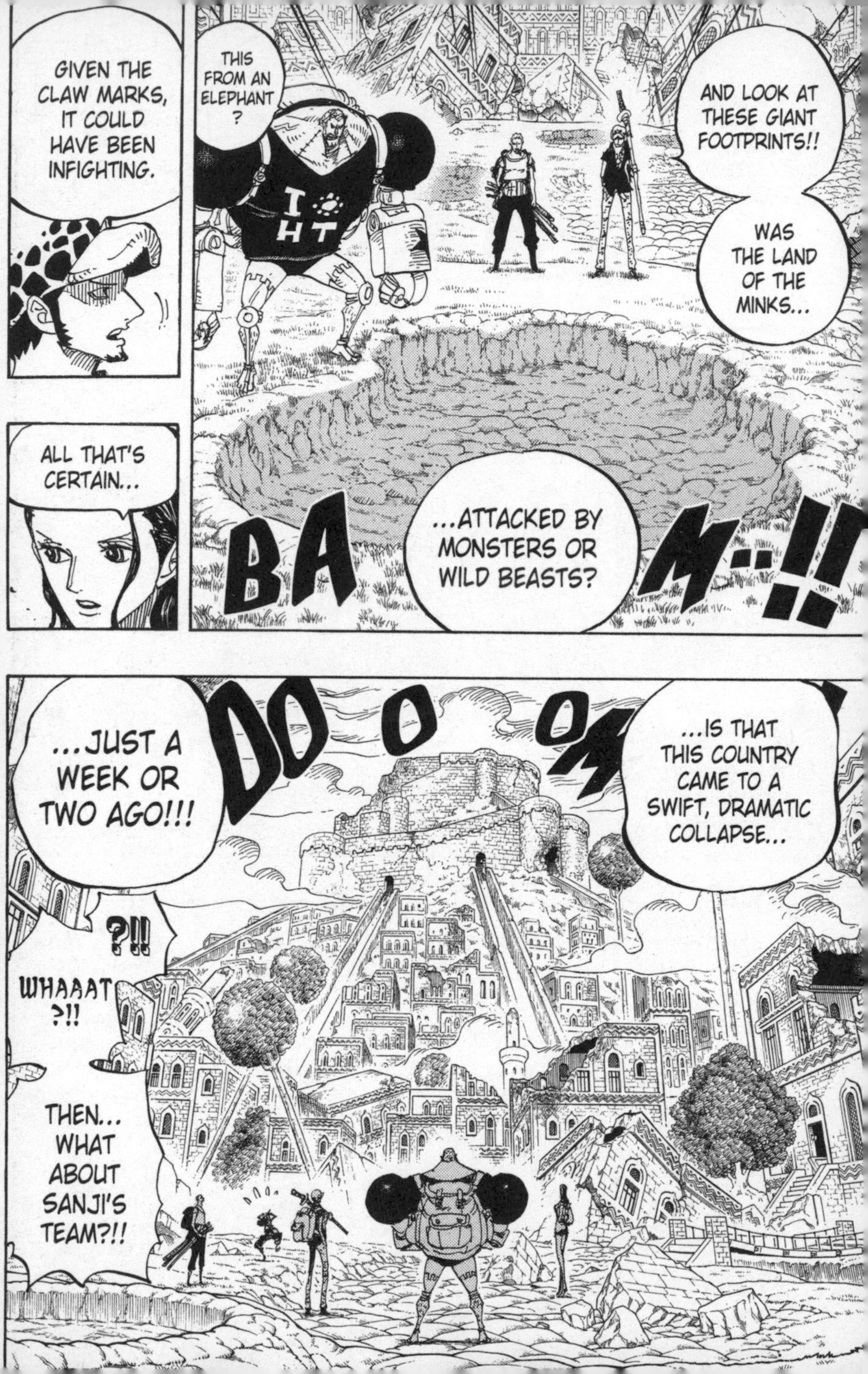
AND LOOK AT THESE GIANT FOOTPRINTS!!
WAS THE LAND OF THE MINKS...
THIS FROM AN ELEPHANT?
...ATTACKED BY MONSTERS OR WILD BEASTS?
BA M..!!
GIVEN THE CLAW MARKS, IT COULD HAVE BEEN INFIGHTING.
ALL THAT'S CERTAIN...
...IS THAT THIS COUNTRY CAME TO A SWIFT, DRAMATIC COLLAPSE...
DO O OM
...JUST A WEEK OR TWO AGO!!!
?!!
WHAAAT?!!
THEN... WHAT ABOUT SANJI'S TEAM?!!

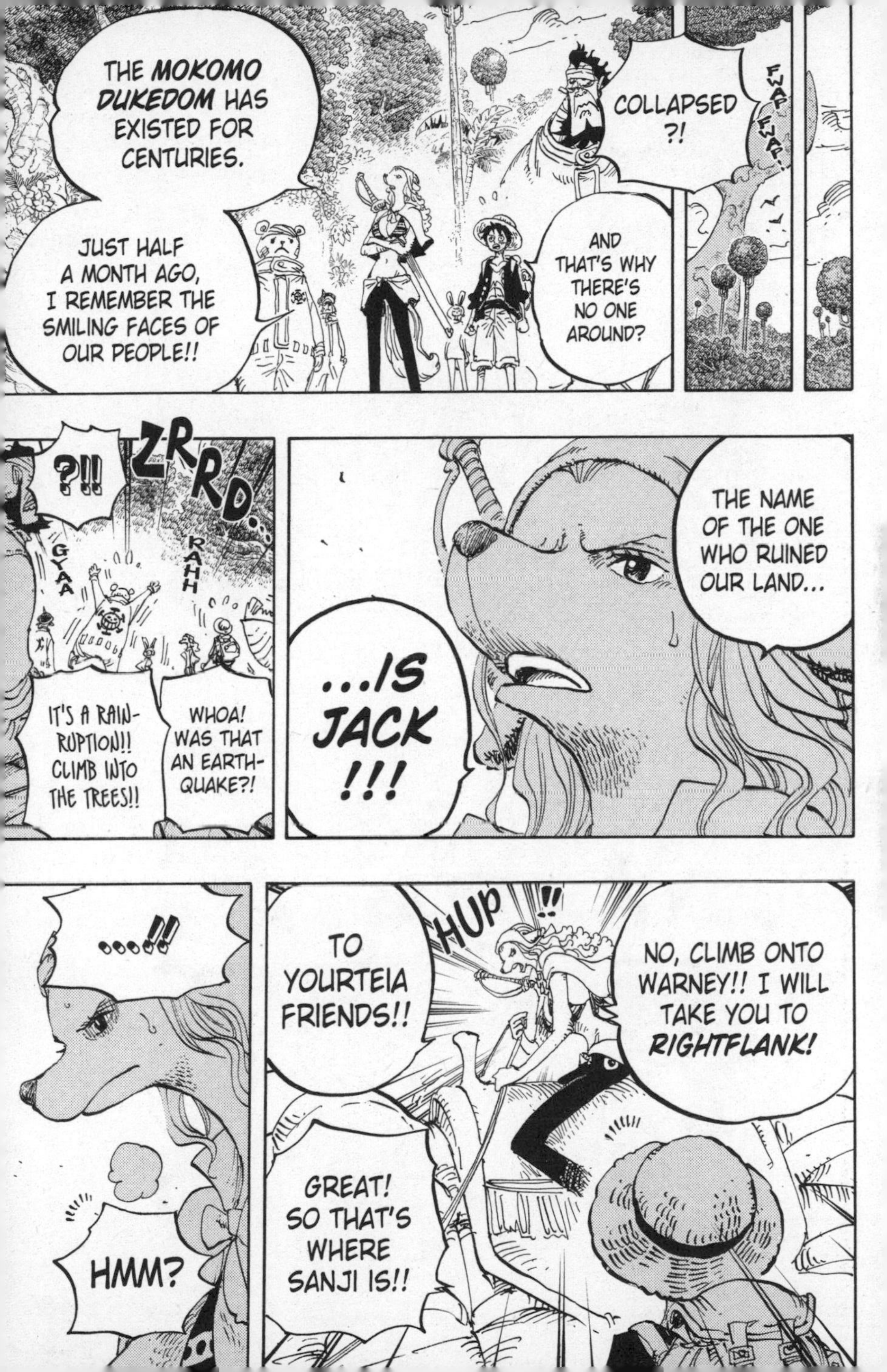

FWAP FWAP
COLLAPSED ?!
AND THAT'S WHY THERE'S NO ONE AROUND?
THE *MOKOMO DUKEDOM* HAS EXISTED FOR CENTURIES.
JUST HALF A MONTH AGO, I REMEMBER THE SMILING FACES OF OUR PEOPLE!!
THE NAME OF THE ONE WHO RUINED OUR LAND...
...IS JACK !!!
?!!
ZRRRD...
RAHH
GYAA
WHOA! WAS THAT AN EARTH-QUAKE?!
IT'S A RAIN-RUPTION!! CLIMB INTO THE TREES!!
HUP
!!
NO, CLIMB ONTO WARNEY!! I WILL TAKE YOU TO *RIGHTFLANK!*
TO YOURTEIA FRIENDS!!
GREAT! SO THAT'S WHERE SANJI IS!!
.....!!
HMM?

SBS Question Corner (Masamichi Kobayashi, Gunma)

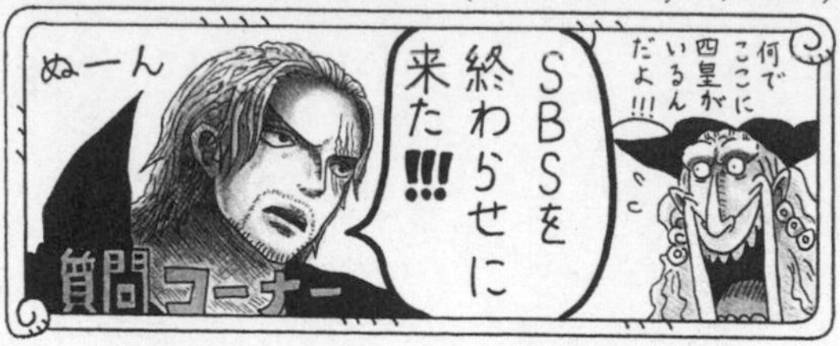
何でここに四皇がいるんだよ!!!
SBSを終わらせに来た!!!
ぬーん
質問コーナー

Q: I have a request. Please draw the childhood versions of the Don Quixote Family!
--Invincible Gum-Gum

A: Okay, sure. I'll skip the ones I've already drawn as kids.

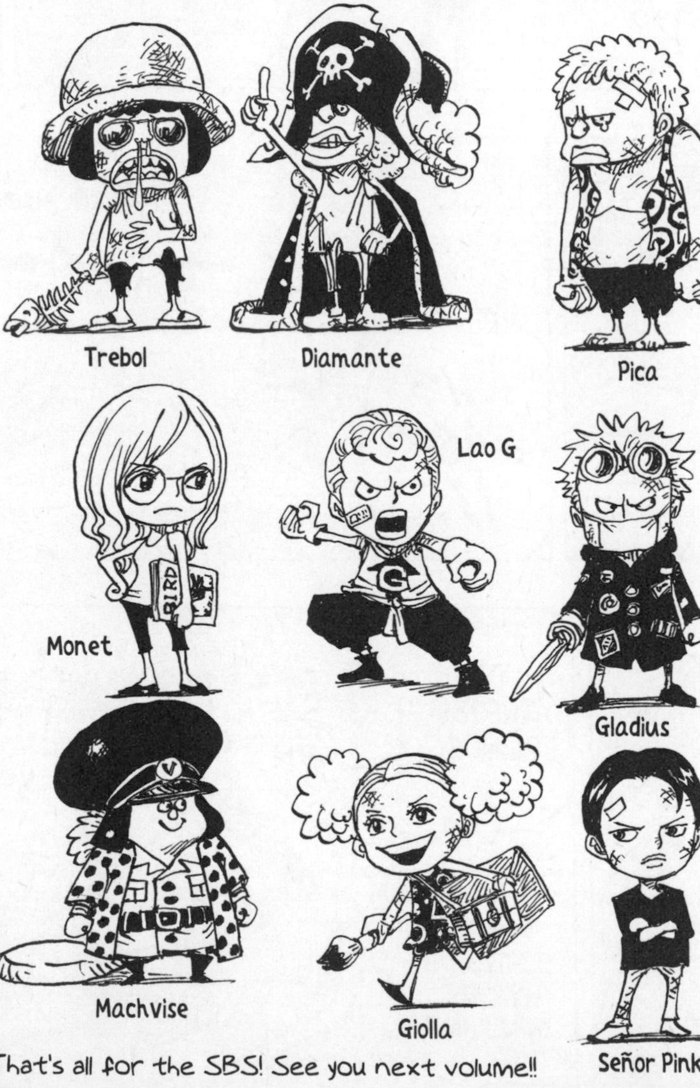
Trebol
Diamante
Pica
Lao G
Monet
Gladius
Machvise
Giolla
Señor Pink

That's all for the SBS! See you next volume!!

# Chapter 806:
# AT RIGHTFLANK FORTRESS

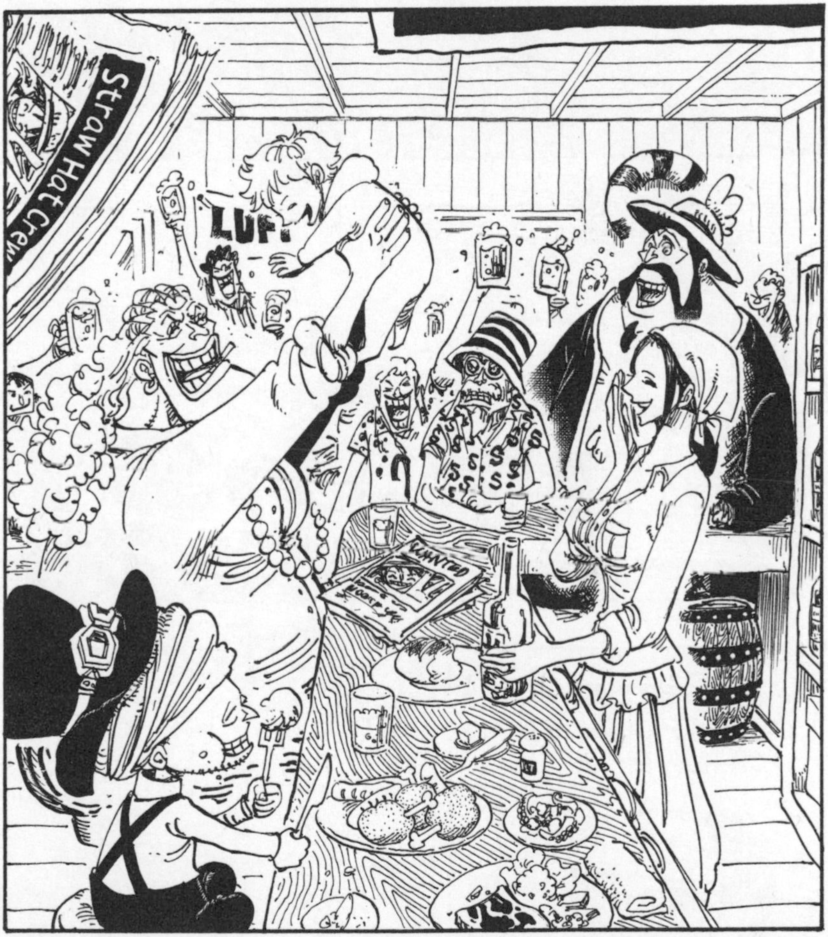

Straw Hat Crew
LUFF
WANTED


DECKS OF THE WORLD, 500-MILLION-MAN ARC, VOL. 2: "WINDMILL VILLAGE"

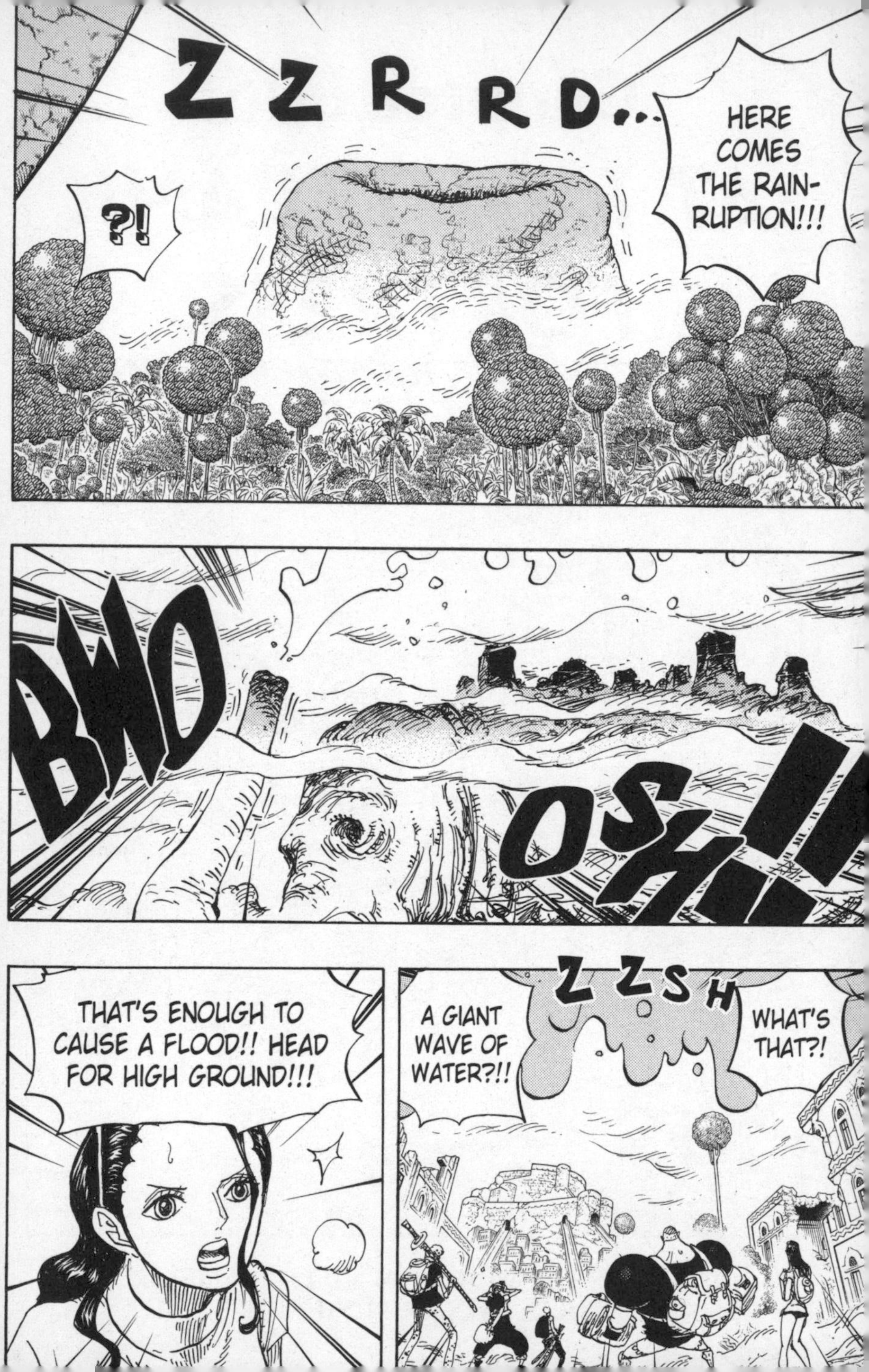
ZZRRD...
HERE COMES THE RAIN-RUPTION!!!
?!
BWOOSH!!
WHAT'S THAT?!
ZZSH
A GIANT WAVE OF WATER?!!
THAT'S ENOUGH TO CAUSE A FLOOD!! HEAD FOR HIGH GROUND!!!

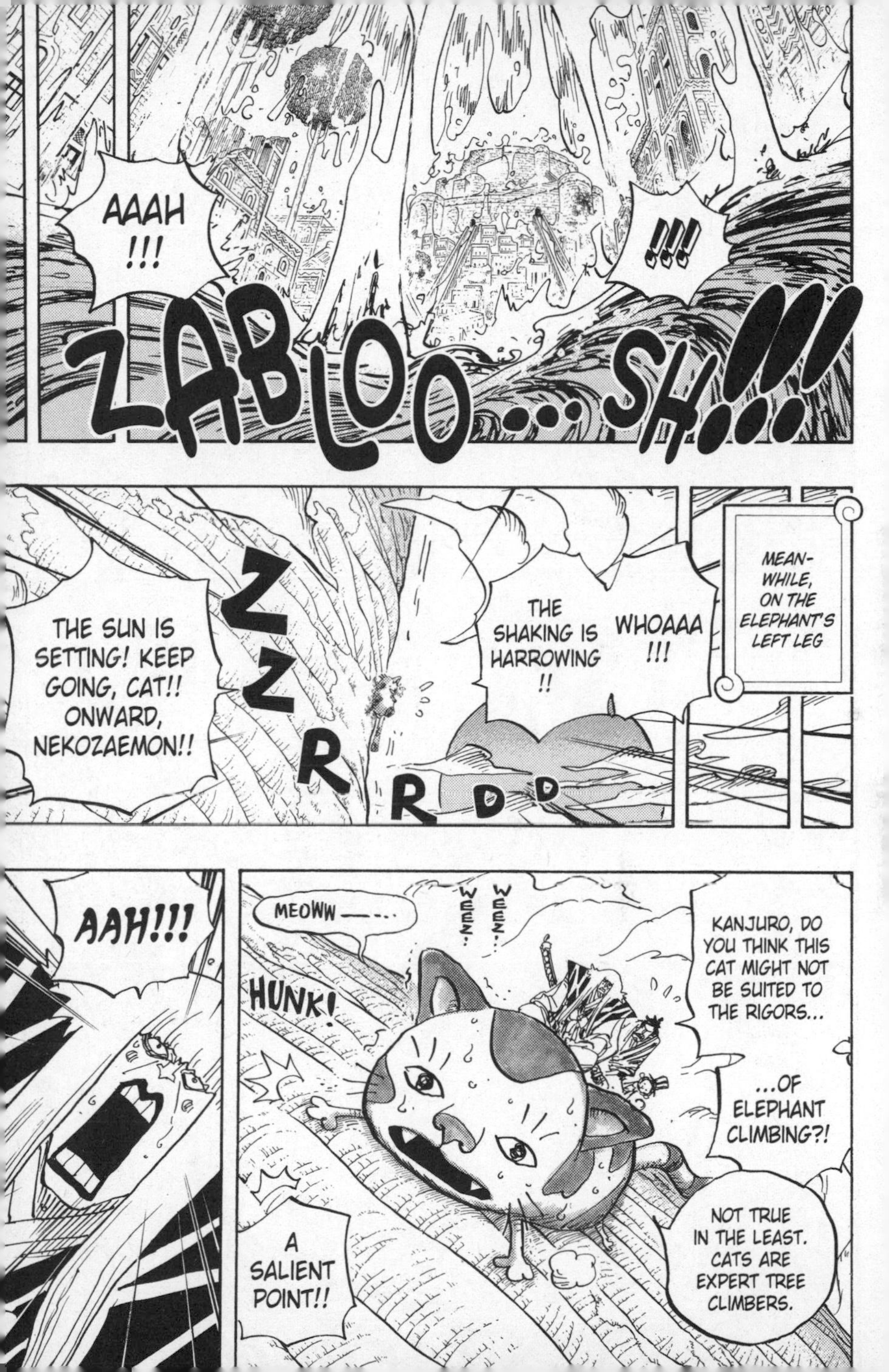
!!!
AAAH !!!
ZABLOO...SH!!!
MEAN-WHILE, ON THE ELEPHANT'S LEFT LEG
WHOAAA !!!
THE SHAKING IS HARROWING !!
ZZRRDD
THE SUN IS SETTING! KEEP GOING, CAT!! ONWARD, NEKOZAEMON!!
KANJURO, DO YOU THINK THIS CAT MIGHT NOT BE SUITED TO THE RIGORS...
WEEZ... WEEZ...
MEOWW ———...
HUNK!
...OF ELEPHANT CLIMBING?!
NOT TRUE IN THE LEAST. CATS ARE EXPERT TREE CLIMBERS.
A SALIENT POINT!!
AAH!!!

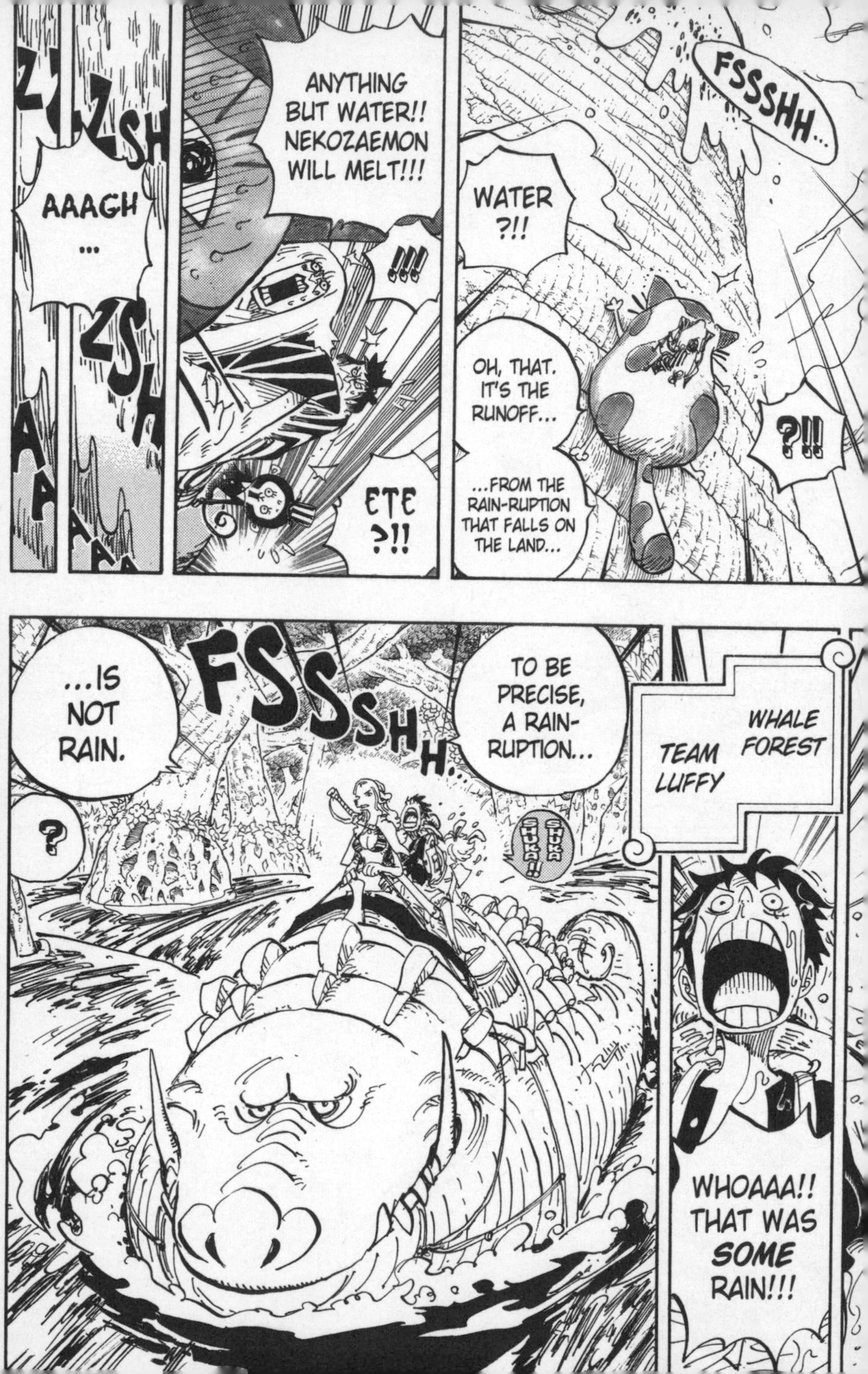
FSSSHH...
WATER ?!!
?!!
OH, THAT. IT'S THE RUNOFF...
...FROM THE RAIN-RUPTION THAT FALLS ON THE LAND...
ANYTHING BUT WATER!! NEKOZAEMON WILL MELT!!!
!!!
ETE ?!!
ZZSH
AAAGH ...
ZSH
AAAA
WHALE FOREST
TEAM LUFFY
WHOAAA!! THAT WAS *SOME* RAIN!!!
TO BE PRECISE, A RAIN-RUPTION...
FSSSHH...
...IS NOT RAIN.
?
SHUKA SHUKA

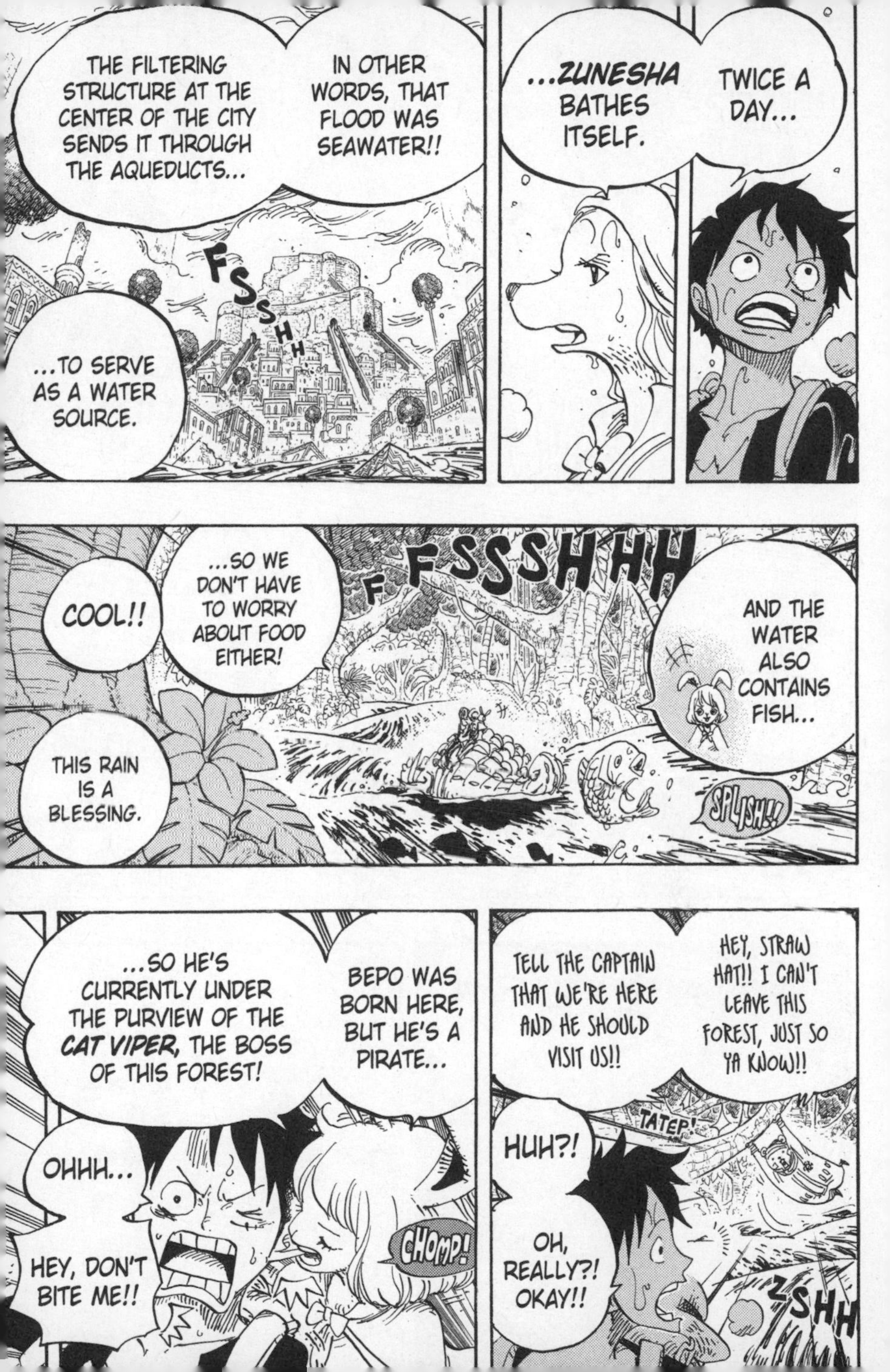
TWICE A DAY...
...ZUNESHA BATHES ITSELF.
IN OTHER WORDS, THAT FLOOD WAS SEAWATER!!
THE FILTERING STRUCTURE AT THE CENTER OF THE CITY SENDS IT THROUGH THE AQUEDUCTS...
FSSHH
...TO SERVE AS A WATER SOURCE.
AND THE WATER ALSO CONTAINS FISH...
SPLISH!!
FFSSSHHH
...SO WE DON'T HAVE TO WORRY ABOUT FOOD EITHER!
COOL!!
THIS RAIN IS A BLESSING.
HEY, STRAW HAT!! I CAN'T LEAVE THIS FOREST, JUST SO YA KNOW!!
TELL THE CAPTAIN THAT WE'RE HERE AND HE SHOULD VISIT US!!
TATEP!
HUH?!
ZSHH
OH, REALLY?! OKAY!!
BEPO WAS BORN HERE, BUT HE'S A PIRATE...
...SO HE'S CURRENTLY UNDER THE PURVIEW OF THE CAT VIPER, THE BOSS OF THIS FOREST!
OHHH...
CHOMP!
HEY, DON'T BITE ME!!

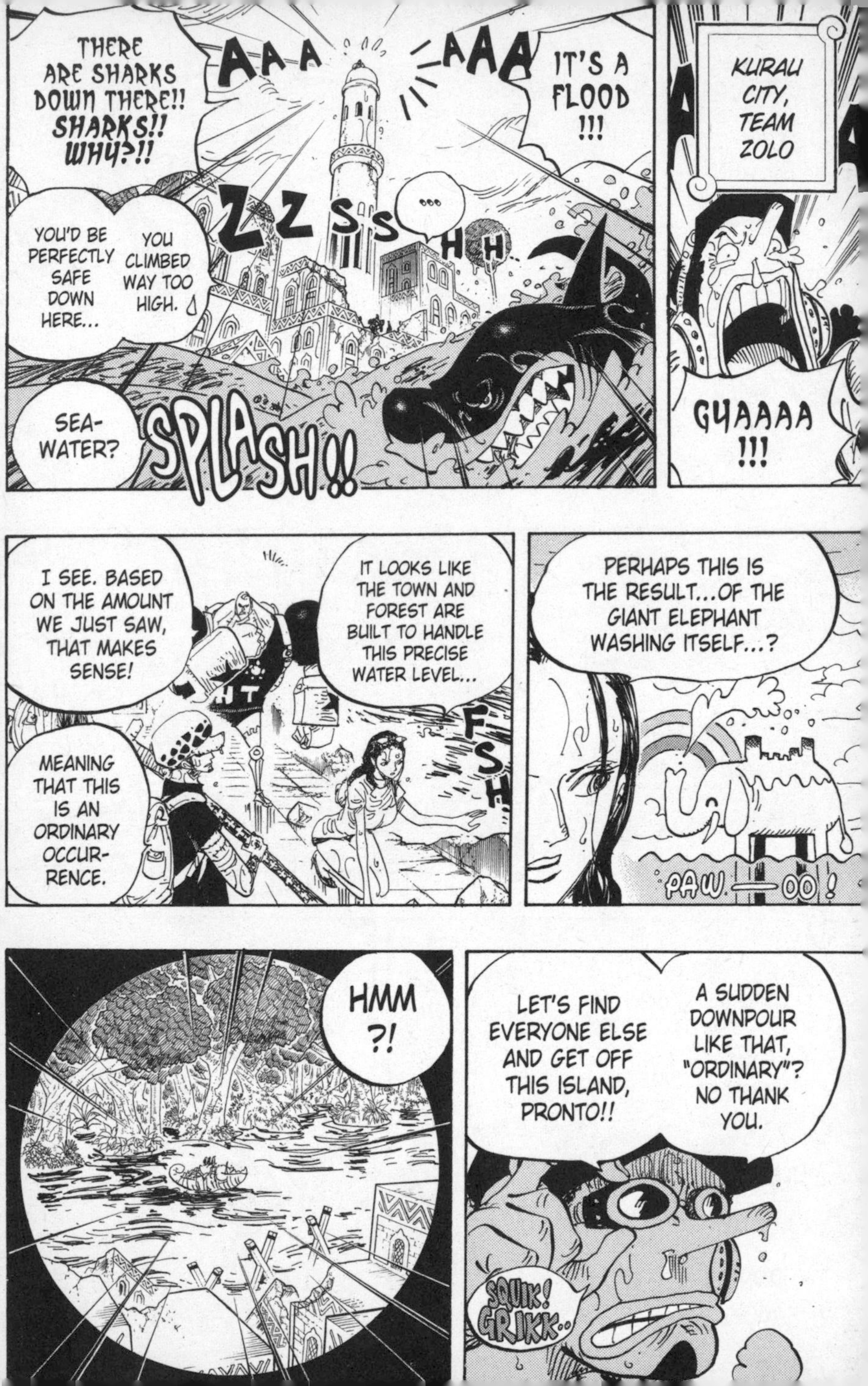
KURAU CITY, TEAM ZOLO
GYAAAA!!!
AAA AAA
IT'S A FLOOD!!!
THERE ARE SHARKS DOWN THERE!! SHARKS!! WHY?!!
ZZSSHH
...
YOU CLIMBED WAY TOO HIGH.
YOU'D BE PERFECTLY SAFE DOWN HERE...
SEA-WATER?
SPLASH!!
PERHAPS THIS IS THE RESULT...OF THE GIANT ELEPHANT WASHING ITSELF...?
PAW-OO!
IT LOOKS LIKE THE TOWN AND FOREST ARE BUILT TO HANDLE THIS PRECISE WATER LEVEL...
I SEE. BASED ON THE AMOUNT WE JUST SAW, THAT MAKES SENSE!
FSSH
MEANING THAT THIS IS AN ORDINARY OCCURRENCE.
A SUDDEN DOWNPOUR LIKE THAT, "ORDINARY"? NO THANK YOU.
LET'S FIND EVERYONE ELSE AND GET OFF THIS ISLAND, PRONTO!!
SQUIK! GRIKK..
HMM?!

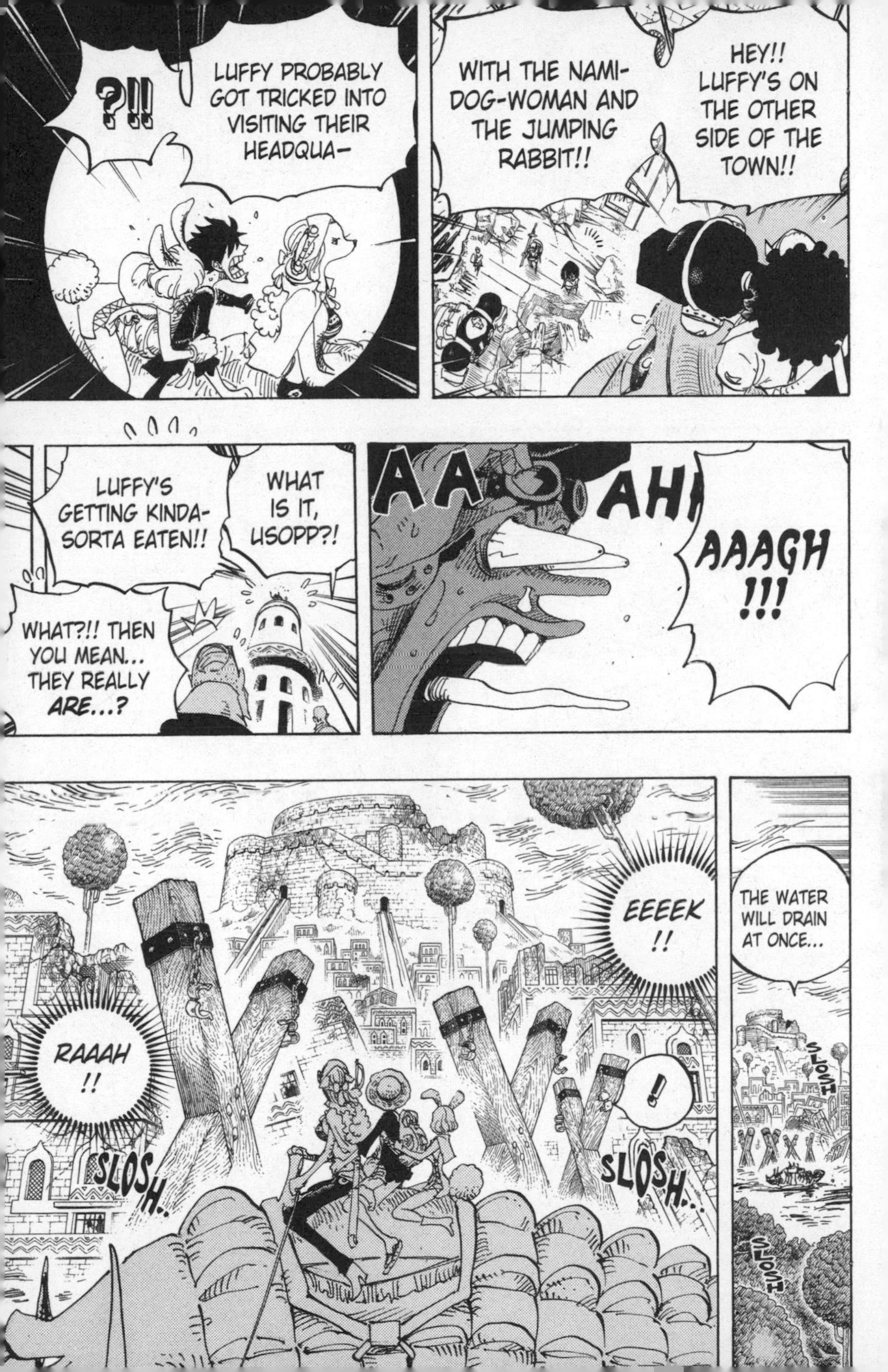
HEY!! LUFFY'S ON THE OTHER SIDE OF THE TOWN!!
WITH THE NAMI-DOG-WOMAN AND THE JUMPING RABBIT!!
LUFFY PROBABLY GOT TRICKED INTO VISITING THEIR HEADQUA—
?!!
AAAGH!!!
AA AH
WHAT IS IT, USOPP?!
LUFFY'S GETTING KINDA-SORTA EATEN!!
WHAT?!! THEN YOU MEAN... THEY REALLY ARE...?
THE WATER WILL DRAIN AT ONCE...
SLOSH
SLOSH
EEEEK!!
!
SLOSH...
RAAAH!!
SLOSH..

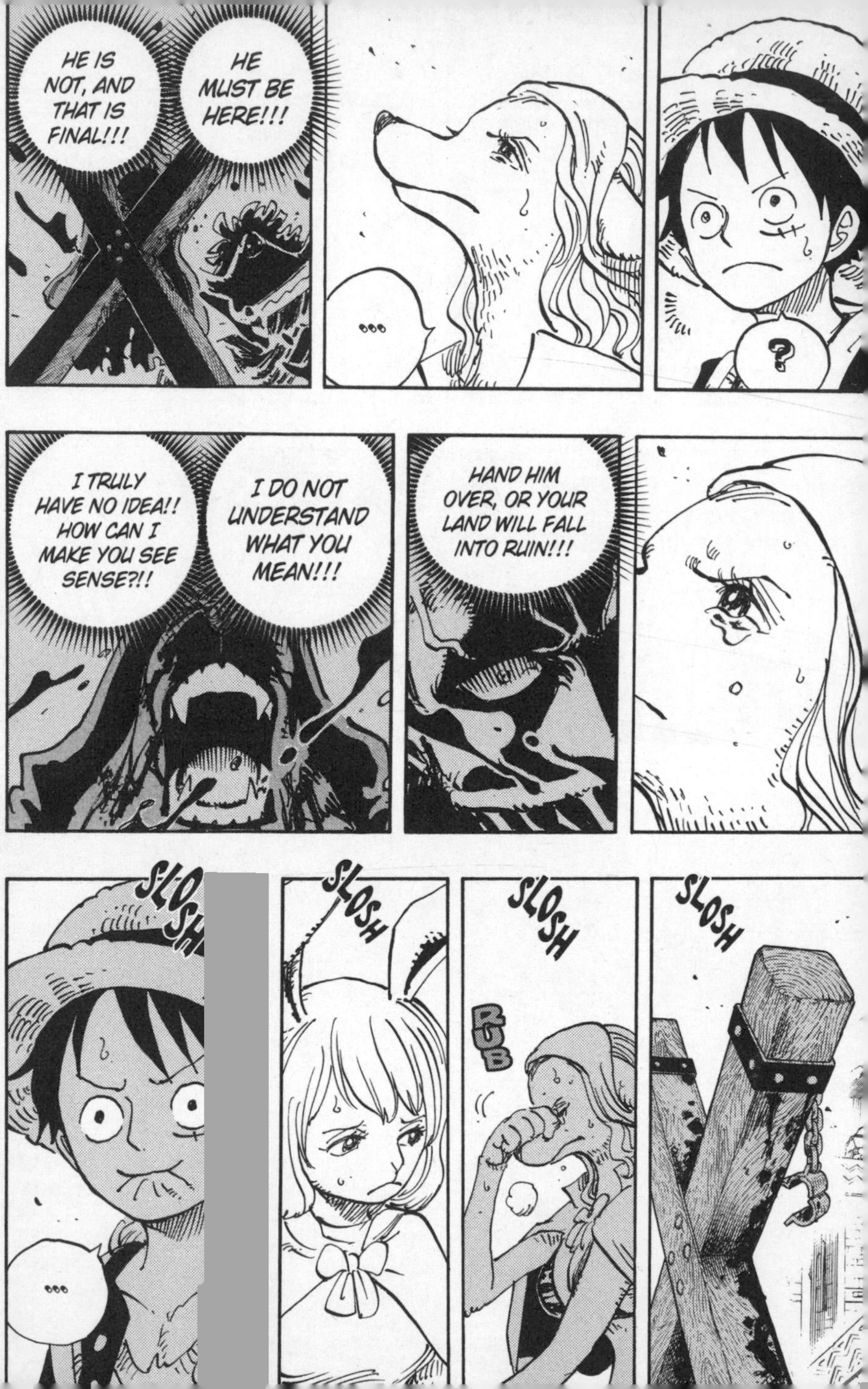
?
...
HE MUST BE HERE!!!
HE IS NOT, AND THAT IS FINAL!!!
HAND HIM OVER, OR YOUR LAND WILL FALL INTO RUIN!!!
I DO NOT UNDERSTAND WHAT YOU MEAN!!!
I TRULY HAVE NO IDEA!! HOW CAN I MAKE YOU SEE SENSE?!!
SLOSH
SLOSH
RUB
SLOSH
SLOSH
...

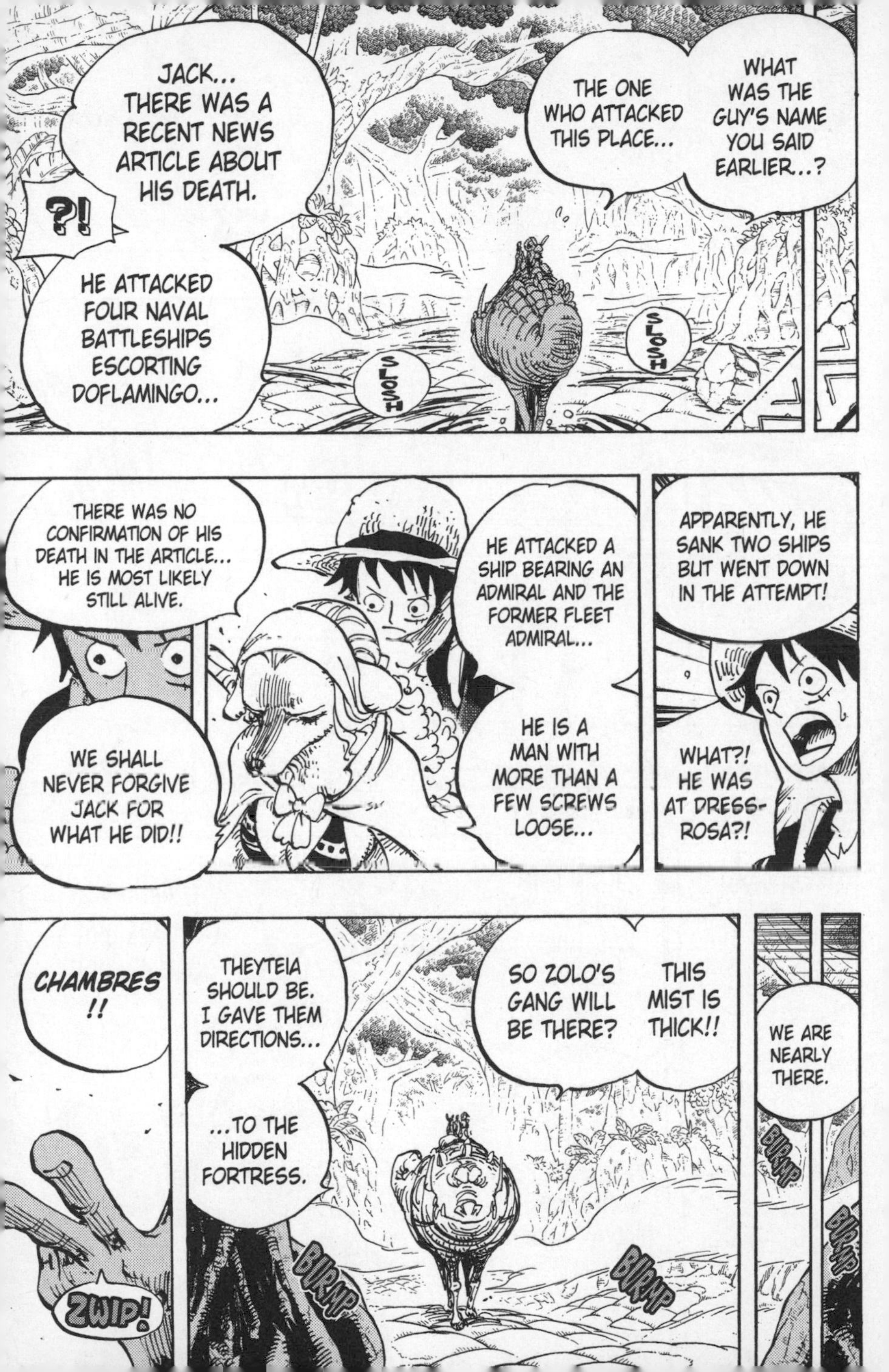
WHAT WAS THE GUY'S NAME YOU SAID EARLIER...?
THE ONE WHO ATTACKED THIS PLACE...
SLOSH
SLOSH
JACK... THERE WAS A RECENT NEWS ARTICLE ABOUT HIS DEATH.
?!
HE ATTACKED FOUR NAVAL BATTLESHIPS ESCORTING DOFLAMINGO...
APPARENTLY, HE SANK TWO SHIPS BUT WENT DOWN IN THE ATTEMPT!
WHAT?! HE WAS AT DRESS-ROSA?!
HE ATTACKED A SHIP BEARING AN ADMIRAL AND THE FORMER FLEET ADMIRAL...
HE IS A MAN WITH MORE THAN A FEW SCREWS LOOSE...
THERE WAS NO CONFIRMATION OF HIS DEATH IN THE ARTICLE... HE IS MOST LIKELY STILL ALIVE.
WE SHALL NEVER FORGIVE JACK FOR WHAT HE DID!!
WE ARE NEARLY THERE.
BURMP
BURMP
THIS MIST IS THICK!!
SO ZOLO'S GANG WILL BE THERE?
THEYTEIA SHOULD BE. I GAVE THEM DIRECTIONS...
...TO THE HIDDEN FORTRESS.
BURMP
BURMP
CHAMBRES !!
ZWIP!

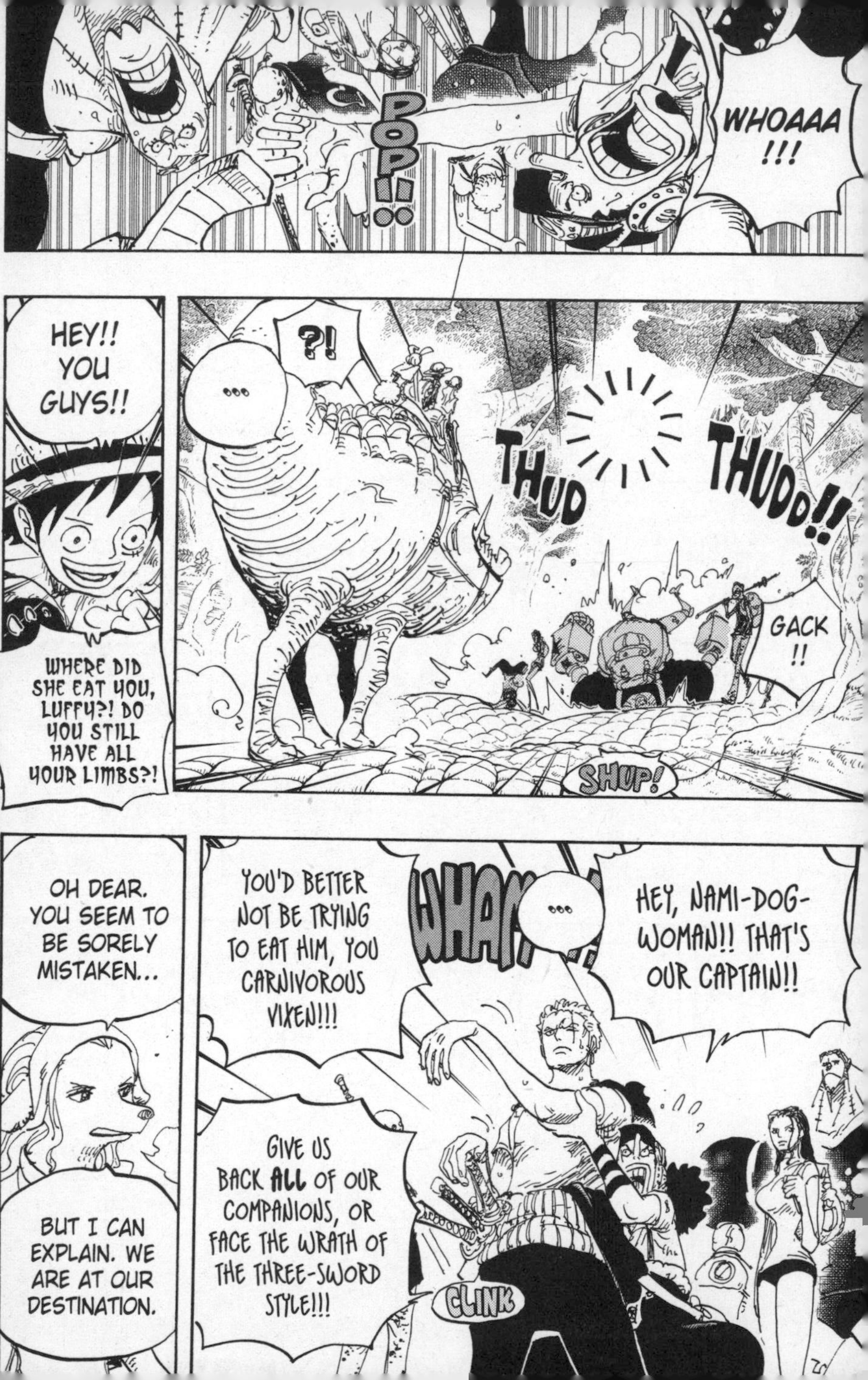
WHOAAA!!!
POP!!
?!
...
THUD
THUDD!!
GACK!!
SHUP!
HEY!! YOU GUYS!!
WHERE DID SHE EAT YOU, LUFFY?! DO YOU STILL HAVE ALL YOUR LIMBS?!
HEY, NAMI-DOG-WOMAN!! THAT'S OUR CAPTAIN!!
...
YOU'D BETTER NOT BE TRYING TO EAT HIM, YOU CARNIVOROUS VIXEN!!!
GIVE US BACK **ALL** OF OUR COMPANIONS, OR FACE THE WRATH OF THE THREE-SWORD STYLE!!!
CLINK
OH DEAR. YOU SEEM TO BE SORELY MISTAKEN...
BUT I CAN EXPLAIN. WE ARE AT OUR DESTINATION.

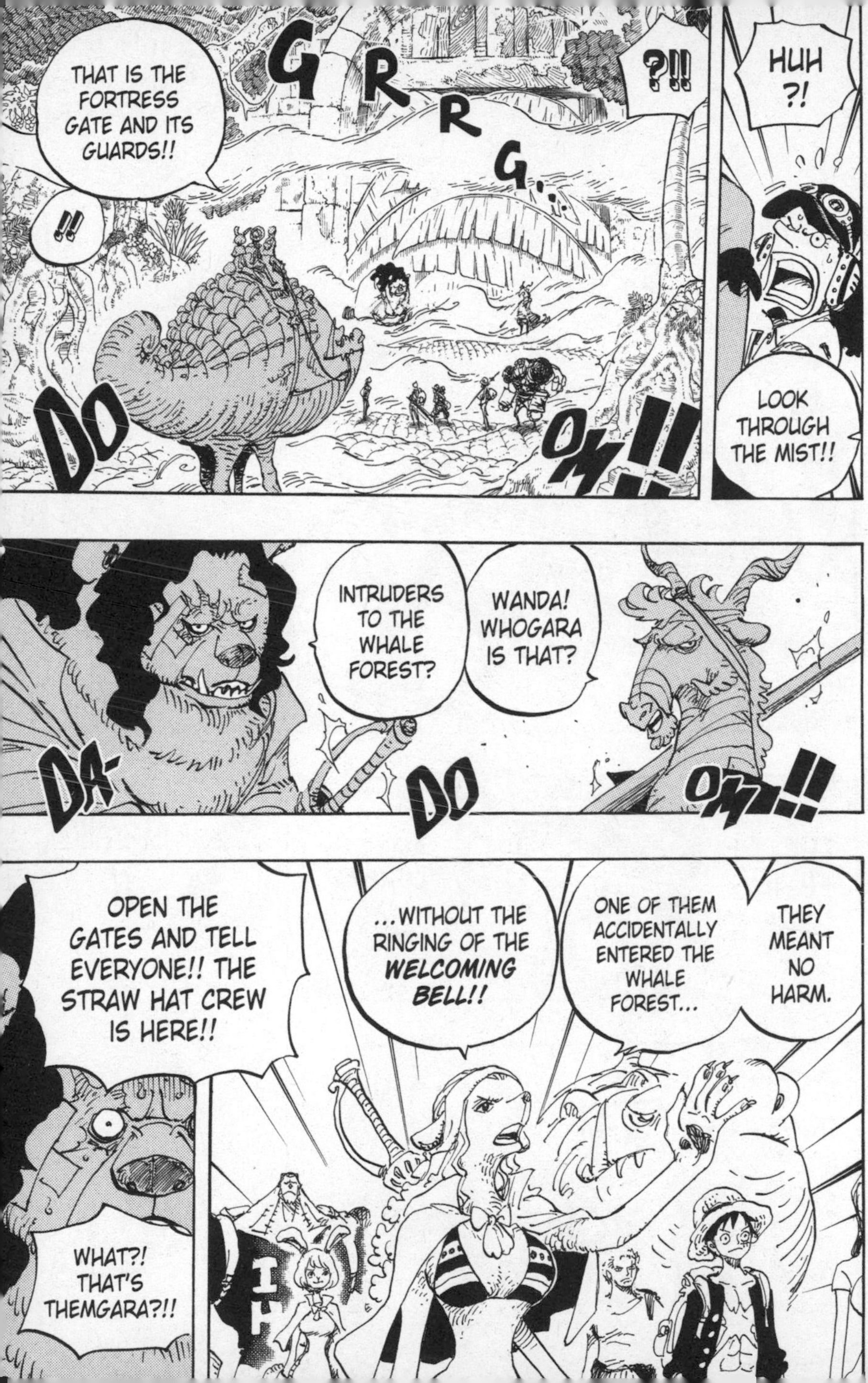
HUH ?!
LOOK THROUGH THE MIST!!
?!!
GRRRG...
THAT IS THE FORTRESS GATE AND ITS GUARDS!!
!!
DOOM!!
WANDA! WHOGARA IS THAT?
INTRUDERS TO THE WHALE FOREST?
DA-DOOM!!
THEY MEANT NO HARM.
ONE OF THEM ACCIDENTALLY ENTERED THE WHALE FOREST...
...WITHOUT THE RINGING OF THE *WELCOMING BELL!!*
OPEN THE GATES AND TELL EVERYONE!! THE STRAW HAT CREW IS HERE!!
WHAT?! THAT'S THEMGARA?!!

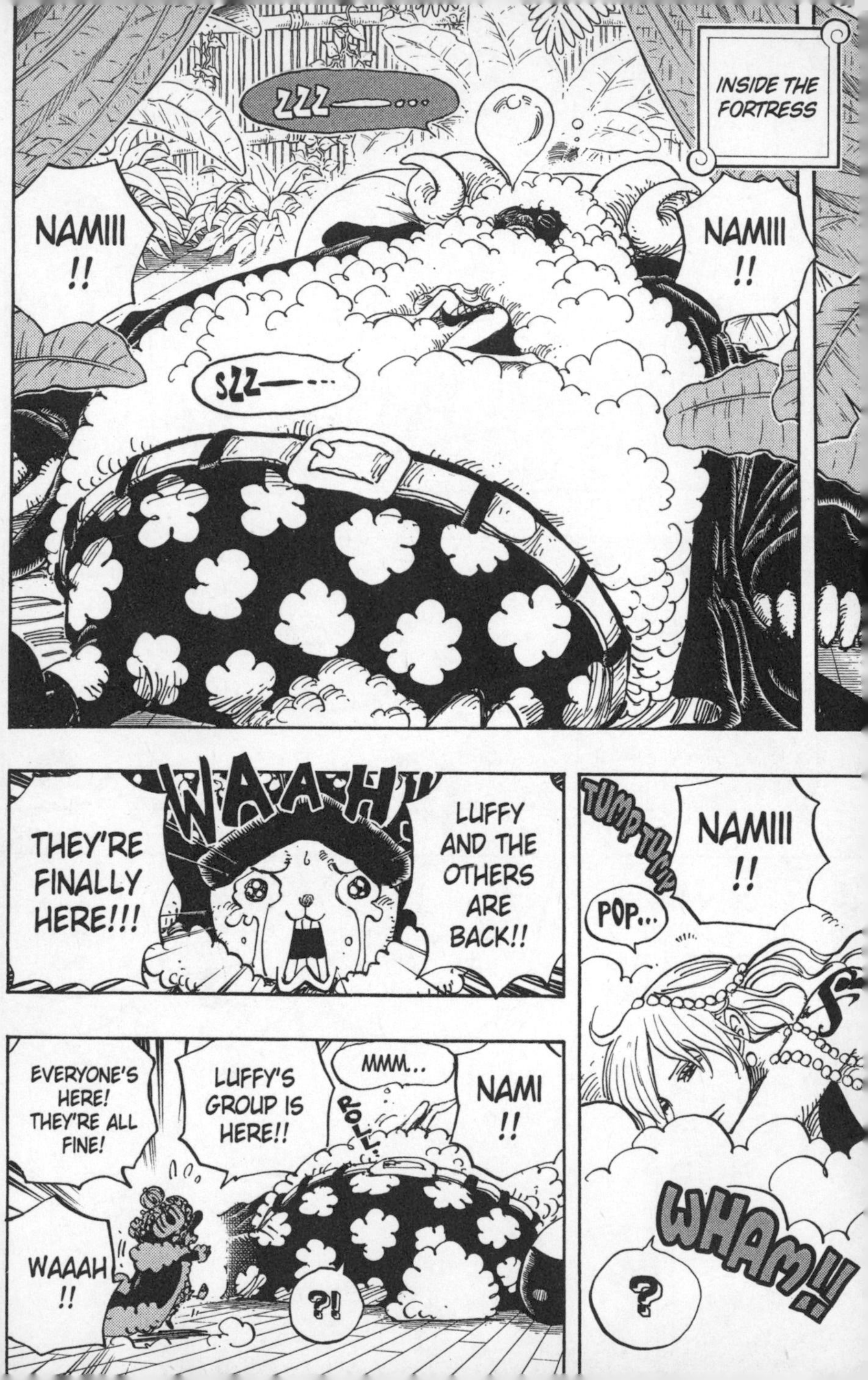
INSIDE THE FORTRESS
NAMIII !!
ZZZ—...
NAMIII !!
SZZ—...
TUMP TUMP
NAMIII !!
POP...
WHAM!!
?
WAAH
LUFFY AND THE OTHERS ARE BACK!!
THEY'RE FINALLY HERE!!!
MMM...
NAMI !!
ROLL
LUFFY'S GROUP IS HERE!!
EVERYONE'S HERE! THEY'RE ALL FINE!
WAAAH !!
?!

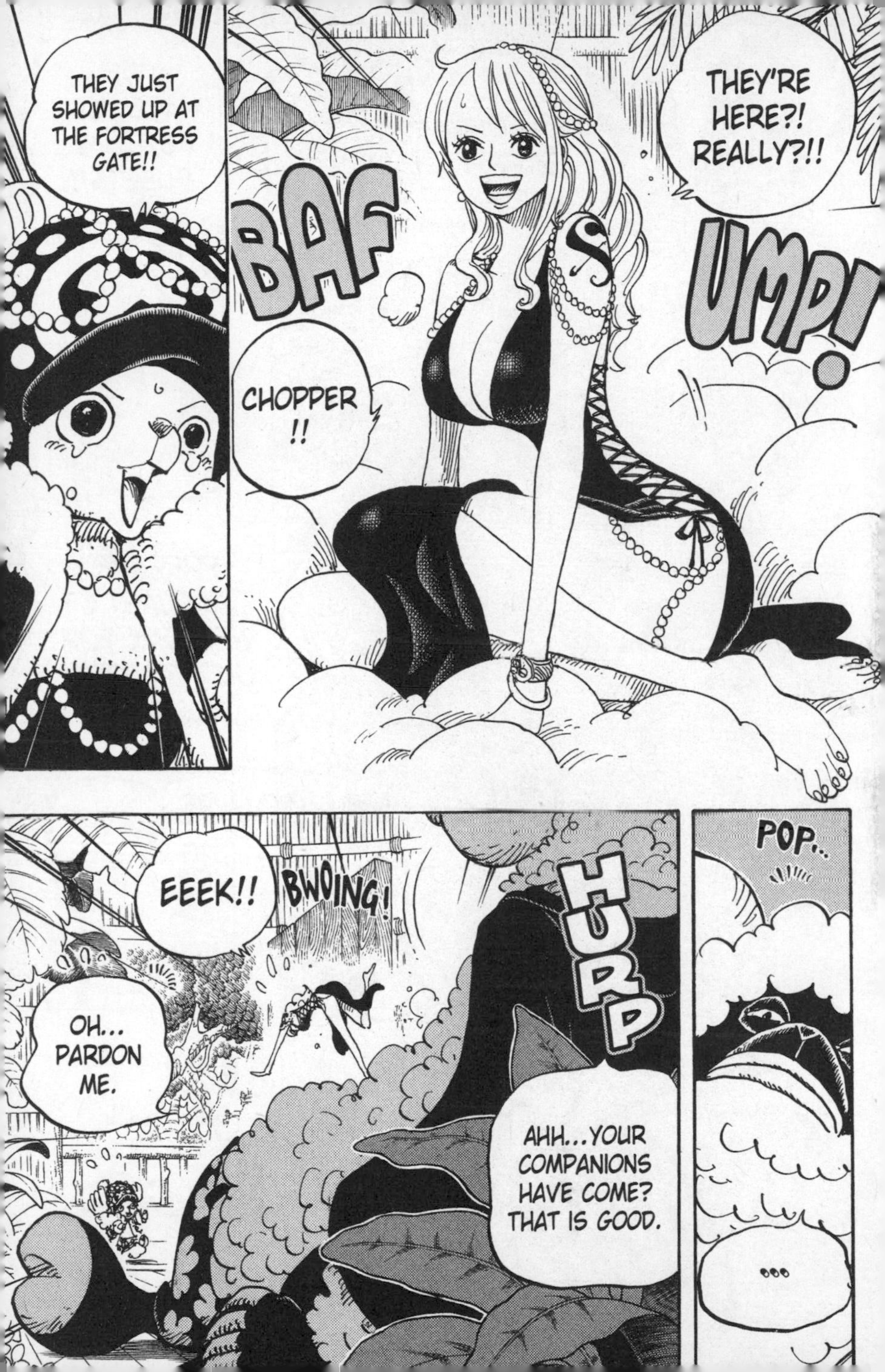
THEY'RE HERE?! REALLY?!!
UMP!
BAF
CHOPPER !!
THEY JUST SHOWED UP AT THE FORTRESS GATE!!
POP...
...
HURP
BWOING!
EEEK!!
OH... PARDON ME.
AHH...YOUR COMPANIONS HAVE COME? THAT IS GOOD.

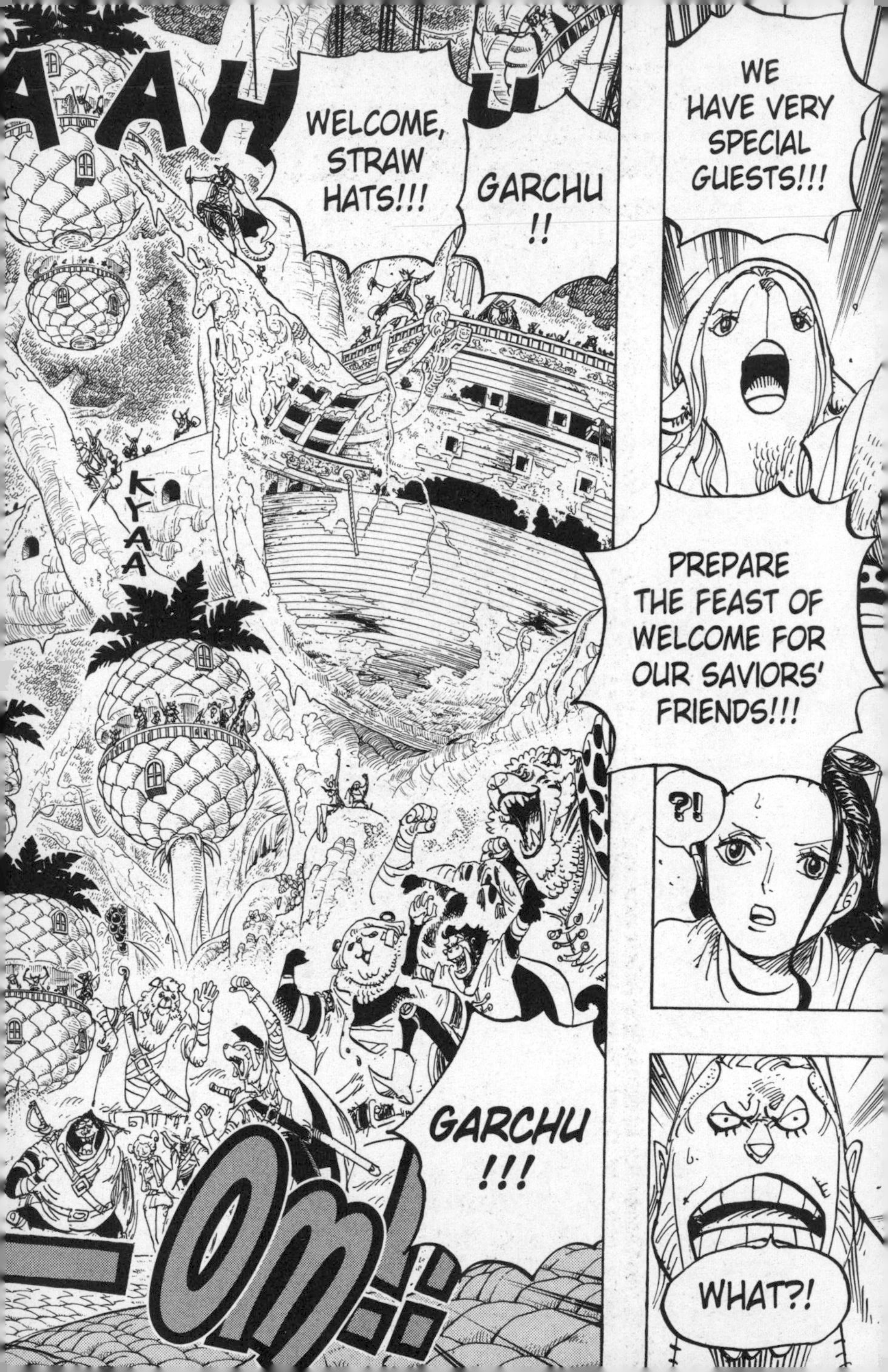
WE HAVE VERY SPECIAL GUESTS!!!
PREPARE THE FEAST OF WELCOME FOR OUR SAVIORS' FRIENDS!!!
?!
WHAT?!
GARCHU!!
WELCOME, STRAW HATS!!!
KYAA
GARCHU!!!

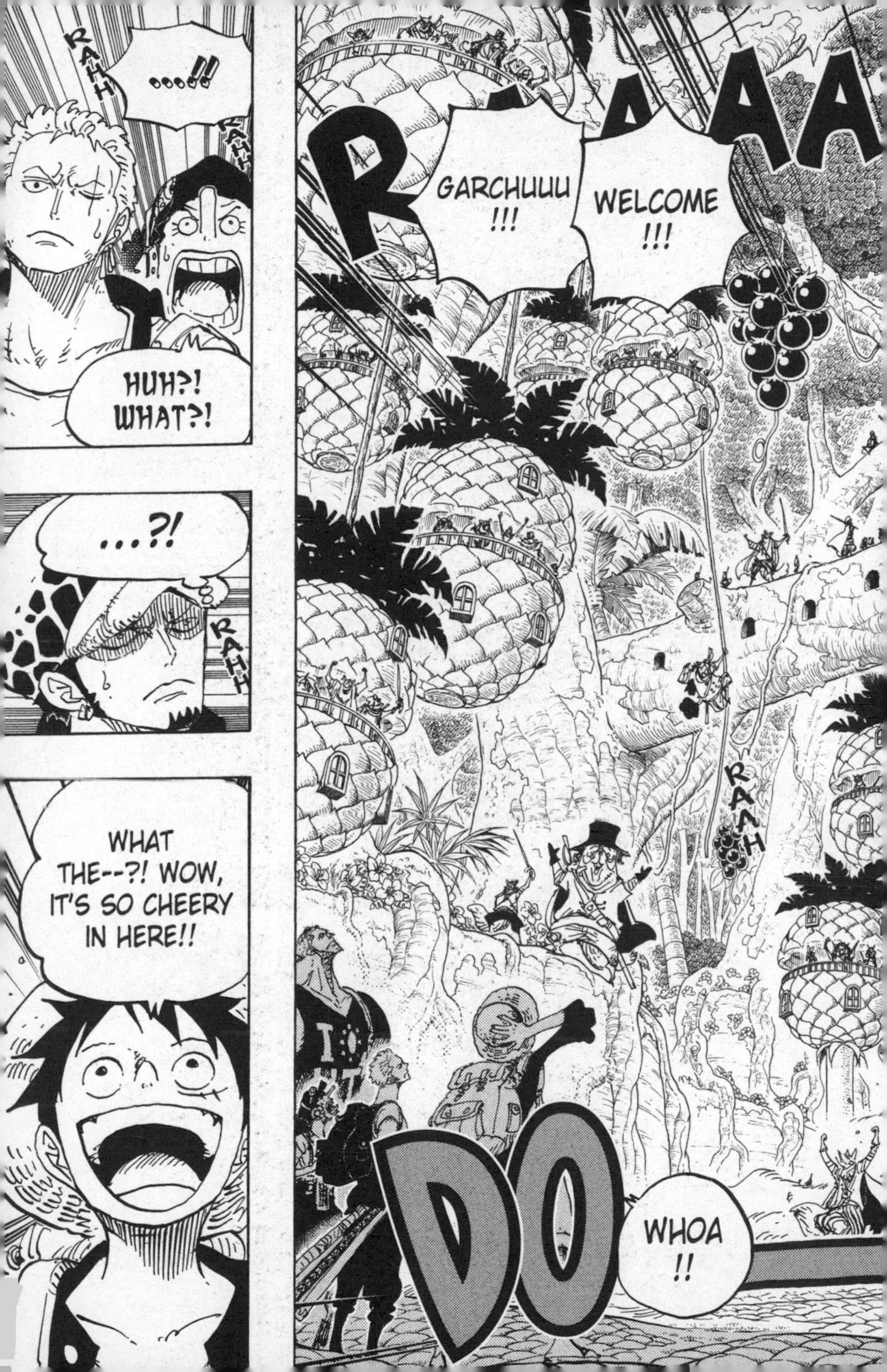
RAAAA
WELCOME !!!
GARCHUUU !!!
RAAH
WHOA !!
DO
RAHH
....!!
RAHH
HUH?! WHAT?!
...?!
RAHH
WHAT THE--?! WOW, IT'S SO CHEERY IN HERE!!

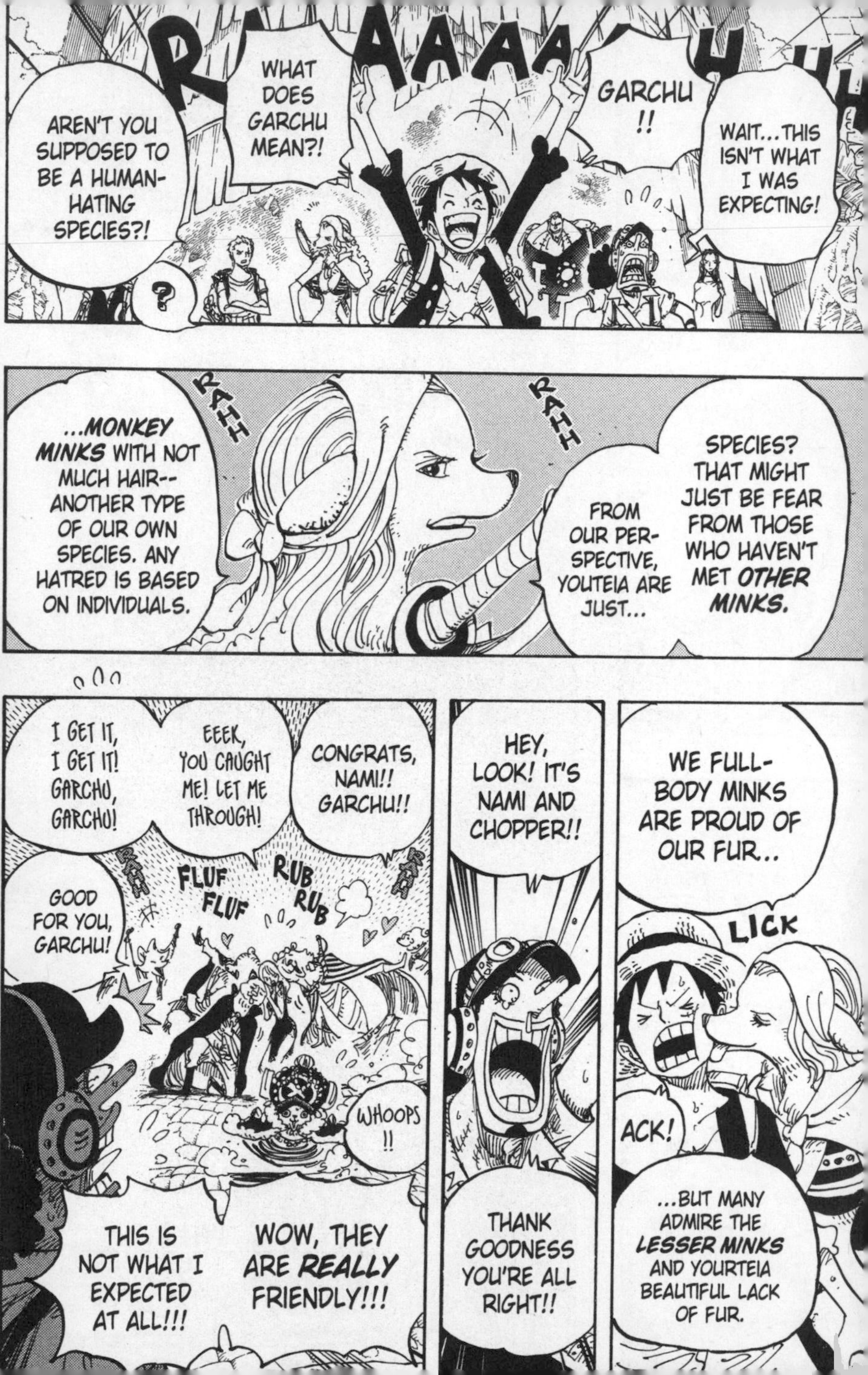

WAIT...THIS ISN'T WHAT I WAS EXPECTING!
GARCHU !!
WHAT DOES GARCHU MEAN?!
AREN'T YOU SUPPOSED TO BE A HUMAN-HATING SPECIES?!
?
SPECIES? THAT MIGHT JUST BE FEAR FROM THOSE WHO HAVEN'T MET *OTHER MINKS.*
FROM OUR PER-SPECTIVE, YOUTEIA ARE JUST...
RAHH
...*MONKEY MINKS* WITH NOT MUCH HAIR-- ANOTHER TYPE OF OUR OWN SPECIES. ANY HATRED IS BASED ON INDIVIDUALS.
RAHH
WE FULL-BODY MINKS ARE PROUD OF OUR FUR...
LICK
ACK!
...BUT MANY ADMIRE THE *LESSER MINKS* AND YOURTEIA BEAUTIFUL LACK OF FUR.
HEY, LOOK! IT'S NAMI AND CHOPPER!!
THANK GOODNESS YOU'RE ALL RIGHT!!
CONGRATS, NAMI!! GARCHU!!
EEEK, YOU CAUGHT ME! LET ME THROUGH!
I GET IT, I GET IT! GARCHU, GARCHU!
RUB RUB
FLUF FLUF
GOOD FOR YOU, GARCHU!
WHOOPS !!
WOW, THEY ARE *REALLY* FRIENDLY!!!
THIS IS NOT WHAT I EXPECTED AT ALL!!!

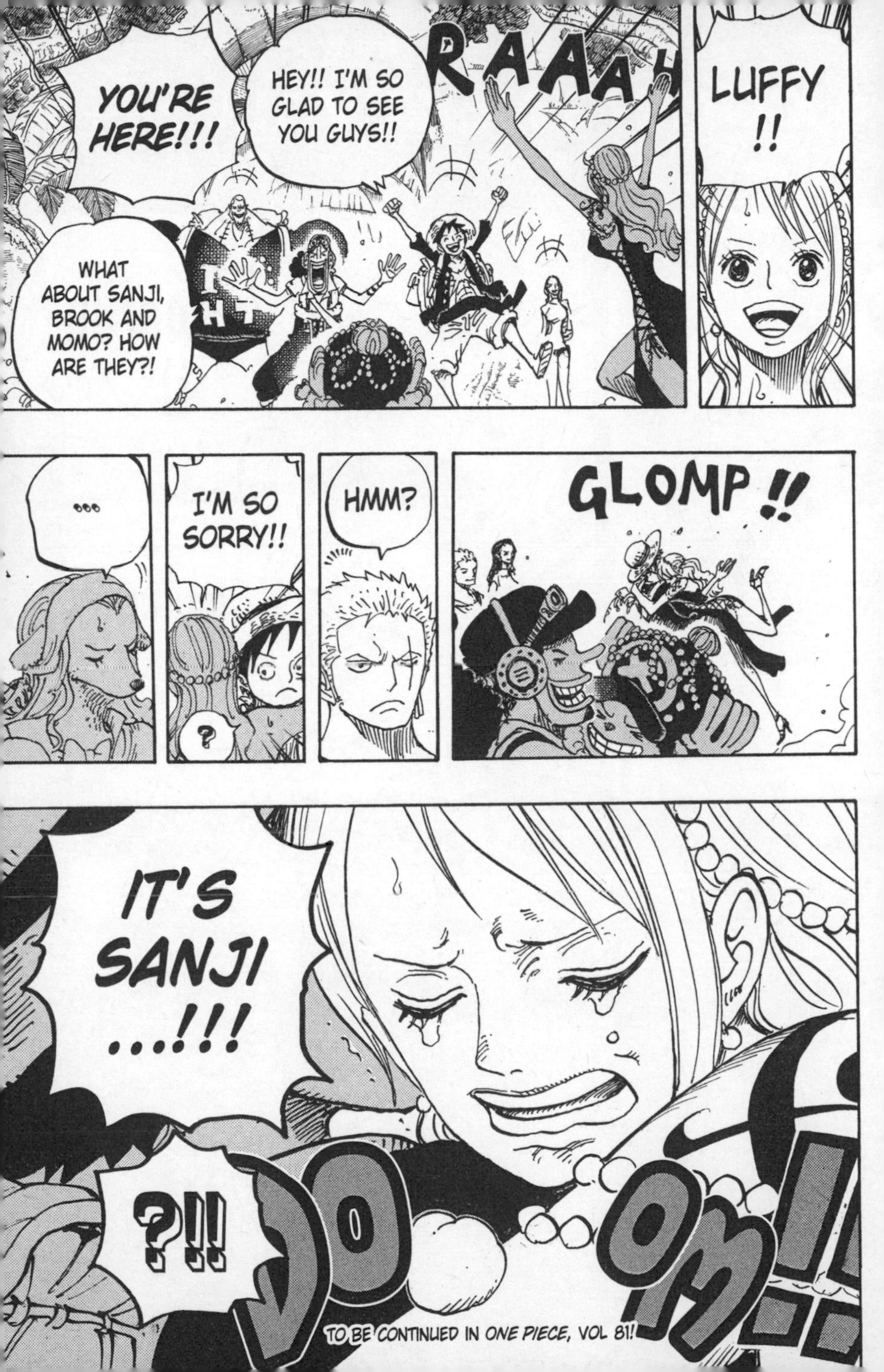
LUFFY !!
RAAAH
HEY!! I'M SO GLAD TO SEE YOU GUYS!!
YOU'RE HERE!!!
WHAT ABOUT SANJI, BROOK AND MOMO? HOW ARE THEY?!
GLOMP !!
HMM?
I'M SO SORRY!!
?
...
IT'S SANJI ...!!!
?!!
TO BE CONTINUED IN ONE PIECE, VOL 81!

# COMING NEXT VOLUME:

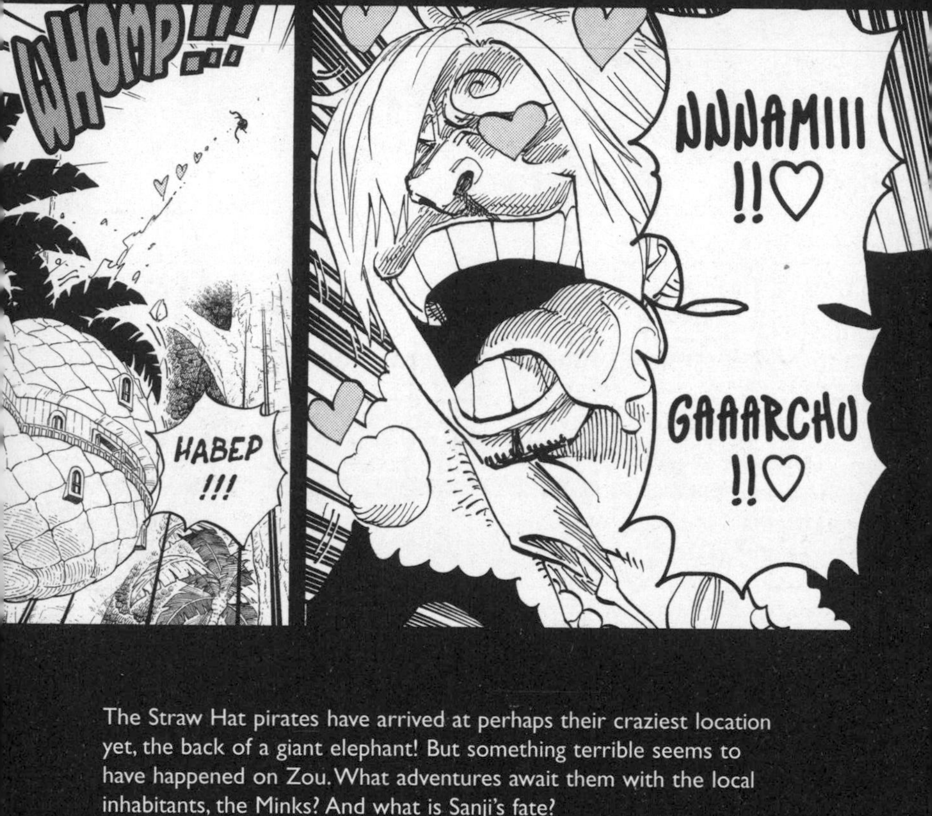
NNNAMIIII !!♡
GAAARCHU !!♡
WHOMP!!!
HABEP !!!

The Straw Hat pirates have arrived at perhaps their craziest location yet, the back of a giant elephant! But something terrible seems to have happened on Zou. What adventures await them with the local inhabitants, the Minks? And what is Sanji's fate?

## ON SALE FEBRUARY 2017!

# NARUTO

Story and Art by
**Masashi Kishimoto**

## *Naruto is determined to become the greatest ninja ever!*

Twelve years ago the Village Hidden in the Leaves was attacked by a fearsome threat. A nine-tailed fox spirit claimed the life of the village leader, the Hokage, and many others. Today, the village is at peace and a troublemaking kid named Naruto is struggling to graduate from Ninja Academy. His goal may be to become the next Hokage, but his true destiny will be much more complicated. The adventure begins now!

## WORLD'S BEST SELLING MANGA!

RATED T TEEN ratings.viz.com

SHONEN JUMP

VIZ media

NARUTO © 1999 by Masashi Kishimoto/SHUEISHA Inc.

www.shonenjump.com

www.viz.com

# Seraph of the End
## VAMPIRE REIGN

STORY BY **Takaya Kagami** ART BY **Yamato Yamamoto**
STORYBOARDS BY **Daisuke Furuya**

## Vampires reign—humans revolt!

Yuichiro's dream of killing every vampire is near-impossible, given that vampires are seven times stronger than humans, and the only way to kill them is by mastering Cursed Gear, advanced demon-possessed weaponry. Not to mention that humanity's most elite Vampire Extermination Unit, the Moon Demon Company, wants nothing to do with Yuichiro unless he can prove he's willing to work in a team—which is the last thing he wants!

## THE LATEST CHAPTERS SERIALIZED IN WEEKLY SHONEN JUMP

OWARI NO SERAPH © 2012 by Takaya Kagami, Yamato Yamamoto, Daisuke Furuya /SHUEISHA Inc.

www.shonenjump.com

www.viz.com